1988

The Age of
William Wordsworth

The Age of
William
Wordsworth

CRITICAL ESSAYS ON THE

ROMANTIC TRADITION

EDITED BY

Kenneth R. Johnston
and Gene W. Ruoff

RUTGERS UNIVERSITY PRESS
New Brunswick and London

Library of Congress Cataloging-in-Publication Data

The Age of William Wordsworth.

Bibliography: p.
Includes index.
1. Wordsworth, William, 1770–1850—Criticism
and interpretation. 2. Romanticism—England.
I. Johnston, Kenneth R. II. Ruoff, Gene W.
PR5892.R63A34 1987 821'.7 87-313
ISBN 0-8135-1243-3
ISBN 0-8135-1244-1 (pbk.)

Contents

Introduction

The essays collected here have been written to make the life and works of William Wordsworth (1770–1850) more generally available to educated nonacademic audiences in America. Although such a goal presupposes a need, it would be difficult to prove that Wordsworth is less well known in the public mind than any other poet. The adjective "Wordsworthian" may in fact call forth more definite and valid conceptions than, say, "Chaucerian" or "Miltonic," thanks primarily to a few of his short lyrics on daffodils and daisies so often reprinted they are as familiar as the air we breathe. But although there are probably more good poets writing, giving readings, and publishing in America today than at any time in our history, the most common image summoned up by the idea of a "well-known" poet is a memory of the elderly Robert Frost struggling to read *We Are the Land's* in a stiff breeze at John F. Kennedy's inaugural in 1960. Wordsworth, then, may be a relatively familiar entity in a relatively unknown universe.

Ironically, the situation is one with which Wordsworth was well acquainted, and one he spent much of his life trying to rectify. In his young manhood, he felt that the reading and appreciation of poetry was degenerating into an upper-class drawing room activity, hardly distinguishable (he said) from the discrimination of grades of sherry. Wordsworth lived in the beginning of the age of mass literacy and realized that mass entertainments might become a threat to more worthwhile entertainments like poetry: "the works of Shakespeare and Milton, are driven into neglect by frantic novels, sickly and stupid German Tragedies, and deluges of idle and extravagant stories in verse" (preface to *Lyrical Ballads,* 1800). We need only substitute romance novels, soap operas, horror movies, and rock videos—and add Wordsworth's works to those of Shakespeare and Milton—to recognize our own cultural era as essentially similar.

But there is one area of our civilization in which Wordsworth and poetry are far better known now than they were two hundred years ago: the domain of public education, especially higher education. This simply did not exist in its present American form in Wordsworth's time. And in the literary departments of our colleges and universities, Wordsworth's stock is very high indeed. As he himself confidently predicted (with characteristic egoism), he now revolves among the largest stars of the universe of poetry in English: if less bright than Shakespeare and Milton, and perhaps Chaucer, no dimmer than Spenser or Byron or Pope or Tennyson. He outshines all the rest, even on the western side of the Atlantic, where he must share the skies of immortality with Whitman, Dickinson, and Frost.

Here we have a paradox, which the present volume of essays is intended to address: like poetry itself, Wordsworth is little known, or known erroneously, outside the academy; but inside the walls of colleges and universities his reputation is inviolable, though hardly—such is the nature of academic life—uncontested. Late in his life, when in England he had finally become famous, an old Romantic among the emerging generation of Victorian sages, he said he would prefer the designation of "teacher" over any other description of his career. Thus he would be heartened by his strong position in the bastions of Anglo-American academia. Yet he would be both troubled and amazed by societies in which academic experience is, on the one hand, available to historically unprecedented portions of the general population and, on the other hand, seems radically cut off from, or discontinuous with, everyday social reality. In the cultural situation of modern literature, college and university English departments must always guard against becoming academic equivalents of those upper-class drawing rooms from which Wordsworth sought to liberate a truly democratic poetry.

The exhibition "William Wordsworth and the Age of English Romanticism," which was the originating occasion of these essays, was funded generously by the National Endowment for the Humanities, which offered a direct grant and also matched the substantial private donations raised by each of three sponsoring venues: the New York Public Library, Indiana University, and the Chicago Historical Society. In addition, photographic copies of the exhibition were created on display panels, which are distributed through state humanities councils to public libraries, schools, and other appropriate locations, where they may be used in conjunction with public lectures and forums, poetry readings, and other humanities programs. Finally, whatever profits are realized by the sale of this book will be donated to the upkeep and expansion of the Wordsworth Heritage Library in Grasmere, England.

These events and artifacts are all part of a large public humanities endeavor devoted to the idea that literary culture should be made widely and popularly available to any interested citizen in the world's most powerful democracy. In a very real sense, this is the kind of program that Words-

worth and his fellow Romantic writers—American as well as British—
would have applauded, representing a future toward which many of their
best imaginative efforts were directed. And it is appropriate that such a large
program on English Romanticism be mounted with Wordsworth as its
focus, because he more than any other English poet is identified with the
Romantic effort to make poetry an everyday, common, democratic experience. That poetry should be written in "a language really spoken by men,"
that its subjects are best selected from the incidents and characters of ordinary life, and that a poet "is a man speaking to men . . . carrying everywhere
with him relationship and love"—these are beliefs, strongly expressed in
the preface to *Lyrical Ballads,* that will always redound to the fame of
Wordsworth, no matter how often critics point out that his own practice
sometimes swerved from this ideal. Over a century ago, John Stuart Mill
called Wordsworth "the poet of unpoetical natures," as compared with
more traditionally "beautiful" poets like Shakespeare, Milton, or Keats. But
we are all unpoetical natures now, relatively speaking, in a world more utilitarian than Mill could have imagined, and his faint praise has become an
honorific that helps to explain Wordsworth's enduring and rising reputation.

The year 1960 could provide a convenient starting date from which to
document Wordsworth's steady rise to academic preeminence. At that time,
when the editors of this volume were about to embark upon graduate studies, Wordsworth was indeed well known as one of the major English poets
—so well known there seemed to be little disagreement about him, and as
little enthusiasm for studying him. As on the occasion of the centenary of his
death a decade earlier, in 1950, and as in the still-prevailing popular image
of him today, he was regarded as a Romantic nature poet whose love of nature was a good deal more philosophical and serious (and therefore, in academic eyes, valuable) than it had seemed to be to Matthew Arnold in 1864.
In that year, Arnold had complained, in his introduction to a very influential
anthology of Wordsworth's best poetry, that Wordsworth, like all the Romantic poets, "did not know enough" and that his poetry was best appreci-
ated for its simple, spontaneous, refreshing naturalism, and by avoiding as
much as possible the abstract, philosophical systematizing Wordsworth increasingly poured into his creations, especially after the "great decade" of
1797–1807, which Arnold posited as the creative center of his entire career.

The first century of Wordsworth scholarship, starting from the time of his death, may well be viewed as a response to Arnold's claim, and by 1960 it had been exhaustively demonstrated that Wordsworth knew—or implied, or invoked, or borrowed from Coleridge—a great deal more philosophy, mainly of the German Idealist and British Empirical varieties, than Arnold had given him credit for—probably a great deal more than Arnold himself knew. And, just as this primary intellectual or philosophical project seemed finished, so too did the other pertinent aspects of academic study of a great artist's work. His texts had been established by Ernest de Selincourt and Helen Darbishire and published in an impressive five-volume edition by Oxford University Press between 1941 and 1949, painstakingly revised in the 1950s. Mary Moorman had published the first volume of her still-standard biography in 1957 and was hard at work on the second (published in 1965). In 1953, M. H. Abrams had published his seminal study of Romantic expressionism, *The Mirror and the Lamp,* in which Wordsworth figured centrally. This book seemed the end product of a line of critical argument Wordsworth himself had begun with his controversial preface of 1800 and its now-famous tag phrases about poetry being "the spontaneous overflow of powerful feelings" and the result of "emotion recollected in tranquility," which generations of school children and English majors had come to accept as universal definitions of all poetry.

A quarter of a century ago, then, Wordsworth was so well known and well established in the academy that he seemed decidedly old hat. All that has changed, and changed radically, in the last twenty-five years. Already by the time of the bicentenary of his birth in 1970, "Wordsworth" had become a fighting word. His texts, his biography, his poetry, his philosophy and politics, the very nature of his worth as a poet, have all been rendered problematic, even though his position as the fourth and latest of the greatest poets in English seems more secure than ever. The editions of de Selincourt and Darbishire, which once seemed as imperishable as the mountains of Westmorland, have been challenged and replaced, particularly by the volumes of the Cornell University Wordsworth project, which seek to restore the poems to their earliest forms and set forth for patient examination all the revisions and encrustations to which Wordsworth subjected his canon throughout his long life. Mark Reed's monumental efforts to establish a precise chronology of the poet's life, sometimes with day-by-day precision, have produced two volumes to date (through 1815) and have created the groundwork for new biographical studies more searching and accurate than

Moorman's. The results of this enterprise have reached into the college classroom, with the result that today our students read versions of poems, or even entire poems, not known to exist in the late fifties or early sixties, such as *The Ruined Cottage* and the two-part *Prelude* of 1799.

The situation is equally dramatic in critical interpretation and valuation of Wordsworth's verse. In the fifties and sixties, Wordsworth's poetry was read pretty straightforwardly, with some honorable exceptions, as descriptive, philosophically meditative verse. Though practicing poets from Byron and Shelley to Ted Hughes and Seamus Heaney have always paid tribute to the great imaginative power of his poetry, he was not much in favor with the New Critics, who were then consolidating their position in American universities and who favored in general a tight, dry, ironic, "modernist" sensibility of the sort exemplified by T. S. Eliot in the twentieth century and by John Donne in the seventeenth. Taking Wordsworth literally at his words' worth, the New Critics found in him little irony (largely true), mainly affirmation (partly true), and no ambiguity (false). But since then, Wordsworth's poetry has been massively reinterpreted by a wide variety of astute and subtle critics until he sometimes seems the very paradigm of another kind of modernism than the New Critics liked to recognize: that is, the sensibility ill at ease with the modern world but striving, against all odds and sometimes even against itself, to make affirmative, forward-looking statements of "something evermore about to be."

By a historical accident that has not yet been fully explained (but about which Romanticists are somewhat smug), much of the advanced theoretical criticism in America in the last two or three decades has centered upon Romantic texts for its arguments and evidence, as one can see simply by citing the names of some of the leaders in these critical movements: Harold Bloom, Paul de Man, Northrop Frye, Geoffrey Hartman, M. H. Abrams, E. D. Hirsch, J. Hillis Miller. Though these critics could hardly be said to agree with each others' methods or valuations of specific texts, they all do share a concentration upon, and respect for, Romantic poetry. Perhaps it was their reaction against their own professors' antipathy to Romantic poetry that turned them toward it for revisionist readings—though in that case one would have to acknowledge that such New Critics as Cleanth Brooks and Robert Penn Warren, and even Eliot himself, had always found much of permanent value in Wordsworth's work, even if their sympathies did not extend as generously to Shelley, Blake, or Byron.

The present volume is a modest attempt to make available to a more general public some of the fruits of this massive critical revaluation of Wordsworth's work. Contributors have been urged to address a generally educated literate audience and to forsake the privileged academic perspective from which they write for their colleagues in the study of Romanticism. Wordsworth once remarked that great writers must create the taste by which they are to be enjoyed, and something of the same challenge faces academic Wordsworthians if they are to make their "new" poet more widely known. We hope that we have succeeded, even though in some respects our address to the public or "general reader" must be like that of the proverbial blind men who tried to define an elephant by touch.

One thing is certain: compared to other available collections dealing with Wordsworth, this volume is remarkable for its range of interests. In a large sense, the study and evaluation of Wordsworth's achievement must always be marked by widely different readings, since few poets have lived so long, or written—and revised—so much, as he did. Our contributors represent a wide spectrum of American and British Romanticists, covering at least two scholarly generations: some began their work on Wordsworth and English Romanticism over half a century ago, while others have only recently completed their doctoral studies. The range of approaches, and of conclusions, is equally various. Wordsworth is the poet of polarities, not only that most famous one between Mind and Nature, but of many others as well: simple/profound, radical/conservative, normal/bizarre, good/bad. The poet of nearly biblical power, in such lines as "My mind turned round as with the might of waters" is also the poet of apparently ridiculous literalisms like "I've measured it from side to side, / 'Tis three feet long and two feet wide." Contributors to this volume were selected for the excellence of their work and for their interest in a public project connected with Wordsworth, not for their alignment with any critical perspective on these polarities the editors might have set down.

Our first part, "Wordsworth and the Romantic Era," places Wordsworth in the cultural and political contexts of his age. David Erdman examines Wordsworth's experience in Revolutionary France and presents a young man whose political sympathies are even more radical, and active, than has been previously suggested. Stephen Parrish and Joseph Wittreich examine his attitude toward his era from two rather more elevated perspectives, different yet ultimately complementary: the artist as satirist and as prophet. Michael Cooke explores the meanings of pleasure and play for the period. Finally, James Chandler's essay counterbalances Erdman's with a detailed examination of the fascinating process by which Wordsworth, youthful republican and enthusiast for reform, became known to a younger generation as the very type of apostasy from the cause of liberty.

The second part is devoted to "Wordsworth and the Forms of Romantic Art." Stuart Curran's essay traces Wordsworth's development in mastering, using, and revising the poetical traditions he inherited, a process easily lost sight of in readers' (and teachers) too uncritical acceptance of the dogmas of original expression Wordsworth set forth in his famous preface. Kenneth Johnston's essay follows in the same direction, exploring a major paradox in Wordsworth's development, that his famous *Lyrical Ballads* were written partly as a result of his failure to write the grand epic poem he and Samuel Taylor Coleridge believed he must write to fulfill his poetic destiny. Beth Darlington shows Dorothy Wordsworth, the poet's sister and lifelong companion, to have been both more of an artist than traditional biographers have allowed and a less frustrated one in her relation to her brother than some contemporary feminist critics have been willing to admit. Jack Stillinger and Jonathan Wordsworth demonstrate that Wordsworth's influence on his younger contemporaries Keats and De Quincey was both more pervasive and more positive than is generally recognized. Karl Kroeber sets forth in some detail the most plausible grounds for a meaningful comparison between Wordsworth's poetry and the art of an exact contemporary, J.M.W. Turner, England's greater painter, whose Romanticism is often impressionistically compared to Wordsworth's. Thomas McFarland concludes the section by exploring the formal principles of one of Romanticism's finest achievements, the longer lyric.

In the final part, "The Heritage of the Age of Wordsworth," Carl Woodring examines what Wordsworth variously meant to his immediate successors in the Victorian era, and David Simpson, a native Briton, documents Wordsworth's reputation in nineteenth-century America. Gene Ruoff compares Wordsworth's achievement to that of Maria Edgeworth, much more successful and well-known than he in their lifetime but now obscured because she wrote in the then-devalued form of the novel, the very form which ultimately overturned the cultural hegemony of poetry. Morris Dickstein concludes the volume by exploring Wordsworth's appeal to our modern, Freudianized sensibilities, as the poet whose masterpiece is an epic-length examination of "the growth of my own mind."

We hope that this volume, like the exhibitions of which it was originally a part, will find multiple audiences. Although it does not depend upon the exhibition whose name it echoes, the collection should enrich the appreciation of those readers fortunate enough to see it. For the general reader, appreciative of Romantic poetry in general and Wordsworth's in particular, but perhaps put off by outmoded academic experiences of him, the volume will provide a useful introduction to some of the new ways in which the poet and his age are being understood. Most of the essays will be accessible to undergraduate students, and all of them will be useful to graduate students. Finally, we hope that our colleagues in the academy, who have done much to challenge and extend our consideration of the poet and his times, will find much here that is both new and interesting to them. We thank our distinguished contributors on behalf of the exhibition project, "William Wordsworth and the Age of English Romanticism," which this volume will reinforce, and on behalf of the Wordsworth Heritage Centre in Grasmere, England, which will be the beneficiary of all profits from its sale.

A portion of Kenneth R. Johnston's work on this volume was accomplished on time provided by a Fellowship for Independent Study and Research awarded by the National Endowment for the Humanities.

Gene W. Ruoff's work on the Wordsworth project, of which this volume is one consequence, was supported by time made available through a Senior Fellowship of the Institute for the Humanities at the University of Illinois at Chicago. Linda Vavra ably assisted his final editorial work on the collection.

Both editors are grateful for the friendly and efficient support of the staff of Rutgers University Press, especially Leslie Mitchner, who has overseen the project from its inception. Our copy editor, Janet S. Mais, performed wonders in bringing the individual essays into stylistic conformity.

KENNETH R. JOHNSTON
GENE W. RUOFF

Chronology

1770   Wordsworth born 7 April at Cockermouth, Cumberland.

1771   Birth of Dorothy Wordsworth, 25 December.

1778   Death of mother, Ann Wordsworth (nee Cookson).

1779   Wordsworth enters Hawkshead Grammar School near Esthwaite Lake.

1783   Death of father, John Wordsworth.

1787–1791   Wordsworth attends St. John's College, Cambridge.

1789   Bastille stormed 14 July; outbreak of the French Revolution.

1790   Wordsworth's summer walking tour of France, Switzerland, Italy, and Germany, with Robert Jones.

1791   Wordsworth's walking tour of North Wales, where he climbs Mount Snowden.

1791–1792   Wordsworth leaves for France in late November; passes through Paris en route to Orléans (c. December–January) and Blois (c. February–September); revisits Paris (c. October–November) on return to England (by December 22). French Republic proclaimed 22 September 1792. Anne Caroline Wordsworth, illegitimate daughter of Wordsworth and Annette Vallon, baptized at Orléans, 15 December 1792.

1793   Wordsworth publishes *An Evening Walk* and *Descriptive Sketches*; writes but does not publish "Letter to the Bishop of Llandaff," attacking liberals turning against the French Revolution.

Reign of Terror begins. Trial and execution of Louis XVI and Marie Antoinette, January; France declares war on Britain 1 February.

1794   Danton and Robespierre executed; Terror ends; Directorate established.

Coleridge and Robert Southey meet, plan to establish "Pantisocracy" on the Susquehanna River in America; publish *The Fall of Robespierre.*

1795   Wordsworth receives small legacy from Raisley Calvert; settles with his sister Dorothy in Racedown, Devonshire (c. September 1795–July 1797); meets Coleridge and Southey.

1796   Wordsworth writes but does not publish verse drama, *The Borderers.*

1797   Wordsworth and Dorothy move to Alfoxden, Somerset (July 1797–June 1798).

1798   *Lyrical Ballads* published anonymously by Wordsworth and Coleridge; includes *Tintern Abbey* and *Ancient Mariner.*

French invasion of Egypt; battle of the Nile.

1798–1799   Wordsworth and Dorothy spend winter in Goslar, Germany, where he composes "Lucy" poems and earliest *Prelude* materials.

1799   Wordsworth and Dorothy move to Dove Cottage, Grasmere; *Two-Part Prelude* composed.

Napoleon returns from Egypt, overthrows Directorate. Suppression of societies in England sympathetic to French revolutionary principles.

1800   Second edition of *Lyrical Ballads* published, with Wordsworth's controversial Preface; second volume added, which includes *Michael, The Brothers,* and "Lucy" poems.

1802   Wordsworth composes many famous lyrics, including *To the Cuckoo, Resolution and Independence*, and beginning of *Intimations Ode*; travels to France during the Peace of Amiens to resolve matters with Annette (July–August); marries Mary Hutchinson 4 October.

Coleridge publishes *Dejection: An Ode* in *Morning Post* on Wordsworth's wedding day (and his own anniversary).

French reoccupy Switzerland.

1803   War resumes between France and Britain; invasion of Britain threatened; Jefferson purchases Louisiana Territory from France.

1804   Wordsworth completes *Intimations Ode*, begins major expansion of the *Prelude*.

Coleridge moves to Malta for his health.

Napoleon proclaimed Emperor.

1805   Wordsworth completes thirteen-book version of the *Prelude*.

Death at sea of Wordsworth's brother, John (see *Elegiac Stanzas*).

1806   Coleridge returns to England.

1807   Wordsworth publishes *Poems in Two Volumes*, including *Intimations Ode, Resolution and Independence*, and the series of sonnets on England's war with France.

France invades Portugal and Spain.

1808   Wordsworths leave Dove Cottage but remain in Grasmere.

1809   Wordsworth publishes *Tract on the Convention of Cintra*, a protest against settlement of Peninsular Wars.

1810   Wordsworth publishes *Guide to the Lakes*; estrangement from Coleridge.

1812   Deaths of two Wordsworth children, Catharine and Thomas.

1813   Wordsworth becomes Distributor of Stamps for Westmorland; family moves to Rydal Mount, their home for the remainder of Wordsworth's life.

        Southey becomes Poet Laureate.

1814   Wordsworth publishes the *Excursion*.

        Fall of Paris, abdication of Napoleon.

1815   Wordsworth publishes *The White Doe of Rylstone* and first collected edition of *Poems*.

        Napoleon returns from Elba, Battle of Waterloo.

1817   Coleridge publishes *Sybilline Leaves* and *Biographia Literaria*.

1819   Wordsworth publishes *Peter Bell* and the *Waggoner*.

1820   Wordsworth publishes *Duddon Sonnets* and *Vaudracour and Julia*.

1822   Wordsworth publishes *Ecclesiastical Sketches*.

1835   Wordsworth publishes *Yarrow Revisited and Other Poems*.

1842   Wordsworth publishes *Poems Chiefly of Early and Late Years*.

1843   Wordsworth becomes Poet Laureate.

1847   Death of Wordsworth's daughter, Dora.

1850   Wordsworth dies 23 April; *Prelude* published in July.

Wordsworth and the Romantic Era

The Dawn of Universal Patriotism
William Wordsworth among
the British in Revolutionary France

DAVID V. ERDMAN

Bliss was it in that dawn to be alive,
But to be young was very heaven!
—Wordsworth, *Prelude*

"I went over to Paris," said the poet Wordsworth to an interviewer late in his life, "at the time of the revolution in 1792 or 1793, and so was *pretty hot in it*; but I found Mr. J. Watt [Jr.] there before me, and quite as warm in the same cause. We thus both began life as ardent and thoughtless radicals; but we have both become, in the course of our lives, as all sensible men, I think, have done, good sober-minded Conservatives." We note that in retrospect Wordsworth was vague about the year and that he felt his reaction had occurred gradually. His first full, poetical account, in *The Prelude*, was only gradually revised into conservative sobriety over the years (and never published during his lifetime), but it was cautiously vague about the identity of the "cause" and the degree of his own involvement, even in the earliest drafts. About both, however, a great deal of circumstantial evidence can now be assembled.[1]

Fourteen years after the beginning of the American Revolution, the people of Paris, on 14 July 1789, stormed the prison-fortress of the Bastille, and the exciting news of a French Revolution spread through the world. That "Robbert-Den" was soon reduced to a rubble of souvenir stones, and its key crossed the Atlantic to lie on George Washington's hall table. By the time of the Revolution's first anniversary, in July 1790, citizens of many nations joined in celebrations, at home or—the happy few who could travel—in the streets and halls and gardens of French cities and villages. Young William Wordsworth and his college classmate Robert Jones, ending their third year at Cambridge, managed by a beautiful coincidence to arrive in the harbor city of Calais exactly on the thirteenth (having passed their examinations in June). Joining the celebration, "In a mean city, and among a few," they saw "How bright a face is worn when joy of one / Is joy of tens of millions" (*Prelude*, bk. 6, lines 358–360). As they went on they were welcomed in every village to join "Dances of Liberty" and regaled by travelers from Paris with tales of the "great Spousals newly solemnized" there. Indeed, so universal was the rejoicing and the welcome extended to all who bore the honored "name of Englishmen" that Jones and Wordsworth instead of following the crowd to Paris walked straight toward the highest natural and historical symbol of liberty, the Alps. There, indeed, Wordsworth's "heart leaped up when first" he looked down like that freedom fighter William Tell on "a green recess, an aboriginal vale" in Switzerland (*Prelude* 6.396, 448).

A year later, having finished college, Wordsworth spent the summer with Jones, this time walking in Wales (where they *could* have met some of the Welsh correspondents of the Jacobin Clubs). Then, after some career discussions in Cambridge and London, Wordsworth sailed alone for France, with letters of introduction to several potential friends in Paris and to Helen Maria Williams in Orléans. His career explanation was (in his sister Dorothy's words) that he intended to "pass the winter for the Purpose of learning the French Language which will qualify him for the office of travelling Companion to some young Gentleman."[2] His slender present means were a portion of inheritance from the proceeds of their grandmother's estate.

Reaching Paris, Wordsworth made a swift round of the attractions, which included both the Assembly and the Jacobin Club, where the debates and hectoring gave him the impression that the "revolutionary power" was tossing "like a ship at anchor, rocked by storms"—a storm that produced "hissing factionists with ardent eyes" and "Joy, anger, and vexation, in the midst of gaiety" (*Prelude* 9.50ff.). He had clearly come predisposed to find a revolution in progress and the joy and anger properly directed. He shortly left Paris and went on down the Loire valley to Orléans—where he found neither Helen Williams nor, as he had half expected, his friend Jones.

He soon introduced himself to an English family who had built a cotton mill in Orléans, and he assured his lawyer-brother Richard (who was handling the inheritance) that he would now have entrée to "the best society"; but he had to add, "I find almost all the people of any opulence are aristocrates and all the others democrates." He had imagined "there were some people of wealth . . . favorers of the revolution," but there was "not one to be found." He moved on to Blois, probably disappointed about the millowner and perhaps advised by the "2 or 3 officers of the Cavalry" whom he had met in his Orléans boardinghouse. For in Blois he found, among more military men, a true revolutionary, Michel Beaupuy, who gave him a sophisticated indoctrination in the purposes and dynamics of the Revolution.

Feeling like young Dion of Syracuse, who had been instructed by Plato in "philosophic war," Wordsworth clearly wished to transform himself into a true "democrate." This was not Blake's "mental war" but an application of science ("philosophy") to strategy and tactics. Plutarch tells how the tyrant of Syracuse was indoctrinated (not very successfully, it must be noted) by a combination of lessons in geometry—and a commando raid upon his kingdom. An application would be to consider whether the British monarchy might be democratized by legislation or might require a military invasion. Before the end of this year, 1792, most of the British in Paris would become involved in—or flee from—preparations for a French descent upon London, or Dublin.

These were not matters to be mentioned in letters to England, nor the fact that there was an active Jacobin Club in Blois, which subscribed to two revolutionary periodicals, the *Annales patriotiques* and the *Courrier* edited by Antoine-Joseph Gorsas, with whom Wordsworth became acquainted. But Wordsworth kept in touch with his college friends William Mathews and Jones, and in May he reported grim news of an insurrection in the revolutionary army. The revolutionary general Theobald Dillon had been attacked by his own troops when they were routed by the Austrians: "An ignominious flight, the massacre of their general, a dance performed with savage joy round his burning body, the murder of six prisoners, are events which would have arrested the attention . . . of the most barbarous savages" (*Letters: Early Years* 77). Clearly, wiser generals were needed, "commanding geniuses," to use a term Coleridge applied both to poets and to warriors. That Wordsworth's sympathies continued on the radical side for many years is evident from his implying, in his 1802 sonnet *I grieved for Buonaparte,* that Napoleon *might have been* a savior of the Revolution.

In 1792 Wordsworth must have known, from conversations with the officers he lived among, that many Belgians, Liègeois, Germans, Dutch, and Savoyards were forming legions in France—and must have been impressed by the fact that several British and American sympathizers were volunteering to join the French army against the counterrevolutionary forces which had begun to invade the nation. When he saw his countrymen stepping forward in this emergency, was there not in Wordsworth's character a strong urge to step into an active post of command? After all, what had he most wanted to make his career when he left Cambridge? Consider how he answered that question when interviewed by note-taking neighbors in his seventy-fifth year:

> He said that after he had finished his college course, he was in great doubt as to what his future employment should be. [What he did, of course, was to go to revolutionary France, where the action was.] He did not feel himself good enough for the Church . . . the struggle between his conscience and his impulses would have made life a torture. He also shrank from the law, although . . . told . . . that he was well fitted for the higher parts of the profession. [On the other hand] he had studied military history with great interest, and the strategy of war; and he always fancied that he had talents for command; and he at one time thought of a military life, but then he was without [the necessary political] connections. He mentioned this to show how difficult it often was to judge of what was passing in a young man's mind.

In 1803 he had offered to join the Grasmere Volunteers—but dropped out when not asked to take command.

Since he ended up a poet, it is difficult to entertain the image of Wordsworth as a philosophical warrior. It was a rather different sort of "connections" that led him to room with military men in Orléans and Blois and turn to the French officer Michel Beaupuy for Platonic insight. His interest in the Grasmere Volunteers; his grieving for Bonaparte (until that hero had himself crowned emperor by a pope, revealing that he lacked the domestic roots of moral virtue which could have made him the savior instead of destroyer of the Revolution); his celebration of the *Character of the Happy Warrior* as one whose "moral being" is his prime care and who, "if he be called upon" to face great issues of "good or bad for human kind," will be strong enough even in the "heat of conflict" to keep "the law in calmness made";[3] even his ardent pamphlet on the Convention of Cintra, accusing the British cabinet of betrayal of the Spanish people fighting on a battlefield that consisted of "the floors upon which their children have played"—all these pointers, because they have been overlooked or perceived as mere figures of speech, have not quite established—as they should have done—the poet Wordsworth as a would-be man of action.[4]

Too strongly influenced by Wordsworth's own conservative protestations—and by a continuing strain of conservative patriotism among British historians—his youthful radicalism has come to be seen, by whole generations of scholars and common readers, as a matter of attitudes and sympathies without active involvement. In some not altogether cryptic passages in *The Prelude,* nevertheless, the poet does seem to be depicting himself in a critical stage of the French Revolution as "inly" contemplating (if only he had sufficient command of the French language) the idea of offering himself as a philosophical Napoleon. Realizing from his study of history that "tyrannic power is weak," he never gave up the notion (he says) that history can be drastically changed by a Brutus or such liberators as the Athenian Harmodius and Aristogiton, assassins of tyrants (*Prelude* 10.198–200). He thought "How much the destiny of man had still / Hung upon single persons: that there was . . . / One nature . . . / That, with desires heroic and firm sense, / A spirit thoroughly faithful to itself" could be "as an instinct among men"—and "at this time" (when he was in France) he would "willingly" have taken up service in a "cause so great, however dangerous" (*Prelude* 10.155–169; 152–154).[5]

Writing this account of his 1792 ruminations ten years later, Wordsworth frames them in the political context of the September massacres which followed the Parisian overthrow of the monarchy in the uprising of

10 August, but he conflates this "moment" with the Robespierre crisis a year later, and we are all too ready to leap to the conclusion (as many writers would subsequently do) that the September bloodiness shook Wordsworth out of his youthful bliss about the Revolution.

But in the wider context we must realize that Wordsworth's sequential response to the immediately famous "days" of August and September 1792 could not have been much different from the responses of the other British in Paris that autumn. And it should be helpful to turn for a moment for documentation to the responses of Wordsworth's friend James Watt, who was equally "hot" and who seems, as the war fears and the violence increased, not to have cooled at all.

When Watt arrived in Paris early in the year, he and his companion, with letters of introduction from Joseph Priestley, were very civilly received by "Mr de la Rochefoucauld"—an aristocrat who had already dropped his title—who introduced them to Mr. Lavoisier, at whose house they met several "first rate Chemists." But "not a word of Chemistry was there spoken, they are all mad with politics: we have not met anywhere with such a set of enragés." In July, Tom Wedgwood, another Anglo-Franc writing from Paris to his father, reported: "I lodge here in the same house with young Watt— he is a furious [enragé] democrat . . . Watt says that a new revolution must inevitably take place, and that it will in all probability be fatal to the King, Fayette, and some hundred others. The 14th of this month will probably be eventful." And then this: "He means to join the French Army in case of any civil rupture." Here was another "philosophical" warrior.

The "second revolution" did take place, on 10 August, without fatality to the King or Fayette, but with blood shed when the "600 men from Marseilles who know how to die" marched upon the Tuileries to liberate the King (defended by Swiss mercenaries). This was a planned and visibly "necessary" affair; if the "people" were to rule, the King could not remain sealed off from them. This action troubled only the few committed "enemies of the people." But less than a month later came (unplanned, unless invisibly: one could subsequently condemn any enemy as having plotted it) the September massacres. For James Watt's reaction, we have his letter to his father of 5 September, the fourth day of the massacres: "I am filled with involuntary horror at the scenes which pass before me and wish they could have been avoided, but at the same time I allow the absolute necessity of them. In some instances the vengeance of the people has been savage & inhuman." He gives the instance of a princess dragged naked through the streets and her head "stuck upon a Pike . . . and shown to the King & Queen."

The apparently inevitable sequel, seeming to come as a surprise to all, was the discovery that France had become a Republic! On 21 September, Wordsworth, still in Orléans, is believed to have attended a celebration in honor of the shining new Republic of France. In Paris that afternoon, the members of the National Assembly, suddenly looking around, saw that the quorum present had the authority to constitute themselves the new Convention, "an assembly of philosophers occupied with preparing the happiness of the world," as one speaker declared. The fall of the Bastille had been a glorious day, but this was a transformation. Rejoicing at the new Republic was joined by celebrations of the success of the revolutionary armies at Valmy, on 20 September, which halted the congregated might of French royalists and Prussians led by the Duke of Brunswick's "starry hosts" (as Blake called them).

Wordsworth defines this as "the time in which enflamed with hope, / To Paris I returned" (*Prelude* 10.38–39). And there he found a new swarm of British visitors, already beginning to talk of a renewal of the English, Irish, Scottish, and Welsh revolutions that might bring all free nations into a harmonious "philosophical" commerce. Theoretically Wordsworth was on his way to London, to draw upon his bit of inheritance (because he and Annette Vallon, in Blois, were expecting the infant who arrived in December and was named Caroline). But he stayed for many weeks, inevitably caught up in the rejoicing of the gathering British, who by November could organize themselves as a philosophical vanguard for the liberation of the British Commonwealth, or whatever other goals they variously envisioned.

On 29 September the Convention established a committee to write a constitution for the new Republic; its members would include Tom Paine, who had come over from England just in time, recommending as he left that the British people summon a Convention of their own. Paine apparently had the impression that the British people were also ready for a great leap. And indeed many shared that impression. The French Revolution had been from the beginning what Gwynn Williams, in his *Artisans and Sans-culottes*,[6] calls "an energising myth," though "it stood at some distance from the British popular movement." Then suddenly "that distance abruptly disappeared," and in late September new members began to "pour into the divisions" of the London Corresponding Society—and of every society which was unmistakably "popular," precisely at that moment when "respectable" sympathisers were falling away in droves. . . . For the British popular movement, the French Revolution which counted was that of 10 August 1792 followed by a French Convention and a Republic based on manhood suffrage, with a sansculotte as its most vivid image.

To the head of the movement . . . swept the London Corresponding Society, Burke's "Mother of all Mischief." Its constitution was almost *Rousseau-ist* in its direct democracy and unlimited numbers, its penny weekly subscription, local division, its members' right to recall delegates and to ratify committee decisions. Members took it seriously. (67–71)

Wordsworth's British associates in Paris must have felt right in the midst of this upsurge, for an increase in the numbers and the commitment of British visitors was a part of the same breakthrough. A few had come over at each stage of the Revolution, to watch the excitement or share in it. But Paine and the British radicals who accompanied him this September were the crest of a large wave. By November 1792 there were in Paris enough English republicans—a suitable term for the common spirit among them—to organize themselves formally as "The Friends of the Rights of Man associated at Paris," informally the "British Club," with a Directory in which John Oswald, a Scottish member of the Jacobin Club and, by now, commander of a volunteer battalion, served at times as secretary. (Wordsworth, who used Oswald's name and some particulars of his career in his *Excursion* and *Borderers,* could conceivably have done so without ever meeting him or even seeing him in action, since his legendary career was widely known in both London and Paris; yet a Paris meeting is most likely.) Paine was both helping write a republican constitution and cooperating with the war office to obtain French assistance for an uprising of armed volunteers in Dublin. Oswald was now officially drilling volunteers in Paris and probably instructing other drillmasters. He probably also found time to introduce Dr. William Maxwell, a delegate from the London Corresponding Society *and* Horne Tooke's older Society for Constitutional Information, to Minister of War Servan, in late August.

Maxwell offered to equip a company of sharpshooters with rifle-bored guns—as he later explained in a letter to Servan's successor, Pache. Maxwell returned to England "to negotiate in Birmingham for the supply of pikes, guns and daggers,"[7] payment for which he had agreed should be deferred till the end of the war. Among the sympathetic British who had to stay home but expressed their sympathy concretely was Robert Burns, who sent cannon which, as an exciseman, he had taken from a smuggling vessel he had helped to capture. (He had sent these to Paris in February, actually, considerably in advance of the main wave.)[8]

The increasingly serious group of British in Paris in this period left very little record of their political discussions, and even the British spy reports of their doings survive mainly in meager summary. Conversations in the well-known salons of Helen Maria Williams and her lover, John Hurford Stone, and of such whiggish Parisians as Lavoisier and Manon Roland are seldom more than sketchily reported; knowing that Watt and Oswald visited them—and conjecturing that Wordsworth did too—tells us little of what they talked about. But the British Club members left a fair amount of evidence of their views—though rather little of their intentions. Oswald's public declaration in February 1793—in a Jacobin Club meeting the record of which has only recently surfaced—to the effect that a group of French Jacobins had been planning an invasion of England in October implied that there had been British among them.

Most of what we know of the organization and composition of the British Club comes from spy reports and the researches a century ago of John G. Alger.[9] Having met with increasing seriousness after November, the club gave formal notice in the *Moniteur* of 5 January of its formation and its intention to meet twice a week, as apparently it had been doing for some time. The British spy, Captain George Monro, reported on 17 December that "Mr. Frost has left his house [White's Hotel, meeting place of the club] and seldom makes his appearance. He is, however, one of the society"; also that the "party of conspirators" have definitely "formed themselves into a society." The poet Robert Merry had presided over a meeting the day before, and a Dr. George Edwards had arrived to join Maxwell.[10]

Dr. Edwards, an admirer of Franklin's theories of medicine, would present his works and an outline for a constitution to the Convention in 1793. Joining Maxwell may have meant joining him in the French army, or perhaps simply joining his English faction in the society (i.e., those focusing on England). On 27 December (on the other hand) Monro reported that "many of the party had become friends of royalty"—wanting to keep a role for a king in the British Constitution if not the French? Or simply opposing the guillotining of King Louis (their more probable position)? Doubtless there were some, on days when they could believe that a liberal reform of the British Constitution was a likely prospect, who had come to believe, as they fraternized with the French people, in the approach of a Federation of the Free Nations of Britain, the United States of America, and a Republic of France. (The very idea terrified Edmund Burke.) But there were still many "who would stand at nothing to ruin their country," that is, who still hoped for a British revolution. On the last day of the year Monro described the remnant of the club as "beneath the notice of any one, struggling for consequence among themselves."

Alger, summarizing further, reports thus: With few exceptions they were "heartily tired of politics and addresses. Tom Paine's fate [he was tried in London in absentia 18 December and declared an outlaw] and the unanimity of the English [against France—no London sansculottes were showing their faces] has staggered the boldest of them, and they are now dwindling into nothing." On 11 January 1793 another address was advocated by Paine but was so warmly opposed that "the dispute nearly ended in blows. I cannot tell how it ended, as things are kept very secret" (Alger, *Paris*, 330–331).

Henry Redhead Yorke tells us the particulars. The address invited the Convention to liberate enslaved England. He opposed it, and "we carried it"—that is to say, the address was rejected—"by a majority of one." It was, however, again brought forward, whereupon Yorke and Johnson (a young surgeon from Derby, who had accompanied Yorke to Paris) drew up a remonstrance and seceded. This second address was presented to the Convention on 22 January (the day after Louis's execution), but I have not found it in the National Archives.

Alger proceeds to make a tally of the club membership at this time:

Thomas Muir, the Scotch advocate afterwards transported to Botany Bay [for his part in organizing a "National Convention" in Scotland in December], arrived in Paris on the 20th January 1793, and no doubt joined the club. . . . Sampson Perry, militia surgeon and journalist, who, to avoid a press prosecution, fled to Paris in December 1792, must also have belonged to the club. Paine, invited to the Hotel de Ville to dine with Petion, Dumouriez, Santerre, Condorcet, Brissot,

Danton, Vergniaud, Sieyes, and others took Perry with him. Perry also made acquaintance, at the receptions of Madame Lavit, with Cloots, Couthon, Herault, David, and Laignelot, a Paris deputy. This last ultimately procured his release. Perry, at the instance of Herault, sent a female relative and her friend to England, with letters to Sheridan and other Opposition leaders, in the view of initiating an agitation for peace.

(Alger, *Paris,* 361–362)

(Actually, the British Club did not collapse until the spring of 1793, and then not simply because the members could not agree on a course of action, but because war between Britain and France was swiftly rendering the options for any concerted action problematic; members fled home, or joined the French army, or remained in Paris in increasing isolation. When the "year of the French" finally came, militarily, in 1797, the thrust was invasion—of Ireland, with only a brief feint toward England—and not much insurrection anywhere.)

Perhaps the focus of the spies for the British government, some of whose reports for 1792 survive, was strategically the wisest one. Though toward the end of 1792 there was alarming news that the American poet Joel Barlow had offered the services of British shoemakers to keep French armies shod, the British spies seem to have been more concerned about the menace of revolutionary propaganda than about military assistance. A letter summarizing spy reports for Lord Auckland, British ambassador to Holland, reports Paine's appointment to the "executive government" (i.e., the Constitution Committee) and describes Dr. Priestley as "the great adviser to the present ministers, being consulted by them on all occasions" (Priestley did not even go over to France). But most alarming is the spy's discovery that

there are also 8 or 10 other English and Scotch who work with the Jacobins and in great measure conduct their present manoeuvres [Frenchmen, presumably, could not have been clever enough]. I understand these gentlemen at present are employed in writing a justification of democracy [!] and an invective against monarchy which is to be printed at Paris, and dispersed through England and Ireland. The names of some of them are Watts and Wilson, of Manchester; Oswald, a Scotsman; Stone, an Englishman, and Mackintosh who wrote against Burke.[11]

What were these British advisors to the Jacobins preparing to publish? I can see two possibilities. A manifesto which justified the Revolution had been drafted by Oswald for the Jacobin Club in September, and its propagation doubtless occupied several such gentlemen. But the still-impressive and in those days alarming work that was being printed in English and advertised in the *Chronique du mois* (a monthly of which Oswald and Paine were among the editors) was a "revised" edition of John Oswald's *Review of the Constitution of Great Britain,* "printed at the English press by Gillet" (an associate of J. H. Stone, who would later use the "English Press" rubric for a shop of his own).

Indeed Oswald's book seems the only likely project these gentlemen were concerned in printing for dispersal "through England and Ireland," the zones of potential revolution, during this autumn. It may be that some of the summarized spy reports did specify both the title and the author's name, thus lighting the fuse that fired Burke's outcry in Parliament the following March against the dissemination by John Oswald of the dangerous doctrine of "democracy" and the hideous concept of liberation from "the yoke of property."

For the rest of 1792, the inspiring formation of the French Republic continued to restrain animosities among spokesmen of the Voice of the People (i.e., politicians), for the single Enemy to be slain was Louis XVI, whose "trial" took the center of attention, while the military situation remained auspicious. And on 6 November the French won a victory that seemed to promise a future of peace, if not relaxation. Here Thomas Carlyle succeeds, in language culled from the contemporary record, in being extremely faithful to what we now call the "perception" of what was happening and to the enthusiasm that inspired the British in Paris to call for a celebration:

The Sixth of November 1792 was a great day for the Republic; outwardly, over the Frontiers; inwardly, in the *Salle de Manege* [meeting hall of the Convention].

Outwardly: for Dumouriez, overrunning the Netherlands, did, on that day, come in contact with Saxe-Teschen and the Austrians; and Dumouriez wide-winged, they wide-winged; at and around the village of Jemappes, near Mons. And fire-hail is whistling far and wide there, the greant guns playing, and the small; so many green Heights getting fringed and maned with red Fire. And Dumouriez is swept back on this wing, and swept back on that, and is like to be swept back utterly; when he rushes up in person, the prompt Polymetis; speaks a prompt word or two; and then, with clear tenor-pipe, "uplifts the Hymn of the Marseillese, *entonna la Marseillaise,*" ten-thousand tenor or bass pipes joining; or say, some Forty-thousand in all; for every heart leaps at the sound; and so with rhythmic march-melody, waxing ever quicker, to double and to treble quick, they rally, they advance, they rush, death-defying, man-devouring; carry batteries, redoutes, whatsoever is to be carried; and, like the fire-whirlwind, sweep all manner of Austrians from the scene of action. Thus, through the hands of Dumouriez, may Rouget de Lille [composer of the hymn] . . . be said to have gained . . . a Victory of Jemappes; and conquered the Low Countries.

(Thomas Carlyle, *The French Revolution,* 538–539)

When the news of victory reached the Hall of the National Convention, a committee was reporting on "the Crimes of Louis." When the news reached the British living in Paris, they issued a call for a celebration on Sunday the eighteenth at White's Hotel. There they sang, danced, drank toasts—and signed a manifesto of solidarity to be read to the Convention. This British manifesto apparently originated as a response by the fraternal nations appealed to in the Oswaldian Jacobin manifesto of 3 October. But by a coincidence of timing, when it was made public on 28 November, it appeared to be an immediate answer, by those assembled at White's, to a decree issued to the world by the Convention on Monday, 19 November, offering brotherhood and assistance to all peoples seeking freedom.

The toasts drunk at White's (as officially announced by the club) were not fourteen (the French magic number) but thirteen (the American), though they were *meant* to be fourteen. I number them for convenience:

[1] The French Republic, founded on the rights of man,
[2] The French armies, and the destruction of tyrants and tyranny,
[3] The National Convention,
[4] The Coming Convention of England and Ireland [N.B.],

[5] The Union of France, Great Britain, and Belgium, and may neighbouring nations join in the same sentiments,

[6] The Republic of Men, accompanied by an English song to the air of the "Marseillaise," composed by an English lady—probably the woman who sang it, Helen Maria Williams, Wordsworth's "contact",

[7] The dissolution of the Germanic Circle and may their inhabitants be free,

[8] Abolition of hereditary titles throughout the world (proposed by Lord Edward Fitzgerald and Sir R. Smyth),

[9] Lord E. Fitzgerald and Sir R. Smyth,

[10] Thomas Paine, and the new way of making good books known by royal proclamations and by prosecuting the authors in the King's Bench,

[11] The Women of Great Britain, particularly those who have distinguished themselves by their writings in favour of the French revolution, Mrs. [Charlotte] Smith and Miss H. M. Williams,

[12] The Women of France, especially those who have had the courage to take up arms to defend the cause of liberty, *citoyennes* Fernig, Anselm, &c [this would have to include Théroigne de Mericourt and Etta Palm],

[13] Universal Peace, based on universal liberty.[12]

The most formal action of the banquet at White's Hotel was the signing of an Address to the National Convention by fifty British citizens resident in Paris, chosen by votes of the whole group (about a hundred persons in all). Among those present but not nominated we are certain of Tom Paine, not chosen since he was a member of the Convention being addressed; Helen Maria Williams, who sang; and Henry Redhead Yorke. Almost certainly Sampson Perry was there, and Thomas Christie of the London Coresponding Society; possibly Wordsworth, but not Mary Wollstonecraft (who arrived in Paris too late).

Some reports add that "Sir Robert Smith and Lord E. Fitzgerald renounced their titles, and a toast was proposed by the former . . . : The speedy abolition of all hereditary titles and feudal distinctions" and that "General Dillon proposed 'The people of Ireland; and may government profit by the example of France, and Reform prevent Revolution.'" (This "reform" proposal was dropped from the official list, obviously to keep the focus on revolution.)

A report to London by the British spy Monro noted that Maxwell, one of those present, was still negotiating with the war minister for the command of a company in the French service. Monro had not noticed that among the several French officers and deputies at the banquet was the Irish general Arthur Dillon, of the French war office. We know that Dillon was in contact with Stone and Paine and, probably, Oswald. In January 1793 Oswald would advocate—in confidence to the French war office—an invasion of London, Oswald and Dillon agreeing on the figure of sixty thousand troops to be subsidized by France.

The completely predictable event of 21 January, the execution of King Louis XVI (with Oswald's volunteers, men and women, dancing around the guillotine), led swiftly to declarations of war and the cessation of free travel across the Channel, which many of our activists had not foreseen as inevitable, having focused their expectations on a different goal. With historical hindsight it has been easy to conclude that those in France or England who congratulated each other on the close approach of a union of free nations were unrealistic—blind or stupid, or at least badly misinformed. Future historians may easily draw similar conclusions about the peace movements of the present—if any live to write history.

The air was, indeed, full of misinformation—and anxiety about it. In the White's Hotel address we find a paradoxical combination of confidence in majority British sentiment and a need to have a poll of that opinion. In subsequent meetings of the British Club—which continued, more or less secretly, for a month or two after the declarations of war against each other by the governments of France and Britain in early February—the guiding spirits of the club again and again decided (a) that a British revolution was now inevitable and (b) that one or two of them should hurry back to London, or Dublin, to find out the state of the political atmosphere. This sending of delegates had begun early in the winter; it is plausible to conjecture, though no evidence can be found, that Wordsworth's sudden acting upon his oft-delayed decision to go back to London in December to raise cash, even while the birth of his child was approaching, was understood by Oswald and others of the club to be coincident, at least, with the wish for a fresh poll.

As François Furet observes, in *Interpreting the French Revolution,* the

outbreak of the war between the French Revolution and the rest of Europe is probably one of the most important and telling *problems* [emphasis added] in the history of the Revolution. The war . . . was *accepted* rather than desired by the European monarchies, despite pressure from the emigres and the French royal family. By contrast, it was desired in France by the court and the social forces that hankered after the Ancien Regime; but in the winter of 1791–2 those forces were far too weak. . . . In reality [by the winter of 1792–1793] it was the Revolution that, over Robespierre's objections, wanted to go to war against the kings. The Revolution, yes. But . . . which one?[13]

Jacques-Pierre Brissot was one of the revolutionaries who saw everything to gain in war with Britain and who often overpowered the counterarguments of Robespierre. And while the legend that Wordsworth while in Paris was a Brissotin rests on shaky evidence—he lived to contradict an assertion that he had lived in the same building as Brissot—it does seem likely that in this winter Wordsworth's interest in philosophical war would align his thinking with the military philosophizing of the staunchest members of the British Club, who continued on into the spring their increasingly quarrelsome dispute as to whether to begin the British Revolution in London or in Dublin—and whether to join it by invitation or start it by an invasion.

Ironically it was a maneuver of the British government that filled the London and Paris journals in December 1792 with misinformation easily mistaken for evidence that insurrections were sweeping England and Scotland. London papers reported that (while nobody else seems to have been looking) attempts had been made to storm the Bank and the Tower of London, à la the storming of the Bastille and, say, the Tuileries. And armed battalions were reported as supporting an elected Convention of Catholics in Ireland. The purpose of these reports was to justify summoning the militia in all counties, a necessary prerequisite for the calling of an emergency session of Parliament to vote funds for war with France (the same stratagem had been used preceding the American war, in December 1774).[14]

Thus, just as Wordsworth was moving from Paris to London, in early December or possibly late November 1792, the British who had rejoiced at the destruction of the Bastille were now regaled with tales of a similar threat to the Tower, a similar emblem of tyranny. Some members of the British Club even managed to get a placard pasted up on dead walls in *London*, dated "Paris, December 4." To me this poster smacks of Oswaldian philosophy—perhaps temporarily Wordsworthian. I like to surmise, not quite seriously, that the poet who in a few months would be writing a pamphlet justifying the execution of Louis (which he decided not to publish, having discovered the less-than-insurrectionary mood prevailing in London after all)—I like to imagine that his mission for the club was to arrange for the printing and posting of these placards as soon as he got to London. They must have been torn down by "loyal" British and their spies soon after posting, but one copy has survived, worth quoting in full:

FRIENDS OF THE RIGHTS OF MAN ASSOCIATED AT PARIS,
DECEMBER 4, FIRST YEAR OF THE FRENCH REPUBLIC

We whose names are subscribed to this declaration, for the greater part natives of Great Britain and Ireland, and now resident in Paris, sensible of the duties we owe to our countrymen, as well as to the general cause of liberty and happiness through the world, have formed ourselves into a society for the express purpose of collecting political information and extending it to the people at large in the several nations to which we belong.

We are happy that our temporary residence in this enlightened and regenerated capital enables us to become the organ of communicating knowledge on the most interesting subjects, of administering to the moral improvement and social happiness of a considerable portion of our fellow-men, and of undeceiving the minds of our countrymen, abused by the wretched calumnies of a wicked Administration who, in order to perpetuate the slavery of the English, have made it their business to stigmatise the glorious exertions of the French.

We begin with an open and unequivocal declaration of the principles which animate our conduct, and precise definition of the object we mean to pursue, that no individual in any country may mistake our motives or be ignorant in what manner to address us. We declare that an equal Government, unmixed with any kind of exclusive privileges, conducted by the whole body of the people or by their agents, chosen at frequent periods and subject to their recall, is the only Government proper for man; that the British and Irish nations do not enjoy such a Government; that they cannot obtain it until a National Convention be chosen and assembled to lay its foundations on the basis of the Rights of Man; that to effect this great and indispensable object we

will use all the means which reason, argument, and the communication of information can supply; that we will endeavour to remove all
national prejudices which it has been the interest of tyrants to excite in
order to separate and enslave the great family of Man; that we invite
individuals and societies of every name and description in the above
nations and elsewhere to a manly and unreserved correspondence with
our society; and we pledge ourselves to them and to the universe that
no composition or sacrifice extorted from the fears of expiring Oppression shall seduce or deter us from persevering with firmness and
constancy in the discharge of the important duty we have undertaken.

Here follow the signatures.

No signed copy survives, but the signers must have included Paine,
Barlow, . . . and Wordsworth? The language is impersonal, but all must
have agreed to the sober emphasis on enlightenment. The alternative between a government conducted by the people or by their representatives in-
dicates the gap in theory that divided the British and Irish in Paris, the gap in
strategy being imposed by the fact, one would suppose, that the Irish already had their insurrectionary battalion, in arms, in Dublin, while it would
require invading battalions from France to liberate London.

The intellectual battle was still on when Wordsworth returned to London in December, and he would have found the universal patriots there as
positive as those he had left behind in Paris. And even the official British response to the guillotining of King Louis, even the public eruption of mutual
war, failed to deprive the British in London of hope and moral righteous-
ness. "In France," wrote one of these in a pamphlet justifying the execution
of Louis, a tyrant and murderer, "royalty is no more; the person of the last
anointed is no more also, and I flatter myself I am not alone, even in this
kingdom [the author's italics], when I wish that it may please the almighty
neither by the hands of his priests nor his nobles . . . to raise his posterity to
the rank of his ancestors and reillume the torch of extinguished David." The
author of this "regicide" pamphlet (as Burke would have called it) was
William Wordsworth.

2

Wordsworth as Satirist of His Age

STEPHEN M. PARRISH

"I have long since come to a fixed resolution to steer clear of personal satire," avowed Wordsworth in 1806; "this is a rule which I have laid down for myself, and shall rigidly adhere to."[1] This avowal helps to make an essay on Wordsworth as a satirist seem about as bleakly promising as a celebration of wit and humor in *The Excursion,* or a study of Wordsworth's Bawdy. Whatever image of Wordsworth we favor—the poet of Nature, the ardent lover, the chronicler of human suffering, the apostle of the One Life, the Tory Humanist—we are likely to envisage a somber manner, a sober mask, inner feeling subdued to the decorum of programmatic or confessional verse, or to the proprieties of public prose. If we recall Hazlitt's description of this countenance, we are more apt to be struck by its strength and ugliness, or by "the severe, worn pressure of thought about his temples," than by what Hazlitt discerned as a "convulsive inclination to laughter about the mouth."[2]

Our impression of high seriousness, elevated above the low satiric mode, can be reinforced by a glance at Wordsworth's ranking of his predecessors. Chaucer, to be sure, took his place in the cluster of four names at the top,[3] but the great satirists who dominated the century of Wordsworth's maturation are shown scant respect. Though Wordsworth sometimes revealed close acquaintance with the poetry of Dryden and Pope, the only notice he gives it in the compact little outline of English literature embedded in the 1815 "Essay, Supplementary to the Preface" takes the form of a characteris-

tic attack, concentrated on a rendering of night in Dryden's *Indian Emperor*
and a moonlight scene in Pope's *Iliad:* "A blind man, in the habit of attending accurately to descriptions casually dropped from the lips of those
around him, might easily depict these appearances with more truth. Dryden's lines are vague, bombastic, and senseless; those of Pope, though he had
Homer to guide him, are throughout false and contradictory." And in the
preface to which this essay is "supplementary," Wordsworth relegates Satire to the sixth and last of the classes into which he divides poetic writing,
remarking that satire rarely had "sufficient of the general in the individual to
be dignified with the name of poetry."

But to allow these dismissive remarks to shape our image of Wordsworth
is to miss, or undervalue, some of the most powerful and brilliant strains in
his writing, verse and prose alike—the strains of sardonic criticism, scorn,
and open contempt, often barely modulated by civility, in which he couched
the strongest of his political, social, and literary convictions. A fair specimen
is his early, little-read, "imitation" of Juvenal, much of which remains in
manuscript. The occasion of his 1806 pledge to eschew satire was Francis
Wrangham's request for permission to publish the pieces of Juvenalian verse
the two friends had worked on together more than ten years earlier. Like all
good satire, this verse makes pointed use of animal imagery. The targets of
Wordsworth's satiric attack ranged from the King himself and the Queen—
or perhaps their daughter of the same name—

> Insatiate Charlotte's tears, and Charlotte's smile
> Shall ape and scaly regent of the Nile—

to British diplomats—

> What has this blessed earth to do with shame
> If excellence was ever Eden's name?—

to bishops, politicians, lesser public figures, and an assortment of barons
commencing with "thundering Thurlow":

> Must honour still to Lonsdale's tail to bound?
> Then execration is an empty sound.
> Is Common-sense asleep? has she no wand
> From this curst Pharaoh-plague to rid the land?[4]

We should remember that the plan of the great *Recluse*, formed in 1798,
was to give "pictures of Nature, Man, and Society," with Wordsworth (ac-

cording to Coleridge's understanding) "assuming something of the Juvenalian spirit as he approached the high civilization of cities and towns, and
opening a melancholy picture of the present state of degeneracy and vice."[5]
But by 1806 Wordsworth not only refused Wrangham permission to publish his Juvenalian verses but begged him to destroy them. Their raw crude-
ness may stem from Juvenal, but the satiric impulse behind them found
other outlets, even in the gentler years of *Lyrical Ballads,* when Wordsworth is thought to have moderated his antiestablishment feelings. *A Poet's
Epitaph,* modeled on a poem by Burns, satirizes a range of professions and
offices, this time generalized, in terms of sardonic hyperbole. The politician,
seeking to approach the poet's grave, is given ironic advice:

> —First learn to love one living man;
> *Then* may'st thou think upon the dead.

The lawyer is similarly rebuffed, urged to "carry to some other place"

> The hardness of thy coward eye,
> The falsehood of thy face.

The bishop, mocked as a "man of purple cheer"—"A rosy man, right
plump to see"—is permitted to approach, but "not too near." The poem
reaches a fresh level with the brilliant stanzas attacking the scientist and the
moral philosopher, the primary objects of the poet's bitter contempt in the
1800 edition:

> Physician art thou? One, all eyes,
> Philosopher! a fingering slave,
> One that would peep and botanize
> Upon his mother's grave?
>
> Wrapp'd closely in thy sensual fleece
> O turn aside, and take, I pray,
> That he below may rest in peace,
> Thy pin-point of a soul away!
>
> —A Moralist perchance appears;
> Led, Heaven knows how! to this poor sod;
> And He has neither eyes nor ears;
> Himself his world, and his own God;

> One to whose smooth-rubb'd soul can cling
> Nor form nor feeling great nor small,
> A reasoning, self-sufficing thing,
> An intellectual All in All!
>
> Shut close the door! press down the latch:
> Sleep in thy intellectual crust,
> Nor lose ten tickings of thy watch,
> Near this unprofiable dust.

If this is the kind of satiric writing Wordsworth meant he had given up when he made his avowal to Wrangham in 1806, we can only feel regret at the loss. Such a sure command of the language of scorn and the metaphors of futility, of littleness, of vanity (the "sensual fleece," and "intellectual crust," and the "smooth-rubb'd soul" are as richly complex as they are pointedly simple) could have ranked Wordsworth as a major satiric voice, had he chosen to allow that to happen. But the regret need not obscure Wordsworth's achievement as a satirist. From almost the beginning of his career he showed a liking and a flair for satire, and to trace the intermittent appearance of his satiric manner and voice is to recognize their distinctive pungency and range.

As we could expect of a poet so closely touched by the French Revolution and its aftermath, a good deal of Wordsworth's satiric scorn was directed against political and social targets. The growth of satiric elements in his early writing was slow, but persistent. When in 1794 he revised *An Evening Walk*—in its first published form a relatively conventional locodescriptive poem infused with Virgilian tones—"Landscape [became] *paysage moralisé*," in the words of the poem's recent editor, James Averill, and "a glow-worm [became] the implied emblem of Wordsworth's poetic and political situation":[6]

> Oh! may'st thou, safe from every onset rude,
> Irradiate long thy friendless solitude,
> So Virtue, fallen on times to gloom consigned,
> Makes round her path the light she cannot find,

And by her own internal lamp fulfills,
And asks no other star what Virtue wills,
Acknowledging, though round her Danger lurk,
And Fear, no night in which she cannot work.

The companion poem published in 1793, *Descriptive Sketches*, offers melancholy pictures of human suffering inflicted partly by harsh Nature, partly by disease and penury, "Labour, and Pain, and Grief, and joyless Age," and partly by war and tyranny, so that

—The mind condemn'd, without reprieve, to go
O'er life's long deserts with its charge of woe,
With sad congratulation joins the train,
Where beasts and men together o'er the plain
Move on,—a mighty caravan of pain.

The poem closes with a prayer that has both Virgilian and Popeian overtones (muted in later revision) and offers a dark view of the human condition:

Oh give, great God, to Freedom's waves to ride
Sublime o'er Conquest, Avarice, and Pride,
To break, the vales where Death with Famine scowr's,
And dark Oppression builds her thick-ribb'd tow'rs;
Where Machination her fell soul resigns,
Fled panting to the centre of her mines;
Where Persecution decks with ghastly smiles
Her bed, his mountains mad Ambition piles;
Where Discord stalks dilating, every hour,
And crouching fearful at the feet of Pow'r,
Like Lightnings eager for th' almighty word,
Look up for sign of havoc, Fire, and Sword.

The neoclassical language of polemic here is sharpened in *Salisbury Plain*, written in the following year or two as a poem of social protest, attacking the pression of the poor that resulted not only from war but from the tyranny of social injustice:

Insensate they who think at Wisdom's porch
That Exile, Terror, Bonds, and Force may stand:

That Truth with human blood can feed her torch,
And Justice balance with her gory hand
Scales whose dire weights of human heads demand
A Nero's arm. Must Law with iron scourge
Still torture crimes that grew a monstrous band
Formed by his care, and still his victim urge,
With voice that breathes despair, to death's tremendous verge?

The invocation that closes this poem is not a prayer but a revolutionary call
to action:

Heroes of Truth pursue your march, uptear
Th'Oppressor's dungeon from its deepest base;
High o'er the towers of Pride undaunted rear
Resistless in your might the herculean mace
Of Reason; let foul Error's monster race
Dragged from their dens start at the light with pain
And die. . . .[7]

The sentiments behind these verses are spelled out in a series of letters
that Wordsworth wrote to William Mathews in 1794 and 1795 and in the
unpublished "Letter to the Bishop of Llandaff" of 1793. In the letters to his
friend Mathews, Wordsworth speaks in a straightforward way and declares
himself to be a republican. He disapproves, he says, of monarchy and aristo-
cratic government and is hostile to all "hereditary distinctions and privileged
orders," as he offers his services as a political commentator in a proposed
new magazine.[8] The kind of comments he might have written is revealed in
the "Letter to the Bishop of Llandaff," in which Wordsworth addresses, he
supposed, an apostate from liberal causes; he draws from time to time on
resources of irony and indignation that begin here to mark his satiric manner. He opens by expressing the fear that his lordship may have slipped
while crossing the allegorical bridge of life portrayed by Addison and
"fallen, through one of the numerous trap-doors, into the tide of contempt
to be swept down to the ocean of oblivion."[9] He goes on to reproach the
bishop with delicate sarcasm for overreacting to the execution of the French
king. "At a period big with the fate of the human race, I am sorry that you
attach so much importance to the personal sufferings of the late royal mar-
tyr and that an anxiety for the issue of the present convulsions should not

have prevented you from joining the idle cry of modish lamentation which has resounded from the court to the cottage."

The letter constitutes a wide-ranging indictment of the monarchy, of "hereditary authority," of "arbitrary distinctions among mankind" ("stars, ribbands, garters, and other badges of fictitious authority"), of the coercive power of tyrannical government, of restrictions on the liberty of citizens, of abuses even in the Church and the courts ("I congratulate your lordship upon your enthusiastic fondness for the judicial proceedings of this country. I am happy to find you have passed through life without having your fleece torn from your back in the thorny labyrinth of litigation"). In its pointedly direct address to its victim, it achieves a sardonic eloquence that sharpens whenever Wordsworth touches on the principles closest to his heart: the reliable common sense of the common man. "Left to the quiet exercise of their own judgment do you think that the people . . . would cry out as with one voice for a war from which not a single ray of consolation can visit them to compensate for the additional keenness with which they are about to smart under the scourge of labour, of cold, and of hunger?"

For reasons that now seem clear, Wordsworth never ventured to publish this letter. In the climate of the day, it could have been dangerous, and his views of the French Revolution soon began to change. Fifteen years passed before he allowed a political tract to appear over his own name (Kenneth Johnston has begun to identify anonymous essays in the *Philanthropist* of 1795 as plausibly Wordsworth's). *The Convention of Cintra* (1809) is prefixed with an epigraph from Bacon that constitutes an apology for satire: "Bitter and earnest writing must not hastily be condemned; for men cannot contend coldly, and without affection, about the things which they hold dear and precious."[10] The things that Wordsworth held precious in 1809 were of a rather different order from those he cherished in 1793, but both his published political essays now seem surprisingly bloodthirsty in their endorsement of action in a righteous cause. Despite his explicit avowal to William Mathews in 1794—"I am a determined enemy to every species of violence"—in 1793 he appeared to excuse the excesses of the French Revolution with a blandly reconciling analogy: "The animal just released from its stall will exhaust the overflow of its spirits in a round of wanton vagaries, but it will soon return to itself and enjoy its freedom in moderate and regular delight." And in *The Convention of Cintra* the British generals in Spain are bitterly taxed for their failure to employ the weapons of fire and sword:

"The French army was not broken? Break it then—wither it—pursue it with unrelenting warfare—hunt it out of its holds."

The political sentiments that animated the stream of *Sonnets Dedicated to National Independence and Liberty* in 1802 and 1803 when England lay briefly under the threat of French invasion were patriotic, and their hortatory manner keeps them from becoming primarily satiric. But their power occasionally arises from satiric elements—vignettes of political servility in France, or images of the "fen of stagnant waters," the "Bogs and Sands," to which England has been reduced. Later political writings like the 1818 *Addresses to the Freeholders of Westmorland,* or the "Postscript" of 1835 on the subject of the poor laws and the slave trade hardly add to Wordsworth's credentials as a satirist, owing to their general tone of earnest sobriety, but flashes of a sardonic voice hint at what the poet remained capable of. They show best in Wordsworth's indictments of folly—that is, of the political opposition. Henry Brougham (in 1818) is taxed for "labouring to ingraft certain sour cuttings from the wild wood of ultra reform, on the reverend, though somewhat decayed, stock of the tree of Whiggism." His party is accused of confusing liberty with license, independence with

> the explosive energy of conceit—making blind havoc with expediency. . . . The independence which they boast of despises habit, and time-honoured forms of subordination; it consists in breaking old ties upon new temptations; in casting off the modest garb of private obligation to strut about in the glittering armour of public virtue; in sacrificing, with jacobinical infatuation, the near to the remote, and preferring to what has been known and tried, that which has no distinct existence, even in imagination.[11]

This, the *Second Address to the Westmorland Freeholders,* culminates in a sardonic contrast between "rash Politicians . . . the worst enemies of mankind" and landscape gardeners, who are sensible enough to govern their "elegant art" by principles of balance and propriety.

But "political satirist" is too limited a phrase to do justice to Wordsworth's satiric range, and it can mislead us by suggesting that the poet moved along any sort of conventional path. The truth is that his deepest reaction against the follies and abuses of his age arose more against the Industrial Revolution than the French Revolution. Wordsworth's disquiet about the urbanization of English manners, as of the English countryside, runs as a persistent theme through the greatest poetry of his great decade. It is revealed not only in the procession of unsophisticated country characters, often victims of social wrongs, that moves through his poems, but in the carefully articulated program for experimental verse drawn up in the prefaces to *Lyrical Ballads*. The poet who turns to rural occupations and manners and to rustic and common life to find "the essential passions of the heart," "the elementary feelings of mankind," is expressing a kind of revulsion from much of the modern world, and the nature of that revulsion is nowhere more eloquently spelled out than in an early paragraph of the 1800 Preface, constituting a powerful indictment of the way the times were moving:

> For a multitude of causes unknown to former times are now acting with a combined force to blunt the discriminating powers of the mind, and unfitting it for all voluntary exertion to reduce it to a state of almost savage torpor. The most effective of these causes are the great national events which are daily taking place, and the encreasing accumulation of men in cities, where the uniformity of their occupations produces a craving for extraordinary incident which the rapid communication of intelligence hourly gratifies. To this tendency of life and manners the literature and theatrical exhibitions of the country have conformed themselves. The invaluable works of our elder writers, I had almost said the works of Shakspear and Milton, are driven into neglect by frantic novels, sickly and stupid German Tragedies, and deluges of idle and extravagant stories in verse.

This indictment trails off with a melancholy reflection on "the magnitude of the general evil" and with doubts about the adequacy of the poems that follow to reform the "degrading thirst after outrageous stimulation" which has been generated by industrial urbanization.

The poems by which Wordsworth hoped to counteract the general evil celebrate the virtues and trace the misfortunes of survivors of an earlier, pastoral, age. While it is war and drought that bring on the suffering of people like Margaret in *The Ruined Cottage* ("A happy land was stricken to the heart"), the suffering of old Michael is linked directly to the immersion of his son in "the dissolute city," where he "gave himself to evil courses" and succumbed to the weight of "ignominy and shame." In the letter to Charles James Fox which he wrote to accompany presentation copies of *Lyrical Ballads*,[12] Wordsworth alluded specifically to *Michael*, elaborating on the "calamitous effect" of recent alterations in the style and conduct of English life. He singles out "the spreading of manufactures through every part of the country . . . workhouses, Houses of Industry, and the intervention of Soup-shops &c. &c." (It is worth observing that the parallel letter drafted by Coleridge to send to William Wilberforce contains no such talk of the encroachments of modern civilization).[13] Other scattered allusions to these events could be collected (though we might mercifully overlook the aged Wordsworth's complaint, in 1845, about the intrusion of railroads into the Lake District, which reads like a parody of his early patriotic sonnets: "Is there no nook of English ground secure / From rash assault?").[14] Peter Bell exhibited, for instance, a kind of natural savagery reinforced by "whatever vice the cruel city breeds." (Mary Lamb once wondered whether Wordsworth could possibly believe that a "liver in towns had a soul to be saved"). And the world which is too much with us, the world of getting and spending in which "we lay waste our powers," is clearly the world of industrial commerce.

But Wordsworth's major satiric portrayal of the urban wasteland is, of course, to be found in book 7 of *The Prelude*.[15] The movement of this book resembles that of a locodescriptive landscape poem: we are taken on a series of daytime and evening walks through scenes that evoke moral reflection. But there is another principle of order that governs the structure of the book. Before we reach London at all, we are invited to share the visions of magic and romance that danced in a Hawkshead schoolboy's mind—"marvellous things," "fond imaginations," all of them enticing, charged with wonder. When these dreams and illusions give way to reality, we enter a world that seems as unreal as the visions had been—a world of artifice and imitation, of "mimic sights that ape / The absolute presence of reality." These sights range from the dazzling parade of "specimens of Man" to spectacles that seem parodic of normal human behavior and human relationships. In a powerful crescendo they culminate in a Parliament of Monsters that stands as an emblem of the city itself, a "hell / For eyes and ears,"

> anarchy and din
> Barbarian and infernal! 'tis a dream,
> Monstrous in colour, motion, shape, sight, sound,

a "Swarm," a "blank confusion." The climax of the long crescendo points in strikingly modern terms to the most terrible feature of the urban waste-land: loss of individual dignity, and worse, loss of identity:

> An undistinguishable world to men,
> The slaves unrespited of low pursuits,
> Living amid the same perpetual flow
> Of trivial objects, melted and reduced
> To one identity, by differences
> That have no law, no meaning, and no end.

The steady movement of book 7 from enticing illusion, through deceiving appearances of reality, and finally to grotesque surrealism points up the ironic contrast between Bartholomew Fair in London and the charming vil-lage fair in Grasmere that follows, at the opening of book 8. Wordsworth's ironic intent is unmistakable. Each fair has its animals (the "company of dancing Dogs," the "chattering monkeys," "The Horse of Knowledge and the learned Pig" in London are set against the bleating sheep and lowing heifer in Grasmere), its beggar, its blind man, its musician, its peddlers (in Grasmere a "sweet lass of the valley" blushingly offers fruit from her father's orchard), its showmen, its crowds (only "a little Family of Men, / Twice twenty, with their Children and their Wives" in Gasmere); and the artfully developed ironic contrasts between them illuminate the meaning of the poet's progress from book 7 to book 8—from the dismal world of ur-ban man back to the pastoral world of nature remembered from childhood.

Heavier, pitiless irony is marshaled in two London portraits that Words-worth sardonically classifies under "entertainments" or "public Shows" to be enjoyed in the city. Both take on ironic resonance from the "sad incom-petence of human speech" cited toward the close of the previous book, as the poet struggled to communicate his feelings at having crossed the Alps. The first portrait, of William Pitt "the Younger" speaking in the Commons, is about as thick a piece of sarcasm as Wordsworth ever fashioned:

> Silence! Hush!
> This is no trifler, no short-flighted Wit,
> No stammerer of a minute, painfully
> Deliver'd. No! the Orator hath yoked
> The Hours, like young Aurora, to his Car;
> O Presence of delight, can patience e'er

Grow weary of attending on a track
That kindles with such glory? Marvellous!
The enchantment spreads and rises; all are rapt
Astonish'd; like a Hero in Romance
He winds away his never-ending horn,
Words follow words, sense seems to follow sense;
What memory and what logic!

The second portrait, equally withering, moves from the Parliament to the
Church and celebrates the virtuosity of a vain, pretentious young preacher:

There have I seen a comely Bachelor,
Fresh from a toilette of two hours, ascend
The Pulpit, with seraphic glance look up,
And, in a tone elaborately low
Beginning, lead his voice through many a maze,
A minuet course, and winding up his mouth,
From time to time into an orifice
Most delicate, a lurking eyelet, small
And only not invisible, again
Open it out, diffusing thence a smile
Of rapt irradiation exquisité.

The portrait closes with sardonic admiration of

. . . the Crook of eloquence with which
This pretty Shepherd, pride of all the Plains,
Leads up and down his captivated flock.

We can hardly miss the ironic contrast between the slick, oral virtuosity
of this urban shepherd in book 7 and the dumb, inarticulate eloquence of
Wordsworth's real shepherds in book 12, men "Shy and unpractis'd in the
strife of phrase," who are at home only in another sort of language,

. . . the language of the heavens, the power
The thought, the image, and the silent joy:
Words are but under-agents in their souls.
(1805 *Prelude*, bk. 12, lines 270–272)

If the broad currents of Wordsworth's satire rose from his reaction to the growing effects of the Industrial Revolution, one of the most persistent streams that runs through the poetry of his great decade centered on a particular manifestation of the follies and abuses of society. This manifestation would have been of special importance to a poet concerned to trace the growth of his own mind, for it involved the growth of a child's mind, the nurture of a maturing sensibility. Wordsworth seems not to have been committed to any one of the theories of education that claimed adherents in the last decade of the eighteenth century and the first decade of the nineteenth, but some of his simplest verse left no doubt about the kinds of theory he opposed, and this verse constitutes a satiric indictment of some of the major philosophical premises of his age. Wordsworth's fervent espousal of what we might call "organic" philosophies of man and nature, as against prevailing philosophies of "mechanism," comes close to the vital center of the Romantic revolution, once suggestively characterized by Alfred North Whitehead as "a revolution on behalf of value."[16]

The earliest important expression of Wordsworth's views on the nurture of the mind appears in his review of the growth of his own youthful mind under the ministering tutelage of Nature. Asserting in what we now call the "two-part" *Prelude*, composed in 1798 and 1799, that the mind of man is created and developed like a "strain of music," Wordsworth sardonically mocks a mechanistic analysis of the human organism:

> But who shall parcel out
> His intellect by geometric rules,
> Split like a province into round and square;
> Who knows the individual hour in which
> His habits were first sown, even as a seed;
> Who that shall point as with a wand and say,
> This portion of the river of my mind
> Came from yon fountain?
>
> (1799 *Prelude* 1.242−249)[17]

The mockery runs on with an image of a museum collection, to embrace the glibly articulate analytic philosophers who would

> ... class the cabinet
> Of their sensations and in voluble phrase
> Run through the history and birth of each
> As of a single independent thing.

The contrast, here, between the images of the mind as a river and the mind as a display case of scientific specimens reveals with perfect clarity a central development of Romantic thought.

In the 1798 *Lyrical Ballads* Wordsworth had set forth in rather more jocular fashion some of the underlying premises of *The Prelude*'s gentle mockery. Setting up a dialogue between a believer in books as a source of moral instruction and a believer in the unmediated tutelage of "Nature," Wordsworth put into the latter voice the memorable stanzas that have hung so hauntingly in the ear of generations of readers:

> The eye it cannot chuse but see,
> We cannot bid the ear be still;
> Our bodies feel, what'er they be,
> Against or with our will.

> Nor less I deem that there are powers,
> Which of themselves our mind impress,
> That we can feed this mind of ours,
> In a wise passiveness.

These stanzas from *Expostulation and Reply* are reinforced by two more in the same voice from *The Tables Turned* which seem to anticipate the biting satire of *A Poet's Epitaph*:

> One impulse from a vernal wood
> May teach you more of man;
> Of moral evil and of good,
> Than all the sages can.

> Sweet is the lore which nature brings;
> Our meddling intellect
> Misshapes the beauteous forms of things;
> —We murder to dissect.

Though these sentiments are exaggerated for dramatic and poetic effect, the voice is authentically Wordsworth's.

When he turned, in the expanded *Prelude* of 1804–1805, to an account of the role of books in his own education, Wordsworth delivered a satiric attack on some fashionable and popular educational theories deriving from Rousseau, Maria Edgeworth, and others. The first part of the attack was a self-congratulatory expression of gratitude on behalf of Coleridge and himself for having been allowed as children to read as their fancy led them:

> Where had we been, we two, beloved Friend,
> If we, in lieu of wandering, as we did,
> Through heights and hollows, and bye-spots of tales
> Rich with indigenous produce, open ground
> Of Fancy, happy pastures, rang'd at will!
> Had been attended, follow'd, watch'd, and noos'd,
> Each in his several melancholy walk
> String'd like a poor man's Heifer, at its feed
> Led through the lanes in forlorn servitude.
>
> (1805 *Prelude* 5.233–241)

Gratitude is followed by sarcasm, as Wordsworth goes on to offer a portrait of a child brought up by the formulas of current educational theory:

> . . . the monster birth
> Engender'd by these too industrious times.
> Let few words paint it: 'tis a Child, no Child,
> But a dwarf man; in knowledge, virtue, skill;
> In what he is not, and in what he is,
> The noontide shadow of a man complete.

The "few words" devoted to lampooning this repellent prodigy of learning stretch out compulsively to fifty lines of rather heavy and labored irony. Morally perfect, drilled in science, fashionably sceptical, the boy speaks in discourse "Massy and ponderous as a prison door," and

> Can string you names of districts, cities, towns,
> The whole world over, tight as beads of dew
> Upon a gossamer thread.

The portrait ends with two images drawn from the world of nature from which the little monster has been insulated. One alludes ironically to

> Each little drop of wisdom as it falls
> Into the dimpling cistern of his heart;

the other elaborates on the "vanity" that claims the center of this "life of lies" controlled by officious and tireless proctors: if any pure or natural impulse should inexplicably rise in the little prodigy's mind,

> Some busy helper still is on the watch
> To drive him back and pound him like a Stray
> Within the pinfold of his own conceit.

So much for education in the formative years. Wordsworth's view of university education was more benign, owing probably to the fact that he felt little touched by it. Cambridge never became much more than what it seemed to be at first sight, a dream, and Wordsworth the dreamer. It was a place where he was left free to grow without much interference from academic discipline, a place that allowed him to educate himself. The tutors who tried to impose what discipline there was are satirized in pitiless images:

> . . . grave Elders, Men unscour'd, grotesque
> In character; trick'd out like aged trees
> Which, through the lapse of their infirmity,
> Give ready place to any random seed
> That chuses to be rear'd upon their trunks.
> (1805 *Prelude* 3.574–578)

When Wordsworth goes on to project a fanciful image of what Cambridge might have been—"a Sanctuary for our Country's Youth"—he renders it ironically as a refuge for beasts and birds. The place that could have offered

> A habitation sober and demure
> For ruminating creatures, a domain
> For quiet things to wander in, a haunt
> In which the Heron might delight to feed
> By the shy rivers, and the Pelican
> Upon the cypress spire in lonely thought
> Might sit and sun himself—

turns into a festival of gaudy distractions:

> Alas! alas!
> In vain for such solemnity we look;
> Our eyes are cross'd by Butterflies, our ears
> Hear chattering Popinjays.

The force of feeling behind this satiric indictment should not be muted by its wit or its lyric form. Nor should we miss the deeper importance of Wordsworth's concern about education. For education is what develops literary taste (which is not innate, but acquired), and the depraved condition of taste in England makes up a major theme of Wordsworth's great critical prefaces. A taste for poetry, he had wryly declared as early as 1800, is a vitally serious matter, and not to be talked of as if it were a taste for rope dancing, or a taste for sherry. By 1815 he had learned the hard truth (articulated first by Coleridge) that every great poet, "as far as he is great and at the same time *original*," (and Wordsworth clearly aspired to both adjectives) "has had the task of *creating* the taste by which he is to be enjoyed."[18] The road before him may be smoothed by other writers, but "for what is peculiarly his own, he will be called upon to clear and often to shape his own road:—he will be in the condition of Hannibal among the Alps." This task was hardly made easier by arbiters of taste like Samuel Johnson, who receives (in the little 1815 résumé of English literary history) the full weight of Wordsworth's satiric scorn. Johnson's *Lives of the Poets* reflects the abstract reputation with which the taste of his age had endowed the writers of England. "We open the volume of Prefatory Lives, and to our astonishment the *first* name we find is that of Cowley!—What is become of the Morning-star of English Poetry? Where is the bright Elizabethan Constellation?" Where is Chaucer? Spenser? Shakespeare? These, Wordsworth laments, "we have *not*." And who do we have? The names toll contemptuously through three lines of print: "we have Roscommon, and Stepney, and Phillips, and Walsh, and Smith, and Duke, and King, and Spratt . . . ," all "writers in metre utterly worthless and useless" except to show "what a small quantity of brain" it takes to win popular admiration.

The Romantic revolution of taste was nowhere more firmly established than in this important, undervalued essay, which appeared before Coleridge's *Biographia Literaria,* before Keats had left medical school, before Shelley had published any verse except *Queen Mab* and a few scattered lyrics, before Blake was known to anyone beyond his circle, before Hazlitt had begun to collect his influential literary essays, before De Quincey had come into view outside of Westmorland. Wordsworth's essay (which, with the 1815 Preface, stimulated Coleridge to put the *Biographia* together) ranks with the prefaces to *Lyrical Ballads* as central documents of the most important critical revolution of the century.

Like all revolutions, this one was achieved by attacking and overthrow-

ing the intellectual and philosophical premises of the age before it, and satire was the natural method of attack. If Wordsworth consciously tried to
suppress his own satiric powers, they remained at work through nearly the
whole range of his writing. Even *The Prelude,* as Ford Swetnam perceptively
showed, is virtually a chorus of satiric voices: "Wordsworth uses satire to
underline some of the most crucial ideas and values of the poem, and . . .
also uses the changing tone of the satire to dramatize the spiritual progress
of the poem's narrator."[19] This spiritual progress emblemizes the philosophical progress of an entire age. Matthew Arnold's patronizing dismissal
of what Wordsworthians were pleased to call their Master's "philosophy"[20]
has, here and elsewhere, helped to obscure the real nature of Wordsworth's
philosophical achievement. By internalizing his own complex but powerful
reactions to the French Revolution and the Industrial Revolution and then
projecting these reactions in verse and prose, Wordsworth did more than
any other English writer to bring about the profound and sweeping revolution of sensibility that opens the modern age.

3

"The Work of Man's Redemption"
Prophecy and Apocalypse in Romantic Poetry

JOSEPH A. WITTREICH, JR.

I know that the multitudes walk in darkness. I would put into each man's
hand a lantern to guide him.   —Wordsworth, *Letters*

Revelation points to the purity and peace of a future world; but our sphere of
duty is upon earth.   —Wordsworth, "Postscript," *1835*

When C. S Lewis is preposterously wrong, he is usually, like Dr. Johnson on
such occasions, provocatively so. For example, as he scrutinizes the whole
question of literary influence *"in the fullest sense,* the sense it bears when we
say that *Paradise Lost* is influenced by Homer or Virgil," he suggests that
very few English writers have undergone an influence of *that* sort from any
book of the Bible. He mentions Martin Tupper's *Proverbial Philosophy,*
The Book of Mormon, even Blake's prophetic books, simply as the exceptions that confirm his rule. The reference to Blake, however, does allow
Lewis to observe the beginnings of such an influence in the Romantic period: it excited an interest in, a taste for "this sort of thing."[1]

Not since the Puritan Revolution had there been so much prophesying—
or so much writing on the prophecies, secular and sacred, the focal point of
which always seemed to be the Apocalypse of St. John, whose prophecy, it
was thought, was now being brought to fulfillment by the French Revolution. Robert Southey caught something of this eschatological excitement

when, in a letter of 1824, reflecting back on those revolutionary years, he remarked, "Few persons, but those who lived in it, can conceive or comprehend what the meaning of the French Revolution was, nor what a visionary world seemed to open upon those who were entering it. Old things seemed passing away, and nothing new was dreamt of but the regeneration of the human race."[2] Wordsworth not only shared in but fueled this enthusiasm as he looked ahead to "a sublime movement of deliverance," declaring in *The Convention of Cintra,* "Let . . . the human creature be rouzed; . . . let him rise and act. . . . Regeneration is at hand." In *Reply to Mathetes,* he represented the poets as morning stars, awakening men from sleep and mobilizing the energy of the multitudes for some glorious end. The excitement was contagious; poets were caught up in it; and Milton himself, along with John of Patmos, was regularly summoned to preside over this volatile phase of history when the first paradise seemed ready to be lost in the splendors of a second.

The Romantics did not discover prophecy—they recovered it—and, in the process, restored poetry to the once but no longer secure foundations of Scripture. At different times, of course, first this scriptural book, then that, predominated; but during the Romantic period it was the prophetic books that commandeered attention, and a specific one: the Book of Revelation. That is not surprising, given Romanticism's predisposition to use this book as a mirror of its own history and its prompting of artists to use this same book as an aesthetic model or as the cipher for a poetics. What is surprising is the extent to which Romantic poetry, allying itself with a tradition of apocalyptic prophecy, often casting itself in this mold, recoils from apocalypse, turning a tradition that had always afforded a critique of culture into a tradition that would now critique itself. And what is still more surprising, perhaps, is the extent to which both St. John and Milton themselves seem to authorize such an enterprise. Both seem to comprehend that apocalyptic is but one of an array of attitudes a writer might assume while writing prophecy, which credits the present with a responsibility for shaping the future that apocalypse glimpses. Prophecy ascribes to man, to human consciousness, the task of making the future that apocalypse, in its despair, consigns to a God in whom it vests the power of effecting what man is otherwise powerless to realize. If prophecy is an invasion of the mind, an agent in the expansion of human consciousness, apocalypse (as it was then widely understood) is an assault upon history, a deus ex machina device for achieving what is humanly unattainable.

The very idea of apocalypse has been used, and abused, as a code word for Romantic ideology, which exalts imagination in poetry, symbol and myth in poetic style, and which perceives an integrated world in nature. As foundation stones of Romanticism, apocalypse and prophecy are a joint presence in its literature, revealing the extent to which that literature is self-reflexive and furnishing in conjunction a critique of the very ideology that literature would foster and of the self-representations that it would promote. The ideological critique that some would perform from the outside, or that they see being performed by the second generation of Romantics upon the first, is more often than not an embedment within Romantic literature itself, which summoning up commonplaces of prophetic and apocalyptic traditions also submits those commonplaces to scrutiny, even sometimes to harsh interrogation. Jerome McGann says it best when he observes that "Romantic poetry incorporates Romantic ideology as a drama of contradictions which are inherent to that ideology. In this respect Romantic poetry occupies an implicit—sometimes even an explicit—critical position toward its subject matter." And as McGann goes on to observe:

> Changed circumstances . . . pushed the later Romantics, in particular Byron and Shelley, into a more seriously problematic relation to the Romantic ideas of the poet-as-*vates* and the special privilege of art. In them the so-called Romantic Conflict went much deeper than anything by the earlier Romantics, and this later problematic eventually contributed to the breakup of Romanticism as a coherent movement.[3]

Blake and Wordsworth may seem to be little more than purveyors of a modified, secularized apocalyptic tradition that in the poetry of Coleridge comes under a careful review, thus paving the way for the sharpening attention and deepening criticism of this tradition afforded by Byron, Keats, and the Shelleys. Even with Blake and Wordsworth, however, though more covertly, the commonplaces of prophetic and apocalyptic traditions, as well as commonplace attitudes toward both, are being interrogated from the inside with the result that such interrogation, as well as the critique that it engenders, may be seen—indeed *should* be seen—as an aspect of the dialectic playing itself out, with increasing intensity, within Romantic literature itself.

To be sure, commentators on the Apocalypse, then as now, were preoccupied with questions of genre, form, and structure and often resolved those questions into analogies that worked deconstructively, that had the effect of dismantling the Book of Revelation of its supposed ideology and of denying the various claims so often made for it. The Book of Revelation is like an epistle, a prophecy, an apocalypse, a history, drama, or pastoral, a great painting, or a musical composition. But each analogy seemed to explode in the face of contrary evidence. The letters are not private but public communications admonishing not individuals but symbols. John's book is a prophecy here of the past and there of the present or future; it is a prophecy modulating into apocalypse yet resisting either classification by virtue of the uncertainty of its time reference. It seemed, at least in part, to be apocalyptic; yet unlike other apocalypses it was not written pseudononymously and did not appear to be deterministic in its philosophy or even, according to some, eschatological, for it does not catapult us beyond history. Seen from this perspective, the Book of Revelation empties apocalyptic of its customary attitudes and content. It is also a drama with an ever-shifting cast of symbolic characters, but drama interiorized and conflict developed through contary perspectives rather than contending players. The apocalyptic theater is, first and foremost, a mental theater. It is tragedy subsumed in comedy, history anticipated rather than fulfilled, and pastoral overwhelmed by lamentation—dark age, not golden age, pastoral. It is now a poem, now a picture. It is now a system of hieroglyphics, now a picture gallery—and now a fully orchestrated symphony of mental music. Here it is sound, there vision, and this dialectic of senses is repeatedly interrupted by narration. But it is also a clogged narrative with a recapitulatory structure, a temple become a labyrinth. Still, what appears to be an example of anti-form is actually a difficult and dazzling order. Expectations built then broken—that repeated rhythm is not a flaw in this work, but an essential motive therein.

The Apocalypse is a subversive book—and most subversive, as Vasily Rozanov has shown, of its own supposed ideology. For once the stars are torn from the firmament and the world is in ruins, once weeping and lamentation have ceased, tears have been wiped away, and there is a reign of peace, what is brought forth is not life in heaven but life on earth: "the joy of living on earth, *precisely on earth*. . . . The Apocalypse presents, calls for, and demands a new religion. . . . It shouts 'at the end of time' . . . for 'the last age of humanity.' "[4] The movement of the Apocalypse was not beyond but back into time and history, and in aligning themselves so closely with the prophetic Milton, the Romantics found an important conduit for John's "apocalyptic" message.

No evasion, no idealization of history, Romantic prophecy emerges from Miltonic prophecy, appropriating its tenets and discoveries. When, in *Milton*, Blake quips, "Say first! what mov'd Milton" (pl. 2, line 16) he does so by way of remembering what Milton says first in *Paradise Lost*, that it was in response to an ancient prophecy in heaven that Satan moved against Adam and Eve and that Paradise was lost, and, remembering this, by way of playing upon the irony that Milton now moves in response to a prophecy which he understands, only gradually, and by which the lost paradise will be restored. Prophecy has often had negative consequences on history, a fact Milton himself underscores by ending *Paradise Lost* as it began, with a prophecy whose vision of history, not full of glad tidings, is fraught with the misery, fever, and fret of human existence; a prophecy in which the veil on coming centuries is rent, opening a window on the history of the poet's own time. Prophecy of the past masking as prophecy of the future is actually being written in the present tense. The example of Milton in old age, having fallen on evil days and evil tongues, compassed round by danger and darkness but not enslaved, dramatizes the situation of the prophet, one of exile and cultural alienation, provoking him into self-scrutiny and scrutiny of history and then into quarreling with both, and heightening his political concern and urgency, even if paradoxically such concern and urgency seem diminished by his self-reflection and analysis. Milton made clear to the Romantics, through the examples of both *Paradise Lost* and *Samson Agonistes*, first that prophecy which seems to be a revelation of the poet to the world is, in fact, a revelation of the world to itself, and second that even if poetic prophecy harbors apocalyptic desires (and perhaps *most* when it harbors such desires), the poet-prophet must tell the story of what went wrong, monstrously so, with the story itself seeming always to ravage the apocalyptic myth, distancing history from it and forcing a readjustment of expectations in the wake of damaged hopes and dashed promises.

In Milton's last poems, no less than in the Apocalypse itself, apocalypse is brought under scrutiny and becomes an object of criticism; it is repre-

sented as an irony curling back upon itself. That is, the Apocalypse presented itself to the Romantics as what we would call today a very Derridean, deconstructive book: "We cannot and must not forgo the *Aufklärung*,
in other words, what imposes itself as the enigmatic desire for vigilance, for
lucid vigil. . . , for elucidation, for critique and truth, but for a truth that at
the same time keeps within itself some apocalyptic desire, this time a desire
for clarity and revelation, in order to demystify or, if you prefer, to deconstruct apocalyptic disourse itself."[5] Both John and Milton appear to devise
a system for delivering us from apocalyptic systems, and in such a way as to
make the Apocalypse a very congenial book for those who felt, as Wordsworth did in *Home at Grasmere,* that poetry should now divest itself of "all
Arcadian dreams, All golden fancies of the golden age, / The bright array of
shadowy thoughts from times / That were before all time, and are to be /
Ere time expire" (lines 625–628).

What is distinctive about Romantic poetry is the disjunction of prophecy
and apocalypse within it, together with its compulsion to move prophecy
beyond poetics into the realm of ideology, where prophecy and apocalypse,
losing their identity, acquire distinction; where in poetry there is now a dispersion of prophetic voices. Not all these voices sing of joy; some murmur
ominously, and others, uttering odious truth, send forth songs of misery and
woe. Some would exalt the English nation; others would shake her shores.
In the great poetic prophecies of English Romanticism, these various voices
are orchestrated, now with this and now with that one predominating; and
of these prophecies *The Prelude* is still the premiere example. Long before
its publication and immediately after hearing a recitation of it, Coleridge, in
To William Wordsworth (1806), recognized *The Prelude* for what it is: a
"prophetic Lay" (line 3), more than historic, about the building up of the
human spirit. Here Wordsworth joins with Blake in depicting the formation
of the prophetic character—the same agonizing, arduous process unfolded
in Blake's prophetic writings from *The Marriage of Heaven and Hell*
through *Jerusalem.* As Byron and Shelley were later to do, he turns the prophetic poet into an oracle, making of him the image of a better time and
making him issue a prophecy that begins and ends in the mind of man.

Not just Blake and Wordsworth, but all the Romantics, are preoccupied
with the vatic stance and maintain ties with prophetic tradition—with what
is, from their perspective, inseparable from the Milton tradition. Blake and
Wordsworth are the most firmly bound to this tradition, exploring the pos

sibilities for prophecy in the modern world. Shelley, however, particularly in *Prometheus Unbound*, manifests a tendency, also evident in the poetry of Coleridge and Byron, to investigate the limitations of prophecy by way of rendering more precisely its efficacy for the new age. And that same tendency is there, even more emphatically, in the poetry of Keats.

Of the Romantics, Keats is the poet least rooted in prophetic tradition; yet he is also the poet who gathers into sharpest focus the turns and counterturns of Romantic poetry, its fleeing from and then flying back into vision, as well as the perennial problem of whether the poet speaks oracularly or merely gives vent to his dreams: "Was it a vision, or a waking dream? / . . . —Do I wake or sleep?" (lines 79–80). That question is posed, not just here in *Ode to a Nightingale,* but in *The Fall of Hyperion,* where visionaries and dreamers are identified only to be denigrated (ironically by the "High Prophetess" [bk. 1, line 145]) for not thinking of the earth. Subsequently, in lines Keats apparently meant to cancel, Moneta instructs the poet: "The poet and the dreamer are distinct, / Diverse, sheer opposite, antipodes. / The one pours out a balm upon the world, / The other vexes it" (1.199–202). *The Fall of Hyperion* begins by distinguishing between Poets and Fanatics, between those who are engaged by and disengaged from the world. What gnaws at Keats clearly is that those who fly after their visions may also be flying from social and political responsibility: the fanatic, paradoxically, surrenders the ideology of prophecy. In the very act of making such distinctions, though, Keats opens a gulf between poets and visionaries, between poetry and prophecy, that the other Romantics had sought to bridge. Coleridge called any distinction between the artist and the visionary a coldblooded hypothesis; and Shelley wrote his *Defence of Poetry,* in part, to argue for the interconnectedness of poetry and prophecy, his objective thus being to make "poetry an attribute of prophecy." But as with Keats, so with the rest of these poets: they are impelled to scrutinize prophecy, to examine its limitations; and they conclude that this tradition is cause both for celebration and for criticism.

Part of the allure of prophecy is that poetry could be fashioned to fit its outline without ever being circumscribed by it. Prophecy seemed to correlate with Blake's—with the Romantics'—idea of one central form containing all others; it was a mixed genre, a composite or global order. It was also a difficult order hammered out of a multiplicity of perspectives and organized around a system of synchronisms, a consequence of which was that prophecy was often plotless and always radically redundant. This mode was especially agreeable to poets like Wordsworth who were in constant search of new combinations of forms, who made an idealism of sundry forms commingling, and whose objective through form was to present the parts as parts with a feeling for the whole, to construct new patterns out of the elements of previous patterns and thereby reactualize the text within the text. Wordsworth does this in *The Prelude* by allowing the final episode on Mount Snowdon to recapitulate all of the poem's earlier hilltop and mountaintop experiences. The very logic of prophecy calls for the surrender of usual notions of sequence and succession, for their displacement by synchronic structures, and cajoles poets into searching for new and more intricate forms of intertextuality. Indeed, those new forms of intertextuality provide the principles for interleaving one's own poems and for integrating them into the one poem, which is the poet's own canon—Wordsworth's Gothic cathedral to which all his poems are architecturally significant and for which they are mutually supportive.

The special allure of the Revelation prophecy is that it posed the crucial questions for an aspiring poet-prophet. Was prophecy possible, and could it be profitable in the new age? Did the spirit of the age neuter or nurture prophecy? And what exactly are the literary activities of the prophet, hence of the poet who is an aspiring prophet? Is John simply a compositor, setting forth another's vision? If so, is he actually redacting another's prophecy, or is he rather editing it? If an editor, is it only another's prophecy that he is preparing; or does he instead stitch together various prophecies, making an anthology of the scattered fragments of many others' visions? Or, if John is the author of this prophecy, is he an active or passive recipient of his vision? Does he record here one continuous vision, or separate visions received at different times and even at times distant from another? The answers to these questions, in a very important way, determine the authenticity, as well as the authority, of any given prophecy and affect the form it will assume, as well as the truth claims made for it. But most important, perhaps, is the question of the relationship between prophecy and apocalypse and of the relationship of their own poetry to the traditions of both. Prophecy may supply the form, the poetic casting; but apocalypse seems always to be the deep concern, functioning here as subtext and there as co-text. Prophecy may become self-reflexive; but its turn upon itself is usually preliminary to its turning against apocalypse, a tradition whose thrust was into future history and then beyond and whose subject, it seemed, was God, not man.

Witness the example of Coleridge, whose own dedication to the art of prophecy manifests itself in such poems as *Religious Musing,* which, referring to the Book of Revelation, itself culminates in a vision; or in *The Destiny of Nations,* which Coleridge calls "A Vision" and in which he speaks of prophets as "Fit instruments and best, of perfect end" (line 468); and in *Ode to the Departing Year,* which in its dedicatory letter allows that "among the Ancients, the Bard and the Prophet were one and the same character" and which also finds Coleridge explaining, "although I prophesy curses, I pray fervently for blessings." The prophetic role here assumed by Coleridge, the poem's epigraph makes clear, is that of a Cassandra; and the epigraph, as Coleridge explains, is there to remind us that "we see but *one* side, and are blind to noon day evidence on the other." Mankind, with its single vision, lets the prophets like Cassandra go unheeded. Still, the difficulties with prophesying are twofold: typically, prophecy is addressed to an audience without the eyes to see and the ears to hear; yet the prophet himself is thwarted by himself—by his failure to achieve vision despite his straining for and yearning after it, or by its loss, by the poet's own difficulty in articulating the vision and in creating the paradise the vision decrees. But the prophet is also thwarted by his medium, which is marked by both obscurity and fragmentariness. These limitations of prophecy offer the grounds for exploration in Coleridge's first collection of his poetry, *Sibylline Leaves* (1817). Through his title, Coleridge relates a whole gathering of poems to prophetic tradition and, furthermore, indicates his own comprehension of the problem of prophesying in the new age.

That enigmatic title brought notice to these Cumaean murmurs, seemingly tossed about by all the winds of heaven, and even sent one of Coleridge's contemporaries to a dictionary, whereupon the following explanation was elicited from him:

"Sibylline", says our Dictionary, means "of or belonging to a Sibyl or Prophetess": the word cannot therefore, we hope, be appropriated by Mr. Coleridge, who is not so humble a poet as to assume, voluntarily, the character of an old woman. But on refreshing our classic memory we grasp the very essence and soul of this mysterious title. The Sibyl wrote her prophecies on leaves; so does Mr. Coleridge his verses—the prophecies of the Sibyl become incomprehensible, if not instantly gathered; so does the sense of Mr. Coleridge's poetry; the Sibyl asked the same price from Tarquin for her books when in 9, 6, and 3 vols; so does Mr. Coleridge for his, when scattered over sundry publications, and now as collected into one—as soon as the Sibyl had concluded her bargain she vanished, and was seen no more in the regions of Cumae so does Mr. Coleridge assure us he will be seen no more on Parnassus—the Sibylline books were preserved by Kings, had a College of Priests to take care of them, and were so esteemed by the people, that they were seldom consulted; even so does Mr. Coleridge look to delight Monarchs, his book·will be treasured by the Eleven Universities, and we venture to suppose that it will be treated by the public . . . pretty much in the same way with the ravings of his Archetype.[6]

However cunning, this explanation disregards the serious dimension of Coleridge's title: its intention of thrusting all these poems within the orbit of prophecy and, simultaneously, of identifying the problems felt by a poet who would now assume the role of prophet. In this regard, Coleridge's own note on his title is revelatory: "The following collection has been entitled *Sibylline Leaves*," he says, "in allusion to the fragmentary and widely scattered state in which they have been long suffered to remain." It is the "fragmentary . . . state" of these poems, then, to which Coleridge draws our attention and which he thereby invites us to ponder. Doing just that, E. S. Shaffer notices that the preface to *Kubla Khan* "is not an excuse for a fragment, but a presentation of credentials for writing apocalyptic, for assuming the prophetic role. . . . The prefatory 'Vision in a Dream' becomes a kind of authenticator of the poet's right to present the prophetic lays of a 'John.'"[7] Many of Coleridge's poems are, like *Kubla Khan*, both "A Vision" and "A Fragment": they come forth, in the words of *Religious Musings*, "in fragments wild / Sweet echoes of uneartly melodies" (lines 347–348) and are all "Monads of the infinite mind" (line 408), particles of the divine vision. Each poem is an atom belonging to one body, pursuing its own self-centered end while contributing at the same time to a larger totality. Just as in *The Destiny of Nations*, the large vision is composed of "fragments many and huge" (line 144), which, once assembled as in *The Picture*, "Come trembling back, unite, and once more / The pool becomes a mirror" (lines 99–100). There is method in Coleridge's fragments.

Coleridge's title implies a theory of the fragment, inviting the reader to perceive these poems as deliberately fragmentary and to find in them a metaphor for evolving consciousness and being. Yet the title is also a reminder that the oracles of the sibyls were consulted on occasions of disaster, their purpose being not to predict the future but instead to counsel men in how to avert a national danger. Through his title, therefore, Coleridge also points to the legislative function of his poems, to their potentiality as a transforming power both on individual men and on national history. In this connection, Coleridge would probably expect us to recall something of the history of the sibylline oracles. The pagan sibyls were replaced first by Hebrew, then by Christian ones. In each moment of replacement, the old form is retained while the content is altered; the old form indicates the concern of the newer oracles (whether they be Hebrew or Christian) with a "pagan" audience and, furthermore, implies the oracles' purpose of conversion: they would bestow light on mankind and prepare a new way for him to follow. Always ethical and historical in their interest, the oracles, once Christianized, turn from the past to future history. In the process, sibylline literature merges into apocalyptic literature, prophecy and apocalyptics now joining together and remaining in early Romantic literature closely allied. They are irrevocably allied in Blake's poetry—in the correlation of *Milton* and *Jerusalem,* for example—and also in the early Coleridge as evidenced by the most startling of his prophetic poems, *The Rime of the Ancient Mariner.* Yet by Wordsworth and Byron, prophecy and apocalypse are segregated, their long-enduring alliance broken, for purposes of redefining relationships and revising inflections. By the Shelleys, on the other hand, apocalyptics itself is distinguished from millenarianism: they reject the former, at least as an eschatological conception, while countenancing the latter. Keats, for his part, deepens the Romantic critique of apocalyptics into a critique of the visionary ideology in which prophecy itself had established its moorings.

In various of her novels, Mary Shelley provides a link between Coleridge's thinking on prophecy and that of Byron and her poet-husband. Fragments of discourse, ostensibly edited by Victor Frankenstein, then by Captain Walton, and arranged by Mary according to the logic of her vision within a dream, *Frankenstein* has been described as "obviously and notoriously a 'prophetic' book";[8] and it clearly belongs to what was destined to become a tradition of the apocalyptic novel. More interesting for our purposes, however, is *Valperga,* which postulates that prophecy is about the self that is also the object of its contemplation and which, through two

Cassandra-like heroines, explores the burden of prophecy. Mary Shelley concludes, it would seem, that it is a test of the true prophet that he should not be heard, that the prophecy itself go unheeded. In *The Last Man,* there is a reflection, in the introduction, on the 1818 visit of Mary and Shelley to the sibyl's cave; and that reflection, in turn, sets forth the idea that the leaves found in the cave are fragments of prophecy, the raw materials that require shaping into a unified and intelligible vision. That is precisely the role that Mary, having in her imagination revisited the cave and picked up leaves from it, performs in the writing of her novel. With Mary, the whole prophetic tradition, previously withheld from women, breaks in upon a newly emerging female literature. The voice of Moses and all the patriarchal prophets here gives way to the voice of the sibyl, mingling with that of Milton, who was himself a critic of patriarchal religion and culture.

This is Mary's account of her visit to that cave:

At length my friend, who had taken up some of the leaves strewed about, exclaimed, "This *is* the Sibyl's cave; these are Sibylline leaves." On examination, we found that all the leaves, bark, and other substances, were traced with written characters. What appeared to us more astonishing, was that these writings were expressed in various languages. . . . We could make out little by the dim light, but they seemed to contain prophecies, detailed relations of events but lately passed; names, now well known, but of modern date; and often exclamations of exultation or woe, of victory or defeat, were traced on their thin scant pages. This was certainly the Sibyl's cave. . . . We made a hasty selection of such of the leaves, whose writing one at least of us could understand; and then, laden with our treasure, we bade adieu to the dim hypaethric cavern. . . .

During our stay in Naples, we often returned to this cave. . . , and each time added to our store. Since that period. . . , I have been employed in deciphering these sacred remains. Their meaning, wondrous and eloquent, has often repaid my toil, soothing me in sorrow, and exciting my imagination to daring flights, through the immensity of nature and the mind of man. . . .

I present the public with my latest discoveries in the slight Sibylline pages. Scattered and unconnected as they were, I have been obliged to add links, and model the work into a consistent form. But the main substance rests on the truths contained in these poetic rhapsodies, and the divine intuition which the Cumaean damsel obtained from heaven.

I have often wondered at the subject of her verses, and at the English dress of the Latin poet. Sometimes I have thought, that, obscure and chaotic as they are, they owe their present form to me, their decipherer. As if we should give to another artist, the painted fragments which form the mosaic copy of Raphael's Transfiguration in St. Peter's; he would put them together in a form, whose mode would be fashioned by his own peculiar mind and talent. Doubtless the leaves of the Cumaean Sibyl have suffered distortion and diminution of interest and excellence in my hands. My only excuse for thus transforming them, is that they were unintelligible in their pristine condition.

. . . the merits of my adaptation and translation must decide how far I have well bestowed my time and imperfect powers, in giving form and substance to the frail and attenuated Leaves of the Sibyl.

What is important, Mary claims, is a decipherer—someone to integrate and explain and give continuity to the fragments. Prophetic works are, by definition, fragmentary, the particles of a vision that receives articulation and definition only to the extent that an author of prophecy is able to make its fragmentary parts cohere, each with the others. The journey into the cave is the journey into the self, into one's own mind; and the leaves are fragments of that mind which, once integrated, brings light out of darkness. The episode is another rendering of Byron's promotion of self-knowledge and of Shelley's proclamation that prophecy begins and ends in the human mind.

Byron's most conspicuous evocation of prophetic tradition occurs in his preface to *The Prophecy of Dante,* where he identifies as his literary models not just "the Prophecies of Holy Writ" but also "Cassandra of Lycophron, and the Prophecy of Nereus," having already explained in a letter to John Murray, dated 29 October 1819, that Dante, here speaking in his own person, will embrace "all topics in the way of prophecy—like Lycophron's Cassandra." Through these references to prophetic tradition, Byron implies a criticism of prophecy, thereby forging his own statement on the problems of prophesying in the modern world. Apollo had bestowed on Cassandra the spirit of prophecy; but in her prophesyings (first of the ruin of Troy and then of the death of Agamemnon) she was unheeded. Because it is not listened to, Byron is saying, prophecy makes nothing happen and, because of the failings of mankind, has never possessed the legislative power so often ascribed to it. The truth of prophecy, hence their acknowledgment of the prophet, steals upon men tardily, "strik[ing] their eyes through many a tear / And mak[ing] them own the prophet in his tomb" (canto 4, lines 153–154). Byron's critique here is underscored by his reference to the prophecy of Nereus, who checks the waves, halts Helen's ship, and foretells her cruel fate. The point of this prophecy, as related in one of the Horatian poems—that Helen in her adultery will become the destroyer of a nation— is enlarged upon in a succeeding poem, where blame is affixed not so much to Helen as to the fury of the lion that exists in all men and that motivates them to run their ploughs over, and thereby destroy, the world.

With considerable calculation, Byron allows *Marino Faliero* and *The Prophecy of Dante* to front one another in the same poetic volume, where a cautious commitment to prophecy emerges out of a devastating critique of apocalypse; where a world of fallen vision is paradoxically redeemed by vision, by the emergence of a prophetic consciousness. Byron is reported to have had a highly particularized knowledge of the New Testament, especially of Revelation, and to have talked about the Apocalypse as a curiously perplexing book. Both poems use the Book of Revelation to deliver their pointedly prophetic message, which is a message against apocalypse, even in *The Prophecy of Dante* where "the hue / Of human sacrifice . . . / Troubles the clotted air" (2.76–78), where "still Division sows the seeds of woe" (2.134), but where all that is necessary is for the avenger to stop avenging. *Marino Faliero* climaxes in a Christian vision of apocalypse, with the avenging angel emptying the vials of wrath in the harlot city of Venice— climaxes in a violent swirl of largely negative apocalyptic imagery. Here apocalyptic impulses are shown defeating human freedom and leaving the poet on a rock of desolate despair. The apocalyptic vision at the end of *Marino Faliero* crowds upon the prophetic eye of Dante, the latter poem reinforcing the conclusion of the former one, that apocalypse, which often had been a device for tempering disillusion with hope, has become an instrument instead for intensifying despair with a sense of doom. If prophecy offers a potential release from the tragedy of history, apocalypse causes history to lean back again upon tragedy, making history indistinguishable from tragedy.

Apocalypse is an idea in and an illusion of history, which needs shattering, and is also a spirit in man, which needs restraining, an avenging passion which requires bridling. This, in turn, becomes Byron's highest hope for prophecy: that it may forestall an apocalypse in the world and become the principal agent in individual redemption, effecting those discoveries, first in *The Prophecy of Dante* and then in *Childe Harold's Pilgrimage,* which enable the poet, finally, to accede to the prophetic office and to enlighten mankind as an oracle. Byron's point here is like Wordsworth's in *Home at Grasmere:* the poet is not born into the consciousness of the prophet but must struggle to achieve it; he is not summoned by God but beckoned by history to prophesy. Both poets may be said to begin in the same attitude, the one Wordsworth assumes in *Home at Grasmere:*

> No prophet was he, had not even a hope,
> Scarcely a wish . . .
> The lot of others, never could be his lot.
>
> (15–16, 18)

Like Wordsworth, Byron reaches the discovery that, indeed, he can be an oracle to his fellow man. Only gradually does the poet succeed to the prophetic office, and only then (and then, at least for Byron, in only a very limited sense) does he become an oracle and, like Wordsworth in *The Prelude,* an epic hero. This principle animates *Don Juan*—a poem that begins with the declaration "I want a hero" (Canto 1, st. 1) and that ends in the discovery that the poem's narrator *is* its hero.

It is too simple to conclude that, speaking "with an ironic countervoice," Byron "opens a satirical perspective on the vatic stance of his Romantic contemporaries."[9] Rather, he foregrounds the undersong—its doubts, misgivings, suspicions—of all Romantic prophecy; but also, in admitting to the prophetic consciousness as a potentiality of the poet, Byron joins with Blake, Wordsworth, and the Shelleys in the Romantic celebration of the artist as a culture-hero. Like Blake in *The Marriage of Heaven and Hell,* Byron exploits the radical possibilities of eschatological satire. But unlike Coleridge, Byron, in *Childe Harold's Pilgrimage,* claims no muse for his "lowly lay" (Canto 1, st. 1); he dissociates himself from "the phrensy" of prophetic tradition and refuses "to soar," preferring instead to gaze beneath the "cloudy canopy" and to proclaim "the Muses' seat . . . their grave" (1.40–42). On the face of things, Byron is doing just what Hazlitt accused him of doing, "reversing the laws of vision," in a poem whose "broken magnificence," in the words of John Wilson, is but the surface expression of a larger intention to assemble the "fragments of a dark dream of life"[10] and stand them up against all the coherent visions of utopia made of hopes that have become like ashes in the mouth, and founded upon the supposition that man is becoming instead of that he is ceasing to be. It is not that Byron is simply anti-utopian; rather, he would exchange utopias of escape for those of realization.

Byron's strategy, both here and in *Don Juan,* is like Coleridge's: to present a poem whose parts are shattered fragments of a whole, a poem that will be like "a broken mirror, which the glass / In every fragment multiplies; and makes / A thousand images of one that was" (3.33). That strategy Byron justifies through his explanation that man "seest not all; but piecemeal . . . must break, / To separate contemplation, the great whole" (4.157). "Our outward sense," he says, "Is but of gradual grasp"; and so only if we grow with its growth can "we . . . dilate / Our spirits to the size of that they contemplate" (4.158). And Byron's purpose, like Coleridge's, is conversion and liberation of a "race of inborn slaves, who wage war for their chains, . . . rather than be free" (4.94). Yet that purpose in Byron's poetry becomes highly restricted. A poem like *The Rime of the Ancient Mariner,* for example, couples prophecy and apocalypse; it is about the surrender of hope and betrayal of vision, about the consequences of not keeping faith in time of trouble. Betraying his vision, the mariner as false prophet consigns others to eternal death and himself to death-in-life; he keeps others from the marriage feast. Yet even if he has slain his vision, thereby deferring apocalyptic consummation, the whole experience survives to form a prophecy, a warning prophecy that, if heeded, will open upon the naturalized apocalypse of Wordsworth's *Tintern Abbey,* with the alienation of the one poem giving way to the communion of the other. The love of nature leads to the love of man, and the apocalypse in nature prophesies an apocalypse in history. In contrast, a poem like *Childe Harold's Pilgrimage* not only makes prophecy an end in itself but tightens its compass so greatly that, while still encircling and so pertaining to the individual, it no longer contains and thus loses all contact with, all pertinence for, history.

In *The Ghost of Abel,* Blake chides Byron for this perversion of prophecy, for this denial of the eschatological possibilities implanted from the very beginning in that tradition. Implicit in Shelley's poems, which repeatedly enter into dialogue with Byron's, is this same criticism, in the infinitely more restrained formulation of his preface to *The Revolt of Islam:* "There is a reflux in the tide of human things which bears the shipwrecked hopes of men into a secure haven after the storms are past. Methinks, those who now live have survived an age of despair." Shelley's fine discrimination of history and eschatology may prevent him from restoring prophecy and apocalypse to union, but he does restore millennial expectations to prophecy. His poetry everywhere intones the counsel of *Prometheus Unbound:* "to hope till Hope creates / From its own wreck the thing it contemplates" (act 4, lines 573–574), although even here the prospect of a new Promethan man seems brighter than that for a new golden age in history. Demogorgon's words are reminiscent of those more prosaic lines in *The Prelude* where Wordsworth declares that "Man is only weak through his . . . / . . . want of hope where evidence divine / Proclaims to him that hope should be most sure" (bk. 10, lines 161–163). They recall, too, Byron's 1821 *Memoranda* statement, "What is Poetry?—The feeling of a Former world and Future"—a statement that causes the poet to invoke the prophets and thereupon to observe, "If it were not for Hope, where would the Future be? . . . in all human affairs it is Hope—Hope—Hope."

Prometheus Unbound, the greatest and surely the most hopeful of Shelley's prophetic utterances, seems to argue that for the great artist, for Prometheus, revolution is not enough: the great artist, of which Prometheus is the prototype and Shelley an ectype or copy, must also reconceive, create anew, the essential framework of the world. In Shelley's countermyth to Aeschylus's, Prometheus achieves his apotheosis as poet-prophet. He is the maker of the prophecy that, emanating from him, also ends in him. The archetypal prophet, like Blake's Los, Prometheus is also the emblem of prophecy: "He gave man speech, and speech created thought / . . . and the harmonious mind / Poured forth in all-prophetic song" (act 2, sc. 4, lines 72, 75–76). The associations here exploited by Shelley are the same ones that Sidney, in his *Apologie for Poetrie,* had focused for the Renaissance: Prometheus is the prototypical poet, "the first light-giuer to ignorance"; he is a type of the poet as *vates* who is all that Prometheus's name, as Sidney interprets it, implies—"a diuiner, Fore-seer, or *Prophet*"—and who, considering what may be and should be, apprehends and thereupon paints for mankind a new ideal. "These bee they," says Sidney, "that, as the first and most noble sorte [of poet], may justly be called *Vates.*" Similar associations, of course, are developed by Byron in *The Prophecy of Dante,* where the poet is depicted as a prophet, a "new Prometheus . . . / Bestowing fire from heaven, and then, too late, / Finding the pleasures given repaid with pain" (4.14–16); they are also inferred by Mary Shelley and recorded in her notes to Percy's poem, where she describes Prometheus as "the prophetic soul of humanity" and the final act of his poem as a "rejoicing in the fulfillment of the prophecies."

Those associations may be inferred from *Prometheus Unbound* because they are embedded in its text, having first been gathered into focus by its epigraph. There reference is made to Amphiarus, who becomes the spokesman for Zeus, a false prophet who is a mouthpiece for and an upholder of orthodoxies; and that reference implies a contrast with Prometheus, who is the overthrower of Zeus, a prophet who, undermining orthodoxies, would remake the world. Myth opposes myth in *Prometheus Unbound,* where Shelley's supporting strategy is to create a new oracle, a new prophecy, that will subvert the old oracle, the old prophecy. Yet this new prophecy, for all its apocalyptic rumblings, is not an "apocalypse." What follows the appeal "Tear the veil!" and the declaration "It is torn" (act 1, line 539) is a revelation; but that revelation promises nothing that is final, complete, conclusive. History may be brought to an apotheosis, but it may also slide back into its former self.

Early readers of *Prometheus Unbound* understood something of this, declaring the poem's subject to be "the *deliverance* of Prometheus"—his "transition . . . from a state of suffering to a state of happiness; together with a corresponding change in the situation of mankind."[11] Modern criticism has finely honed that perception, freeing Shelley of the charge of mindless millenarianism and aligning him with Swedenborg and Blake, for whom an apocalypse is, first of all, a mental event—man's summoning of himself to judgment—and possibly a causal, yet conditional, event whereby a man, through regeneration, may redeem the universe, even if only temporarily. The poem's revelation, as Harold Bloom acknowledges, is "that apocalypse can roll over into the fallen state again"; or as Earl Wasserman says even more insistently, "Shelley has not promised an apocalypse for man."[12] All he does do, through his invocation of the Book of Revelation, is to assure us that not John of Patmos's God, but only the human mind, once it becomes unbound, can suppress the serpent, seal the pit, and summon up a new heaven and a new earth in history. Insistently we are reminded by the Spirits of act 1, as Prometheus is reminded, that they "bear the prophecy / Which begins and ends in thee" (1.690–691, 706–707, 799–800). This is to say no more, and no less, than that prophecy is the creation of the human mind it both reflects and transforms; prophecy is a mirror of the very thing it contemplates and a model of that which it would create.

There is, moreover, an intricate and rich intertextuality joining *Prometheus Unbound* to *The Cenci* and jointing them as companion poems. The Book of Revelation is a vital part of that intertextuality, moving through the substratums of Shelley's tragedy and on the surface of his lyrical drama, serving the one poem as subtext and providing for the other a co-text, with Shelley seeming to insist that the Apocalypse, with its contrary perspectives and paradoxical formulations, furnishes both negative and positive images for history, even for post-Christian history, and that it also applies to history indefinitely, where its paradigmatic events occur over and over again, here with tragic and there with liberating consequences. If, as Byron thought, liberation is the poetry of politics, liberation is also the politics of prophecy out of which Romantic poetry is made. Here, inward commotions of the mind find their counterpart in the convulsive movements of history, the winning of inward freedom promising social betterment and prognosticating the improvement of history.

It has been said that prophecy is the central metaphor for *modern* poetry; prophecy is, in fact, the central metaphor for much poetry of the Western world, ancient and modern—Virgil's and Dante's, Ariosto's and Tasso's, Spenser's and Milton's. And more: prophecy is, arguably, the ur-form of most major poetry of English Romanticism. If the critical reorientation accomplished by an earlier generation of criticism made an orthodoxy of F. R. Leavis's proposition that the "Romantic poets have among themselves no attachments of the kind that link the poets in the line from Donne and Ben Jonson to Pope and the line from Pope to Crabbe,"[13] the dominance of prophecy in Romantic poetry exposes the heresy in that "orthodoxy." Prophecy poses, against Leavis's "line of wit," a line of vision; and the Romantics' adoption of prophecy, sometimes viewed as a device for mystifying their poetry and for escaping history, is, more exactly, their instrument for the demystification of poetry and for encountering history.

The apocalyptic component in Romantic poetry is a deliberate factoring into it of error, a way of giving poetic presence to error. Historically, apocalypse was always subject to misreading, misinterpretation, egregious misrepresentation. No less than Milton, and as much to their credit, the Romantics, in aligning themselves with apocalyptic prophecy—with this tradition of misunderstanding—tie themselves to the possibility of error, all the while hoping, of course, to render the possibility less probable. In Romantic prophecy, as in Milton's last prophetic poems, apocalypse is a presence that the poetry evades until the dream can be internalized; yet such a strategy has also been misconstrued as revoking the promise of history by centering its promise in the self. What with Milton became the central concern of literary prophecy—and what Milton's poetry itself made the crucial issue for Romantic prophecy—was learning to perceive sequential apocalypses, of history and of individuals (usually in that order) as an inverted sequence, the elements of which were interdependent. Apocalypse could therefore continue its grip on poetic desire by marking the space, sometimes huge space, between expectation and fulfillment—the space "between" being the space of the poem and being filled with the realization that prophecy, which had always been a critique of culture, might also, and just as appropriately, become a critique of itself. Poetry, in the process, acquires a prophetic wisdom of its own and, in its encounter with and sometimes ravaging of the apocalyptic myth, yields up a Poets' Revelation.

It should come as no surprise that *The Prelude*, which Howard Nemerov describes as "a series of mountain climbs, with vision at the top of each mountain, climaxed by the grand vision from Mount Snowdon," should also harbor what Nemerov presents as the essential prophetic wisdom of the poet, that he "doesn't foretell the future, he makes it, he brings it to pass, he sings it up."[14] The true prophet, assuming he is a poet, need not hurl himself into the future; for his real concern will be with seeing the present clearly, with effecting an unveiling of it. In this refined sense, *The Prelude* is an apocalyptic poem, although, in this context, it must be allowed that one of the chief critical disputes involving this poem is whether it represents a false or true apocalypse, whether finally it portrays an apocalypse at all or, as Jonathan Wordsworth argues, presents the poet as "a borderer . . . between the unregenerate present and the millenarian future."[15] Even more than *The Prelude, The Recluse* displays apocalyptic hesitancy, with Wordsworth at once engaging and disengaging the apocalyptic myth in such a way as to make the Apocalypse a co-text of his poetry and, simultaneously, a subtext of history—in such a way as to produce an unveiling of the mind while leaving nature and the world of history still partially veiled. Blake is the only Romantic poet to present a united vision of apocalypse in the mind and in history. By Wordsworth and the other Romantics, such visions become progressively, explicitly disunited until by Shelley they are reintegrated in the vision of *Prometheus Unbound,* where the very idea of apocalypse is radically redefined. Wordsworth may have disclaimed the honor of being a poetic guide to the other poets of his age, but in matters of prophecy and apocalypse he was emphatically a guide, especially for the poets of the second generation, whose apocalyptic hesitancy is transferred to prophecy and who, even if they become regenerate, thus offering a hope that can be generalized to mankind, become increasingly tentative about their prophetic posture and claims, producing a poetry that is now rife with apocalyptic deferrals.

For pre-Miltonic poets, it may have been possible to use the Apocalypse to hide the terrors of history and thereby evade eschatological despair, to temper the terrors of the present with the promises of a better future. Earlier ages, as Carl Jung observes, "could ignore the dark side of the Apocalypse, because the specifically Christian achievement was not to be frivolously endangered. But for modern man, the case is quite otherwise: We have experienced things so unheard of and so staggering that the question of whether such things are in any way reconcilable with the idea of a good God has become burningly topical. [The Apocalypse] is no longer a problem for experts in theological sermons, but a universal religious nightmare."[16] Milton was not only the first of the modern poets but the first of them to feel compelled to justify God's ways to men. He made such efforts "burningly topical" in an age that made a nightmare of the Apocalypse, and Milton so represented it in *Samson Agonistes.*

We now know the history of apocalypse—and of the Apocalypse—in the post-Renaissance and modern world: of how that scriptural book, its total mythology and its eschatological visions, became historized and secularized, interiorized and humanized. Carl Becker records one phase of this history: the process whereby "the utopian dream of perfection, having been long identified with . . . life eternal in the heavenly city . . . was at last projected into the life of man on earth and identified with the desired and hoped-for regeneration of society."[17] M. H. Abrams continues this story about how the heavenly city acquires earthly foundations by augmenting it with an account of how the Apocalypse becomes imploded in Romantic poetry.[18] But there is also an episode in this tale that, omitting Byron and marginalizing Keats, Abrams does not relate. And it is a tale dear to the hearts of the Romantics who could not, or would not, laugh off "the trauma of history"; for whom, if I may continue to adapt David Roskies' chapter titles as a shorthand,[19] Jerusalem became a ruined city; whose poetry, in turn, made a "liturgy of destruction" and of "the self under siege." When the poet's homeland becomes a ruin, when its cities are places of nightmare, when the poet himself is a ruin among ruins, there is a new tale deriving from a narrowing of options: he may express blind faith or eschatological despair; he can implode history or watch it explode before his eyes.

In such a world, the apocalyptic myth and its eschatological visions exasperate; they do not edify. And not only are claims to vision submitted to scrutiny and often rendered suspect, but the myths encapsulated within vision come under review. Apocalypse, one of many forms of revelation, is wrenched away from prophecy, of which it is a species; and eschatological visions, when not made to clash with, are often wrested from their apocalyptic form. If not always, certainly by the time we reach the early years of the nineteenth century, poets comprehend the importance of distinguishing apocalyptic form from apocalyptic content and then of discrimating ideologically between apocalypse and prophecy.

In Romantic poetry, not only does eschatology come in for parody, but the visionary himself is reviled. It may be, as Bernard McGinn insists, that without a pattern of crisis/judgment/vindication, there is no eschatology.[20] That may be the very point of a symbolic structure like *Frankenstein,* where each of its three parts ends in judgment—of Justine, of the Monster, of Frankenstein himself—but where there is no accompanying vindication. In some Romantic literature, eschatological paradigms are invoked only to be eroded, while the visionary is censured rather than celebrated. Eventually, as Roskies remarks, all the redemptive ideologies (Judaic, Christian, even Marxist), each seen as an extension of the other, are discredited. Utopias become dystopias and then disappear from historical writings, redemptive ideologies flee from literature, and civilization moves into apocalyptic crisis. Yet even when the Romantics cannot embrace the Apocalypse and its eschatology, they call up both, not to crowd out, but to center, reality.

The Apocalypse can be used to departicularize history and, by identifying the present with the final days, can turn the present into a dead end. But the Apocalypse can also be used, as so often the Romantics did use it, to

particularize the historical moment, to distance the present from the pro-
phesied end and thereby make a future possible. Paradoxically, the Apocalypse, which could be used to blot out the present, could also be used to
engender in the present a sense of belonging in time; it *could* be used to
afford the present moment its fullness by imparting meaning to it in terms of
the promised end.

   One can always, it seems, under the pretense of lifting the veil, find en-
coded in present history a system of implied allusion that makes it coincide
with the apocalyptic paradigm. But this is also an evasion, a reneging on responsibility. For as Roskies proposes of nineteenth- and twentieth-century
writers (and what he says is not just true of *Jewish* writers), quite apart from
creating an absolute identity between the present crisis and the apocalyptic
end, they remember that the present occupies a place in the midst of time
and allow it to gather meaning from an eschatological perspective. That
perspective is enabling; for through it we may come, in Roskies' words, "to
know the apocalypse, express it, mourn it, and transcend it" by fashioning
catastrophe into something else, by turning images of destruction into new
acts of creation.[21] Such was the agenda of poetry in the Age of Wordsworth
— an age that believed with the Wordsworth of *The Prelude* that poets must
now exercise their skills "Not in Utopia . . . / Or some secreted island . . . /
But in the very world, which is the world / Of all of us, — the place where,
in the end, / We find our happiness, or not at all!" (11.139–144). If the
Apocalypse had been a book about and for achieving transcendence, if its
myth had hitherto encapsulated a world beyond time, beyond its corruption
and change, in its Romantic revision that book is brought down to earth,
and in the process its myth, relieved of its illusions, is retrieved for, and
newly accommodated to, history.

4

Romanticism
Pleasure and Play

MICHAEL G. COOKE

Except for hard-core traffickers in nostalgia, the present has one advantage over the past: its ways seem natural, while past ways seem incidental to their time, and merely preliminary. It may be startling, for those of us who still dwell on poetry, to find that our easy association of poetry with elevated pleasure is rather latter-day. There was a time when *use* dominated in the common idea of poetry. And before that there was a time when direct social participation (perhaps we could call that an unconscious use) was the order of the day.

Horace was the first of the ancients to analyze not just how poetry worked, but what it worked for. In the *Ars Poetica* (lines 333–334) he sets up two sweeping classes of poets, two exhaustive objects for poetry: *aut prodesse volunt aut delectare poetae*. The poet, we would say, reaches out to teach or to give pleasure (or both at once, Horace adds, but we don't keep that in mind). By dichotomizing "teaching" and "pleasure" Horace has led the world in giving teaching an excessively stern image, if not a bad name.[1] Certainly teaching has not held its ground with pleasure as the goal of poetry, having become something like the serviceable lizard among the cherished flowers in the garden. By the beginning of the nineteenth century, Shelley is forthrightly declaring, "Didactic poetry is my abhorrence" (preface to *Prometheus Unbound*), and Schiller calls didactic poetry a contradiction in terms (*widersprechend*). And the twentieth century first reduces the dynamism of teaching to a passive element of "meaning" in poetry, then dismisses that meaning. Archibald MacLeish asserts that the poem "should not mean, but be," and T. S. Eliot makes meaning a bone tossed to quiet the watchdog of conventionality.

Pleasure, meanwhile, seems to have come canonically into its own. Coleridge declares that "the proper and immediate object of poetry is the communication of immediate pleasure" and further intones: "The species of composition, which represents external nature, . . . or the human mind,—both in relation to human affections—so as to produce immediate pleasure— / and the greatest quantity of immediate pleasure in each part, that is compatible with the largest possible [sum] of Pleasure in the whole."[2] There has even emerged a side poetics to justify the pleasure people take in work of a tragic cast and thus to staunch any flow of embarrassment or guilt that might arise from the appearance of enjoying the representation of hardship and doom. In his essay "Of Tragedy," David Hume discriminates between the feelings of the tragic figure and those of the witness or audience and effectively suggests that it is the tragic figure who takes a narrow and self-serving view of suffering, while the audience is high-minded in appreciating the justice and rhetorical grace with which that suffering is articulated (*Four Dissertations* [1757]). Hume, whose views are in sympathy with Burke's *Philosophical Inquiry into . . . the Sublime and Beautiful* (1757), might seem to carry the justification of tragedy to the borders of ruthlessness when he implies a connection between the tragic figure and a guilty criminal; the culprit quakes when Cicero speaks, and quakes the more dreadfully as Cicero the more powerfully speaks; but the audience's pleasure waxes apace, at the fusion of justice and beauty.

It is worth stressing the sharp difference between Aristotle's view of tragedy and Hume's. For Hume, there is no pity and fear, no identification with the victim of tragedy. For Aristotle there is no pleasure, but only the purgation of what might be seen as pleasure's antitheses, the aforementioned pity and fear. More important, Aristotle looks at tragedy in a personal vein, with the audience going through simultaneous but several purgations; Hume proposes a collective response, according to community values, with the tragic victim (or culprit) alone in a personal posture. A social bearing only implicit in Aristotle is forthright in Hume. In this respect, Hume also distinguishes himself from Horace, putting "pleasure" in a social context, where Horace puts "instruction."

Hume's justification of pleasure is not of course properly Romantic. For one thing, it is too straightforwardly social, too comfortable in its knowledge and its judgment. The Romantic approaches social good more circuitously, more uncertainly, and more menacingly; as Friedrich Schlegel says, "Whoever wants to be educated, let him educate himself. This is rude; but it can't be helped" (*Critical Fragments,* no. 86). The importance of Hume for Romanticism emerges really in the latter's failure, despite Coleridge's absolute affirmation, to embrace Hume's defense of poetic pleasure. A kind of discomfort persists in the presence of pleasure. Among the Romantics, Byron perhaps excepted, we seem to find a surplus of intensity (a.k.a. *Sturm and Drang*), and of gravity, and idealism—in sum, a short shrift for pleasure and play. A young ass is not frolicsome or cute, but an occasion for sad, edifying sentiments. A jaunt in the woods (à la Wordsworth's *Nutting*) or in the city (à la Blake's *London*) betrays savage exploitive impulses lurking in the breast of a clownish youth or elicts a harshly melancholy, accusative air.

The discomfort with pleasure as the end of poetry stands out in Wordsworth's preface to *Lyrical Ballads* (1800) and manifests itself as he is in the thick of presenting pleasure as the goal of his own work; "The pleasure which I hope to give by the Poems now presented to the Reader. . . ." In fact, Wordsworth breaks new ground by making pleasure not just the end but the origin of poetry. A "Poet," he declares, is

> a man *pleased* with his own passions and volitions, and who *rejoices* . . . in the spirit of life that is in him; *delighting* to contemplate similar volitions and passions as manifested in the goings-on of the Universe. . . . To these qualities he has added . . . an ability of conjuring up in himself passions, which are indeed far from being the same as those produced by real events, yet (especially in those parts of the general sympathy which are *pleasing and delightful* do more nearly resemble the passions produced by real events, than anything which, from the motions of their own minds merely, other men are accustomed to feel in themselves. (Emphasis added.)

Having thus set up the origin of poetry in pleasure, Wordsworth proceeds directly to establish the formal connection and identity between origin and end. The poet, as it were mentally conjuring, wishes "to bring his feelings near to those of the persons whose feelings he describes . . . , and even confound and identify his own feelings with theirs; modifying only the language which is thus suggested to him by a consideration that he describes for a particular purpose, that of giving pleasure." In a rousing finale to this veritable disquisition on pleasure, he declares that "the poet writes under one restriction only, namely, the necessity of giving immediate pleasure to a human Being possessed of that information which may be expected from him, not as a lawyer, a physician, a mariner, an astronomer, or a natural philosopher, but as a Man."

It is surprising, after this, to run into misgivings about pleasure, a sense that it might bring us to impairment and disrepute. But that is precisely where Wordsworth takes us: "Nor let this necessity of producing immediate pleasure be considered as a degradation of the Poet's art." This puritanical assumption that pleasure might entail degradation seems to come out of the blue. Wordsworth goes on to assert, "It is far otherwise," but the mere voicing of the doubt tends to blight the principle of pleasure that has luxuriated through the passage. Clearly more is at work than Wordsworth's inveterate habit of putting a negative statement to counter a hearty positive assertion, as where the third verse-paragraph of *Tintern Abbey,* following the visionary claim that "we see into the life of things," goes abruptly to the question "If this be but a vain belief. . . ."

In a sense, given what he has set out to do, Wordsworth cannot afford to leave the reader too soon satisfied with the sense of "pleasure," even in the adjusted Humean mode. He appears to be speaking about the volume at hand: "The pleasure which I hope to produce in the reader by the Poems." In actuality, though, he is using the present volume as an Archimedean fulcrum to tilt the entire world of poetry into a new dispensation. It is not enough for him to get the reader to take pleasure in the new work, or new approaches, that he is presenting. Presumably that would leave old pleasures intact, from Horace to Hume. But Wordsworth desires to make the reader see the entire span of poetry in a new light, according to new standards: "If my conclusions are admitted, and carried as far as they must be if admitted at all, our judgements concerning the works of the greatest Poets both ancient and modern will be far different from what they are at present."

The word he uses, virtually as a slogan for this mission, is "pleasure." It is a term of reassurance, conciliation, and seduction in what might be taken as a threatening situation of newness. But behind the seduction the case *is* being made. Pleasure is being redefined, and the reader's mind turned into new conceptions, through pleasure. What Wordsworth says of poetry he is exemplifying in prose, but with one major difference: the concept rather than the experience of pleasure must take effect here. Lionel Trilling's ground-breaking essay "The Fate of Pleasure" recognizes the immense weight of Wordsworth's commitment to pleasure but does not look into its intrinsic thrust toward a new definition and a new set of relations for the concept of pleasure itself.[3]

Wordsworth's recalibration of pleasure starts at the simplest level. It is the product of self-recognition and self-confidence: "Being possessed of that information" which everyone has, irrespective of career or calling, "as a Man." This initial egotism constitutes a bond with all the rest of readers or their egos, so that the pleasure of the self at once increases and fuses with the pleasure of the category to which that self belongs.

For Wordsworth, much more is at stake. Self-recognition, self-confidence, and self-categorization are as virtues both obvious and insufficient. They constitute both a base and, Wordsworth seems to think, a danger. He introduces the fear of "degradation" precisely at this point, at the second, ostensibly universal level of pleasure. Degradation, we must infer, is relative; Wordsworth is not being a spoilsport about pleasure but proceeding according to Vladimir Solovyov's conception of asceticism as the choice of the higher over the lower good.[4] What, then, is the higher good, the peculiar pleasure Wordsworth envisions? We shall see that he moves, in a few brief steps, from an apparently aesthetic position to a psychosympathetic one and finally to a comprehensive spiritual and moral one.

First, Wordsworth calls pleasure, or the necessity of producing pleasure in poetry, "an acknowledgement of the beauty of the universe." But this acknowledgment itself occurs "in the spirit of love" and proves a "homage" to the "native and naked dignity of man." When Wordsworth further says that "pleasure in poetry pays homage" to the "grand elementary principle of pleasure," he is not lapsing into stunned tautology but placing the individual case in its categorical matrix. The question of beauty joins indissolubly with love and dignity, and these rest intrinsically on a principle which, as meriting the epithets "grand" and "elementary," seems both homely and sublime.[5] Wordsworth is fitting many complex elements into a small compass, moving us from familiar ground by familiar steps to rather unexpected positions. He goes beyond Shelley's unacknowledged legislator—the keynote of the preface is an *insistence on acknowledgement*—and makes the poet "the rock of defence for human nature; an upholder and preserver, carrying with him everywhere relationship and love" and binding "together by passion and knowledge the vast empire of human society, as it is spread over the whole earth, and over all time."

If we were not pursuing Wordsworth's definition of pleasure, it would be fitting to ask if these comprehensive professions of unity and sympathy and value can be accepted from the poet who at about the same time was penning "I traveled among unknown men," with its post–French Revolution reaction of insularity. But the question is not how well Wordsworth held to his position; rather, it is how he conceived of it. And his conception of pleasure moves from "animal sensations" to "moral sentiments," from the single person at a single moment to all persons at any time. Herein lies Wordsworth's objection to the "discoveries of science," which are intrinsically "remote."

This conception of pleasure sustains itself in Wordworth's criticism and obiter dicta over the years. In a letter of 1814, Wordsworth breaks "poetic passion" down into "two kinds: imaginative and enthusiastic [on the one hand], and merely human and ordinary [on the other hand]" (*Middle Years*, vol. 2, p. 617).[6] In the "Essay, Supplementary to the Preface", he enunciates the position that there is "an enthusiastic, as well as an ordinary sorrow; a sadness that has its seat in the depths of reason, to which the mind cannot *sink* gently *of itself*, but to which it must descend by treading the depths of thought" (emphasis added). In fact, the polarization of "imaginative" and "ordinary," as of "enthusiastic" and "ordinary" (where *enthusiastic* has the root meaning of "containing divinity") exactly picks up the famous lines in *Tintern Abbey:*

> . . . sensations sweet,
> Felt in the blood, and felt along the heart,
> And passing even into the purer mind
> With tranquil restoration.

The only difference is that *Tintern Abbey* spells out the passage that connects the polar positions and thus makes a continuum where casual reading might see only sequence or division.

James A. W. Heffernan has suggested that the Restoration critic John Dennis provided the Romantic poet Wordsworth with the distinction between "ordinary" and "enthusiastic" passions.[7] As we know, Wordsworth freely acknowledges that Dennis "well observed" the "two kinds" of poetic passion (*Middle Years* 2.617), but this is not tantamount to *equating* Dennis's thought and Wordsworth's. Dennis, I would say, contributed to Wordsworth's idea just what a gold or ruby wholesaler would to a Buccellati or a Fabergé. That is to say, Wordsworth created out of what Dennis wrote something the latter had never dreamed of. Let us hear Dennis on "Enthusiastik Passion": "[These are] caus'd by Ideas [i.e., revived sense impressions, à la Hobbes] occurring to us in Meditation and producing the same Passions that the Objects of those Ideas would raise in us if they were set before us in the same light that those Ideas give us of them." Apart from the phrasal thicket of the prose, this sounds very much like Wordsworth, or vice versa. But such an impression does not hold up if we allow Dennis to go on and illustrate his point:

> The Sun mention'd in ordinary Conversation, gives the Idea of a round flat shining Body, of about two foot diameter. But the sun occurring to us in Meditation, gives the Idea of a vast and glorious body, and the top of all the visible Creation, and the brightest material Image of the Divinity. I leave the Reader to judge, therefore if this Idea must not necessarily be attended with Admiration; and that Admiration I call Enthusiasm. So Thunder . . . in common Conversation, gives an Idea of a black Cloud, and a great Noise. . . . But the Idea of it occurring in Meditation, sets before us the most forcible, most resistless, and consequently the most dreadful Phaenomenon in Nature: So that this Idea must move a great deal of Terror in us, and 'tis this sort of Terror that I call Enthusiasm.
>
> (*Critical Works* [1704], vol. 1, pp. 338–339)

It seems, here, appropriate to father not the preface to *Lyrical Ballads* on Dennis, but rather Edmund Burke's *Philosophical Enquiry into the Origin of Our Ideas of the Sublime and the Beautiful.* Dennis is dealing with varieties of the sublime (admiration and terror) under the heading of "enthusiasm." He envinces utter innocence in relation to the Wordsworthian sense of "pleasure," or in relation to Wordsworth's deep and intrinsic link between recollection of "absent things" and identification with the human lot. In short, Wordsworth uses the word "meditation," as Dennis does, and distinguishes between "ordinary" and "enthusiastic" passion, as Dennis does; but he transforms Dennis's words, giving them a different setting and form and end and value. Ultimately, Wordworth shows how the enthusiastic inheres in the ordinary, or forms a continuum with it. Dennis truly divides the two, whereas Wordsworth only distinguishes them from each other, keeping a necessary connection without making that connection automatic or inevitable.

To recapitulate, it is the pattern of the preface to oscillate between some simple notion of pleasure, such as "animal sensations," and some complex extension and revision of that notion toward "moral" relations. To the very end, Wordsworth is telling us that we have a right, like Mr. Hardcastle, to want to be pleased in the ways we've grown used to; he calls this, ambiguously, "honourable bigotry." But he at once proceeds to try to convert the bigots, to enlarge and ennoble pleasure: "It is possible for poetry to give other enjoyments, of a purer, more lasting, and more exquisite nature. . . . If my purpose were fulfilled, a species of poetry would be adapted to interest mankind permanently, and likewise important in the multiplicity and quality of its moral relations."

If we look back to Horace and Hume, it is manifest that Wordsworth summons us, in the perennial name of pleasure, to something singular and new. If we look forward, to Pater for example, it becomes clear that something had a singularly brief historical span. In his essay on Winckelmann in *The Renaissance*, Walter Pater delivers himself as follows: "Let us understand by poetry all literary production which attains the power of giving pleasure by its form, as distinct from its matter." The concern with form might seem on one level reminiscent of Wordworth's emphasis on meter in the preface, but the reliance on form alone carries us eons from Wordsworth. What Pater omits is precisely the generic valence, the psychic authority, the moral engagement, and the articulate human essence that Wordsworth so painstakingly and so passionately fosters in his definition. What Pater omits is in that sense the Romantic conception of pleasure.

One further word may help to pinpoint Wordsworth in the multitudinous discourse on pleasure. Wordsworth in effect treats pleasure as a mental event rather than as an emotional-physiological one. This in a way leads on to Freud, who in *Beyond the Pleasure Principle* announces that "the course taken by mental events is automatically regulated by the pleasure principle." But Wordsworth is far from shunning the authority of sensation and feelings, while Freud is at pains to do so, calling "the meaning of the feelings of pleasure and unpleasure which act so imperatively upon us. . . the most obscure and inaccessible region of the mind." Thus despite the fact that both Wordsworth and Freud presume that poetry and mental events, respectively, will result in an overbalance of pleasure, they are not talking about the same thing. Freud says that "the pleasure principle follows from the principle of constancy." It is a manifestation of an individual mental economy, indeed of an isolated one. Wordsworth on the other hand makes pleasure a sine qua non of human "relationship and love." Put another way, where Freud sets up an opposition between pleasure and the increments of reality in human experience and, further, between pleasure and the ego's "development into more highly composite organizations," Wordsworth intrinsically identifies pleasure with both.

This idea of pleasure is of supreme importance in engaging with English Romantic poetry. Keats in his maturer work breaks away from a hedonistic-competitive notion of pleasure and achieves a vision analogous to Wordsworth's when, in *Hyperion: A Fragment,* he declares sorrow "more beautiful than beauty's self." Like Wordsworth he goes beyond the aesthetic ("beauty's self") to the emotional-psychic ("sorrow") and makes of the latter a supra-aesthetic state. Ultimate beauty inheres in a vision of sympathy and prevailing human value, by way of identification with the state of the victim and an assumption of responsibility for it. In *The Romantic Will,* I have argued that Keats uses *The Fall of Hyperion* to join humanity and divinity at the point of suffering, and it is important to see the beauty, and thus the pleasingness, of suffering there.[8] Keats in effect carries pleasure, reconstituted, into the two seemingly inhospitable reaches of disaster and sublimity. But that is precisely what Wordsworth envisions in promising always "an overbalance of pleasure." He is not dichotomizing the soul into pleasure and pain and putting a meter (except for a poetic meter) on each. Rather, he is transforming the pain that we topically feel into the sense of strength and satisfaction and scope that we experience generically, ubiquitously, in seeing pain under the control of form, in language compatible with our own, and borne up by a lucid image or event.

In a cryptic way Byron conveys an equivalent understanding of the metaphysical, as opposed to the mathematical, primacy of pleasure when he pronounces that it is good "to feel that we exist, even though in pain." And Coleridge, at the end of *This Lime-Tree Bower, My Prison,* as he recovers from an isolating and thus dehumanizing and denaturalizing pain, reaffirms both pleasure and poetry in the Wordsworthian utterance "No sound is dissonant which tells of life." Here again the aesthetic is reconceived, and the caw of the rook, a sound that might by itself seem unpleasant, is prevented from being so, in relation to its human and metaphysical freight (it "tells of life").

Wordsworth's theory of pleasure is complexly derived. It includes ready sensation and aesthetic sensitivity and a moral sense of a deep and pervasive identification with the human state. It defines the human state in terms of its insistent weight and perennial incompleteness and inundation, attraction, and dereliction. Though it is necessary to point out the fact that Wordsworth can be very insular and ungenerous, the fact is that his theory of pleasure enters virtually into much of his poetry. The second verse paragraph of *Tintern Abbey,* where he summarizes the scene above the unkempt abbey as a collection of "beauteous forms," gives a virtual model for the position of the preface. The movement of the paragraph from "beauteous forms" to "the life of things" is complex and worthy of scrutiny.

The "forms," of course, have a daring Platonic freight, but to begin with they are physical objects that, seen and visualized, cause the pleasure of "sensations sweet." These sensations prove far from simple; they have a sort of Platonic career, being "Felt in the blood, and felt along the heart," and "passing even into the purer mind, / With tranquil restoration." Such an effect remains clearly personal, introspective. Wordsworth proceeds to show how the "beauteous forms" link him ideally to all mankind and all of nature; he shifts the subject from "I" to "we," and "we" are identified with a capacity, beyond confusion and pain, for a "deep power of Joy," where "We see into the life of things."

It is easy to be misled by the chronological pattern of *Tintern Abbey* into conceiving of several, distinct phases of experience, even several, distinct spheres of emotion and reflection in the Wordsworthian scheme. Indeed, Wordsworth appears to introduce a calculus of then and now:

> That time is past,
> And all its aching joys are now no more,
> And all its dizzy raptures. Not for this
> Faint I, nor mourn, nor murmur; other gifts
> Have followed; for such loss, I would believe,
> Abundant recompense.

But I suggest that *Tintern Abbey* is not a poem of sequence and—if we consider the Platonic undertones—progressions; rather, it is a poem of manifestation or revelation, bringing forth what inheres in a state without being always recognized or known. As Friedrich Schiller observes in his letters *On the Aesthetic Education of Man,* the "physical state" and the "aesthetic stage" may be "two periods in theory," but "in practice they more or less merge one into the other." Wordsworth does not describe two separate and distinct states of then and now. To the contrary, the present is a more complex and more inclusive version of the past. The "presence that disturbs . . . with the joy / Of elevated thoughts" contains the very paradox and ambivalence we see in the boy who, bounding "like a roe" over the mountains, seems somehow to be flying from "something that he dreads." The moment of material pleasure is both precious and dangerous.[9] For while it is a gift in itself, it must also serve as a stage and clue. "Elevated thoughts" must be added, and "animal movements" yield to a contemplative and spiritual "presence." The poem shows "coarser pleasures" and "present pleasure" as a part of ultimate pleasure, on the one hand "elevated" and on the other "chasten[ed] and subdue[d]." Pleasure becomes the comprehensive condition of the human being, fusing early and late, sensation and thought, joy and sorrow, elevation and chastening. It is a generic term for being substantially human, irrespective of specific conditions. When Wordsworth speaks of "the still sad music of humanity, / Nor harsh nor grating," we may rightly recall Coleridge intoning that "no sound is dissonant which tells of life."

We must also see that the Romantic impulse to generalize and abstract pleasure, after being brought to its symbolic extreme, is from there brought back down to concrete existence. That is to say, Wordsworth supplants "the sounding cataract" with "the still sad music of humanity"; he supplants what directly exists with something invented and sustained in the mind. This is the typical movement of pleasure from local to universal, from sensational to conceptual. But in conceiving of humanity in terms of music, Wordsworth also focuses and embodies that abstraction. Every person contributes to the music; every person represents it. And if it is sad music, that only deepens its pleasure, which is not the pleasure of sensory satisfaction in sound but the pleasure of being and belonging to something great expressed in the phenomenon of sound.

To dwell a moment longer on Wordsworth, we may recognize this sort of pleasure in *I wandered lonely as a Cloud,* which needs to be understood in terms of a human emblem. The poem in fact suggests sound in words like "jocund" and "glee," but the paramount fact is that three changes occur: aimless motion ("wandered") gives way to dancing; obscurity and gloom ("clouds") give way to light and gaiety ("stars . . . twinkle," "sprightly dance"); and loneliness gives way to community. And all at the sight of the "golden daffodils." In effect, the daffodils prove to Wordsworth that isolation and privation are incidental and that, even at the very border of the barren and threatening lake, community flourishes. The "bliss of solitude" is subtly self-contradictory, being based on the knowledge, when one is "vacant" and "pensive," that the full and joyous world is ready to hand (or to mind); and one is tempted to wonder if Wordsworth is implying that the daffodils were dancing to see him, as he exults to see them. Certainly he and they become one "jocund company."

It is not customary to compare this poem to *Tintern Abbey.* Wordsworth himself did not seem to put it among his higher poetic achievements, speaking of it as an "impression . . . upon the imaginative faculty" rather than "an *exertion* of it" (*Poetical Works,* vol. 2, p. 507).[10] Clearly *Tintern Abbey* represents a considerable "exertion" of the imaginative faculty. Next to it, *I wandered lonely as a Cloud* seems slight enough. But where this little poem lacks the scope, it cannot be said to lack the characteristic nucleus of *Tintern Abbey,* for it also grows from an ordinary topical incident that reverberates in time and, through time, produces a change in value for itself as for the poet:

> I gazed—and gazed—but little thought
> What wealth the show to me had brought.

"The show" amounts to more than shows. The poem enters into the theater of Wordsworth's spirit, the original incident restoring itself and the witness in exactly the way incidents in *Tintern Abbey* do. In fact, the incident restores the witness to his humanity—the great motif and rallying cry of the preface to *Lyrical Ballads*—from a barren and depressed state in nature and in himself. That, too, links *I wandered lonely as a Cloud* with *Tintern Abbey.* And that is what gives singular depth to the "jocund company" and singular resonance to the poet's heart filling with pleasure and dancing with the daffodils. The pleasure is not incidental and picturesque, not "ordinary" in the Dennis-Wordsworth sense, but rather proves abiding, meditated, and rooted in devotion to humanity in the singular sense that Wordsworth enunciates.

The status of pleasure in the Romantic order is intimate and complex, and one would say surprisingly so. But pleasure, as we have seen it unfold, looks typical of the pardoxicality of the period; as Wordsworth says, it is both "grand" and "elementary." It is a pleasure in the grand and elementary that informs and justifies the domestic resolution of Friedrich Schlegel's revolutionary novel *Lucinde*. And it is likewise this pleasure that justifies and redeems Faust's forbidden plea: "stay, thou art so fair." No aesthetic bias moves him here, but the obscure humility of being able, at last, to attach himself to something finite and perishable, recognizing at once its power and its inevitability in his nature.

On the face of it, the concept of play seems no less remote from supposedly typical Romantic concerns—with revolution and the gravity of life—than does the concept of pleasure. One is tempted to look upon the mischief associated with the theater episode in Jane Austen's *Mansfield Park* as an index of the undesirability of play. Or perhaps one observes, in the revelry preceding the Battle of Waterloo stanzas of *Childe Harold*, canto 3, signs of impropriety and unconsciousness of the world's demands. Even the Wordsworthian boys, stealing rides in rowboats or birds from other people's snares, skating or riding on horseback, or impersonating and inspiring owls around Winander, all carry the same admonition: that play must cease and entails discomfort and punishment (even, cryptically, death).

But difficulty with any of these cases of play is more a matter of style than of intrinsic quality. Each involves play divorced from a context, from the proper scope and relations of experience. There is another kind of play in Romanticism, more complex and more satisfying, if also, like Romantic pleasure, less amusing for the moment. The adult Byron playing with the "mane" of the ocean at the end of *Childe Harold 4* exemplifies such play. It combines the action of the boy with the consciousness of the man, the wry daring of the man with the confident spontaneity of the boy, the self-absorption of the boy with the humility and visionary breadth of the man. In other words, play reflects the choice and power to act in a context wherein only the self is controlled, where everything is clear but nothing final, so that every step becomes a demonstration, an experiment, and a discovery.

The scope of play in Romanticism is best seen in Schiller's *On the Aesthetic Education of Man.*[11] Schiller sets out to expatiate on Art and Beauty, but straightway asserts "a direct connexion with all that is best in human happiness, and no very distant connexion with what is noblest in our moral nature" (3). This has at first the smack of tendentiousness, of that very application which Schiller seems elsewhere to repudiate, terming "self-contradictory . . . the notion of a fine art which teaches (didactic) or improves (moral): for nothing is more at variance with the concept of beauty than the notion of giving the psyche [Gemut] any definite bias" (157). But it is possible to see why Schiller bridles at "moral" art while summoning art to "what is noblest in our moral nature." Clearly Schiller will accept the moral valence of art not in any behavioristic or programmatic sense but only in terms of the strongest manifestations of human values and relations. Conventional morality dictates and binds; the "aesthetic," as Schiller sees it, "leads to the absence of all limitation" (151) and is "the consummation of humanity" in that it can "release us" into a "lofty equanimity and freedom of spirit" (153).

Given Schiller's huge claims for the aesthetic, it may come as a surprise to find him holding up as the end of beauty the formal concept of the "play-drive" (101, passim). But Schiller foresees our surprise and explains himself:

Man . . . is neither exclusively matter nor exclusively mind. Beauty, as the consummation of his humanity, can therefore be neither exclusively life nor exclusively form. . . . It is the object common to both drives [for life and for form], that is to say, the object of the play-drive. This term is fully justified by linguistic usage, which is wont to designate as 'play' everything which is neither subjectively nor objectively contingent, and yet imposes no kind of constraint either from within or from without. Since, in contemplation of the beautiful, the psyche [Gemut] finds itself in a happy medium between the realm of law and the sphere of physical exigency, it is . . . removed from the constraint of the one as of the other. . . . Life becomes of less consequence once human dignity enters in, and duty ceases to be a constraint once inclination exerts its pull; similarly our psyche [Gemut] accepts the reality of things, or material truth, with greater freedom and serenity once this latter encounters formal truth, or the law of necessity, and no longer feels constrained by abstraction once this can be accomplished by the immediacy of intuition. In a word: by entering into association with ideas all reality loses its earnestness because it then becomes of small account; and by coinciding with feeling necessity divests itself of its earnestness because it then becomes of light weight. (103, 105)

This is a neat if protracted account of the operation whereby "the play-drive" becomes an apt vehicle for transmitting the idea of beauty. But there are undesirable side effects; both life and form, reality and necessity, bringing beauty in their train, prove to be of small account (*klein*) and of light weight (*leicht*).

No wonder Schiller comes out in the manner of Wordsworth worrying about our reaction to his ideal of pleasure: "You may long have been tempted to object, is beauty not degraded by being made to consist of mere play and reduced to the level of those frivolous things which have always borne this name?" Actually, it proves to be the case that, as Wordsworth uses "pleasure" in a specific material sense and also in a comprehensive, abstract one, so does Schiller use "play." In the former, local material sense, "play" might mean a degradation of beauty, but in the latter, abstract sense it is "of all man's states and conditions the one which makes him whole and unfolds both sides of his nature at once" (105).

Thus Schiller can fly in the face of our preconceptions with the claim that with "the agreeable, the good, the perfect, . . . man is merely in earnest; but with beauty he plays" (105). He hastens to add that "the beauty we find in actual existence is precisely what the play-drive in actual existence deserves; but with the ideal of beauty set up by Reason, an idea of the play-drive, too, is enjoined upon man, which he must keep before his eyes in all his forms of play" (107).

Put in other terms, the distinction between local or topical play and ultimate, abstract play means that humankind may never invest itself wholly in the moment of play, in any mere manifestation of its capacity and need for play. At the same time it may not make light of those moments, as neither capacity nor need can be embodied except through them. If such moments render reality "of small account" and necessity "of light weight," the upshot is not belittlement but freedom from superstitious portentousness in the face of reality, and freedom from a sense of oppression before it. There would result, then, a superior sense of proportion and perspective and competence of humankind. Rendered small, reality does not run like a juggernaut down the path of perception and value; does not run humanity into the earth. The moment of play, as it addresses the capacity and need for play, saves humankind from being overwhelmed, giving it the world of experience and duty in a form capable of being wielded with assurance and grace. This is the basis for Schiller to turn oxymoronically upon himself, with his exaltation of play itself over earnest play (*ein ernstes Spiel*). This is the basis for his contention that "man only plays when he is in the fullest sense of the word a human being, and he is only fully a human being when he plays" (107).

We live in an age that exalts both pleasure and play, but only for their powers of concrete absorption and practical distraction. Accordingly we are likely to balk at the austere intellectuality and idealism that Wordsworth and Schiller bring to these concepts. Part of our difficulty would stem from our view of history, part from our view of psychology or personality.

Both Wordsworth and Schiller conceive of pleasure and play, respectively, as a source of transcendence. As Wordsworth avers, "a great poet [as purveyor of pleasure] . . . ought, to a certain degree, to rectify men's feelings, to give them new compositions of feeling, to render their feelings more sane, pure and permanent, in short, more consonant to nature, that is, to eternal nature, and the great moving spirit of things" (*Early Letters*, pp. 295–296).[12] But such an approach to poetry and experience *sub specie aeternitatis* does not consort with the way we see humankind in history. William Barrett sums up the modern position: "Man is totally within history and . . . there are no suprahistorical points of view from which he can step outside of his world in order to be the Platonic spectator of it. . . . The more deeply we investigate human culture the more deeply we find man in each age immersed in his own time." There is only, Barrett affirms, "historical man in an actual or definite situation."[13] It is no wonder that, in *Ringolevio*, Emmett Grogan should tacitly upend Schiller's posture: "thieves and revolutionaries play for keeps, the artist . . . for fun."[14]

In the domain of psychology, again, we find an implicit denial of the objectivity and graciousness and idealism that Wordsworth ascribes to pleasure and Schiller to play. If we look at the fact that the Romantic writers tie their highest values to art, and if we then consider the interpretation of art in the psychoanalytic tradition, the opposition comes out graphically. Ernst

Kris in his *Psychoanalytic Explorations of Art* emphasizes the communicative valence of art but founds effective communication on the displaced gratification of what the audience experiences as forbidden interests and desires.[15] Recent practitioners have been at pains to revise and amplify the vision of psychoanalysis, but even here the ennobled prospect of pleasure and play have little scope. Meredith Anne Skura speaks sensitively of psychoanalysis as providing "a new scale of possible discriminations," and she speaks sensitively also of play, in her study *The Literary Use of the Psychoanalytical Process*.[16] But play is a *space*, rather than a state; it is what D. W. Winnicott calls transitional space between solipsism and reality.[17] Skura is not wholly satisfied with the formula and declares that "art is neither reality itself nor an escape from reality." Still, the distance between her modernist outlook and the romantic vision can be measured in her definition of play: "True play begins only when the child realizes the difference between killing a father doll and killing a father, or when the patient recognizes the difference between merely disagreeing with the analyst and having fantasies which turn disagreement into a crushing attack" (189). The question arises: Do not Dennis's and Wordsworth's "ordinary" people play, and not just subhomicidal children and the mentally disturbed? Even more to the point, do not "enthusiastic" and creatively "imaginative" people play? And what becomes of play when the "transition" is complete? Is there nothing for it but to abide by St. Paul's bleak advice to put away childish things?

Johan Huizinga's famed and seminal study, *Homo Ludens* (1949) might be thought to proffer an argument against any reductive notion of play. In actuality, it is only apsychoanalytic. Huizinga declares that "civilization does not come *from* play like a babe detaching itself from the womb: it arises *in* and *as* play, and never leaves it." He is really dealing with the ordinary forms of experience, the customs and patterns and formulas that envelop, as much as express, the human being, in what Peter L. Berger calls the *social construction of reality*.[18] For Huizinga, "play" ranges from *panem et circenses* to chivalric tournaments and the *corrida*. It boils down to a kind of super glue for the body politic. It is striking that he nowhere mentions Schiller or takes up the play of mind and spirit, of judgment and aspiration and magnanimity that Schiller conceives. The proposition that "animals play just like men" makes it clear that Huizinga would not have understood Schiller.

The difficulty is not that Huizinga is utilitarian and Schiller idealistic. To the contrary, Huizinga is merely utilitarian and Schiller is both utilitarian and idealistic. For Schiller, play is the point of fusion between life and form, reality and necessity. It is thus an inclusive concept rather than a specific phenomenon, just as for Wordsworth pleasure, the point of fusion between personality and humanity, immediacy and history, is an inclusive concept rather than a specific phenomenon.

And yet a marked difference appears between pleasure and play as Wordsworth and Schiller, respectively, expound these concepts. In brief, the difference lies in Wordsworth's emphasis on sophisticated immersion, Schiller's on fine-tuned aloofness. Perhaps that difference arises from Schiller's grounding in philosophy, where Wordsworth takes a more pragmatic approach; certainly Schiller, though claiming to come without "the support of authority and borrowed strength," falls back on "Kantian principles," especially on Kant's idea of disinterest as the hallmark of the aesthetic experience. Certainly much of the *Aesthetic Education* could pass for a gloss on Kant's definition of beauty as "the form of the purposiveness of an object, so far as this is perceived in it without any representation of a purpose." But we need to recall that Schiller means play to be "capable of bearing the whole edifice of the art of the beautiful, *and of the still more difficult art of living* [emphasis added]" (107, 109).

What finally keeps Schiller and Wordsworth apart occurs at the level of illustration, where the German thinker who was so preoccupied with classical antiquity turns to the statue of the putative Juno Ludovisi, while the English poet who was so preoccupied with life as ordinarily lived turns to the world about him. It is striking, though, that Schiller's description of the classical figure resists, if it does not contradict, his ideal of equilibrium (*Gleichgewicht*). Here is how he articulates this ideal; the Greeks

banished from the brow of the blessed gods all the earnestness and effort which furrow the cheeks of mortals, no less than the empty pleasures which preserve the smoothness of a vacuous face; freed those ever-contented beings from the bonds inseparable from every purpose, every duty, every care, and made idleness and indifferency the enviable portion of divinity—merely a more human name for the freest, most sublime state of being. (109)

But as he continues, Schiller seems closer to the ennobling sympathy and strife that Keats presents in the Hyperion poems and that Wordsworth propounds in the preface to *Lyrical Ballads:*

> It is not Grace, nor is it yet Dignity, which speaks to us from the superb countenance of a Juno Ludovisi; it is neither the one nor the other because it is both at once. While the woman-god demands our veneration, the god-like woman kindles our love; but even as we abandon ourselves in ecstasy to her heavenly grace, her celestial self-sufficiency makes us recoil in terror. The whole figure reposes and dwells in itself, a creation completely self-contained, and, as if existing beyond space, neither yielding nor resisting; here is no force to contend with force, no frailty where temporality might break in. Irresistibly moved and drawn by those former qualities, kept at a distance by these latter, we find ourselves at one and the same time in a state of utter repose and supreme agitation, and there results that wondrous stirring of the heart for which mind has no concept nor speech any name. (109)

It is not enough to say that Wordsworth might call it "pleasure" in his edified and all-embracing sense and that Schiller himself has been calling it redeemed "play." Both "pleasure" and "play" will give rise to conceptual tensions and gaps because they are less analytic than hortatory ideas; they summon the age out of habits that are comfortable and efficient, and thus they problematically oppose what Wordsworth calls an "honourable bigotry."

Surely Wordsworth and Schiller appear to be right in making their pitch. As Schlegel says, the fact that "the age isn't ready" doesn't mean that a given thing "shouldn't happen," for "if something can't yet be, then it must at least always continue to become" (*Athenaeum Fragments,* no. 334). But even at such a rate, resistance may develop (in a few short decades Cardinal Newman will come out against pressing even valid ideas upon an unready age). In *Don Juan* Byron invites the reader to a new pleasure of self-discovery, and the age was scandalized; Byron indulges and invites the reader to share in a kind of play with accepted values and forms, and that led to offense. The age may have felt that he was less inviting it to play than playing with it. And yet we can see, for example in the work of Byron's allusions (*alludere,* to play), that Byron meant to awaken the age *from* its dream of security in the covenant of the rainbow and *to* its hard, exhilarating engagement with the true colors of reality:

> . . . like nothing that I know
> Except itself;—such is the human breast;
> A thing, of which similtudes can show
> No real likeness,—like the old Tyrian vest
> Dyed purple, none at present can tell how,
> If from a shell-fish or from cochineal.
> So perish every tyrant's robe piece-meal.
> (*Don Juan,* Canto 16, st. 10)

It would seem a sheer concession to the contemporary social context that, for all the momentousness that Wordsworth and Schiller see in pleasure and play, they pay so little attention to its erotic dimension. In *Nutting,* of course, Wordsworth forthrightly links pleasure and eroticism:

> Tall and erect, with tempting clusters hung,
> A virgin scene!—A little while I stood,
> Breathing with such suppression of the heart
> As joy delights in, and, with wise restraint
> Voluptuous, fearless of a rival, eyed
> The banquet. . . .

He speaks further of "that sweet mood when pleasure loves to pay / Tribute to ease; and, of its joy secure, / The heart luxuriates. . . ." He even seems to treat play as a variant of pleasure: "beneath the trees I sat / Among the flowers, and with the flowers I played. . . ." But in his holding forth on pleasure in the preface to *Lyrical Ballads,* he offers up one scant comment on the subject: "This principle [of similitude in dissimilitude] is the great spring of the activity of our minds, and their chief feeder. From this principle the direction of the sexual appetite, and all the passions connected with it, take their origin: it is the life of our ordinary conversation."

It is small wonder that James Hogg chose to take a cut at Wordsworth's stilted evasion: "for on similitude / In dissimilitude, man's sole delight, / And all the sexual intercourse of things, / Do most supremely hang."[19] Again, in the "Essay, Supplementary to the Preface of 1815," a passing reference is made to pleasure and eroticism: "With the young of both sexes,

Poetry is, like love, a passion; but, for much the greater part of those who have been proud of its power over their minds, a necessity soon arises of breaking the pleasing bondage; or it relaxes of itself." Here the pleasure of eroticism is reduced to a metaphor, and at that a metaphor of transience, as though it represented the simple order of sensation rather than the complex, abstract order of value.

If Wordsworth elides the erotic, Schiller almost ignores it. The passage on the Juno Ludovisi contains his clearest approach to it, and that takes the form of a metaphor, not of transience, but of transcendence: "While the woman-god demands our veneration, the god-like woman kindles our love; but even as we abandon ourselves in ecstasy to her heavenly grace, her celestial self-sufficiency makes us recoil in terror." This is an extreme reaction and noteworthy not just for breaking Schiller's drumbeat of equilibrium and indifference but also for being the solitary substantial exemplification of his theories to be found in the text. Could it be that the erotic is being held down, throughout, under a lid of equilibrium? Or is it marginal and therefore unlikely to meet the central qualifications of the argument? With Wordsworth, does not his own metaphor suggest that his continuing as a poet and a lover of poetry gives evidence of a submerged, or sublimated, eroticism?

In the light of these questions, it is proper to call in Schopenhauer to comment on Schiller's fusion of life and form and on Wordsworth's fusion of sensation and the norms of life. For Schopenhauer makes it clear that the erotic may be the most common and the most compelling and the most profound instance of those fusions. The very title of Schopenhauer's essay, "The Metaphysic of the Love of the Sexes," suggests the immediate and the eternal, the individual and the abstract. But Schopenhauer's argument does more, coming uncannily to resemble what Wordsworth and Schiller both argue for, a meeting which is revelatory for our innermost need and power, a meeting between the simplest sort of personal spontaneity and the ultimate, most abstract sense of perfection we can approach, as person *and* as participant in the race. Schopenhauer's idea, let us briefly recall, is that passionate love between a man and a woman represents our deepest, unconscious, way of searching for compensation and correction for our defects, and thus also nature's unremitting way of searching for the consummation of our being. In effect, then, Schopenhauer, like Schiller and Wordsworth, is seeing both the poignant subjection of human experience to its quotidian moments and the attainment through those moments of something permanent and ideal.[20] In this light, Schopenhauer comes to seem less a critic than an alternative version of the Romantic inquiry into the trials of perfection. Pleasure, and play, along with the erotic, must be recognized as givens of all human experience, but they may be regarded as Romantic when they cease to be functions or actions and enter into the field of ideal relations, conditions whereby we recognize and pursue, as personalities and as members of the human race, a fulfillment that seems both imminent and impossible, both supreme and fraught with degradation and terror.

"Wordsworth" after Waterloo

JAMES K. CHANDLER

In announcing Wordsworth's death, on 23 April 1850, at age eighty, the *Democratic Review* had just the following coldhearted comment:

> We must acknowledge that we are not impressed with any very heavy sense of sorrow, for we cannot include him in the list of those who, like Burns, Byron, and Shelley, have secured the lasting worship of the people by their immortal aspirations for, and soul-inspiring invocations to, Liberty. Unlike those great spirits, Wordsworth passes from amongst us unregretted by the great body of his countrymen, who have no tears for the salaried slave of Aristocracy and pensioned parasite of Monarchy.[1]

This did not represent a consensus of English opinion. Matthew Arnold, in his famous *Memorial Verses* that same spring, would speak eloquently for those Victorians who regretted Wordsworth's passing. But the fact that such an obituary could be written at all tells us something about the state of Wordsworth's political reputation in certain circles by 1850, whether or not those circles encompassed "the great body of his countrymen." Among Chartists and other Victorian reformers, the heirs of the radicals of the 1790s and of 1815–1819, Wordsworth loomed as a once-legendary hero turned legendary traitor, a "renegado" to his political faith. He was not the only poet to be so castigated in the nineteenth century. The figure of the

Romantic-poet-turned-renegado was also associated closely with the other Lake Poets, Coleridge and Southey, but Wordsworth has come to enjoy dubious preeminence. He has been singled out from the others not because his conservatism was more extreme (I doubt that it was) but more probably because he lived the longest and because he was both the most considerable poet and the most committed young radical of the three.

My aim here is to inquire into the genesis of this important cultural formation, the legend of Wordsworth as renegado. I do not seek to challenge the legendary claim about Wordsworth's tergiversation. Rather, I want to consider the various early narratives about the making of the legendary renegado within a narrative of the making of that legend. I want to trace the legend's development, to raise questions about why it emerged when and how it did, and to venture some answers to those questions. The initial motive for this inquiry, I should say at the start, arises from a discrepancy between my conviction about when Wordsworth's political reversal must have occurred (i.e., at the outset of the decade in which he wrote his greatest work, 1797–1807) and when it is usually represented as occurring (i.e., well after that decade) in the legendary accounts. For reasons which will become clear, the years immediately following the defeat of Napoleon demand closest attention, but the best known articulation of the myth in question takes us again, briefly, toward midcentury.

Robert Browning's *The Lost Leader* (1845) is a poem in two stanzas, but the first gives us most of the relevant details:

> Just for a handful of silver he left us,
>   Just for a riband to stick in his coat—
> Found the one gift of which fortune bereft us,
>   Lost all the others she lets us devote;
> They, with the gold to give, doled him out silver,
>   So much was theirs who so little allowed:
> How all our copper had gone for his service!
>   Rags—were they purple, his heart had been proud!
> We that had loved him so, followed him, honoured him,
>   Lived in his mild and magnificent eye,

> Learned his great language, caught his clear accents,
>> Made him our pattern to live and to die!
> Shakespeare was of us, Milton was for us,
>> Burns, Shelley, were with us,—they watch from their graves.
> He alone breaks from the van and the freemen,
>> —He alone sinks to the rear and the slaves![2]

Four decades later still, when Browning was himself a member of the Wordsworth Society, he apologized for the harshness of the poem's depiction of Wordsworth's "great and venerable personality."[3] By then, it had exerted considerable influence on the poet's reputation, as the echoes in the *Democratic Review's* obituary already seem to attest. Yet for all of its harshness, the poem remains relatively unspecific in its references. One can see this in the operation of the central pronouns—*we, they,* and *he*—all of which appear in the poem without antecedents. As for the first two pronouns, part of the poem's task seems to be to define the relation between "us" and "them" mutually within the poem. As for the other pronoun, one cannot even say for sure that "he" is Wordsworth in the first place. Indeed, the erasure of the antecedent for "him" is a matter explicitly taken up in the second stanza: "Blot out his name, then, record one lost soul more, / . . . Life's night begins: let him never come back to us!" (lines 21–25). By joining "them," so the logic of the pronouns seems to run, "he" can no longer be named among "us," and "we" and "they" are now in one sense defined by the use of "his" name. In another sense, however, "we" continue to know that "he" is Wordsworth (even without recourse to the letters in which Browning says that Wordsworth was his model) just as Browning's very first readers, whether or not they agreed, must have known. The poem's ironies seem to depend upon precisely such a paradox, that we know just whose name is now lost from our registers. One of the *effects* of this strategy is that the poem's critique becomes all the more powerful when, on the strength of so slight a sketch of so dastardly a traitor, everyone is prompted to think of just one writer. One of its *implications* is that, if Browning is able to presume upon such recognition, then clearly Wordsworth's reputation must already have stood low in the eyes of many politically minded observers, even before Browning took him down another peg.

Wordsworth had recently accepted a civil-list pension (1842) and the laureateship (1843), but the story goes back much further than that. As early as Hazlitt's stunning 1821 essay "On the Consistency of Opinion," we already find a tactic rather like Browning's: that essay first takes up its topic in apparently general terms, naming no names, but when Hazlitt finally gets around to mentioning Wordsworth (and then Southey and Coleridge), it becomes clear that he has presupposed reference to their cases all along.[4] By 1821, Hazlitt himself had already written against Wordsworth's and Southey's apostacies in several other contexts, and so of course had some influential poets. One who did his share in shaping Wordsworth's nineteenth-century reputation was Byron.[5] In the first canto of *Don Juan* (pub. 1819), Byron sardonically "commanded" his reader not to "set up Wordsworth, Coleridge, Southey." If the reasons he goes on to offer are not exactly political— "Because the first is crazed beyond all hope, / The second drunk, the third so quaint and mouthey"—his attacks on them in letters of this period and in his dedication to *Don Juan* are pointedly so. Byron had come, through a complicated set of associations, to connect what he saw as the fanatical poetic system building of the Lake Poets with their succumbing to the Legitimist ideology that attended the Restoration of European monarchy after Napoleon's defeat. The Lakers are "renegado rascals" in his correspondence, and Southey is "my Epic Renegade" in the dedication to *Don Juan*.[6] Although the attack on Southey's politics stems partly from personal vendetta having to do with Southey's comments on Byron's "League of Incest" in Venice, Byron is no less mordant about Wordsworth's politics.[7] Still, the dedication had no great influence in 1819 because its publication was suppressed throughout Byron's lifetime (though it did have a small readership through John Murray, Byron's publisher). Nor would Wordsworth emerge singly as the clear leader of the Lakers until after the humorous controversy over his *Peter Bell* in the spring and summer of 1819,[8] an affair that engaged the imagination of another famous poet who shaped Wordsworth's public image.

The very title of Shelley's rich satire *Peter Bell the Third* reminds us first of all that the attacks on Wordsworth's most widely reviewed poem began even before it was published. In Shelley's satiric mythology, Peter Bell the First is a reference not to Wordsworth but to the sight-unseen parody of Keats's friend, John Hamilton Reynolds. In his parodic dedication to Thomas Moore, Shelley conceded that the first Peter was "the Rat," for attacking what he had not read, but called the second Peter "the Apostate" and then went on in the poem itself to criticize Wordsworth's politics and character more trenchantly than even Byron had done.[9] Shelley's recondite allegorizing of Wordsworth's career suggests that he, too, could already take for granted the view that Wordsworth had turned renegade. Indeed, though the matter is too complex to take up here, Shelley's Byronic satire in *Peter Bell the Third* actually turns against itself in the end and, in so doing, actually anticipates some of the key points of Wordsworth's reception history as I trace it here.

The fact that Shelley could take so much for granted about Wordsworth's reputation, and the attention that *Peter Bell* attracted when it was published in 1819 can be explained in part by two notorious episodes of 1817–1818. Working backward from 1819, the first of these is Wordsworth's involvement in the 1818 Westmorland election. Despite the excellent scholarship that has been done on this event in Wordsworth's biography,[10] students of the Romantic period tend to underestimate its larger impact. The Tory Lowthers, whom Wordsworth supported, represented the interest of Lord Lonsdale, Wordsworth's patron, which had gone unchallenged for decades. The Westmorland seat could only have been threatened by a formidable opponent, and Henry Brougham, a Westminster Whig-Radical with a national reputation, seemed just that. "Westmorland soon became the centre of interest for the whole country," as Brougham's biographer writes, and besides the innovation of Brougham's personal canvassing, the election was also "probably the first outside London which was reported on, day by day, in the Press."[11] Wordsworth's support for the Lowthers, moreover, was by no means nominal or passive. The documentation and correspondence that survive for the election indicate that he was both an active campaigner and a key advisor for the Lonsdale camp. An indication of Wordsworth's perceived influence in the election can be found in Brougham's extended attack on him in his public speech at Kendal on 23 March.[12] The election was close, and Wordsworth's support may even have decided it in favor of the Lowthers.

The second event behind the *Peter Bell* controversy was the 1817 affair of *Wat Tyler*, Southey's radical play about the leader of the peasant revolt against Richard II. Composed in 1794, it lay unpublished for twenty-three years until it was issued in a pirated edition that happened to appear in the midst of Southey's series of attacks on reform. Southey sought legal recourse to have the embarrassing work suppressed, but, in the event, Lord Eldon ruled that property rights were irrelevant to seditious writings. More pirated editions appeared, more articles about Southey's conduct. The level of national publicity for this entire episode anticipated that of the Westmorland election in the year to follow.[13] The press had a field day with Southey's reputation, and on 14 March the case was even discussed on the floor of Commons, when William Smith, the Opposition member for Norwich, brought it up during the debate on the Seditious Meetings Bill. According to the report cited by Southey himself, Smith had come to the House that day equipped with a copy of *Wat Tyler* in one pocket and, in another, a copy of the *Quarterly Review* issue which contained one of Southey's recent tirades against the reformist press. Before reading an appropriate pair of passages from each text, Smith introduced them with a short prefatory remark, recorded in Hansard thus:

> The hon. member . . . adverted to that tergiversation of principle which the career of political individuals so often presented. He was far from supposing, that a man who set out in life with the profession of certain sentiments, was bound to conclude life with them. He thought there might be many occasions in which a change of opinion, when that change was unattended by any personal advantages, when it appeared entirely disinterested, might be the result of sincere conviction. But what he most detested, what most filled him with disgust, was the settled, determined malignity of a renegado.[14]

This was not the first use of the term renegado in a political context in England, but it is the one that touched off the first flurry of indignation over its use, not least on the part of the Lake Poets themselves.[15]

When the *Wat Tyler* affair erupted, Southey was clearly the central target for charges of tergiversation, and indeed he had been such a target for several years.[16] But the affair is relevant here because it called attention, by association, to Wordsworth's position in 1817, and though it centered on Southey, it crystalizes the idea of confronting a poet directly with earlier writings he would have forgotten. It is nonetheless also true that no early work of Wordsworth precisely counterpart to either *Wat Tyler* or *Joan of Arc* was available to reformers in the Regency period, and this, as we shall see, has implications for the peculiar way in which his career is reviewed.

Wordsworth's political reputation among reformers was not completely unscathed before 1817. In 1816, the year when Southey began attacking the reform movement in explicit prose, Wordsworth published his *Thanksgiving Ode* volume of political poems. The title poem, about the victory at Waterloo, eventually became notorious in radical circles for its bloody prayer to a martial Almighty:

> But thy most dreaded instrument,
> In working out a pure intent,
> Is Man—arrayed for mutual slaughter,—
> —Yea, Carnage is thy daughter![17]

Byron, Shelley, and Hazlitt all got around to mocking this particular stanza. But though far-reaching, the influence of this poem was delayed. The volume was not widely reviewed when it appeared and seems to have gone completely unnoticed by the radical press. The really important political critique of Wordsworth in 1816 was to be found in Shelley's *Alastor* volume, in two poems that were composed before the *Thanksgiving Ode* appeared: the title poem and the sonnet *To Wordsworth*. With these poems, we reach something that might in two senses be viewed as a point of origin for the legend presupposed and passed on by Browning.

The first and more trivial sense is that Shelley's poems constitute the earliest clear "source" of Browning's poem. In view of what is know about Shelley as Browning's chief poetic examplar generally, there is every reason to see the sonnet as a model for Browning's poem about Wordsworth:

> Poet of Nature, thou has wept to know
> That things depart which never may return:
> Childhood and youth, friendship and love's first glow,
> Have fled like sweet dreams, leaving thee to mourn.
> These common woes I feel. One loss is mine
> Which thou too feel'st, yet I alone deplore.
> Thou wert as a lone star, whose light did shine
> On some frail bark in winter's midnight roar:
> Thou hast like to a rock-built refuge stood
> Above the blind and battling multitude:
> In honoured poverty thy voice did weave
> Songs consecrate to truth and liberty,—
> Deserting these, thou leavest me to grieve,
> Thus having been, that thou shouldst cease to be.

Lost leadership is very much the poem's guiding theme, and the tone of the poem toward its subject, both the early reverence and the later regret, anticipates the tone of Browning's. The personal stake that Shelley avows in Wordsworth's poetry as a moral force is again, as in Browning, considerable, though Shelley addresses his lost leader in the "I" of personal confession rather than the "we" of social solidarity. The charge of apostasy is leveled most directly in the concluding lines of the poem, where a deft syntactic ambiguity turns the whole apostrophe into a kind of elegy thirty-five years before the fact. Wordsworth ceases to be *thus*—as he was—but, by virtue of not being thus, he thus ceases to be at all.

In *Alastor* Shelley elaborates this death-in-life figure into a full-scale narrative allegory of a Romantic poet's narcissistic abdication of social responsibility. Shelley here, like Browning later, declines to name the poet who forms the subject of the discourse, though he does not presuppose recognition in the way that Browning does. In addition to providing the sonnet (where Wordsworth *is* named) as a gloss on *Alastor,* he marks off his subject with an elaborate set of echoes and allusions to Wordsworth's poetry: even more intensely than in the explicit sonnet, *Alastor* uses Wordsworth's own language to frame its indictment of him. The most signal of the allusions are the epigraph from *The Excursion* and the verbal echoes that bracket the central narrative in the introductory and concluding lines. As in the sonnet *To Wordsworth,* the allusions point primarily to the *Intimations Ode*— "natural piety," "obstinate questionings," "loss 'too deep for tears.'"[18] The explicitness and fresh sense of disappointment in the sonnet, together with the elaborate allusive marking in both poems, suggest that Shelley is dealing with a myth, not already made, but very much in the making.

But there is another, more important sense in which the sonnet *To Wordsworth* and *Alastor* mark a kind of origin for Browning's legend. Both of these poems were composed in the second half of 1815, in the months immediately following the Battle of Waterloo (18 June). In taking us back to the close of the Napoleonic wars, they lead us to what I am going to suggest is the large generative circumstance for the first published attacks against Wordsworth as a renegade. The eleventh canto of *Don Juan* gives us Byron's famous comparison of his own career with Napoleon's: "Even I"

> Was reckoned, a considerable time,
> The grand Napoleon of the realms of rhyme.

> But Juan was my Moscow, and Faliero
>   My Leipsic, and my Mont Saint Jean seems Cain
>   (sts. 55−56)[19]

The retreat from Moscow in late 1812, the Battle of Leipzig in 1813, and Waterloo (which occurred near Mont-Saint-Jean) constitute the three major events in Napoleon's fall from the eminence he had enjoyed in most of Europe. Byron suggests that these three events can be analogized to the three ambitious works he published from 1819 to 1821, which occasioned his fall from the eminence he had enjoyed in fashionable England. In what follows I will suggest that Wordsworth's fall from eminence in reformist England has a different relation to the events of Napoleon's downfall, a *historical* rather than a *metaphorical* one. Napoleon's defeat, that is to say, can be seen as the oblique occasion for Wordsworth's appearance before the world in the role of the renegado.

There is some ambiguity about how we date Napoleon's fall. One can look at 1812−1815 or focus more narrowly on 1815. A case can certainly be made for taking the former view. During the negotiations of 1814 in the aftermath of Leipzig, Napoleon's hegemony was believed by some to have been decisively terminated. Amelia Sedley's father in *Vanity Fair,* we recall, is represented as holding that belief so firmly that he staked his entire fortune on it and thereby went bankrupt when Napoleon returned to power in the spring of 1815. The belief in the peace of 1814 was not completely implausible; Sedley is not supposed to be a stupid man. But he *is* portrayed as a desparate man, and Thackeray suggests, with the benefit of hindsight, that he should have known better—should have known, as many did, that the final defeat of Napoleon was yet to be accomplished. In any case, I take 1815 to mark that decisive end, just as I take Shelley's late-1815 representations of Wordsworth in the *Alastor* volume as the decisive beginning of the Wordsworth legend.[20] With certain qualifications, one can go far to substantiate the view that Waterloo was as decisive for Wordsworth's political reputation as it was for Napoleon's political life.

For students of Wordsworth's career, the year 1815 is often taken to mark quite a different event: the publication of his two-volume collection of poems and, more notoriously, the two self-aggrandizing critical essays he wrote for them. Since these embattled prefaces aim to defend the poet against attacks on his work that had been initiated many years earlier, one must say precisely what is involved in calling 1815 a pivotal year for Wordsworth's reputation. The crucial point is that, although Wordsworth had been under critical fire for years, I seek to establish the first attack on him *as a renegado*, as one who has deserted a political cause. Very few of the early attacks on Wordsworth's poetry were explicitly political. They tended rather to focus on his poetic system and on his obsessive commitment to it. He was said to be perverting his genuine talent on account of a methodical mania for reforming taste. This distinction between the perverse poetic systematizer and the politically quietist turncoat was later erased in the celebrated lampoons of Byron and Shelley. Its importance becomes clear when one considers that those earlier reviews that *were* to any degree political in their critique of Wordsworth's system building tended to attack him from the other side. They suggested that Wordsworth's poetic "experiments" showed a dangerous tendency to innovation, populism, and even iconoclasm. Such charges can even be found in the early responses of Francis Jeffrey, the editor of the Whig *Edinburgh Review* and the critic perhaps most responsible for Wordsworth's defensive essays of 1815. In the maiden volume of the *Review* (1802), in fact in the very review that identified and christened the Lake Poets as a school, Jeffrey was explicit on this score. Having discussed "the qualities of style and imagery," which "form but a very small part of the characteristics by which a literary faction is to be distinguished," he turns to the "subject and object of their compositions, and the principles and opinions they are calculated to support," which "constitute a far more important criterion":

> A splenetic and idle discontent with the existing institutions of society, seems to be at the bottom of all their serious and peculiar sentiments. . . . The present vicious constitution of society alone is responsible for all these enormities: the poor sinners are but the helpless victims or instruments of its disorders, and could not possibly have avoided the errors into which they have been betrayed. Though they can bear with crimes, therefore, they cannot reconcile themselves to punishments. . . . While the plea of moral necessity is artfully brought forward to convert all the excesses of the poor into innocent misfortunes, no sort of indulgence is shown to the offences of the powerful and rich.[21]

Writing as a progressive Whig, in a journal literally bedecked with the Buff and Blue, Jeffrey does not stand altogether at odds with such views, though he clearly implies that they are excessive. These are not, in any case, the "principles and opinions" with which Byron would associate the "style and imagery" of the Lakers after Waterloo. Moreover, something close to Jeffrey's early characterization of Wordsworth survives intact through the most important of the responses to *The Excursion* in 1814.

After John Wilson Croker's review of Keats's *Endymion*, Jeffrey's review of *The Excursion,* with its acerbic minimalism ("This will never do"), is perhaps the most notorious of the nineteenth century. Yet not even this hostile Whiggish reviewer, at this later date, was attacking Wordsworth for the political positions taken in his poem. It was not the ideas, but the perverted system of taste by which they were given expression, that Jeffrey found repugnant. Still less was Jeffrey attacking Wordsworth for having changed his ideological coloration. On the contrary, the very burden of Jeffrey's argument is that the author of *Lyrical Ballads* (1798, 1800, 1802) and the 1807 *Poems* is now so firmly entrenched in the positions he took in those eary volumes that he is past change: "A man who has been for twenty years at work on such matter as is now before us, and who comes complacently forward with a whole quarto of it after all the admonitions he has received" must be "beyond the power of criticism."[22] This theme, that Wordsworth's "case" is now hopeless, is struck repeatedly here, and it is later echoed in Byron's epithet, "crazed beyond all hope," in *Don Juan.* With characteristic logic, Jeffrey actually announced in this review that since Wordsworth *was* now beyond hope of change, he would no longer try to reform him in the pages of the *Edinburgh Review.* Jeffrey was as good as his word for eight years, foregoing comment even on such ripe targets as *Peter Bell* in 1819. He did not in fact review another of Wordsworth's publications until 1822, at which point he pronounced that the "Lake School of Poetry . . . is now pretty nearly extinct."[23]

Nor does even the radical Hazlitt cast Wordsworth as a political traitor in his review of *The Excursion.* It is true that at one point he expresses mild disagreement with the specific form of Wordsworth's hopes for the future. Quoting a passage (on the subject of the French Revolution) that shows "the same magnanimity and philosophical firmness" as he finds elsewhere in the poem, Hazlitt remarks: "In the application of these memorable lines, we should, perhaps, differ a little from Mr. Wordsworth; nor can we indulge with him in the fond conclusion afterwards hinted at, that one day *our* triumph, the triumph of humanity and liberty, may be complete" (*Collected Works* 10:119; Hazlitt's italics).[24] Such comments evidently regard Wordsworth as a political ally, and a valuable one. Hazlitt's primary reservation about Wordsworth's view is that it is unrealistic: "All things move, not in progress but in ceaseless round; our strength lies in our weakness; our virtues are built on our vices; our faculties are as limited as our being; nor can we lift man above his nature more than above the earth he treads" (119). Whatever censure these remarks imply is clearly tempered by an admiration for what Hazlitt represents as Wordsworth's sympathetic hopefulness. When Hazlitt resumes the review in the next number of the *Examiner,* he calls Wordsworth not only a "great poet" and a "deep philosopher" but also a "fine moralist"—presumably as fine a moralist as ever (121). Hazlitt does enter some incisive criticisms, and these were the reasons for Wordsworth's peevish dissatisfaction with the review. But they are not allegations of retrograde political purposes. They are closer to Jeffrey's complaints, perhaps even closer to those that Coleridge would enshrine in the *Biographia Literaria* two years later. They have to do with the encumbrance of the poem's "load of narrative and description"; with dramatic improprieties, such as the use of the Pedlar as a rustic character; and with Wordsworth's idealizations of the rustic character generally.[25]

Since, in the context of the contemporary reform movement, the ideological tendencies of *The Excursion* seem to me quite retrograde, I must confess to a certain degree of surprise in what Jeffrey and Hazlitt have to say about it. But this sense of surprise can be objectified in the form of a historical contradiction if we turn attention to the record of one major exception to this sort of response to the poem. Mary Shelley's journal contains the following entry for 14 September 1814: "Shelley . . . brings home Wordsworth's *Excursion,* of which we read a part, much disappointed. He is a slave."[26] Here is minimalism of a very different kind, for unlike Jeffrey's "This will never do," the Shelleys' terse sentence implies a criticism that is explicitly ideological and that sees a decisive reversal in Wordsworth's views. Shelley and Jeffrey draw diametrically opposed views of this moment in Wordsworth's career, and from political perspectives which, though not identical, might both be called at least broadly reformist. What makes this especially astonishing is that *The Excursion* is perhaps the most fully discursive and explicit poem about politics and society that Wordsworth published in his lifetime;

it offers a full account of the Solitary's experience of the French Revolution as well as several long speeches about the national welfare. This is therefore a contradiction that bears scrutiny.

Jeffrey thinks the innovative and populist Wordsworth is essentially un-changed in *The Excursion* and rejects it for being, if anything, only more Wordsworthian than ever. The problem Jeffrey faces is how to account for what he must have regarded as Wordsworth's sudden change by, say, 1816 (with the publication of the *Thanksgiving Ode*) or by 1818 with the explic-itly Tory *Address to the Westmorland Freeholders*. This is a problem be-cause, placed side by side, *The Excursion* and the two addresses are by no means ideologically incompatible, as readers familiar with both texts know well. Wordsworth wrote in the first address of the issues that had divided the two major parties of the age:

> In matters of taste, it is a process attended with little advantage, and often injurious, to compare one set of artists, or writers, with another. But, in estimating the merits of public men, especially of two parties acting in direct opposition, it is not only expedient, but indispensible, that both should be kept constantly in sight. The truth or fallacy of French principles, and the tendency, good or bad, of the Revolution which sprang out of them; and the necessity, or non-necessity—the policy, or impolicy, of resisting by war the encroachments of republi-can and imperial France; these were the opposite grounds upon which each party staked their credit: here we behold them in full contrast with each other—To whom shall the crown be given? On whom has the light fallen? and who are covered by shade and thick darkness?[27]

It is clear from his rhetoric which side Wordsworth takes in 1818, but the rhetoric of the Wanderer in book 9 of *The Excursion,* scarcely less explicit than Wordsworth's in the address makes it clear that the sides taken are the same. It is perhaps fortunate for Jeffrey that he had announced an end to his reviews of Wordsworth in this period, for he would have been hard pressed to find something consistent to say.

The contradiction is no less nettling, however, from Shelley's side, for he thinks that the innovative and populist Wordsworth has vanished from *The Excursion* and rejects it for marking a reversal of earlier politics. This is the view of *The Excursion* that sees it in relation to the early Wordsworth as

Smith saw Southey's *Quarterly Review* essay in relation to *Wat Tyler*. The problem with Shelley's view emerges once we ask the question What could he have meant by the early Wordsworth? What, in other words, was the equivalent of *Wat Tyler*—or for that matter, *Joan of Arc*—in the eyes of Wordsworth's contemporaries? It seems to be the work of what Arnold would later call the golden decade, beginning with the *Lyrical Ballads* of 1798. There is virtually no reference by Shelley or anyone else in the Regency period to any of Wordsworth's few published works before 1798, and Wordsworth published only extracts of his own selection from them in his 1815 volumes. As for Wordsworth's unpublished works of the mid-1790s, the "Letter to the Bishop of Llandaff" and the two versions of *Salisbury Plain,* later published in a radically altered version as *Guilt and Sorrow,* these writings would have been totally unknown outside of a very small circle of his friends. Like almost everyone else of his generation, Shelley regarded *Lyrical Ballads* as Wordsworth's songs "consecrate to truth and liberty." (And this is surely the poetry Browning alludes to when he said that Wordsworth's "great language" and "clear accents . . . Made him our pattern to live and to die.") In the playful dedicatory stanzas to *The Witch of Atlas,* Shelley makes a clearly invidious comparison between *Lyrical Ballads* and the "later" Wordsworth of *Peter Bell*:

> My Witch indeed is not so sweet a creature
>   As Ruth or Lucy, whom his graceful praise
> Clothes for our grandsons—but she matches Peter
>   Though he took nineteen years, and she three days
> in dressing.
>
> (Prose and Poetry, lines 33–37)[28]

Shelley would no doubt have included the 1807 *Poems* (the only other volume of poetry published by Wordsworth between 1798 and 1814) in this liberal corpus as well. The *Intimations Ode,* which quickly became the most famous poem in the 1807 volumes, is not, after all, the subject of Shelley's critique in the sonnet *To Wordsworth.* On the contrary, Shelley admits that the pains and losses with which the ode is concerned are "common woes" that he shares as well. It is the loss of Wordsworth, the author of just that poem, that Shelley laments, and this loss must therefore belong to a later period.

In the light of this frame of reference, Shelley's problem, the obverse of

Jeffrey's, is that he must assert the radical change between the political positions of *The Excursion* and of Wordsworth's earlier poetry. One immediate
difficulty with such an assertion is that *The Excusion* parallels quite closely
the unpublished masterwork of the golden decade, *The Prelude;* the two
poems were indeed developed out of the same body of verse, which was
composed at the very dawning of the golden decade in 1797–1798. It is as
hard to mark an ideological reversal between *The Excursion* and, say, *The
Ruined Cottage* (c. 1797–1798) as it is to do so between *The Excursion* and
the *Addresses to the Freeholders of Westmorland.*

Modern scholarship has given us as full an account of Wordsworth's life
and of the stages of his compositions as we probably have for any author
before this present century. Shelley could not have known what we do now,
for example, about the unfolding of the *Recluse* project.[29] On the other
hand, Shelley did know of *The Recluse*'s existence because Wordsworth had
announced it in his prefatory material for *The Excursion* in 1814. There,
Wordsworth had indicated that *The Recluse,* of which *The Excursion*
formed a part, had been in the making for some years, and he had asserted
that his entire oeuvre could be likened to one grand, organically expanding
Gothic church.[30] One would not want to settle for mere *assertions* of continuity on Wordsworth's part, anymore than one would settle for such assertions on the part of a poet like Southey, who argued that *Joan of Arc* and
even *Wat Tyler* itself were ultimately consistent in principle with his later attacks on political reform. As it happens, we have more than mere assertion
to rely on here, for Wordsworth tried in a number of ways to *demonstrate*
that what he did and wrote after the fall of Napoleon was continuous with
what he did and wrote in his golden decade.

First, as we have seen, there are the collected poems he published in
1815. To examine this volume is to see one important aim served by Wordsworth's presentation of his poems. Virtually the entire post-1797 corpus is
arranged in that peculiar system of headings whose incongruity with one
another should not distract us from the idea of the vast unity that they mean
to represent. The poems are also dated, in separate columns, by both year of
composition and year of publication. (No poet, it has been said, ever had a
more loving editor of his work.) Wordsworth's two volumes of 1815 create
the impression of a seamless corpus steadily evolving from the start with
no major chronological breaks. Moreover, to the sequence of political
sonnets *Dedicated to National Liberty and Independence* from his 1807

Poems, some dating to as early as 1802, Wordsworth added a new series of sonnets on political themes — now published for the first time as a "Second Part" ("From the Year 1807 to 1813") for the earlier sequence. The one chronological divide over which Wordsworth erects no obvious bridge is the category which distinguishes the "juvenile pieces." Even here, Wordsworth includes neither of the unpublished *Salisbury Plain* poems, which so occupied him in the mid-1790s, and only a few extracts of his own selection from the less explicitly radical poems he did publish, in 1793, *An Evening Walk* and *Descriptive Sketches*.

The presentation of the poems in his next publication, the *Thanksgiving Ode* volume of 1816, sustains these same purposes, and even adverts to them in a prefatory note: "This Publication may be considered as a sequel to the Author's 'Sonnets, dedicated to Liberty;' it is therefore printed uniform with the two volumes of his Poems [i.e., of 1807], in which those Sonnets are collected, to admit of their being conveniently bound up together" (x). This is clearly an attempt to extend the continuity aimed for in the 1815 volumes by including political poems of the years 1814–1816. Wordsworth's phrase "bound up" to describe the relation of his poems echoes the phrasing of the *Intimations Ode,* whose epigraph expresses the wish that Wordsworth's days could follow one another with the seamless and pious continuity of a line of fathers and children. Here, to take the other half of the Hesiodic formula, he wishes that his *works* should display an analogous continuity. The sentiments of the *Intimations Ode* are in fact made to loom large elsewhere in the 1815 volume, for great pains are taken with the imagery and idiom of the *Thanksgiving Ode* in order that its jingoistic performance should be understood as compatible with the already famous endpiece of the 1807 volumes. Even the architectonic arrangement of poems in the 1816 volume recalls the publication of 1807, for the sequence of sonnets dedicated to liberty followed by the elevated and extended *Thanksgiving Ode* closely approximates the order of the second 1807 volume.

Wordsworth's ultimate act of dramatizing the continuity he asserted in his thought and work over the first two decades of the century was probably his decision, in 1819, to publish *Peter Bell*. For this poem had been the manifesto of his "radical" ballads and had been composed in the flurry of activity that launched him on his major decade in the spring of 1798. In his offending preface Wordsworth proudly announced that *Peter Bell* had first seen the light twenty-one years earlier. Perhaps the strangest of the many

ironies in the present chronicle is that this poem was denounced as the product of a renegado. Such a judgment may have been understandable enough
in Reynolds's attack, since he wrote his poem before Wordsworth's appeared. But Shelley's famous parody was written in the knowledge of the
preface in which Wordsworth explains that originally he composed the
poem twenty-one years earlier, that is, in 1798. Shelley's way of handling
that difficulty is to seize on this assertion as grounds for suggesting that
whatever the poem was in 1798, it was now encrusted with the conservative
opinions of the older Wordsworth—with, for example, the mistrust of
fancy in the prologue or with the corresponding faith in Methodist conversion experiences of the kind that save Peter in the end. But both of these
elements were present in the poem in its earlier form. The revisions Wordsworth made in the twenty-one years since 1798 (Shelley actually shrinks the
period to nineteen years) were not changes in substance; they mainly involved cutting the 1798 poem, "hewing" it, as he said, rather than elaborating it.[31]

The assault on *Peter Bell* in 1819 offers powerful evidence to suggest that
the young Wordsworth of *Lyrical Ballads* was not being read the same way
four years after Waterloo as he had been, say, four years before. The whole
Peter Bell controversy in fact turns out to be an inadvertent and twisted parody of the *Wat Tyler* case two years earlier. In the case of *Wat Tyler,* an
older conservative poet finds that he is being called a renegado because pi-
rates have found and published an earlier radical poem that he had disa-
vowed and would have kept hidden from the world. In the case of *Peter
Bell,* an older conservative poet goes out of his way to publish a poem from
what is thought to be his own early radical period, acknowledging it as his
own both by the constant attention he has given it and by saying as much—
as if to insist that, radical or otherwise in 1798, he has not undergone significant change in his principles since then—and he is called a renegado just
the same!

The making of Wordsworth the Renegade is thus, as I suggested at the start,
a cultural process marked by extraordinary contradiction and confusion. I
think that one simply cannot hope to make headway in sorting through it so
long as one clings to the assumption—shared by Jeffrey, Hazlitt, Shelley,
and a host of other younger contemporaries—that the Wordsworth of

1798–1807 was in any important sense either pro-French Revolution or pro-English reform. By way of elaborating this point, I would like to consider one last hypothesis for saving the liberal view of *Lyrical Ballads* and *The Recluse*. One might wish to contend that Wordsworth's position was indeed liberal, Whiggish, or reformist in 1798 or 1800 and that this position remained the same while the times changed. Here again we can draw a parallel with Southey and the *Wat Tyler* affair. For in his infamous public apologia, the *Letter to William Smith*, Southey invoked the dialectic of social change and personal principle in order to justify his having altered his views on certain issues while, as he claimed, remaining true to his principles. Such an argument is offered at the crescendo of Southey's self-righteous indignation:

> The one object to which I have ever been desirous of contributing according to my power, is the removal of those obstacles by which the improvement of mankind is impeded; and to this the whole of my writings, whether in prose or verse, bears witness. This has been the pole star of my course; the needle has shifted according to the movements of the state vessel wherein I am embarked, but the direction to which it points has always been the same. I did not fall into the error of those who having been the friends of France when they imagined that the cause of liberty was implicated in her success, transferred their attachment from the Republic to the military Tyranny in which it ended, and regarded with complacency the progress of oppression because France was the Oppressor. "They had turned their faces toward the East in the morning to worship the rising sun, and in the evening they were looking Eastward still, obstinately affirming that still the sun was there." I, on the contrary altered my position as the world went round. For so doing, Mr. William Smith is said to have insulted me with the appellation of Renegade.[32]

Like those whom Karl Marx derided for their view of the events of 1848–1851 in France, Southey looks at the second phase of a bourgeois revolution and thinks he sees history moving backward, apparently undoing its initial progress and reconstructing the hierarchies it had earlier dismantled. In such a circumstance, says Southey, holding to principles requires reorientation of attitude.

Yet one could take a different view of what happens in the Napoleonic

era. Overall, one might argue, the period of 1793–1815 carries historical
process forward, albeit in an uneven and dialectical way, and thus makes
possible a new progressive era to follow, a reformist era significantly advanced over the protoreformism of the 1790s. In a context understood this
way, Wordsworth's failure may simply have been that he did not reorient
himself. What was liberal for the 1790s was no longer so in the advanced
context of 1815–1819. The year 1815 in England, in this view, would be
the equivalent of 1848 in France, as commentators have been known to represent it—a year when the proletariat succeeds the bourgeoisie as the revolutionary class and therefore when cultural formations undergo a massive
sense of, to use Southey's notion, reorientation.[33] A liberal position formed
in the 1790s and steadfastly held thereafter might come to seem outmoded
and even conservative precisely for its failure to keep up with such a change
in the configuration of political issues.

The merit of a view like this is that it attempts to relate Wordsworth's
ideological career to the larger course of events—and more specifically that
it takes the year 1815 as a historical moment with powerful claims to the
status of a period boundary, a matter agreed upon by historians as diverse
as Harriet Martineau, Elie Halévy, G. M. Trevelyan, R. J. White, and E. P.
Thompson. But there are two compelling reasons why such a way of relating Wordsworth's career to the events of his times cannot be accepted. The
first is that Wordsworth's writings of the major decade embody, from the
start, ideological purposes that are more a denial than an articulation of the
1790s reformism in which he had once participated. The second is that such
a view of 1815 mistakes the kind of periodizing moment that the end of the
wars represents.

To establish the first claim firmly and unreductively requires far more
space than I can here allow the task, but a few points can be briefly outlined.
One must begin by recognizing that Wordsworth did in fact reverse himself
in the course of his long career. For a particularly stark example, one can
consult the recent edition of *Salisbury Plain* and compare the conclusion of
the unpublished poem of 1794 with that of the published version of the
poem that appeared in 1842: the poem's first conclusion, in which a discharged sailor is eventually destroyed by the society that has turned him
against it, is contradicted in the most direct possible way—by the insertion
of negatives into the final stanza's sentences. Or, to look in the more explicit
formulations of his prose, one could take Wordsworth's encomium on

Burke's politics in the *First Address to the Freeholders of Westmorland* and compare it with his attacks on Burke in his 1793 "Letter to the Bishop of Llandaff." Since he regards Burke both early and late as the central political figure of the age, and since his sense of Burke's doctrine is quite consistent early and late, one has no alternative but to see that Wordsworth has indeed changed his principles between 1793 and 1818. But such a change did not occur *in* 1818, nor in 1816 with the *Thanksgiving Ode,* nor in 1814 with the publication of *The Excursion,* nor in 1813 with Wordsworth's acceptance of the stamp distributorship through Lord Lonsdale. It occurred between 1795 and 1798. One does not find ideological reversals between *The Ruined Cottage* and *The Excursion: The Excursion* was in every sense the extension of what had been worked out in *The Ruined Cottage.* One does not find ideological reversals between *The Prelude* and the addresses to the Westmorland freeholders: Wordsworth versified his encomium to Burke sometime after 1818 and inserted it into book 7 of *The Prelude* to suggest its compatibility with the completed poem. One does find such reversals, however, between the rationalist activism of the conclusion of the first *Salisbury Plain* and the "wise passiveness" recommended by the conclusion to *The Ruined Cottage,* a poem which proves upon analysis to be a kind of rewriting of the suffering recounted in *Salisbury Plain.* Likewise one can see such a reversal between what Wordsworth has to say about poverty, first in the letter to Llandaff and then in the address to "Statesmen" in *The Old Cumberland Beggar.* Or again, between the enlightened views of revolutionary education that were to guide the magazine he planned with William Mathews in 1794 and what we find on the subject of education in even the very early drafts of *The Recluse* and *The Prelude.* Wordsworth's turnabout does not coincide with the death of his poetic program; it coincides with its birth. But since I have argued these matters out in another context,[34] I will pass on here to the second point, the question of what kind of historical moment is represented by 1815.

Thompson and White, to take the most recent of the historians I mentioned above, both see 1815 as introducing a four-year period that they consider pivotal in English social history. Thompson calls this period "the heroic age of popular Radicalism" and argues persuasively that only with the end of the war are the radical elements of the North and South— Manchester and Westminster—finally brought together in a common cause.[35] White says of this same period—"Waterloo to Peterloo"—that "it is, more than most periods, one of rapid transition. . . . A form of society which, with all its ways of living and thinking and feeling, had lasted for some fifteen hundred years, was precipitately giving way to another form which has now lasted for some one hundred and fifty."[36] It is also true, however, that both Thompson and White (and again, they are hardly alone in this view) see the brief period introduced by the close of the war as an epitome of a somewhat larger period of accelerated social transition commencing some time in the 1780s. And the relation between the larger period and its epitome is the key to understanding the kind of boundary that 1815 represents. Here first is White's analysis:

> The precipitate nature of the change [i.e., after Waterloo] was largely fostered by the long war which ended in 1815. The war had at once hastened social change and postponed the attempt to solve the problems to which it gave rise. By focusing the energies of the nation upon a common cause, the war had served to supply the need for a centripetal force in a society which had become increasingly subject to the centrifugal forces of an industrial revolution. . . . A myriad discursive aims and interests had been temporarily harmonized in a common endeavor. The peasant could be dispossessed in the interests of economical farming; the artisan could be overworked and underpaid in the interests of large-scale production; machine-breaking could be identified with the sabotage of munitions; the tepid patriotism of the Whigs could be identified with defeatism, and the angry reformism of the Radicals could be identified with treason. Thus, with some hypocrisy, a good deal of selfishness, and still more double thinking, the war had been won. Peace removed the danger, and the focus. The semblance of organic life was lost, and society reverted to a structure of classes, a multitude of individuals, an undisguised battlefield of governors and governed. (20)

The notion here is that 1815 marks not so much an epoch of new issues and conflicts as a full-scale addressing of issues and conflicts that had been held in suspension by the exigencies, real or imagined, of the war against Napoleon. Thompson makes an analogous argument to similar effect when he speaks of the working-class presence as going underground in the face of government oppression at home and untoward developments in Revolutionary France (the Terror, Napoleon's seizure of power, the bad-faith negotiations at the Peace of Amiens) and then as reemerging with renewed force toward the conclusion of the war.

Both historians offer documentation to show that such a view of the war and its sequel in England was widely shared among those who lived through both. White cites Coleridge's 1817 remark, for example, that the war "had brought about a national unanimity unexampled in our history since the reign of Elizabeth" (20). Such testimony abounds. In the *Second Address to the Westmorland Freeholders*, Wordsworth quotes Henry Brougham's 1817 speech on the meaning of 1815:

> As often as we have required that Parliaments should be chosen yearly, and that the elective Franchise should be extended to all who pay taxes, we have been desired to wait, for the enemy was at the gate, and ready to avail himself of the discords attending our political contexts, in order to undermine our national independence. This argument is gone, and our Adversaries must now look for another.
> (*Prose Works* 3:178)

Wordsworth's competing account likewise makes 1815 a year of moment, but he has a different explanation for why it should be so.

> To the very completeness of this triumph [over Napoleonic evil] may be indirectly attributed no small portion of the obloquy now heaped upon those advisers through whom it was achieved. The power of Napoleon Buonaparte was overthrown—his person has disappeared from the theatre of Europe—his name has almost deserted the columns of her daily and weekly Journals—but as he has left no Successor, as there is no foreign Tyrant of sufficient importance to attract hatred by exciting fear, many honest English Patriots must either find, or set up, something at home—for the employment of those affections.
>
> (*Prose Works* 3:166)

All that is missing from Wordsworth's analysis to make it compatible with Brougham's (and roughly so with White's and Thompson's, for that matter) is the acknowledgement that there may have been a *prior* displacement responsible for the animus against Napoleon with which he begins. It is at least plausible to argue, for example, that public animosity once directed at William Pitt and his ministry was successfully rechanneled in Napoleon's direction. Parts of the France books in *The Prelude* could be taken to show that the substitution of Napoleon for Pitt was a factor even in Wordsworth's own political "growth." In any case, Wordworth's special pleading presupposes a view of contemporary English society that was widely shared: it acknowledges that the government was regarded by many as a kind of foreign enemy, armed, like Napoleon, and with no better sense of the interests of English people at heart.

Such an understanding of the context does not support the view that Wordsworth's position remained the same while the times changed. The times indeed changed in all sorts of important ways, but in respect to the debate over reform, what happens with the fall of Napoleon is that the issues and conflicts of the 1790s reemerge in starker and more fully amplified ways. A debate that had been largely suspended and repressed during the long wars—with some important exceptions such as the development of Westminster Radicalism in the 1800s—was vigorously reopened in circumstances that fostered even sharper disagreements. One measure of the topical continuity with the conflicts of the 1790s is how large Burke and Paine still loomed in political debate. We need only recall Wordsworth's invocation of Burke in his 1818 address and Coleridge's promulgation of Burkean doctrine in the *Lay Sermons* of 1817, or Richard Carlile's celebrated arrest in 1819 for reprinting Paine's pamphlets and William Cobbett's return from America with Paine's ashes in the same year.

The increased intensity of the conflict is perhaps easier to see. Obvious enmity between the government and the governed had already developed under the Pitt regime in the 1790s. It afterward had subsided (or been made to subside), only to rise again with a vengeance. British foreign affairs aggravated the volcanic conditions at home. Looking abroad in 1815, English people saw the restoration of Legitimist monarchs and watched them clamp down more oppressively than ever on popular agitation. To their chagrin, the English also found evidence that the Liverpool administration were willing to ingratiate themselves with those monarchs. Despite the general rejoicing over the triumph of the Alliance against Napoleon, and despite the dutiful public cheers for the Continental despots who were entertained by the Prince Regent and his ministers in the summer of 1815, there was, as

White says, "a widespread suspicion . . . that their English hosts had taken some highly un-English infection from their late allies, a suspicion which was not allayed by the retention of a large military establishment and the participation of Lord Castlereagh in a succession of European Congresses for the restoration of 'tranquillity' in the dominions of the lately restored sovereign" (*Waterloo to Peterloo* 14–15). The size of the standing army seemed to confirm the reformers' worst fears, and a number of the popular petitions to the Prince Regent, like the Nottingham Petition of 1816, put the numbers in context: "in the year 1792, our Military Establishment consisted of only thirty-nine thousand men; in 1816, a year of peace, when the valour of our arms has achieved whatever is necessary for our security, or our honour, it is fixed at One Hundred and Forty-nine Thousand, for purposes, we cannot but suspect, injurious to the Rights of Freemen."[37] The period 1815–1819 is characterized, unlike any other, by confrontation between masses of population on the one side—twenty thousand strong at Spa and Spital Fields in 1816 and 1817, and again at Stockport, Manchester, and other northern cities in 1819—and armed British soldiers on the other. It seems inevitable, in retrospect, that the climax of this tumultuous period should have been a bloody encounter between sixty thousand unarmed English citizens at St. Peter's Square in Manchester and (in support of the local yeomanry) a regiment of English hussars, acting on a magistrate's orders and still adorned with their Waterloo medals.

But it is not just that political oppositions intensify after Waterloo; the very *idea* of political opposition seems to do so, too. The party system, for example, begins to seem outmoded to some, as if it implied something too compromising or insufficiently stark. This is how one must understand Keats's remark to his brother in the long journal letter of 1819, when he writes of the post-Waterloo period in politics: "There is scarcely a grain of party spirit now in England. This is no contest between whig and tory—but between right and wrong. . . . Right and Wrong considered by each man abstractedly is the fashion."[38] One also hears evidence of the sort of situation to which Keats alludes in Hazlitt's writing, for while he could provide a careful analysis "On the Spirit of Partisanship" in 1821, his report on Wordsworth's involvement with the 1818 Westmorland election begins in the mode of what Keats calls "Right and Wrong considered by each man abstractedly": "In this contest between sycophancy and independence, a number of election squibs are of course put forth by both parties. A certain

Poet is said to have taken part in the literary drudgery of the *patronage* side of the question" (*Collected Works* 19:35). In Edinburgh, a "political and literary journal" of this period called *The Scotsman* carried an epigraph from Junius: "This is not the cause of faction, or of party, or of any individual, but the common interest of every man in Britain." But somehow this posed no obstacle to printing a lead article about toryism, on roughly the first anniversary of Peterloo, which began: "Toryism is the evil genius of our country. It repines at all good. It takes every thing that is evil under its patronage."[39] Political name-calling must be as old as politics itself, but this way of thinking about parties seems ingrained in the spirit of Hazlitt's post-Waterloo age.

The two larger points I have tried to establish—the one about Wordsworth's reversal between 1795 and 1797 and the other about the meaning of 1815 as an intensification of oppositions established in the 1790s but submerged, suspended, or confused in the intervening period—now put us in a position to say something about the contradictions involved in the making of Wordsworth's political reputation. The post-Waterloo period forced Wordsworth to show his colors in a way that the period of the Napoleonic wars did not. Wordsworth's Burkean antireformism of the 1798–1807 period is firm enough, but it tends to take disguised and displaced forms and thus to reveal itself only to patient interpretation. He was, after all, still able to snipe at Burke in 1804 in the only surviving comment that we have from him on the subject between 1793 and 1818. But the early 1800s was a period that permitted, perhaps even fostered, such displacement and dislocation in a way that ceased to be true after 1815. One could no longer so easily conceal from the world, or for that matter from oneself, where one stood on the major political questions of the day.

The kind of polarization that begins to sharpen at the close of the wars tends to be self-perpetuating. Fears operating powerfully on both sides help to create the object of their emotion. The fear of conspiracy tends to produce and reproduce the fact of it. In post-Waterloo England, networks of spies were matched against networks of reformist correspondence, and in the eyes of the reformers themselves, the legitimacy of the Holy League abroad begins to find its domestic counterpart in the ideology of the Lake school in their out-of-the-way English province. Wordsworth, for his part, became more strident and defensive in his positions from 1815 to 1819 and also found himself encamped more tightly than ever with Southey and Coleridge. Wordsworth took pains to explain his disagreements with Southey,[40] as Coleridge explained his own with both Wordsworth and Southey in *Biographia Literaria,* but these explanations seem to have been dismissed as the narcissism of fine differences. What impressed the public consciousness was, rather, the way in which all three poets come forth to defend each other in this period. This only made them more vulnerable as a collective target. The assumption was that if you had seen one Renegado Laker, you had seen the lot; and more and more, Wordsworth was the one that you would see. One may regard all this as a loss of political subtlety or as a clarification of class conflict, but one cannot ignore its implications for the cultural history of the period.[41]

In saying that post-Waterloo conditions forced Wordsworth to show his colors, one must be wary of the metaphor, for just as there are increasingly no parties in this period but only "Right and Wrong abstractedly considered," so there are increasingly no colors in this period but only black and white. This "dechromatization" of the political picture is visible in Wordsworth's chiaroscuro treatment of the two parties in his 1818 *Address:* "On whom has the light fallen? and who are covered by shade and thick darkness." It seems inevitable in this context that T. J. Wooler's *The Black Dwarf,* perhaps the most important radical journal of the period after Cobbett's *Political Register,* should have been answered (if feebly) by another political journal, *The White Dwarf,* which Gibbons Merle started in direct and explicit opposition to Wooler. It is true that there was another variation on this theme, with the appearance of John Hunt's *Yellow Dwarf* in 1818. But we must not let the bright color blind us. The long discussion of freedom of the press in the first number was occasioned by remarks of the French Minister Jollivet to the effect that "the Liberty of the Press is less necessary in a Representative Government than in any other." By way of response, the *Yellow Dwarf* goes on to survey the political positions of some poets and philosophers on the issue of press suppression under Restoration regimes, and when it comes to Wordsworth, nothing is left to inference:

As to Wordsworth, another of these poetic deliverers, he is "a full solemne man," and you cannot get much out of him. But we should like to hear his opinion—Aye or No—of Mr. Jollivet's allied notions of liberty and the rights of man. Is this sort of legitimate clapping down under the hatches the deliverance for which he mouthed out deep

toned Odes and Sonnets. . . . If he were to say so, the very echoes of his
favorite mountains, "with thousand-fold reverberation," would contradict him. But he says nothing. His is profoundly silent.

This is not an atmosphere that could sustain the texture of poetic ambiguity
of Wordsworth's major work, the imaginative veiling that both reveals
and conceals his change of political mind. The invidious comparison with
Jeremy Bentham with which the discussion in the *Yellow Dwarf* concludes
makes this even clearer. Bentham, it says, was "by habit a logician, by nature a plain, literal man." He had not, "like Mssrs. Coleridge, Wordsworth,
and Southey, been playing at fast and loose with fiction." To Bentham's
credit, the "Gods had not made him poetical."[42]
    Wordsworth and the Lakers had given poeticality a bad name on the
left—poeticality as distinct from the utilitarian prose in the style of Bentham, from the political and religious parody in the style of William Hone
(whose recent acquittal was covered extensively in the *Yellow Dwarf,* as indeed it was all over), and from the social satire in the style of Byron's *Don
Juan.* Hazlitt, Hunt, and Keats were three who worked to save poetry for
progressive politics in this post-Waterloo period. But it was Shelley whose
campaign was most obviously an attempt to redeem imaginative or "poetical" poetry from the degrading state in which, from his point of view, the
Lakers had left it. Hence the anti-utilitarian strain of his defense of the uses
of poetry in 1821 and, more pertinently, the antisatiric strain in his satiric
parody of Wordsworth in *Peter Bell the Third* in 1819. In that poem, Peter
Bell the Second is not only Wordsworth's poem but Wordsworth himself.
Likewise Shelley is as much Peter Bell the Third as his poem, and as he insists, "they are not one but three; not three but one" (*Shelley's Poetry and
Prose,* 324). The Shelley who launched the first serious political attack on
Wordsworth in the year of Waterloo was thus also the first, in the year of
Peterloo, to register the adverse effects of such attacks, the syndromes of
mutual accusation and isolation they perpetuate. The point is most clearly
made in the "Satire on Satire" fragment of 1820, where Shelley argues that
satiric cursing, like Promethean cursing, helps to form the other in image of
one's worst fears and that satiric damnation participates in the system of
Christian damnation it purports to abhor. In the "Essay on Life," probably
of the same period as *Peter Bell the Third,* Shelley wrote that "the words *I*

and *you,* and *they* are grammatical devices invented simply for arrangement, and totally devoid of the intense and exclusive sense usually attached
to them."[43] At this level of abstraction, the political and moral force of the
point seems lost, but then again, the *entire* force of the point was lost on
Shelley's disciple Browning a quarter of a century later, when he set "us"
against "them" by sealing with a curse the fate of that unnamed "him."

Wordsworth and the Forms
of Romantic Art

6

Wordsworth and the Forms of Poetry

STUART CURRAN

The major British Romantics all made inauspicious debuts in print, especially when compared with their great forebears among the British poets. Spenser's *Shepheardes Calendar* introduced its author to the public with a preface placing him in direct succession to Chaucer and added the celebratory gloss of the scholiast "E. K." for good measure. An unknown and previously unpublished John Milton contributed his masterful verses *On Shakespeare* to the Second Folio of 1632, thereby establishing his claim to very distinguished company. In contrast, William Wordsworth bowed in with the anonymous *Sonnet on Seeing Miss Helen Maria Williams Weep at a Tale of Distress,* published in the March 1787 issue of the *European Magazine.* It begins:

> She wept.—Life's purple tide began to flow
> In languid streams through every thrilling vein;
> Dim were my swimming eyes—my pulse beat slow,
> And my full heart was swell'd to dear delicious pain.

Wordsworth, perhaps understandably, never reprinted the poem, and more understandable still is the delicate silence of his critics on what signs it contains for his future development. In terms of chronology its writing would have to be placed somewhere near the period at the end of book 2 of *The Prelude,* which gives us pause inasmuch as this panting adolescent seems to have no interest in the Nature so warmly extolled there. And even the most generous of bardolaters would have to admit that he has no taste. Yet this poem does directly portend the future and, if we take it at all seriously, reminds us of the literary context within which Wordsworth came of age. For the sixteen-year-old Wordsworth never "saw" Helen Maria Williams weeping; he *read* about it in her *Poems, in Two Volumes* of 1786, particularly in a poem that is a true index of its age, *To Sensibility*. There Miss Williams limns a portrait of the devotee of Sensibility:

> Yet tho' her soul must griefs sustain
>   Which she alone can know;
> And feel that keener sense of pain
>   Which sharpens every woe;
>
> Tho' she, the mourners' grief to calm,
>   Still shares each pang they feel,
> And, like the tree distilling balm,
>   Bleeds, others wounds to heal . . .

Three further quatrains of dependent clauses issue in this conclusion:

> She oft will heave a secret sigh,
>   Will shed a lonely tear,
> O'er feelings nature wrought so high,
>   And gave on terms so dear.

It took Wordsworth a decade to convert such rodomontade into "the burthen of the mystery" and to deepen its lachrymose tones into the timbres of the "still, sad music of humanity"; and to do so was clearly a remarkable achievement. The last third of the eighteenth century has come to be known as the Age of Sensibility, and Wordsworth's poetry is undeniably, also surely unexpectedly, its finest fruit.

When Wordsworth, in the "Advertisement" to the 1798 *Lyrical Ballads*, inveighed against "the gaudiness and inane phraseology of many modern writers" and represented his and Coleridge's volume as containing "a natural delineation of human passions, human characters, and human incidents," he knew whereof he spoke. He had begun his career as an apprentice to that "gaudiness and inane phraseology" and had learned the simple truth that the less adorned the language, the more approximating "the real language of men," the more capable it was of representing the inner sensibility, the utterly human. No other poet in the English language has Wordsworth's capacity to turn monosyllables into the fundamental building blocks of poetry and then, as it were, to wring tears from those rude stones. Examples could be cited almost at random, but among the most revealing are these famous lines from the early version of his *Ruined Cottage:*

> Beside yon spring I stood,
> And eyed its waters till we seemed to feel
> One sadness, they and I. For them a bond
> Of brotherhood is broken; time has been
> When every day the touch of human hand
> Disturbed their stillness, and they ministered
> To human comfort. When I stooped to drink
> A spider's web hung to the water's edge,
> And on the wet and slimy footstone lay
> The useless fragment of a wooden bowl.
> It moved my very heart.

The artlessness of this depiction, its compression of natural sustenance and human dissolution within the objective correlatives of spring and bowl, its fleeting immediacy and the pregnant silence in which it concludes—every element seems as irreducible as the chiseled monosyllables by which they are principally represented. If ever there were a touchstone in English poetry for that "grace beyond the reach of art" Pope prized, surely, we would say, this is it. At his best, Wordsworth always seems beyond the reach of art: spontaneous, natural, fresh, neither bound by old traditions nor vestured in the fashions of his time. Still, it is reasonable to suppose that the art that successfully poses as pure originality may be the most sophisticated there is. That art Wordsworth possessed in abundance.

By way of returning to these two texts, Wordsworth's first venture into print and the passage from *The Ruined Cottage,* let us for a moment contemplate an aspect of his temperament which has seemed so entirely uncharacteristic that, until very recently, it was simply dismissed by generations of readers: his love of geometry. It is most explicitly rendered in nearly a hundred lines at the beginning of book 6 of *The Prelude,* but careful attention to the associations the poet weaves around the subject makes us recognize that geometry constitutes a major theme in the central books of his autobiographical poem, beginning with the dream of the Arab attempting to save two objects from a universal deluge, a shell representing poetry and a stone the Arab says "(. . . in the language of the dream) / Was Euclid's Elements" (bk. 5, lines 87–88), and continuing through Wordsworth's belated if blazing recognition that he never wished to cross the Alps at all but to continue an ascent toward "our being's heart and home / . . . infinitude" (6.604–605). These books enact the poet's rite of passage into adulthood; his troubled attempt to reconcile mortal loss—an old, dessicated soldier, the Boy of Winander dead at eleven, the suicide of Esthwaite Lake—with elements that transcend mortality; the imaginative truths of literature and the universal laws of science that the Arab of his dream races to save from "the fleet waters of a drowning world" (5.137). So acute a sensitivity to mortality has, as Helen Maria Williams suggested in *To Sensibility,* its cost. From that dream "I waked in terror" (5.138), Wordsworth notes in his customarily spare manner.

A lapidary language does seem directly, even organically, related to geometry, equivalent in its concern with expressing the essentially human to the elemental irreducibility of Euclidian logic. Still, such an experiment with diction scarcely represents the limit of literary possibility for a temperament so drawn to abstract structures. In *The Prelude,* indeed, Wordsworth does not explicitly point an analogy between geometry and language, but rather between geometry and multiple, coexistent conceptual systems, a three-dimensional rather than plane geometry. From its principles, he says, he meditated

> On the relation those abstractions bear
> To Nature's laws, and by what process led,
> Those immaterial agents bowed their heads
> Duly to serve the mind of earth-born man;
> From star to star, from kindred sphere to sphere,
> From system on to system without end.
>
> (6.123–128)

This sounds, if we transpose its terms into a literary context, very like a program for metaphysical poetry, charting elaborate correspondences among "kindred" spheres, continuously linking the microcosm and macrocosm, in the manner of a Donne or Herbert. If we immediately recoil from such a notion of Wordsworth, it can no longer be because we conceive him as a poet of mere simplicity or of pure sincerity or as Nature's undiscriminating celebrant. The explications of a generation of critics have revealed a poet of endless complexity, of irresolvable ambiguity: in short, the bard of sensibility, we have learned, had an acute and penetrating mind. Perhaps we are ready to see it as the mind of a geometrician.

The *Sonnet on Seeing Miss Helen Maria Williams Weep at a Tale of Distress* was printed over the signature "AXIOLOGUS." The conventional translation of this word in a Greek dictionary is "deserving mention," and we might be content simply to see here an expression of the young Wordsworth's pride in finding himself honored in print. But so self-conscious an application of a Greek pseudonymn suggests that Wordsworth had something further in mind: perhaps to register his "esteem for the logos," the very act of mental conception itself; or, if we narrow and focus the range of meaning, to indicate his primary concern for the quality a poet weighs and measures, the worth of words—more exactly, a "word's worth." Paradoxically, the elderly sage who might be said to have lived off his name never acknowledged its rich suggestiveness, but that he staked his initial venture into print with a pun conflating his name and assumed vocation must suggest the seriousness of his ambition. Moreover, whether or not its readers would have strained the meaning of this pseudonymn so finely, its very neoclassical formality of closure constructs a modest dike against the deluging tears of the devotees of sensibility, Wordsworth and Miss Williams, in the poem. Even more so does the form of the poem, for, if its diction is beyond justification, even a cursory reading reveals a finely constructed Shakespearean sonnet, one that would stand comparison with the models from which the apprentice poet was working, the *Elegiac Sonnets* of Charlotte Smith. Wordsworth's debut in print is within the conventional mode of the most popular poetic form of the 1780s, the sonnet of sensibility. In the year of its publication also came the debut of another poet under Smith's direct influence, William Lisle Bowles, who gained contemporary prominence within the same form and insured its momentum into the 1790s. It was only after the movement had peaked and declined, exactly two decades after his first publication, that Wordsworth in his own collection *Poems in Two Volumes,* probably without a thought of how Helen Maria William's collection by that title had prompted his career, would establish himself through a profound rethinking of its conceptual properties, its geometry, as the greatest master of the English sonnet after Milton.

The sonnet on Miss Williams reveals a poet alive to contemporary fashion and comfortable in cutting it to his own angularity. The passage from *The Ruined Cottage* suggests a second way, more oblique and even more sophisticated, in which formal elements from a "kindred sphere" insinuate themselves into Wordsworth's poetry. What is it that "moved" the Pedlar's "very heart"? Not yet having heard his tale, we have only a few details of the episode to draw from: a spring, a spiderweb and mossy footstone indicating disuse, "The useless fragment of a wooden bowl." What might move the Pedlar is not just Margaret's dissolution, but a larger conceptual frame in which traditionally it would be placed, the traditions of pastoral and, specifically, of the pastoral elegy. The Pedlar actually invokes this frame a few lines before he recounts his visit to the spring:

> The Poets, in their elegies and songs
> Lamenting the departed, call the groves,
> They call upon the hills and streams to mourn,
> And senseless rocks—nor idly, for they speak
> In these their invocations with a voice
> Obedient to the strong creative power
> Of human passion. Sympathies there are
> More tranquil, yet perhaps of kindred birth,
> That steal upon the meditative mind
> And grow with thought. Beside yon spring I stood. . . .

The spring, beside which the traditional eclogue is enacted, remains. The bower is intact, but the bond of human fellowship, symbolized by the "useless fragment" of the traditional prize bowl of pastoral song, as in the *First Idyll* of Theocritus, has been severed. In this objective correlative of Margaret's decay, all the values of pastoral—its claims for simple pleasance, fellow feeling, the bond with nature, a spontaneous and untroubled art— are called into question. As they are throughout *The Ruined Cottage*. The oblique, because realistic, invocation of pastoral convention sets the stage for a poem deeply imbued with the complex double vision of Theocritean and Virgilian pastoral, which is to say, a mode in which the reality principle of the antipastoral intrudes upon and tests the pastoral ideal. Only if we are attuned to that traditional context are we aware of how significantly Wordsworth centers the poem in the conversation of the two friends, Pedlar and Poet. In a modern equivalent to the *First Idyll* of Theocritus, where the shepherds sing of Daphnis's sorrow and death, the friends seek a way to preserve the pastoral ideal by recounting an instance of its failure; and para-doxically, in the fellowship of their sympathy, they enact that ideal once more. This done, they end the poem with an evening retirement that is again conventional to pastoral poetry, a closure of the garden conceived as a psy-chological entity:

> Together casting then a farewell look
> Upon those silent walls, we left the shade;
> And, ere the stars were visible, attained
> A rustic inn, our evening resting place.

That critics have concentrated on the whys and wherefores of Words-worth's revolution in poetic language is natural: the advertisement and preface to the *Lyrical Ballads* emphasize this element, and it became one of the hotly debated topics within the ferment of British Romanticism. But what is equally clear was that Wordsworth was intent on a similar revolu-tion involving the forms of poetry, and it was one he pursued in ways dis-tinctly similar to his reform of poetic diction. The pastoral offers a case in point. By the third edition of *Lyrical Ballads*, that of 1802, Wordsworth in-dicates that the collection has two principal formal axes: the title became *Lyrical Ballads: With Pastoral and Other Poems*. A number of the poems in the second volume, the ones essentially added to the 1800 edition, bear sub-titles indicating this generic emphasis. *Michael, a Pastoral Poem* is still the full title of this poem in modern editions; on the other hand, *The Brothers, a Pastoral Poem* has lost the generic designation Wordsworth originally gave it. But these, and several others as well, are conceived very much with the is-sues, the themes, even the conventions of early pastoral in mind.

That the poems are so seldom spoken of within the framework of pasto-ral is anomalous because the tradition provides a richly detailed and subtle context for them. And yet paradoxically that context is not invoked be-cause, by and large, we inherit the presuppositions about it that Words-worth sought to subvert. By the later eighteenth century it was clear even in England that pastoral, that celebration of all things natural, had become the peculiar province of the artificial. Marie Antoinette's Petit Trianon was a symbol of the age, virtually mythologized through the pictorial elaborations of Boucher and Fragonard. Pastoral represented the rich on holiday. The realm of the true bucolic was either ignored or made the focus of anti-pastoral invective, as in George Crabbe's *The Village*, where the poor litter the land. Crabbe has a manifest sympathy for their plight, but his is the pity of the moral superior, not one of their kind. Crabbe has no faith in the rustic and no belief in the pastoral except as being that Edenic realm from which our inheritance of original sin has irretrievably barred us. With Wordsworth it is exactly contrary. The folk embody the elemental dignity of the human, and the rhythm of their lives led in concert with nature is the ground bass of our being. However it could appear that the entire course of Western civilization conspired to this democratic end, Wordsworth was in the fortunate position to strip pastoral of its artificial trappings and restore it to something like its representation in Theocritus, Virgil, and Spenser.

The restoration required, of course, something more than simply a reality principle. With Wordsworth, pastoral takes on the weight of an ideological commitment:

> Paradise, and groves
> Elysian, Fortunate Fields—like those of old
> Sought in the Atlantic Main—why should they be
> A history only of departed things,
> Or a mere fiction of what never was?

By the time these lines from *Home at Grasmere* were published with the preface to *The Exursion,* it must have been clear to his contemporaries how very seriously Wordsworth meant them. Still, the pastoral of the Lake District is neither balmy nor fancy-free. The climate is cold and the land hard, and the continual challenge of endurance produced by those conditions is at the same time a test of moral fiber. But the result is a population of "Freemen" who have earned their freedom by labor, who live in symbiotic relation to the elemental laws of nature and, independent, uncorrupted by urban finery, have just enough to live on, a mere sufficiency. That, in Wordsworth's view, should be construed as the stuff of paradise. Yet it is also the locus for tragedy, or at least the charged pathos of Margaret and Michael and Leonard in *The Brothers,* all of whom desire the permanence of the enclosed garden and are confronted instead with the flux of existence.

The seeming incongruity between Wordsworth's ideological commitment to pastoral and the mainly tragic themes he wrests from it is, in effect, the essential pivot within traditional pastoral, and Wordsworth seems to have understood its ambivalent essence in a single glance. That is to say, if we return to Virgil's *Eclogues,* we have on the one hand continual evidence of natural bounty, the values of the simple life, the extrapolation of natural fertility into religious and cultural myth, the centrality of song; but on the other hand there is the impending exile of Meliboeus in *Eclogue* 1, the failures in love of *Eclogues* 2 and 10, and the necessary infirmities of old age in *Eclogue* 9. It is very much to the point to cite such examples, for what gives Wordsworthian pastoral its distinctive resonance is the way in which, within a realistic perspective that had been largely absent from pastoral since Spenser, Wordsworth continually invokes the conventional tropes of pastoral. In the hills of the Lake District, we would suppose, there are no longer singing contests. But that, we realize, is not quite true:

> "Now, Matthew!" said I, "let us match
> This water's pleasant tune
> With some old border-song, or catch
> That suits a summer's noon."

It is so natural that we scarcely notice how borrowed is every device. *The Fountain, a Conversation* is an eclogue imbued with tradition: the dialogue of youth and age ranges effortlessly across the most venerable themes of pastoral. At the same time it seems wholly fresh and in its eighteen stanzas attains a remarkable power. The singing contest becomes a metaphor for the unequal challenges of life. The youth, who proclaims "I live and sing my idle songs / Upon these happy plains," is in concert with the beings of nature:

> The blackbird amid leafy trees
> The lark above the hill,
> Let loose their carols when they please,
> And quiet when they will.

But such spontaneity no longer avails for the aged Matthew. The main instrument of continuity, memory, betrays him:

> My eyes are dim with childish tears,
> My heart is idly stirred,
> For the same sound is in my ears
> Which in those days I heard.

Consciousness separates Matthew from his youthful companion and from nature. The rhythm of natural effulgence, the lulling music of the fountain, is the sound of time, and no human can survive its competition. Yet, it is from the very consciousness of that inequality that art, human art, is made. *The Fountain* ends with Matthew bravely accepting the challenge he cannot win and singing not in the borrowed and, for him, false accents of a child, but rather in the absurdly cracked timbres of the old, whose life force paradoxically makes itself known through an intense desire for what is irrecoverable:

> And ere we come to Leonard's rock,
> He sang those witty rhymes
> About the crazy old church-clock,
> And the bewildered chimes.

As a poem like *The Fountain* exemplifies, Wordsworth's invocation of a form is unobtrusive, and yet the form is thought through intellectually so as to effect an organic, or in this context a three-dimensionally geometric, relation to poetic content. It is as if Wordsworth had come to writing a poem like *The Fountain* not because he recalled a specific schoolteacher named Matthew, nor because he was musing on the inevitable differences in viewpoint between old and young, but because he wondered why in the first place a singing contest should have been a central motif in pastoral poetry and went on from that primary impulse to write this simple poem of complex balances between youth and age, spontaneity and experience, natural ignorance and the artifices of consciousness, human fellowship and discontinuity. The eclogue traditionally embodies this kind of dialectical exploration, and it in turn is an essential aspect of Wordsworth's artistic achievement. The attention paid in recent years to the dramatic element in Wordsworth's poetry is a tacit recognition of how deeply it is informed by the values of pastoral. Indeed, a stronger sense of formal context would have given readers of earlier generations some guidelines for how to read, or not to misread, Wordsworth's intentions in poems like *We Are Seven* or *Anecdote for Fathers*, where the clash of perspectives is as absolute as that between, let us say, the shepherd and goatherd of Theocritus's *Fifth Idyll*. Such poems exist for the sake of the multivalences they embody, and what has seemed innovative on Wordsworth's part, effecting a break with normative practices of the eighteenth century, even perhaps presaging the planned conceptual labyrinths of modernism, is little more than an abstracting of the inherent dynamic of the classical eclogue.

It would be comparatively easy to extend this inquiry into an entire essay, for the simple truth is that Wordsworth was England's greatest pastoral poet, placing his inimitable stamp on traditional materials and influencing practically all writing in the mode after him. But his capacity for going to the heart of a formal problem, or turning into a problem what others took for granted, was apparent even before he began the series of pastoral experiments he started publishing in 1800 The very title of his and Coleridge's joint venture places formal considerations at the center of their concern. Many volumes of poetry published in Britain in the late eighteenth century bear generic titles: *Lyrical Ballads* is unique in presenting its readers not with a mere description of the contents but with a conundrum. A ballad by its nature is not lyrical, unless one converts it into a notion of popular song. Given the decades of ballad research in the wake of Thomas Percy's *Reliques of Ancient English Poetry,* any prospective reader of this collection could be counted on to know, in fact, that ballads are antithetical to the lyrical: communal narratives whose power lies precisely in their emotional detachment from the events they record. "But what if we stop that narrative time?" One overhears Wordsworth thinking: "What are the emotions that are being systematically denied by the formal requirements of the mode?" As usual, the bard of sensibility and the geometrician go hand in hand.

In general, *Lyrical Ballads* concentrates not on what people do but what they are. Or if events are placed to the fore, they are conspicuous by their triviality. The narrator of *Simon Lee* cuts the root of a tree stump; Johnny, the "Idiot Boy," rides the wrong way on a pony. The actions are invariably simple: what underlies or accompanies them in the mind is complex, perhaps unfathomable. The poem at the exact center of the 1798 *Lyrical Ballads* is *The Thorn*, whose main characters are a woman who cries out "Oh misery" and a garrulous sea captain who is obsessed with understanding what motivates her repeated cry: "I cannot tell; I wish I could; / For the true reason no one knows." In its abstract relations the poem mirrors our minds, our desire for certitude, our ultimate lack of assurance. "Action is transitory," Wordsworth wrote in *The Borderers*, but the mental aftermath is very different: "Suffering is permanent, obscure and dark, / And has the nature of infinity." Wordsworth appended these lines to *The White Doe of Rylstone* when he published it in 1815, by way of preparing his readers for an even more radical experiment, a lyrical romance, concerned with the cost of others' actions on a passively enduring woman. The relative lack of success of this poem is owing to its length; in the comparative brevity of his lyrical ballads, Wordsworth embodied a richness of nuance, of psychological delicacy, of acute social portraiture that draws readers constantly to return to them and just as continually to discover them anew.

Again, the attention accorded by the preface to the linguistic revolution embodied in these poems has obscured their radical formal ingenuity. But if we reflect for a minute on the relationship of form and language, form and content, in the 1800 volumes, we must acknowledge how closely intertwined are their concerns. The standard hierarchy of the genres observed in the Renaissance and still regulating literary taste at the end of the eighteenth century would have placed two forms at the very bottom, the vernacular ballad stemming from folk materials and the pastoral, after Virgil the traditional starting point for a poetic career. "To me the meanest flower that blows can give / Thoughts that do often lie too deep for tears": these are the meanest flowers of poetry, composed of the simplest elements, deliberately reduced to a common denominator. They are formally akin to the monosyllables that so frequently represent them: form and content are in absolute alliance. And the axis is more than literary in its implications, as a brief glance at the character of subsequent literary history would immediately indicate. Wordsworth was the most successful of English Jacobins: the great leveler of poetry both in language and in form. The last, he had learned in Sunday School, shall be first; and with a single-minded zeal and the eye of a geometrician, he saw how to make it happen. From now on poetry would be secular and of the people, liberated from the constraints of ideology and class that had been virtually universal in Western history up to this point.

But Wordsworth had no intention of liberating poetry from its traditions. Quite the contrary, his program seems to have been one of liberating poetic tradition from the museum where it had been encased in all its pastness, of breathing new life into what had been assumed to be dead. What we have been observing, indeed, appears to have been a systematic program to show that the conventions of pastoral could be made vitally modern or that folk ballads, if we were to look deeply enough, might contain in a marsupial envelopment the inner life their surface seemed to deny. The same principle can be discerned in every form Wordsworth adapts to his use. Nothing is taken for granted and nothing tossed away. Every element, every conventional association or pattern of ideas, seems held to the light, studied as to innate principle or motive force, and recharged with meaning. This is, perhaps, exactly what one expects of a major poet, of the peer of Spenser or Milton, but, as his unprepossessing initial publication might indicate, Wordsworth is exactly the opposite of those master manipulators of poetic form, so unassuming in his methods that he seldom calls attention to the radical rethinking he is engaged in. Indeed, so natural is his characteristic posture that we are loath even to acknowledge its formality. We might expect a Coleridge or a Shelley to publish a two-volume collection divided into six parts, of which the first would end with a professedly Horation ode and the sixth with the last example of the Greater Pindaric ode in English. We do not expect it of Wordsworth, even though that is the careful, the deliberate balance he achieves between the *Ode to Duty* and *Intimations Ode* in his *Poems in Two Volumes* of 1807. But having observed that symmetrical mirroring, we might be led to see it repeated, in a variety of ways, throughout the collection. And without a doubt, the last having been made first, we would find the most significance in the elaborate balances worked out between, and within, the two series of sonnets published in the 1807 collection, *Miscellaneous Sonnets* and *Sonnets Dedicated to Liberty*.

As unportentous as was Wordsworth's debut in the sonnet form, in the 1807 collection he at once established himself, in contemporary opinion and since, as Milton's legitimate heir as master of the sonnet in English. But his artistic purpose is not confined simply to a fine measuring of the dimensions and inner stresses of the "orbicular body" of verse he once compared to a dewdrop. As the *Sonnets Dedicated to Liberty*, with their continual references to Milton indicate, Wordsworth is concerned to measure his inheritance as well. But it is not merely Milton whose presence is invoked. In the first sequence of *Miscellaneous Sonnets*, the conspicuous accentuation of two balanced triplets recalling Renaissance conventions—*From the Italian of Michelangelo* and *To Sleep*—signals the extent to which Wordsworth is laying claim to an indivisible mantle of poetic succession. Between them the *Miscellaneous Sonnets* and the *Sonnets Dedicated to Liberty*, miniature exercises that they are, embody an audacity that is breathtaking, for as recreations of the Petrarchan and Miltonic modes, they at once subtly invoke the entire history of the European sonnet and, as with the pastoral, recast it in contemporary terms. The Petrarchan sonnet, reduced to the abstract, represents a bridging of polarities between here and there, the mundane and eternal, the stationary and liberated, the finite and infinite. Milton's innovation was to politicize the form, using it to measure the relation, whether one of affinity or of alienation, between the speaker and his culture. Accordingly, in a sweeping view, the two series of sonnets could be divided between Wordsworth's momentary, personal reflections and his sense of public obligation.

But, as we might expect and as a quick comparison of the sonnets on ships or on cloud formations in the first sequence with the opening sonnet of the second—*Fair Star of Evening, Splendor of the West*—immediately reveals, the first mode impinges on its successor, offering us a way of understanding the nature of personal epiphanies that directly relates to their extension into a public realm. The *Miscellaneous Sonnets* as a whole recast the Petrarchan sonnet into psychological exploration. The sense of formal explosion we associate with them is congruent with their inner dynamic, for they enact moments in which the imagination suddenly finds itself drawn forth from the finite moment to be empowered by an energy, whether of a departing ship, a sleeping city, or even a dormant winter garden, that seems to bear the mark of infinity. That imagination is the instrument of a secular equivalent of Christian grace: to quote the end of the first sonnet from Michelangelo, whose Catholic tonalities otherwise seem so inappropriate to this poet, it is "a deathless flower, / That breathes on earth the air of paradise." Yet that energy resides not merely in what the eye can behold. Even more powerfully it resides within the conceptual structures of the mind, within its ideals, its exemplars, its extrapolations of permanent symbols from the chaos of history. It is embodied equally in the contemporary King of Sweden—who "stands *above* / All consequences: work he hath begun / Of fortitude, and piety, and love"—and the deposed, imprisoned Toussaint l'Ouverture, whose "friends are exultations, agonies, / And love, and Man's unconquerable mind"—or in the towering past of Venetian republicanism that shadows its present subservience to Napoleon's empire. Most of all, for one nurtured in a British culture, it is embodied in a single exemplary figure: "Milton! thou shouldst be living at this hour." The despairing exhortation may by its eloquence divert us from the recognition that Milton is, indeed, alive, revivified within the consciousness of his successor, whose claim to wield this grand public rhetoric is based in his adherence to the ideals it once served, out of which it was itself created. This famous sonnet comes at the center of the *Sonnets Dedicated to Liberty* and forms the turning point of the sequence. Through appropriating the power of his predecessor, Wordsworth discovers the means to withstand the vicissitudes of demoralizing events and to arouse his dispirited country to a renewed moral vision and the sense of cultural purpose embedded in its history. Though initially the comparison would seem odd, whether on stylistic or generic grounds, the more one contemplates the dynamic interchanges of the *Sonnets Dedicated to Liberty*, the closer they cohere to the exactly contemporary epic prophecy Blake entitled simply *Milton*, in which he records not just his inspiration by, but more significantly his recreation of, the prophetic spirit of Milton. No less than Blake is Wordsworth an Elisha donning the mantle of Elijah. His achievement is all the more to be wondered at, in that it is accomplished in so miniature, so consciously confining a form.

Though this discussion has itself been confined to the unpretentious forms—the pastoral, the ballad, and the sonnet—in which Wordsworth elected to foment a poetic revolution, it is equally true that his ultimate goal was not a country churchyard but a cathedral, as he expresses it in the preface to *The Excursion*. *The Recluse*, if it had ever been completed, would have been at least as long as the *Divine Comedy*. It seems likely, too, if only from Wordsworth's analogy with a Gothic cathedral, the most complex and venerable of geometric forms, that it would have been a major example of the "composite orders" of generic mixture he refers to in the preface to his 1815 *Poems*. Certainly, one can discern an intermixture of deliberately plebeian genres in *The Excursion*, with the pastoral of its first book (*The Ruined Cottage*) supplemented by locodescriptive verse; by conventional travel poetry; by epitaph and inscription, as in the survey of graves in the churchyard; and by the concluding idyll of the Pastor's family circle. But the more interesting and adventurous generic intermixture is contained in *The Prelude*, where Wordsworth consciously plays against the traditions of the classical genres. Since an entire book could be devoted to the subtleties of this grandiose scheme, only the barest of outlines can be offered here. Yet even a cursory glance at the generic mixture of *The Prelude* is sufficient to reveal both the extent to which it reflects at every turn the same discerning eye looking to the premises on which tradition has founded its manifold forms and the way it recreates the hierarchy of genres along the lines of a realistic psychological progression or maturation.

It has become increasingly common to speak of *The Prelude* as Wordsworth's epic poem, but to do so loosely is to elide exactly how it constitutes itself an epic without heroic exploits, divine machinery, or formative national history. There is, indeed, a hero; yet even Wordsworth acknowledged it "a thing unprecedented in Literary history that man should talk so much about himself." He seems in this remark to have forgotten (or not truly to have known) the as yet untranslated Dante, who, exiled in midlife, essentially asked the same question as Wordsworth—"Was it for this?" (the opening phrase of the 1799 *Prelude*)—and similarly set forth to discover his identity. Yet though Dante might provide certain paradigms (for instance, a final summarizing vision from a great height) against which Wordsworth might measure his own literary purposes, the differences in perspective are signal and are themselves paradigmatic of how Wordsworth had to confront a problematic tradition. Wordsworth's poem is resolutely of this world: there are no excursions out of it, no divine intercession to be relied on, not even this late in the day a definitive classical authority to guide one. And to invoke that earlier authority, Virgil, is at once to realize that there is likewise no arena for the hero to *act* in, no history he can be sure of affecting, and no certain glory to be won. Indeed, as the quandary of the opening book emphasizes, however great his ambition, the autobiographical hero seems to have no epic purpose.

That the purpose is implicit in his life is the driving force of Wordsworth's poem, and thus its employment of epic tradition is appropriately concealed, represented only by implication. For instance, both at the beginning and the end of book 1, Wordsworth alludes to the famous conclusion of *Paradise Lost:* "The earth is all before me" (bk. 1, line 14), "The road lies plain before me" (1.640). He appears to imply that he is to begin his epic endeavors where Milton left his, and clearly the quandary is as much literary as personal. Fittingly, the poem begins *in medias res,* not because epic tradition dictates such an opening, but because, realistically speaking, life does. From such a realistic perspective we can begin to look anew for epic signals and will find them in abundance. There is no Urania, but there is the encouraging, if distantly isolated, presence of Coleridge invoked at crucial points throughout the poem. There is no underworld to descend into, but then the naive youth stumbles to an awareness that, as Shelley was to put it two decades later in ironic relation to Wordsworth himself, "Hell is a city much like London," and he discovers at its center the symbolic "Parliament of monsters" (7.718) of Bartholomew Fair. Wordsworth's geography is measured and mapped, unlike the fearful and sometimes marvelous Mediterranean basin traversed by Odysseus and Aeneas, yet journeying from the southwest of England to its northwestern Lake District, east to Cambridge, and south to London, Wordsworth implicitly frames the breadth of geography, inhabitants, and climates that compose his native land, and the principle is extended in the two ventures to the Continent. Traditional epic catalogs are transformed (and Wordsworth does not see it as comic deflation) into those of a library, with lists of epic subjects in book 1, his childhood reading in book 5, and types of pastoral in book 8 and of romance in book 9. The warfare between England and France is assuredly linked with the destiny of nations, and though Wordsworth is Achilles only insofar as he sits it all out, certainly the French officer Michel Beaupuy is a type of Hector who dies upholding his national ideals. As these examples indicate, Wordsworth uses epic conventions by turning them inside out. The procedure is novel only because it is so demandingly realistic. Otherwise, it is basically the same mode by which Virgil appropriated Homer or by which Milton subverted the ideals of classical heroism.

The epic is traditionally the most capacious of literary forms, not only because it aspires to encyclopedic largeness, but because it also subsumes lesser literary genres. As oblique as is Wordsworth's employment of epic conventions, in this generic envelopment *The Prelude* is conspicuously open. Yet it is also conspicuously odd. Wordsworth's greatest generic innovation, though of a piece with the experimentation we earlier observed, may have been his decision to collapse the traditional hierarchy altogether: his epic breadth is contained within a familiar epistle, a verse letter to Coleride. The epistolary fiction controls the intimacy of tone, the associative logic, and internal rumination of the poem, but on a larger plane it also establishes the work's purpose in a bond of communication between writer and reader, which opens out in the last pages as a regenerating bond among Wordsworth, Coleridge, and their future nation. The epistolary mode is thus both functional and enabling. More localized generic intrusions tend to be ideological or psychological in their value. That is to say, the mock-heroic card game of book 1 by contrast emphasizes the realistic perspective Wordsworth will sustain throughout the work; the descent into the hellish city at the center of the work is accompanied by a descent into satire, an uncongenial mode for Wordsworth and one from which he must be weaned by reimmersion in the pastoral world of book 8. That book, entitled "Retrospect," constitutes Wordsworth's fullest representation of a realistic pastoral as the premise for his ongoing life. As essential as it is, pastoral in turn constantly presses toward the regions of romance, as Wordsworth notes of his youthful education in book 5 and of his early imaginings about London (6.77–115). Literary genres, he suggests through these fluid shifts among them, are really modes of apprehension, coexistent within the mind as within the book of one's mind that is an autobiographical poem. As the record of *The Prelude* begins with the pastoral bower of childhood, slowly moving through the unstable imaginings of romance and deflations of satire to a mature engagement with the destiny of nations, and finally to an assertion of the manifest destiny of one's own nation, so there is built up the composite order of this poem and this imagination, which is to say this exemplary, unitary life, "from kindred sphere to sphere."

The complex crosscurrents of that maturation have been simplified in this abstraction of Wordsworth's attempt to relive his life through literary form, and it may sound much more academic than the process of the poem suggests it to be. Yet if the subtitle of the published poem, "The Growth of a *Poet's* Mind," can be taken with added emphasis on the distinctive nature of this autobiography, Wordsworth's patterning of himself through the inherited forms of poetry is logical. It is the ultimate extension of that geometric abstraction with which he attempted to reconceive the elements of his craft and to revitalize a national literature that had, from his perspective, either sunk into mechanical imitation or veered from it into a specious and sensational novelty. Whether conditioning his mind to a small scale or enlarging its vision to epic proportions, Wordsworth, as if by instinct, consciously shaped as he saw. And what in sum he shaped as well was the subsequent direction of British poetry. If it is initially discomforting to think of the exponent of spontaneity and passion as a supreme artificer, the more one contemplates the idea, the more liberating it becomes. So, in truth, it was for Wordsworth.

The Triumphs of Failure
Wordsworth's *Lyrical Ballads* of 1798

KENNETH R. JOHNSTON

This essay is dedicated to those legions of students who have been led into the wonderful poems of Wordsworth and Coleridge's *Lyrical Ballads* through the awful thickets of Wordsworth's preface to the second edition (1800), and Coleridge's chapters in *Biographia Literaria* (1817) on the *Lyrical Ballads'* origins and intentions. Some few have emerged illumined, and adept in curious literary argument, but many more, in my experience, have come out of the ordeal disgusted, not only with Wordsworth and Coleridge, but also with poetry in general and the well-known tag phrases they have been forced to apply to it: "spontaneous overflow of powerful feelings," "emotion recollected in tranquility," "the language really spoken by men," and so on. I am far from denigrating the literary importance of Wordsworth's and Coleridge's critical arguments. Rather, my aim is to provide an alternative to the still-common pedagogic practice of asking students to discuss some poems from *Lyrical Ballads* in the light of excerpts from Wordsworth's preface or Coleridge's retrospect, or both. Specialists in the field know that the connection between the poems and those prose statements is highly problematic, dubious in some important respects, and on occasion nonexistent or just plain wrong. "How do Wordsworth's poems in *Lyrical Ballads* relate to his preface?" is a question that knowledgeable scholars approach gingerly, behind the academic equivalent of the proverbial ten-foot pole, and may take the better part of a valuable career to answer. Yet students are routinely asked versions of the same question, to be answered in the fifty minutes, or less, of a written exam.

The *Lyrical Ballads* are so important in the history of literature written in English that a small but full-time critical industry has been devoted to them almost since their day of publication, and shows no signs of flagging as their bicentenary approaches. There are many reasons for this, not least of which is the quality of the poems they contain: Wordsworth's *Tintern Abbey* and Coleridge's *Rime of the Ancient Mariner* would appear on almost everyone's list of best poems in the language, certainly as among the best of their kind. But it is not just great poetry that makes *Lyrical Ballads* important. Even more crucial are the critical issues they raise, and these emerge in the connection (or lack thereof) between the poems and the two poets' various prose comments upon them. It is no exaggeration to say that the issues raised, or implied, by *Lyrical Ballads*—namely: What is literature? How is it written? Who writes it? Who is it written for? What are its appropriate subjects and forms?—still constitute for most readers the agenda of modern literature and, perhaps even more so, of modern literary *studies*. There are better poems in the language, and certainly more acute prefaces, but none that establish such clear landmarks for the nature of literature and its institutionalized study in modern democratic societies.

It goes without saying that the questions raised, or provoked, by the poets' explanations have done more to guarantee their volume's immortality than the answers they provided. Such is the nature of criticism: endless conversation, not definitive laboratory demonstration. But, while not denying the value of the two poets' comments on their famous volume, I propose to set them aside temporarily and concentrate on what Charles Lamb called the "living and daily circumstances" of its composition.[1] Lamb disapproved of Wordsworth's intention to add a preface to the second edition, and he was right, as he often was in his down-to-earth reactions to his friend's tendencies toward pomposity. That preface, with its splendid but pugnacious humanism, is at once terribly defensive, frighteningly aggressive, and very long, diverting us from many valuable aspects of the poems it ostensibly introduces, especially their themes and subject matter, by entangling us in a technical literary argument about diction, style, and meter and preoccupying us with a mere "experiment" that is being conducted only to "ascertain, how far, by fitting to metrical arrangement a selection of the real language of men in a state of vivid sensation, that sort of pleasure and that quantity of pleasure may be imparted, which a Poet may rationally endeavour to impart." (This is only part of the preface's second sentence and gives a good foretaste of the heavy sledding lying ahead.) The same objections may be raised to the introductory value of Coleridge's chapters in *Biographia Literaria,* despite their more attractive style. Both texts, it seems to me, distract from the humanitarian and even revolutionary "purpose" of the volume—"the multiplicity, and . . . the quality of its moral relations," to which Wordsworth referred—by concentrating on stylistic matters rather than the "systematic defence of the theory, upon which the poems were to be written," which Wordsworth said he "declined" to give because it would require him to retrace "the revolutions, not of literature alone, but likewise of society itself." In short, *Lyrical Ballads* is a revolutionary document without its requisite revolutionary manifesto—or *with* a manifesto that displaces its revolutionary thrust into matters of poetic methodology.

Of course, in the repressive internal political situation of England between 1795 and 1815, the two poets had good reason to play down the radical political implications of their poems (Wordsworth's much more so than Coleridge's), and their own disillusionment with the course of revolutionary activism in both England and France made it all the more easy for them to do so. But even to modern, first-time readers of the 1798 *Lyrical Ballads,* it is obvious that the great majority of these poems are powerfully disturbing statements about very unfortunate and painfully suffering poor people. They raise important sociopolitical questions, making artistic considerations of appropriate language and subject matter seem irrelevant, somewhat like the effect of Walker Evans's unsettling photographs of southern poor folk in James Agee's classic of the Depression, *Let Us Now Praise Famous Men.* We can gain quicker entrée into this ambience by going behind the volume's prefaces and retrospectives into the "living and daily circumstances" of the poets' other work at the time, particularly their lifelong ambition to create a new masterpoem, to be called *The Recluse,* which would address the new democratic society then painfully coming to birth. It would do so by offering "views" of Man, Nature, and Human Life in which all three elements would be displayed in a redemptive, nonrevolutionary philosophy of progress—a consummation still devoutly to be wished.

It is now well known that the accounts offered by Wordsworth and Coleridge as to how, when, and why the *Lyrical Ballads* of 1798 came to be written differ materially from what the poets were actually doing in that "annus mirabilis" of English Romanticism that began in the summer of 1797 when Wordsworth moved to Somerset to be near Coleridge and ended in the summer of 1798 (18 July, to be precise) when the last of the poems, *Lines Written a Few Miles above Tintern Abbey,* was delivered to the printer. There is nothing very surprising or reprehensible in these discrepancies. Everyone tries to put a good face on things, and artists in particular have a natural predeliction for drawing a strong line of cause and effect between initial inspiration, no matter how haphazard, and final production, especially when, as with *Lyrical Ballads,* the production has a celebrity far beyond the artists' original dreams. The only danger of confusion arises when the artists' account, or creative mythos, becomes accepted, as has also been the case with *Lyrical Ballads,* as objective historical fact. Thus many textbooks and innumerable classrooms continue to project the image of Wordsworth and Coleridge coming together in 1797, igniting a spark of mutual creativity that led wonderfully and inexorably to the publication of *Lyrical Ballads* a year later, and "the rest" (the teachers intone) "is history." But it is not; scholarship knows better, even as the best scholarship acknowledges that all history depends on degrees of creative reconstruction.

John Jordan has masterfully untangled the sequences of aborted plans and false starts toward publication with which Wordsworth and Coleridge kept their Bristol friend, Joseph Cottle, interested throughout that famous year in the idea of publishing the joint, or separate, volumes they might produce, some of which would have contained poems (such as Wordsworth's bleak *Salisbury Plain*) far different from the *Lyrical Ballads* we now know.[2] Mary Moorman and Mark Reed have made it very clear that only during the last three or four months of that year can Wordsworth be said to have been concentrating on the composition of the poems that became his contribution to the 1798 *Lyrical Ballads.*[3] From July of 1797, when he and his sister Dorothy first settled at Alfoxden, through mid-December, he spent most of his time revising his play, *The Borderers,* for sale to a London theater company. Following the complete failure of this project—a fate shared equally with Coleridge's dramatic effort, *Osorio*—he began the new year of 1798 by writing and revising nondramatic, blank verse narrative poems, until in early March he could announce the birth of a new master project, *The Recluse,* which would contain them all. It was only after the first week in March, when William and Dorothy received notice that their tenancy of Alfoxden House was to be terminated (because neighbors had told their landlord they were dangerous radicals: i.e., republicans), and the idea of spending a year in Germany with Coleridge began to seem like a plausible next move, that Wordsworth began to compose many of the poems for *Lyrical Ballads and a Few Other Poems*, to give the book its full title. Then, indeed, the concentration of his creative activity becomes phenomenal and well worthy of inclusion among the splendors of English, or any other, literary history.

Mark Reed has also cast a cool eye on the likely literal validity of Coleridge's received account of the origin of *Lyrical Ballads*, an account published nearly twenty years after the fact, in chapter 14 of the *Biographia Literaria*. In Reed's estimation, Coleridge's famous recipe for the mixture of natural and supernatural modes, which he said he and Wordsworth concocted in 1798, is largely the product of later views and retrospective wishful thinking. Reed also notes in passing that the only literary plan which can be demonstrated as occupying much of the two poets' conscious intention in late 1797 and early 1798 is that of *The Recluse*, a philosophical masterwork "on Man, on Nature, and on Human Life," which Wordsworth said would receive all his "eloquence" for the next year and a half at least.[4] Reed does not describe this other plan, because it is not his object of study, nor have others, either in itself or in its relation to the *Lyrical Ballads*, for the very good reason that it is very hard to find such a plan. The most complete one we have also derives from Coleridge's writings of twenty years later and is if anything even more affected by retrospective views and second thoughts than his account of the origin of *Lyrical Ballads*. But we are now in a better position, by extrapolating from recently published texts of the *Recluse* extant in 1798,[5] to say what its plan or intention was, and, having done so, to see how it relates to a similarly extrapolated (i.e., unprefaced) plan of the 1798 *Lyrical Ballads*. The result of this juxtaposition sets Wordsworth's achievement in that volume in a new light, complementary both to his own and Coleridge's accounts and to the refinements recent scholarship has shed upon them.

The Recluse was many things besides a simple failure or an unrealized literary project. Philosophically, it was an epic project based on the faith that its three constituent topics — Man, Nature, and Society — existed in a mutually positive and ultimately redemptive relationship. A fruitful relationship between the individual perceiving mind and the world of natural phenomena would extend outward by a kind of developmental or evolutionary force into the moral relations of one human being with another in society, or civilization. Artistically, *The Recluse* was to have been, in Coleridge's later words, "the first great *philosophical* poem" in English, meaning that it would supplant the last great *religious* epic in the language, Milton's *Paradise Lost*. Biographically and compositionally, it was Wordsworth's attempt to repay with deepest gratitude Coleridge's recognition of his genius, by writing the cultural masterpiece on which they pinned their hopes of his literary immortality. And historically, it is a central example of one of the deepest impulses of literary Romanticism: to produce an epic work that would have redemptive force for modern, secular man, compensating for the demise of revealed religion by creating the mythical text of a new religion of humanism. Goethe's *Faust*, Whitman's *Leaves of Grass*, Blake's *Jerusalem*, Shelley's *Prometheus Unbound,* and Beethoven's symphonies are all, in their disparate ways, examples of the same impulse, among many others that could be cited.

Given so many large and various burdens, it is not surprising that *The Recluse* failed to get written. Or rather, that it was produced in large, fragmentary sections whose unified relationship has presented a daunting challenge to subsequent readers (as have all other examples of Romantic epic pretensions). But no one who has studied *The Recluse* texts carefully, from William Minto and Emile Legouis in the late nineteenth century, to John Alban Finch, Beth Darlington, Jonathan Wordsworth, and myself in the late twentieth, has been content to accept the easy dismissal that it is a nonexistent failure simply because it was not finally produced in the shape projected by Wordsworth and Coleridge in 1798. Helen Darbishire's witty attempt to dismiss it, as consisting of "little more than a prelude to the main theme, and an excursus from it," is self-refuting, since any poem containing both a poet's posthumous masterpiece (*The Prelude*) and his contemporary magnum opus (*The Excursion*) can hardly, at nearly twenty thousand lines of text, be treated as if it did not exist.[6]

But though some of these dimensions of *The Recluse* must have been the subject of Wordsworth's and Coleridge's conversation and the object of their most ambitious thoughts, the only evidence of its status in 1798 that exists today, on paper, are the four poems which constituted the "1300 lines" of poetry to which Wordsworth referred in announcing the beginning of his new epic task to friends. These poems are now known as *The Ruined Cottage, The Old Cumberland Beggar, A Night-Piece,* and the lines on the

Discharged Veteran which appear at the end of book 4 of *The Prelude*. These poems in their original form give clear evidence of Wordsworth's efforts, difficulties, and initial failure to write the projected *Recluse*. His task, in a nutshell, was to incorporate a metaphysical faith in the existence of spontaneous, unmediated grace—symbolized by images of natural beauty—with an ethics of humane concern for all human beings, no matter how lowly or outcast. And the characters of the first *Recluse* poems show that he set himself to his task in the most difficult way possible, for they represent some of the most miserably suffering human beings observable in England in the late 1790s: an old, senile beggar; an indigent discharged veteran suffering from diseases contracted while on service in the West Indies (subduing slave rebellions on the rich British sugar plantations); and, in *The Ruined Cottage*, the distraught wife, or widow, of another veteran, wasting away through delirium to death as she waits in vain for her husband's return. Around such "views" of Man and Society, Wordsworth was attempting to construct a coherent philosophical framework in which his "views" could be positively interpreted in the light of the beauty and sublimity of visual images of external nature. To justify the ways of man to Nature, as it were.

And by March of 1798 he was failing in this effort. Indeed, his letters to friends announcing the beginning of *The Recluse* and his intention to devote himself to it for the next year and a half must in fact mark the *end* of his first concentrated efforts to compose it, for he did not write any more poetry intended for *The Recluse* until almost two years later, when he began *Home at Grasmere* in celebration of his return to the Lake District with Dorothy after their extremely unhappy sojourn in Germany. Of course, their landlord's notice that they must quit Alfoxden House provided an immediate reason for his breaking off work on *The Recluse*. But there are other reasons as well, reasons so powerful that they must have made the quit notice a welcome relief and the idea of a trip to Germany with Coleridge (to learn more about the German Idealist philosophy which was the main source of Coleridge's ideas for *The Recluse*) look like a noble and necessary detour. In the event, composition and publication of *Lyrical Ballads* was undertaken immediately, in the somewhat dreamy expectation that proceeds from its sale would help defray the expenses of their trip.

But Wordsworth's failure on *The Recluse* in January and February of 1798 was not a failure of poetic power. On the contrary, it was a triumph of poetic power unleashed—but uncontained. *The Ruined Cottage* was the first poem Wordsworth had written which can be called "major" without qualification. Coleridge never forgot its impact on him; it alone may have convinced him that Wordsworth, not he, had the artistic genius necessary to become the author of a culture-wide philosophical epic like *The Recluse*. But *The Ruined Cottage* and the other first *Recluse* poems have a power which tends to knock readers out of the framework of poetry, or art, altogether, making "enjoyment" seem a superfluous if not scandalous consideration (akin to Aristotle's concern over the nature of the pleasure we derive from tragedy), and raising questions about the need for social action which are always potentially revolutionary, and not only in the repressive political atmosphere of England in 1798. Wordsworth's failure was thus not a failure of inspiration, nor of creation, but a failure to fit his productions into recognizable poetic form, especially given the optimistic philosophical burdens *The Recluse* was to shoulder, since these first efforts tended more to contradict than to confirm the operation of a benign grace in human existence. Such a failure is no disgrace but quite the contrary: a noble failure in Romanticism's doomed heroic effort, that art should minister to human need by finding or persuasively establishing a necessary or plausible connection between the world of nature and the world of man, an effort manifested in a variety of ways throughout the nineteenth century's attempt to establish a new religion of art. In short, Wordsworth had arrived at a philosophical impasse, and that is exactly where one does arrive in trying to establish a self-evident and positively meaningful connection between natural processes and human or cultural ones. Nor did Wordsworth abandon his effort precipitously; he spent almost another twenty years, inspired by the idea of *The Recluse,* trying to show how "Love of Nature leads to Love of Mankind." But it does not, at least not in any logically demonstrable way. Ironically, we may be closer today to establishing the necessary loving link between man and nature, by the negative force of the superhumanly compelling logics of nuclear or ecological destruction, than through the optimistic faith in Nature held by the first Romantics.

We might expect the first four *Recluse* poems to have a significant relation to other poems Wordsworth was composing about the same time, and this is exactly what we do find in regard to his contributions to the *Lyrical Bal-*

lads of 1798. The burden of my argument is that we see in Wordsworth's lyrical ballads of 1798 the triumphs of a failure. That is, some very successful poems—successful especially in aesthetic wholeness, poetic closure, and generic identity—that emerged from his failure to get on with *The Recluse*, which carry nevertheless—vicariously as it were—the power of the inspiration behind *The Recluse* even as they disguise some of the troubling philosophical and political implications of that power in slighter, more conventional forms.

Prompted by his landlord's notice and the desire to make some money for his trip to Germany, Wordsworth turned, in early March 1798, from his grand but doomed plans for a philosophical epic poem to the much more satisfying expedient of writing shorter poems—lyrics and ballads—with conventional forms and conventional expectations, which he could finish and feel that his readers would recognize as finished poems, even though he hinted in his preface that they might "look round for poetry, and be induced to enquire by what species of courtesy these attempts can be permitted to assume that title." No reviewer of the volume, even the least favorable, swallowed that bait, or went so far as to declare that its contents were *not poems*. But if they had had the poems' relation to *The Recluse* set clearly before them, many would have done so. Indeed, part of the enduring controversy provoked by Wordsworth's long preface to the second edition of *Lyrical Ballads* in 1800 may be accounted for, not only by the force, splendor, and sheer wrong-headedness of some of his claims, but by the fact that the preface has a rhetorical range and elevation much more appropriate to a grand cultural edifice like *The Recluse* than to the predominantly small and apparently naive poems in *Lyrical Ballads*. The key subject terms of *The Recluse* can frequently be observed in the preface's language, as when Wordsworth refers to "the most valuable object of all writing, whether in prose or in verse, the great and universal passions of men [Man], the most general and interesting of their occupations [Society], and the entire world of nature [Nature]." Similarly, Wordsworth's wonderful description of the ideal character of the Poet, added in 1802, carries much more force in the light of *The Prelude,* his masterpiece "on the growth of my own mind," than it does as an introductory statement to all but the most elevated of *Lyrical Ballads*. This discrepancy between the preface and the poems, rather than the poems alone, provoked reviewers enormously and continuously and is still part of the ongoing cultural life of *Lyrical Ballads* today.

Finished, in the sense of satisfactorily concluded, is precisely what the four *Recluse* poems of early 1798 are *not*, powerful thought they are: finished, that is, in the sense of providing the reader with the persuasive philosophical explanations—that their rhetorical mode of blank verse seriousness leads us to expect—of the kind of world it is that allows such suffering to exist, or the kind of world we should be building to alleviate it. But finished, in the sense of coming to "The End" in a recognizably satisfactory way, is just what Wordsworth's lyrical ballads of 1798 *are*: the same persons and issues are present, but the rhetorical treatment and genres do not lead us to expect a "conclusion" in the sense of a comprehensive philosophical or political explanation.

Wordsworth repeatedly flirts with the difference between these two kinds of endings, or "issuings," as in the lines from *Simon Lee*: "O reader! had you in your mind / Such stores as *silent thought* can bring, / O gentle reader! you would find / A tale in every thing" (emphasis added). The narrator protests that his account of old Simon's pain "is no tale; but should you *think,* / Perhaps a tale you'll make it" (emphasis added).[7] Throughout Wordsworth's contributions to the 1798 volume, words like "think," "thought," and "reason" are used as shorthand substitutes or stand-ins for the absent but implied philosophical system which was to inform *The Recluse,* which would account for the wide discrepancy between natural beauty and human moral ugliness. For example: "*think,* ye farmers all, I pray, / Of Goody Blake and Harry Gill" (emphasis added). The simple ballad form does not lead us to expect that the farmers' thoughts should be represented in the poem, but what if they were? What would be the issue, and where would "The End" be, if all landed farmers in England in 1798 were to think systematically about their responsibility for indigent persons like Goody Blake squatting on their lands? Or again, both the failure and the poignancy of Wordsworth's efforts to write *The Recluse* are refracted through the famous refrain of the *Lines Written in Early Spring*: "If such be of my creed the plan [that Nature is a consciously beneficent force] . . . / Have I not *reason* to lament / What man has made of man?" (emphasis added). Indeed he does, but the form of his poetic utterance also gives him a reason, or a literary convention, for not pursuing such reasons in a lyric celebrating the advent of spring. If he did pursue them, he might have so much "reason" to "lament / What man has made of man" that he would be forced to give up the *plan* of his *creed* (i.e., his philosophical or theological system) altogether. And finally, the philosophical weight of *The Recluse,* present but buried in *Lyrical Ballads,* is manifested with magnificently strange effect in the whole tissue of negative rhetorical constructions by which *Tintern Abbey,* the last and in every sense culminating poem of the 1798 volume, urges itself along to its deeply affirmative conclusion, like a doubter's Lord's Prayer: "If this be but a vain belief," "Not for this faint I, nor mourn nor murmur," "Nor perchance, / If I were not thus taught," "Nor, perchance— / If I should be where I no more can hear / Thy voice," "Nor wilt thou then forget." It is precisely the *dubiety* of thought and belief, of teaching and of faith, that paradoxically underscores *Tintern Abbey*'s natural religion; and it is, I am suggesting, the multilayered and deeply felt presence of the failed *Recluse* just under the surface of almost all Wordsworth's poems in the 1798 *Lyrical Ballads* that helps to account for their strange power—as much as the rationale offered in his preface of 1800.

How could the powerful but invisible relation between these two important poetic projects be demonstrated? It is not of course surprising that the fame of *Lyrical Ballads* has obscured the important place of *The Recluse* in Wordsworth's poetic development, despite the latter's precedence both in chronology and, to a considerable degree, in aesthetic merit. *Lyrical Ballads* is a finished, published document that went through many editions and provoked endless critical controversy, whereas *The Recluse* is a grandiose but largely failed poetical-philosophical idea, no more than half published (part posthumously), and more provocative of ridicule than of critical controversy strictly speaking. Moreover, in marked contrast to my argument that *Lyrical Ballads* and the polemical milieu Wordsworth and Coleridge created around it are in large part a displacement from the goals and hopes originally intended for *The Recluse,* other critics and scholars, commenting on the obvious differences between the two kinds of poetry in question, have drawn the relation between these two texts in much more negative, contrastive terms.[8]

But I believe we can see Wordsworth transferring the vexed but enabling power of *The Recluse*'s philosophical and political burdens and its generic ambiguity (was it to be an epic? a narrative? meditative verse essay?) into the smaller poetic forms and conventions of *Lyrical Ballads* by a single, simple strategy: dividing his work on *The Recluse* into essentially two different types of poems. These are, first, his five lyrics of meditative natural description, all identified with the same initial title word, "Lines," designating their conventionally informal, sketchy, and occasionally epigrammatic quality, and situating their utterance with sometimes exhaustive precision, from the "Lines Left upon a Seat in a Yew-tree, which stands near the Lake of Esthwaite, on a desolate Part of the Shore, commanding a beautiful Prospect" to the "Lines Written a Few Miles above Tintern Abbey, on Revisiting the Banks of the Wye during a Tour. July 13, 1798." Second, there are his ballads or tales, ten in all, about suffering poor people, especially mothers and fathers and children, comprising (with the addition of Coleridge's *Rime of the Ancient Mariner*) most of the poems that are usually understood to be the "lyrical ballads" of the title: that is, more or less mysterious narratives involving ordinary people but written in much more intricate and various rhyme schemes than those typical of the authentic folk ballad. There are, in addition, four "dialogue" poems, printed together in two pairs, which partake of, or point toward, the double thematic aspect comprised by the main division into lyrics and ballads. Wordsworth wrote fourteen of these nineteen poems between March and July of 1798, but my description of his two generic types extends also to the five he wrote earlier: two sets of "Lines" (on the yew-tree seat, and "at Evening"), and three narratives which, though not strictly ballads, anticipate his 1798 experiments in that vein. One of these (*Old Man Travelling*) was, moreover, originally part of one of *The Recluse* poems, *The Old Cumberland Beggar,* and I shall make use of another of these three, *The Convict,* to clinch my argument, by showing how the difficulty in making it conform to this division of the volume is in fact the exception that helps to prove the rule.

Why this division into two markedly different kinds of poems? Let us remember that Wordsworth's task in writing *The Recluse* was to integrate a metaphysics of spontaneous grace—symbolized by images of natural beauty—with an ethics of humane concern for all human beings—signally represented by some of the most miserably suffering persons observable in England in the late 1790s. His understandable failure in this task is masked in *Lyrical Ballads,* even as the effort is continued, by relegating each of its terms to separate poetic types in which the reader's expectation of a comprehensive philosophical explanation is submerged or distracted, even as the central (integrative) issue is alluded to in the various poems' tendency to echo each other's concerns, as in Wordsworth's use of the pointed question

"Have I not reason to lament / What man has made of man?" as a refrain in a lyric celebrating the coming of spring. Furthermore, the "plan" of *The Recluse* (see the table) is present in Wordsworth's calculated placement and juxtaposition of his nineteen poems throughout the 1798 volume—the actual, observable "plan" of *Lyrical Ballads,* one with a much stronger deducible relationship to *The Recluse* than to either Wordsworth's or Coleridge's comments about their controversial volume and its various plans and intentions.

In such a tabulation, Wordsworth's pattern of sequence and alternation is quite clear, especially as one moves backward and forward from the strategically placed pairs of dialogue poems. They are separated by the long

A Plan for Wordsworth's Lyrical Ballads, 1798

Genre	Poem
— [C]	[*The Ancient Mariner*]
— [C]	[*Foster Mother's Tale*]
L	*LINES (on a Yew-tree Seat)*
— [C]	[*The Nightingale*]
B/N	*The Female Vagrant*
B	*Goody Blake and Harry Gill*
L	*LINES (First Mild Day)*
B	*Simon Lee*
D	*Anecdote for Fathers*
D	*We Are Seven*
L	*LINES (Early Spring)*
B	*The Thorn*
B	*The Last of the Flock*
— [C]	[*The Dungeon*]
B	*The Mad Mother*
B	*The Idiot Boy*
L	*LINES (Written at Evening)*
D	*Expostulation & Reply*
D	*The Tables Turned*
B/N	*Old Man Travelling*
B	*Complaint of a Forsaken Indian Woman*
N?/L?	*The Convict*
L	*LINES (above Tintern Abbey)*

Key: B = ballad; L = lyric/"lines"; D = dialogue; N = other narrative; C = Coleridge.

stretch of Wordsworth's parent–child "mad songs" at the very heart of the volume, which has a transitional set of "lines" before and after it, the first lamenting what man has made of man (in contrast to what Nature makes of Spring), and the second (*Lines written . . . at Evening*) lamenting poets' difficulty in celebrating anything in Nature that does not lead to thoughts of death. Furthermore, before the first set of dialogue poems and after the last, there is a roughly inverted parallel sequence, of "lines" merging into ballads, and then of ballads leading out to culminating "lines," in which commentary on the meaning of natural beauty and narrative on the fact of human suffering are effectively counterpointed—presuming, that is, one wants to see and feel the contrast as point–counterpoint and not mere undifferentiated difference. Finally, the two pairs of dialogue poems are pointedly set together *as* pairs in significant ways, and not only by their positioning in the volume. They are considerably lighter in tone than almost all the other poems in the volume, yet they have a discernible function that relates them to the more serious poems, in that they are conversational or anecdotal *enactments* of the principle of dialogue, or dialectic, operative between the other two kinds of poems, thus marking the trail of their legacy from *The Recluse*. The dialogue poems represent internally Wordsworth's two main kinds of contribution to *Lyrical Ballads,* by presenting conversations between speakers representing ordinary, conventional, commonsense views of reality, and speakers representing the extraordinary, unconventional, and even visionary possibilities immanent within ordinary reality. To the extent that they juxtapose fundamentally different views of reality or choices about life, they offer to implicate the reader in the dialogic nature of the entire volume. And they do this in a nice sequence also, since the first two present children confounding the merely calculating logic of "commonsense" adults, while the last two present both sides of an argument between two educated adults on qualitative versus quantitative uses of human time.

As with the four poems written for *The Recluse* in January–February 1798, the narrative element bulks much larger in Wordsworth's contributions to *Lyrical Ballads* than the lyric element. But the explanatory or interpretive burden carried by his ballads of March–July is much less than that of the *Recluse* poems, particularly *The Ruined Cottage* and *The Old Cumberland Beggar,* which nearly break down under the weight of the commentary Wordsworth tries to make them bear. The success or failure of Wordsworth's experiments in narrative technique in his ballads of 1798 has always been one of the most prominent topics in critical discussion of his work. But, by comparison with the narrator–auditor situation in the *Recluse* poems, his lyrical ballads are far simpler, a simplicity Wordsworth achieved by radically reducing, or cutting out altogether, the function of the bystanding auditor who "hears" the tale of woe and "tells" it to the reader. In the *Recluse* poems, this narrator is a sensitive young man, essentially similar to Wordsworth himself, who feels severely threatened by the sadness of the stories he hears. In the original version (1797) of *The Ruined Cottage,* he is devastated almost to the point of nervous breakdown by the story of Margaret's sufferings; in the version of early 1798—the version most properly associated with *The Recluse*—he is shielded from this massive depression by a wise old Pedlar who narrates her tale to him and who, in Wordsworth's additions of 1798, interpolates a message of healing calm that places Margaret's sufferings in a larger vision of ongoing natural processes, symbolized by some weeds and grasses the Pedlar once saw "silver'd o'er" by drops of dew and mist as he passed her ruined cottage.

But in Wordsworth's ballads of 1798 there is little danger of such "contamination" from the suffering object to the narrating subject of the poems, since the narrator is very little present. In most of them, a poor, old, decrepit or deranged person tells his or her life story to a bypassing interlocutor whose presence is barely necessary to get the story going ("I followed him, and said, 'My friend, / What ails you? wherefore weep you so?'") and whose reactions to it are represented very minimally, if at all, in the poem. In the ten ballads (or narratives, more generally, since only seven of them are really in ballad form), the narrative situation ranges from no external narrator at all, as in *The Complaint of the Forsaken Indian Woman,* to the highly involved narrator of *The Convict*—whose high degree of involvement is, I will suggest, the main reason the poem is so unsuccessful. In between, along this narrative spectrum, there are three poems (*The Female Vagrant, The Last of the Flock,* and *The Mad Mother*) with almost no narrator, except to ask the question or set the scene that gets the story going. In the center of this spectrum, we find the highly problematic narrators of *The Thorn* and *The Idiot Boy,* whose character and degree of comprehension of the events they narrate has quite properly been the focus of most of the critical controversy over the success of Wordsworth's narrative experiments. Moving toward the more "involved" end of the narrative range, we have two poems, *Goody Blake* and *Simon Lee,* whose narrator says almost as little as in the former group of three but whose comments seem more weighty because they come at the end as well as the beginning of the story and thus have the effect of an interpretation on the events narrated.

Old Man Travelling is the hardest poem to place on this spectrum, and Wordsworth's treatment of it suggests he was well aware of the specific nature of the difficulty it presents. The narrator says quite a lot at the beginning of this "sketch," heavily interpretive of the "patience" and "perfect peace" of the slow-moving old beggar: but the original last six lines, spoken by the old man, about traveling to visit his dying son in a naval hospital, appear to question so radically the benign interpretation of his life offered by the narrator that the poem, for most readers, is broken into two contradictory parts. Wordsworth recognized this flaw and subsequently excised the last six lines altogether, in keeping with the overall narrative strategy observable in his lyrical ballads (relative to the *Recluse* poems) but in reverse: instead of reducing the role of the narrator to a minimum, he thus reduced the speaking voice of the suffering object to nil. In a very similar way, he created *The Female Vagrant* by cutting it out of a larger poem, *Adventures on Salisbury Plain,* in which the wandering woman meets a fugitive sailor and they spend the night telling each other the story of their unmerited sufferings. This extended narrative is in turn embedded in a Rousseauistic framework which considers suffering in "advanced" societies worse than that in primitive ones because in the latter the sufferers do not know what they are missing, not having fallen from any higher state. But this psychohistorical interpretation is both turgid and tentative, as Wordsworth recognized by not publishing the whole poem until 1842, and then only as an example of his juvenile efforts and under a new title, *Guilt and Sorrow,* which highlights the emotional effects rather than the social causes of the two protagonists' suffering.

The "lines" or lyrics in this descriptive division of Wordsworth's labors on *Lyrical Ballads* are half as many in number and proportionately much shorter than the ballads, as befits their genre, except for their lengthy descriptive titles. They are placed at roughly equal intervals throughout the volume, every three to five poems, thus forming a pattern of hopeful, optimistic belief in the natural beneficence of this world, counterpointing the intervening tales of unrelieved human suffering. Just as Wordsworth keeps *interpretive* commentary to a minimum in his ballads of 1798, so in most of these "lines" he keeps to a minimum any *narrative* explanation of the speaker's situation, so that they tend to become full, or total, interpretive credal statements about "seeing into the life of things" through natural forms.

But the "lines" adhere less purely to this division of poetic kinds than the ballads; as I have already suggested, they tend to echo or hint at the larger cultural, political, and philosophical implications behind the *Lyrical Ballads*. This is clearest in the mournful refrain which cuts across the otherwise self-indulgently playful *Lines Written in Early Spring*: "Have I not reason to lament / What man has made of man?" Similarly, in the closely parallel "lines" on "the first mild day of March," the minimal domestic situation seems to have no historical context at all, except for readers who—and there were many more of these in 1798 than there are today—might think, on hearing of the "living Calendar" the speaker proposes to establish with his sister, about that other new calendar, still in force in Directory France, which changed March to Germinal under the authority of a similar ideology: "Love, now a universal birth, / From heart to heart is stealing." But this speaker specifically excludes the rationalistic universalism of the French Revolution in favor of personal emotion: "It is the hour of feeling"—not, let us say, the Age of Reason.

Wordsworth's "Lines" poems in *Lyrical Ballads* may be said to converge upon the *Lines Written a Few Miles above Tintern Abbey* from many directions and in many ways, all contributing to the greatly conclusive effect of that magnificent poem. It is so complex and masterful a creation that I do not have space enough here to say much about it, except by way of comparison with some of Wordsworth's other "lines" and especially with the badly flawed but deeply similar poem, *The Convict*, which immediately precedes it. Like the two spring lyrics, *Tintern Abbey* alludes to themes from Wordsworth's ballads of suffering, in its references to "vagrant dwellers in the houseless woods" and "the still, sad music of humanity," thus continuing the echo effect by which Wordsworth's beautiful nature lyrics remind the reader of the contrasting themes present in the volume.

The very first set of "lines," those ostensibly written upon a yew-tree seat on a shore in the English Lake District, point suggestively toward the lines above Tintern Abbey, for they describe the failed life history of a young man, "a favoured Being," whose virtuously ambitious hopes closely parallel those of Wordsworth, and with a similar fate. Disappointed in his efforts at worldly success, he retired from the world "With indignation . . . , / And with the food of pride sustained his soul / In solitude." But Nature's beauty could still make him remember "those Beings to whose minds / Warm from the labours of benevolence / The world, and human life, appeared a scene / Of kindred loveliness." Establishing such a sense of "kinship" between a similar triad of Man, Nature, and Human Life was of course the hard mission set for *The Recluse,* and the discouraging attitudes of the world at large to this young man's hopes ("dissolute tongues, and jealousy, and hate, / And scorn") are close enough to those against which Wordsworth says, in *Tintern Abbey,* Nature will protect Dorothy as it has protected him: "evil tongues, / Rash judgments . . . the sneers of selfish men, / . . . greetings where no kindness is."

The moral value of natural beauty is interpreted retroactively for the builder of the yew-tree seat, but in the *Lines Written While Sailing in a Boat at Evening,* Wordsworth attempted a prospective statement of Nature's redeeming power, and the difficulties he experienced are illuminating in the present discussion. These lines tend to break down, or apart, for lack of the poet's ability to find a meaning in his various natural metaphors for human life—the setting sun, the flowing river—that does *not* lead to associated thoughts of death and dissolution. His problems multiply when he switches from talking about nature to talking about poetry, for he finds himself mourning when he wishes to be celebrating: the death of James Thomson, the death (and well-known insanity) of William Collins, the passing of history, "*later* ditties" generally (what Walter Jackson Bate and Harold Bloom have called "the burden of the past" or sense of "belatedness" which fell heavily upon Romantic poets)—all lead to "The End" in a way that Wordsworth wishes to avoid, and he can only pray for a moment suspended out of time, symbolized by the repeated image of the boat's "suspended" oar. The whole lifetime of Dorothy Wordsworth functions as a similar (though considerably extended) moment of suspension at the end of *Tintern Abbey,* but in a more successfully artistic way, thanks to Wordsworth's much more sophisticated handling of his preparatory natural images. He recognized the difficulties that still remained in the 1798 version of the *Lines Written . . . at Evening,* and he solved them in the 1800 edition in a way very similar to his bold excision of the original ending of *Old Man Travelling*: he cut the poem in two parts and in all subsequent editions published them as two separate poems, the first two stanzas with the original title, the last three as *Remembrance of Collins Composed upon the Thames near Richmond.* This drastic surgery did not "solve" the residual philosophical problem of either poem, of course—namely, that love of nature and love of mankind (or of poets in particular) have no necessarily positive connection—but it did have the considerable benefit, for Wordsworth, of isolating the two parts the problem he was wrestling with in his *Lyrical Ballads* in their implicit connection to the *Recluse* project: writing poems of metaphysical faith in the meaning of natural beauty and poems of humane concern about the significance of human suffering. In this sense, his division of the *Lines Written while Rowing in a Boat at Evening* can symbolize his entire division of his work on *The Recluse* into the two main poetic types of the 1798 *Lyrical Ballads*.[9]

Finally, some of the usefulness and, I hope, the validity of this kind of descriptive analysis may be demonstrated by comparing Wordsworth's worst poem in *Lyrical Ballads, The Convict,* with his best one, the lines written above Tintern Abbey. That *The Convict* is Wordsworth's worst is confirmed by the poet's own judgment: he cut it from the second edition of *Lyrical Ballads* and never published it again. It is a sort of companion piece to Coleridge's *The Dungeon*—significantly, in that they are the only two poems in the 1798 volume to approach social commentary directly.

THE CONVICT

The glory of evening was spread through the west;
   —On the slope of a mountain I stood,
While the joy that precedes the calm season of rest
   Rang loud through the meadow and wood.   4

"And must we then part from a dwelling so fair?"
   In the pain of my spirit I said,
And with a deep sadness I turned, to repair
   To the cell where the convict is laid.   8

The thick-ribb'd walls that o'ershadow the gate
   Resound; and the dungeons unfold:
I pause; and at length, through the glimmering grate,
   The outcast of pity behold.   12

His black matted head on his shoulder is bent,
   And deep is the sigh of his breath,

And with steadfast dejection his eyes are intent
    On the fetters that link him to death.   16

'Tis sorrow enough on that visage to gaze,
    That body dismiss'd from his care;
Yet my fancy has pierced to his heart, and pourtrays
    More terrible images there.   20

His bones are consumed, and his life-blood is dried,
    With wishes the past to undo;
And his crime, through the pains that o'erwhelm him, descried,
    Still blackens and grows on his view.   24

When from the dark synod, or blood-reeking field,
    To his chamber the monarch is led,
All soothers of sense their soft virtue shall yield,
    And quietness pillow his head.   28

But if grief, self-consumed, in oblivion would doze,
    And conscience her tortures appease,
'Mid tumult and uproar this man must repose;
    In the comfortless vault of disease.   32

When his fetters at night have so press'd on his limbs,
    That the weight can no longer be borne,
If, while a half-slumber his memory bedims,
    The wretch on his pallet should turn,   36

While the jail-mastiff howls at the dull clanking chain,
    From the roots of his hair there shall start
A thousand sharp punctures of cold-sweating pain,
    And the terror shall leap at his heart.   40

But now he half-raises his deep-sunken eye,
    And the motion unsettles a tear;
The silence of sorrow it seems to supply,
    And asks of me why I am here.   44

"Poor victim! no idle intruder has stood
  "With o'erweening complacence our state to compare,
"But one, whose first wish is the wish to be good,
  "Is come as a brother thy sorrows to share.   48

"At thy name though compassion her nature resign,
  "Though in virtue's proud mouth thy report be a stain,
"My care, if the arm of the mighty were mine,
  "Would plant thee where yet thou might'st blossom again."   52

A large part of the failure of *The Convict* can be explained by reference to Wordsworth's compositional difficulties with *The Recluse,* for it is the only one of his ten ballads or narratives of suffering in which the narrator both directly addresses the suffering person *and* offers directly to comment interpretively on the causes or meaning of his suffering. It is also the only one of the ten in which the suffering person is both physically present and completely silent, resembling, in this respect, *The Old Cumberland Beggar* (and the *revised* form of its "overflow" into *Lyrical Ballads, Old Man Travelling*) and, by extension, *The Ruined Cottage.* The situation in *The Convict* is similar to what would have obtained if the young man in *The Ruined Cottage* had come upon Margaret in the last days of her decline, without the company of the Pedlar or the benefit of his philosophical long views, and had tried to say some kind, reassuring words to her. Thus *The Convict,* which dates from 1796 or earlier, the period of Wordsworth's most intense recoil from his political activism, can help us appreciate how much Wordsworth had already achieved by way of universalized human narratives, as distinct from immediate political protests, in his *Recluse* poems. And *Tintern Abbey,* which, amazingly, follows it immediately at the end of the 1798 volume, though the two poems seem to come from entirely different artistic universes, shows us how much further he could go in this direction, eliding the social stresses inherent in his material while linking them to the humanist myth of natural inspiration which informs his most characteristic poetic voice. There may appear to be a correlation here, between growing political conservatism and increased poetic skill, but it is misleading: Wordsworth was still a strong liberal or humane republican in 1798, though moving consistently away from his earlier radicalism. *The Convict* is in fact more of a "liberal" poem (in the pejorative sense of merely expressing wishful good intentions) than a radical one, but Wordsworth's decision to cut it from his oeuvre is justifiable on artistic grounds—as was his excision of the more truly radical but still bombastic antiwar sentiments from *The Female Vagrant* in 1800.

The Convict opens with its narrator in a mood of regret at what man has made of man, as he turns from "The glory of evening . . . spread through the west," to the stark—and gratuitous—contrast of the convict, seen through "the glimmering grate." To draw this moral tension as tightly as possible, Wordsworth has the narrator move directly from his picturesque viewing station to a conveniently nearby prison, where it even appears (from lines 9–12) that he has deliberately asked for the prisoner to be brought forth for his contemplation. There may have been a conventional fashion for this kind of moralistic tableau vivant, to which Wordsworth alludes in the poem's last two quatrains, but using *Tintern Abbey* as a template for comparison with this narrative situation, we may say that Wordsworth in *The Convict* turns very abruptly from a scene of natural beauty to a highly articulated scene of human distress, thus causing an abrupt shift in tone, which, in *Tintern Abbey,* is managed much more gradually, by building up slowly through the conjectures, objections, and qualifications of his long verse paragraphs until he can smoothly achieve the harmonic moral chord, or tonic, of "the still, sad music of humanity." The convict is also a more palpably pitiable human object than the "vagrant dwellers in the houseless woods" in *Tintern Abbey,* though his narrator has also, already, begun to "see into the life of things," albeit with a less original rhetoric: "my fancy has pierced to his heart, and pourtrays / More terrible images there" (19–20).

Wordsworth intensifies the convict's psychic tortures in the poem's curious long center section (25–40) by comparing them to the pampered treatment received by royal criminals, but by this point in the poem the grotesque contrast between the suffering convict and the glorious sunset has been drawn out so excruciatingly as to destroy altogether its effectiveness *as* a contrast, and we begin to wonder what the point of it all is. It is very much to Wordsworth's credit, and very much a part of his development into poetic greatness, that he begins to wonder the same thing and, moreover, builds his wondering right into the texture of his verse, asking himself, in effect, the most damaging question that can be put to any lyric expression: "So what?" The convict raises his head, dislodging a tear, "And asks of me why I am here." To what does all this delineation of human suffering lead, especially in its explicit comparison with the glory, joy, and calm of Nature described in the first stanza? This question, we should note, is precisely the question Wordsworth does *not* put in the mouths of any of his other suffering human creatures in the ballads of 1798, and for good reason. Imagine what would happen to *The Female Vagrant,* or *Simon Lee, or The Mad Mother,* or *The Last of the Flock* if any of those speakers should suddenly turn, at the end of their story, and ask the narrator what business it is of his, or what he intends to do about it. Disguising or subverting this disturbing possibility was also, in compositional terms, Wordsworth's most likely reason for creating the fictional, problematic, and apparently untrustworthy narrators of *The Idiot Boy* and *The Thorn.*

The narrator of *The Convict* begins his defense of his presence at the convict's cell—really a defense of the entire poem—by insisting that he is not "idle," not, that is, a moral prig blandly congratulating himself on the difference between his situation and that of the convict. The conventional moral lesson—"There but for the grace of God go I"—is not the one Wordsworth intends to draw. Rather, he addresses the convict in something of the prospectively redemptive way in which he addresses Dorothy at the end of *Tintern Abbey*—with obviously greater effectiveness there, since Dorothy is not imprisoned or otherwise in danger. This narrator expresses the same hope for future good, in defiance of conventional moral evils, represented here by hypocritical compassion and virtue, as they are represented in *Tintern Abbey* by jealous misunderstanding, "rash judgments," selfish sneering, and hypocritical "greetings where no kindness is."

But *Tintern Abbey* is a personal religious poem, whose private gestures of retreat from society are self-fulfilling and can thus serve to support its transcendental leaps of faith. *The Convict,* on the other hand, is a public, social poem, and though Wordsworth's rhetorical flourishes are equally grand—raising "the arm of the mighty"—they are fatally subjunctive. He can only wish the prisoner well, presumably by transportation to Australia, the specific form of prison reform probably alluded to in the poem's last line. We may also note that the action proposed for this apparently radical "arm" is expressed in horticultural rather than political terms: "Would plant thee where yet thou might'st blossom again." These are the first words of positive, natural, organic process to enter the poem since the first quatrain and constitute a shorthand symbolism, as we might now recognize, for

Wordsworth's faith in a moral interdependence between the world of nature and the world of mankind.

The long last paragraph of *Tintern Abbey* is also a defense against the speaker's possibly apparent "idleness" by invocation of a heretofore invisible bystanding sibling, the poet's sister. The narrator of *The Convict* tries to establish a similar relationship with the suffering person he contemplates: he "is come as a brother thy sorrows to share." Being one's brother's keeper is always a morally risky business and was especially so for Wordsworth in his poetry business of 1797–1798, by his own design. In his major effort on *The Recluse, The Ruined Cottage,* he had had his young narrator contemplate the ruin of another human being and had portrayed him as being so overcome by emotion at hearing the tale of Margaret that he could not appreciate the Pedlar's story *as* a story at all but instead sought relief in a much more intimate relation to Margaret than that of mere bystanding auditor: he leans over her garden wall, "and it seemed / To comfort me while with a brother's love / I blessed her in the impotence of grief." He is left in just such a position of impotence at the end of *The Convict,* wishfully indulging fantasies of power to no purpose, for lack of a real live sister for him to instruct, or for lack of a wise old Pedlar to instruct him in "that secret spirit of humanity" which still endures despite nature's "calm oblivious tendencies" and makes all the sorrow and grief of human ruin appear "an *idle* dream that could not live / Where meditation was" (emphasis added). This is the kind of meditation Wordsworth had not learned to construct when he finished *The Convict* but which he had learned, to a degree of mastery unsurpassed in the language, by the time he wrote *Tintern Abbey.* Between the two, he taught himself how, through his partly failed efforts to solve the huge philosophical and poetical problems posed by *The Recluse.* In *Tintern Abbey,* William and Dorothy can afford to ignore the sneering rash judgments of erstwhile London friends on their apparently escapist devotion to nature because they know they look on nature morally, "hearing oftentimes / The still, sad music of humanity." But the speaker of *The Convict* is much less successful, has in fact nothing more to say, must almost literally shut up at the point at which his poem ends, rather than concluding it more effectively, because he has attempted to draw *direct* and *immediate* connections between: (a) his appreciation of natural beauty, (b) his sensitivity to human suffering, and (c) his own function as commentator between the two, when he undertakes to respond to that portentous tear that "asks of me why I am here."

These were precisely the triangulated relationships, "on Man, on Nature, and on Human Life," that Wordsworth had, in his *Recluse* poems of early 1798, been trying to integrate and failing to, principally because of the problem of his narrating subject's "contamination" by the *affekt,* or emotional force, of the poor people whose suffering he tried to present objectively and interpret authoritatively. Thus it is not surprising that, learning his rental of Alfoxden was about to be terminated, Wordsworth quickly abandoned his heroic but failing efforts on *The Recluse* and, seizing on the idea of a joint publication with Coleridge that they had been talking about for months, turned gratefully to the smaller ballad and lyric forms of the poems he then composed between March and July, on which very much of his fame has come to rest.

He pursued these *comparatively* easier experiments successfully, even triumphantly, by the nice idea of separating the two themes—natural beauty and human morality—he had been trying unsuccessfully to integrate. The specific agency of separation was the expedient of removing, from between them as it were, his own narrating voice and presence, leaving him with his lyrical ballads of 1798: five sets of "Lines" in which he could expand upon his appreciation for natural beauty but say very little by way of explaining or applying its significance; ten ballads or other narratives in which the presence of the narrating subject is minimal, especially by way of offering explanatory comment on the human suffering he describes; and four dialogue poems, which allow "idle" and "serious" views of reality to address each other without issue but with a clear sense of victory for the "idle" party: "this one day / We'll give to idleness." Instead of fully integrating these themes in a single large poem, he could hope, by the artfully juxtaposed arrangements of his poems, that the reader would supply the necessary "thought," "thinking," or "reason" variously alluded to throughout the volume—in a word, its philosophy. The *Lyrical Ballads* are not *all* triumphant, of course, but even in the worst of them—and perhaps especially in that one—we can see clearly the seams of Wordsworth's magnificent effort of expediency, whereby he snatched his triumphs out of failure.

Some final caveats are in order on the status of the plan for Wordsworth's *Lyrical Ballads* which I have tried to excavate by following clues that lead out from *The Recluse.* As a "discovery" of the 1798 volume's literary coherence, it can only take its place in a long line of more or less persuasive arguments about the nature and quality of Wordsworth's achievement. Defense and criticism of Wordsworth's lyrical ballads is one of the longest running interpretive games in the profession, for the good and serious reasons stated at the outset, and I should be loath as well as presumptuous to try to close it down. Furthermore, my procedure, of looking at the volume from the "living and daily circumstances" of its compositional milieu without extensive prior reference to the claims made by Wordsworth in his preface of 1800, will to some critics seem a glaring and perverse oversight, requiring at the very least another stage of discussion: relating my conclusions to a thorough discussion of the preface's strengths and weaknesses. Nor should my argument be understood as a species of what is sometimes called "volume criticism," wherein the critic attempts to show how the placement and sequence of poems in a volume leads to certain calculated effects in the exfoliation of an organic whole. Quite apart from the fact that a plan which has lain undiscovered for nearly two hundred years cannot claim to be very effective, my own reading habits would disqualify me from making such a claim, since I never sit down and read a volume of poetry straight through from beginning to end. Though I believe the plan here exposed to light is operative on readers' experience of the volume, its interest lies more in its illumination of the texture of Wordsworth's poetic development.

Nonetheless, it is more likely than not that some plan such as the one I propose was working in Wordsworth's mind when he and Coleridge put together the first volume of *Lyrical Ballads*. For better or worse, deeply intricate and superficially obscure organizational plans are entirely characteristic of Wordsworth's practice at every stage of his career. His "Advertisement" for *Poems in Two Volumes* (1807), his preface to *The Excursion* (1814), and, most notoriously, his elaborate system of chronological and generic categories for his collected *Poems* in 1815, all share the same two characteristics: (a) carefully argued defenses of the volumes' plan of organization, which (b) most readers have found unpersuasive or irrelevant to the power of the individual poems in them. He hardly ever used the same plan twice. In the preface to *Lyrical Ballads,* his plan was mainly stylistic and linguistic; in *The Excursion,* it was based on the organic image of a Gothic cathedral; and in the *Poems* of 1815, it was a potpourri of literary, psychological, and topical categories. None of these plans has a more than occasional bearing on the poems in those volumes, unless one is willing to expend a great deal more effort, and sympathy, than most readers have been disposed to.

From a certain perspective, Wordsworth's entire career may be viewed as an effort to find a plan, or a system, capacious enough to contain the extremely various outpourings of his genius. I have been using the word "plan" fairly loosely throughout this essay, sometimes referring only to a plan of action the two poets had in view or a table of contents for their contributions to *Lyrical Ballads*; sometimes the word has a higher literary reference, as in Colerdige's claim to Cottle that his poems and Wordsworth's would, together, achieve an overall unity like that of an ode; and sometimes the word rises still higher, with reference to *The Recluse*, toward the idea of a philosophical or metaphysical *system*. All of these usages are also mingled in Wordsworth's own practice. If it is possible to be a powerfully philosophical thinker without being a particularly systematic one, Wordsworth is a good case in point, as he himself recognized in his defense of the ideal Poet, added to the preface in 1802, in which he asserted the power, steadiness, and sensitivity of a poet's thinking, instead of a "systematic defense" of his poetry and its theory, which he declines to undertake. Coleridge was of course much more systematic in the professional sense, but even he by the standards of academic philosophy (then as well as now) was much less systematic than most English professors give him credit for being, on the basis of his evident superiority to Wordsworth on this score. But behind this aspect of their relationship, too, and for all the brief but intense years of their creative symbiosis, they had the same object in view as they did when they paused, diverted momentarily by politically unsympathetic landlords, to write and organize their famous *Lyrical Ballads*: a huge cultural epic, "on Man, on Nature, and on Human Life," to be called *The Recluse*.

8

Reclaiming Dorothy Wordsworth's Legacy

BETH DARLINGTON

Editing Dorothy Wordsworth's journals for their first separate publication in 1897, William Knight found himself maddened by "numerous trivial details" she reported. Opting to delete some passages, he spluttered defensively, "Nothing is omitted of any literary or biographical value, but there is no need to record all the cases in which the sister wrote 'Today I mended William's shirts' or 'William gathered sticks' or 'I went in search of eggs' etc.!" Quoting this editorial apologia in her own journal, Katherine Mansfield tartly contradicts, "There is! Fool!!"[1] And there was. For Dorothy Wordsworth wove the pattern of her life in this simple homespun. Knight's impatience with her often prosaic style testifies to a certain impatience with her life, exposes his judgment that much of it, too, was trivial and did not bear chronicling. To merit the fuller record, Dorothy Wordsworth would have had to have lived in a different life, to have been someone else.

Thomas De Quincey appears to be the first critic to have imagined another Dorothy Wordsworth. The most famous passage in his delineation of her—a portrait that has proved nearly as evocative to Romanticists as the Mona Lisa to Walter Pater—presents her as he remembered her at their first meeting in 1807:

Immediately behind her [Mary Wordsworth], moved a lady, much shorter, much slighter, and perhaps, in all other respects, as different from her in personal characteristics as could have been wished, for the most effective contrast. "Her face was of Egyptian brown;" rarely, in a woman of English birth, had I seen a more determinate gipsy tan. Her eyes were not soft, as Mrs. Wordsworth's, nor were they fierce or bold; but they were wild and startling, and hurried in their motion. Her manner was warm and even ardent; her sensibility seemed constitutionally deep; and some subtle fire of impassioned intellect apparently burned within her, which, being alternately pushed forward into a conspicuous expression by the irrepressible instincts of her temperament, and then immediately checked, in obedience to the decorum of her sex and age, and her maidenly condition, (for she had rejected all offers of marriage out of pure sisterly regard to her brother and his children,) gave to her whole demeanour and to her conversation, an air of embarrassment and even of self-conflict, that was sometimes distressing to witness. Even her very utterance and enunciation often, or rather generally, suffered in point of clearness and steadiness, from the agitation of her excessive organic sensibility, and, perhaps, from some morbid irritability of the nerves. At times, the self-counteraction and self-baffling of her feelings, caused her even to stammer, and so determinately to stammer that a stranger who should have seen her and quitted her in that state of feeling, would have certainly set her down for one plagued with that infirmity of speech, as distressingly as Charles Lamb himself. This was Miss Wordsworth, the only sister of the poet—his "Dorothy".[2]

De Quincey's less well-known, subsequent reflection, however, introduces an alternative Dorothy Wordsworth, more independent, more rigorously focused intellectually, and more professionally committed to her writing: "it would have been far better had Miss Wordsworth condescended a little to the ordinary mode of pursuing literature: better for her own happiness if she *had* been a blue-stocking: or, at least, if she had been, in good earnest, a writer for the press, with the pleasant cares and solicitudes of one who has some little ventures, as it were, on that vast ocean."[3] Perhaps, modeling herself on such paragons as Lady Mary Wortley Montagu and Mrs. Anna Letitia Barbauld, this accomplished Miss Wordsworth would have troubled herself less to record the gathering of sticks, searching for eggs, and deliveries of dung for the garden at Town End, but would she have deigned to note, "The moon shone like herrings in the water"? In contending that Dorothy Wordsworth should have been someone else and done something else, De Quincey seems to invalidate her actual identity and achievements.

This dilemma is not uncommon for women writers. Recent feminist criticism charts a flagrant pattern of reactions to women's works, which Joanna Russ summarizes in *How to Suppress Women's Writing*: (a) she didn't write it; (b) she shouldn't have written it; (c) she shouldn't have written about that; or finally, (d) she is not really she—an artist—and it is not really it—a work of art.[4] Dorothy Wordsworth has drawn less attention than other women writers of her stature. Mary Ellmann, Ellen Moers, Patricia Meyer Spacks, Sandra Gilbert, and Susan Gubar, to name a few major critics in the field, all debar her in their examination of women writers, perhaps because she was not a published author in her own time (I exclude here her few poems printed in her brother's collections), perhaps because she does not quite conform to the paradigms they establish.[5] When critics do confront Dorothy Wordsworth, however, they are frequently preoccupied by what they deem to be lacking in her writing—what is not on the page rather than what is. She is reproved for not asserting her presence more forcefully in her prose, reprimanded for not being more historical or analytic, or disparaged for not writing poetry instead.

In 1940, equipped with scissors and paste, Hyman Eigerman resolved his disappointment with Dorothy Wordsworth by arranging selections from her journals as vers libre and printing them as *The Poetry of Dorothy Wordsworth*.[6] His ambition was to "establish" Dorothy Wordsworth "as an English poet." To do so, he freely "pruned" words and phrases he judged to be "marring" or "offending." Eigerman's liberties with her texts released burnished imagist poems:

> The lake was covered all over
> with bright silver waves
> That were each
> The twinkling of an eye.
>
> The fire flutters
>   and the watch ticks
> I hear nothing
>   save the breathing of my Beloved.

> Two ravens
> Flew high, high in the sky,
> and the sun shone
> Upon their bellies and their wings
> Long after
> There was none of his light to be seen.
>
> The rocky shore,
> Spotted and streaked
> With purplish brown heath,
> And its image in the water, together
> Were like an immense caterpillar.

Or the occasional aphorism:

> The beauties of a brook or river
> Must be sought,
> And the pleasure is
> In going in search of them.
> Those of a lake
> Or of a sea
> Come to you of themselves.

But by formalizing Dorothy Wordsworth's writing, Eigerman denied a significant quality of the journals. Unweaving her patterns, he sundered those startling flashes of beauty and insight from the context which entwines them in quotidian experience. Some of our pleasure in reading the journals derives from our surprise at suddenly encountering an arresting moment of vision embedded in a chronicle of ordinary daily motions and from our realization that such moments can be a part of the texture of everyday experience.

Although eschewing Eigerman's active measures, Elizabeth Hardwick and Margaret Homans demonstrate how phantom works and a phantom writer continue to entice Dorothy Wordsworth's recent critics. In *Seduction and Betrayal*, Hardwick warns, perceptively, that "a sort of insatiability seems to infect our feelings when we look back on women, particularly on those who are highly interesting and yet whose effort at self-definition through works is fitful, casual, that of an amateur. We are inclined to think they could have done more, that we can make retroactive demands upon them for a greater degree of independence and authenticity."[7] But she proceeds to depict Dorothy Wordsworth as such an eccentric, high-strung neurotic that we marvel at her survival; her journals shrivel to the little jottings of a sickly woman, embarrassingly trapped in childhood.

"There was always something peculiar about Dorothy Wordsworth," Hardwick avers, and reminds us of those "wild lights in her eyes" and her intense, excitable nature; there was "something about her of a Brontë heroine" (146). "Wild, driven," "austere, trembling," with her "extravagant, dangerous temperament . . . living out a precarious dedication," she was "always a little mad and in nothing more so than in her fanatic devotion to her brother" (146, 151, 154–155). Hardwick patronizes her subject: William "realized the need of an 'occupation' for Dorothy, an anchor for her free-flying emotions and impressions" and "spurred" her to keep her journals—as a kind of creative therapy, one supposes, in lieu of tranquilizers (147). Hardwick recalls De Quincey's observation, that Dorothy Wordsworth would have been better off had she written professionally, only to allege that she could never have passed muster:

> She could not, would not analyze. . . . This failure to inspect character and motive incapacitates her for fiction; her lack of a rhythmical ear, her lack of training, and her withdrawal from the general, the propositional, and from questioning made it impossible for her to turn her love of nature into poetry. In her journals there are brief vignettes, good mimicry of countryfolk, but there are no real people—especially she and William are absent in the deepest sense.
>
> We cannot imagine that she was incapable of thought about character, but very early, after her grief and the deaths, she must have become frightened. Her dependency was so greatly loved and so desperately clung to that she could not risk anything except the description of the scenery in which it was lived. (156)

Hardwick castigates Dorothy Wordsworth for not writing something else—novels, or poems—and, if she must write journals, for not writing them by different rules. Nature, Hardwick avows, is "not a sufficient subject for the whole mind. To name it, to paint it with words is indeed a rare gift. But it is a gift almost dangling in the air. It is the final narrowness of the pictorial, the frustration of the quick microscopic brilliance, unroped by generalization" (148). So much for Ernest de Selincourt's judgment that "Dorothy Wordsworth is probably the most remarkable and the most distinguished of English writers who never wrote a line for the general public"!

In *Women Writers and Poetic Identity*, Margaret Homans asks, "How does the consciousness of being a woman affect the workings of the poetic imagination?"[8] Her purpose is "to define the special challenges faced by women who aspired to be poets, and thereby to illuminate both their failures and their successes" (3). Schooled in contemporary French critical theory, Homans grounds her examination of the lives and works of Dorothy Wordsworth, Emily Brontë, and Emily Dickinson in neo-Freudian psychoanalysis. She focuses her study on their relation to the natural world and their language.

Homans believes that "at every point" in her work Dorothy Wordsworth "causes her readers to wonder why she never became a competent or ready poet, at the very least, if not a great poet" (41). She concedes that Dorothy Wordsworth "never quite acknowledged her poet's vocation," but she nevertheless insists on using Dorothy as a case study to investigate the "process that leads to a sense of poetic vocation or identity" (6, 9). She claims to regard Dorothy Wordsworth as a "potential poet" who "redirected [her] best energies towards other forms of writing and of activity," but in fact she discusses her subject as a spoiled poet—as a failure (9). The reasons for her failure are, briefly, that her close relation with nature and her "dislocation from the phallogocentric community caus[e] Dorothy Wordsworth great difficulty in creating a central sense of self in poetry" (36). William's separation from nature "allow[s] him to grow up"; Dorothy, however, resists two potentially creative separations—from her brother and from nature—and cannot. "Fatally, her wishes are all fulfilled, and her faculties have nothing to pursue" (56). Her "refusal to risk" the necessary break finally prevents Dorothy Wordsworth from becoming a poet; hence, her meagre output: fewer than twenty poems, and only five of those published during her life, inconspicuously hidden away in William's works. Her "resistance to poethood," her "evasions of poetic identity," appear to be resistance to individuation, evasions of self-actualization—indeed, of adulthood (41–42). Psychologically, Dorothy Wordsworth remains a child.

But what if Dorothy Wordsworth never really aspired to be a poet? I am

not convinced that she did. Brother John Wordsworth, the "silent poet," as
William called him, shared Dorothy's finely tuned sensibility and her love
for literature, but posterity has not categorized him as a failure or insisted
that he never emerged to adulthood for evading—despite his inclusion in
the phallogocentric community—his poetic identity. Does the fact of her remarking that an especially beautiful scene made her feel "more than half a
poet" prove that Dorothy Wordsworth yearned to be a full, authentic, card-
carrying Poet?

Dorothy Wordsworth wrote nearly all her poems for children. In a letter
of 1806 to Lady Beaumont, discussing two of them, she begs:

> Do not think that I was ever bold enough to hope to compose verses
> for the pleasure of grown persons. Descriptions, Sentiments, or little
> stories for children was all I could be ambitious of doing, and I did try
> one story, but failed so sadly that I was completely discouraged. Be-
> lieve me, since I received your letter I have made several attempts . . .
> and have been obliged to give it up in despair; and looking into my
> mind I find nothing there, even if I had the gift of language and num-
> bers, that I could have the vanity to suppose could be of any use be-
> yond our own fireside, or to please . . . a few partial friends; but I have
> no command of language, no power of expressing my ideas, and no
> one was ever more inapt at molding words into regular metre. I have
> often tried when I have been walking alone (muttering to myself as is
> my Brother's custom) to express my feelings in verse; feelings, and
> *ideas* such as they were, I have never wanted at those times, but prose
> and rhyme and blank verse were jumbled together and nothing ever
> came of it.[9]

Leaving aside Dorothy Wordsworth's decorous, self-effacing modesty in
writing to Lady Beaumont, we still cannot detect a committed desire to be a
poet. Had she felt that, she would have written more verses and would have
tried seriously to learn the craft, even if her results were modest. Understanding prosody is no more baffling or laborious than learning French or
German, which Dorothy Wordsworth did do.

In her *Irregular Verses* written for Julia Marshall in 1827, Dorothy
Wordsworth discloses that in girlhood she

... *reverenced* the Poet's skill,
And *might have* nursed a mounting Will
To imitate the tender Lays
Of them who sang in Nature's praise.[10] (Dorothy Wordsworth's italics)

But, she explains, bashfulness and fear of ridicule inhibited her then. She speaks of no later frustrated urges or restraints. It is true that during the illness that darkened her final years, Dorothy Wordsworth often repeated her verses and revised at least one composition obsessively, but that preoccupation should not persuade us to view her as a might-have-been John Clare or Friedrich Hölderlin.

Homans's argument leaves us in the uncomfortable position of judging a life failed for never achieving what it never attempted and need never have attempted. By that yardstick, we all measure up as failures. I do not believe that Dorothy Wordsworth, any of her family, or close friends—even De Quincey—did regard her life as a failure. For us to do so seems not only presumptuous but also foolish. Had psychoanalysis in the early nineteenth century developed to its current level of sophistication and had Dorothy Wordsworth aired with a doctor from Vienna any repressed resentment against her mother (which Homans detects), or her brother fixation, I am not confident that she would have risen from the couch as Homans's "great poet." But such supposing is pointless. We might remember Alice James's deathbed appeal to her brother William: "When I am gone, pray don't think of me simply as a creature who might have been something else, had neurotic [that is, psychoanalytic] science been born."[11] The request is just.

In venturing toward a clearer appreciation of Dorothy Wordsworth's writing, we might begin by recalling Coleridge's admonition to judge a work of art not by its defects but by its achievements. Dorothy Wordsworth's art is her prose: her letters, her moving and proficient narrative *George and Sarah Green*, but especially her journals. Although in 1810, when her friends the Clarksons urged her to publish her account of the Green family's tragedy, she unambiguously declared, "I should detest the idea of setting myself up as an Author," she nonetheless wrote a great deal.[12] Like many women writers—one could cite Elizabeth Bishop and Adrienne Rich as examples—she preferred open to closed forms; a modest to an egotistical, self-aggrandizing voice; common and concrete rather than unusual, elevated, or abstracted language and images; and subjects close at hand, personal, and domestic rather than remote or detached, subjects that elicited a feeling response rather than an intellectual reaction. Such preferences are a writer's privilege.

"Why do women keep diaries?" Mary Jane Moffat asks in the foreword of an anthology titled *Revelations: Diaries of Women.* "Dissatisfaction with the ways love and work have been defined for the female," she argues,

> is the unconscious impulse that prompts many to pour out their feelings on paper and to acquire the habit of personal accounting on some more or less regular basis. The form has been an important outlet for women partly because it is an analogue to their lives: emotional, fragmentary, interrupted, modest, not to be taken seriously, private, restricted, daily, trivial, formless, concerned with self, as endless as their tasks.[13]

But Thomas Mallon, in *A Book of One's Own,* distinguishes a variety of shifting and overlapping motivations that induce both men and women to keep journals.[14] Peering with Mallon over the shoulders of chroniclers, travelers, pilgrims, creators, confessors, and prisoners, one is struck by the range of relationships people establish with their journals. There are no rules.

Dorothy Wordsworth wrote to record her impressions, not to pour out her feelings, fantasize, explain or justify actions, explore ideas, or chronicle significant events; and as Virginia Woolf remarked, "her eye never failed her."[15] Primarily because Dorothy Wordsworth observed with her own eyes instead of through the filters of established poetic decorum, her images are arresting. Because she wrote quickly and spontaneously, as all great diarists do, rather than self-consciously, by prescribed rules, her words seem direct, never to falter uncertainly or fumble for special effects. A unity of style—the prose is lean, spare, sometimes taut—and a subtle unity of intention mark her journals. The steadiness of her vision reflects a consistently responsive sensibility, and this, too, unifies her writing. Perceptions that elsewhere might have seemed fractured, partial, or disparate form a continuum.

Sometimes we are startled by the vividness of a haunting sound or unexpected sight, often at the conclusion of a day's entry:

> Walked between half-past three and half-past five. The evening cold and clear. The sea of a sober grey, streaked by the deeper grey clouds. The half dead sound of the near sheep-bell, in the hollow of the sloping coombe, exquisitely soothing.
>
> (24 January 1798)[16]

> We amused ourselves for a long time in watching the Breezes some as if they came from the bottom of the lake spread in a circle, brushing along the surface of the water, and growing more delicate, as it were thinner and of a *paler* colour till they died away. Others spread out like a peacock's tail, and some went right forward this way and that in all directions. The lake was still where these breezes were not, but they made it all alive.
>
> (31 January 1802)

> Walked through the wood, and on to the Downs before dinner; a warm pleasant air. The sun shone, but was often obscured by straggling clouds. The redbreasts made a ceaseless song in the woods. The wind rose very high in the evening. The room smoked so that we were obliged to quit it. Young lambs in a green pasture in the Coombe, thick legs, large heads, black staring eyes.
>
> (2 February 1798)

Elsewhere the serenity of a whole day, long gone but timeless, slowly washes over us and lulls us:

> A mild morning, the windows open at breakfast, the redbreasts singing in the garden. Walked with Coleridge over the hills. The sea at first obscured by vapour; that vapour afterwards slid in one mighty mass along the sea-shore; the islands and one point of land clear beyond it. The distant country (which was purple in the clear dull air), overhung by straggling clouds that sailed over it, appeared like the darker clouds, which are often seen at a great distance apparently motionless,

while the nearer ones pass quickly over them, driven by the lower winds. I never saw such a union of earth, sky, and sea. The clouds beneath our feet spread themselves to the water, and the clouds of the sky almost joined them. Gathered sticks in the wood; a perfect stillness. The redbreasts sang upon the leafless boughs. Of a great number of sheep in the field, only one standing. Returned to dinner at five o'clock. The moonlight still and warm as a summer's night at nine o'clock.

(3 February 1798)

This is accomplished writing. The frequent omission of verbs creates a sense of stillness, but participles and subjectless verbs carry the prose forward, as if from underneath its surface. It rises and surges to its central image, where distinctions between earth, sky, and sea blur in uncertainty. Here, in this moment of equilibrium, subjects and verbs join together. Ebbing, the prose repeats a similar pattern of omission and closes in the same mood of stillness with which it began.

The apparent artlessness and simplicity of Dorothy Wordsworth's style disarms conventional criticism. Her most recent biographers, Robert Gittings and Jo Manton, are reduced to claiming that "her unique style" is "no style."[17] As with the writing of Christina Rossetti or Emily Dickinson, mobilizing a critical artillery to confront Dorothy Wordsworth's work proves an awkward and pompous maneuver. Tallying parallels between her journals and her brother's poems, or cataloging her references to moon, sea, or birdsong may seem possible alternatives, but her writing itself stands aloof from these procedures. Finally, they disclose nothing of the sources of the particular strength of her prose.

Listening to the cadences of Dorothy Wordsworth's writing rather than looking at printed words, however, may deepen our understanding of her artistry. For, if traditional poetic meters shackled her talent and allowed her to compose only strained and faltering verse, the rhythms of her prose are measured and masterly. "William and I drank tea at Coleridge's," she matter-of-factly begins her journal entry for 7 March 1798. "A cloudy sky. Observed nothing particularly interesting—the distant prospect obscured. One only leaf upon the top of a tree—the sole remaining leaf—danced round and round like a rag blown in the wind." The final sentence slows the tempo of her account of what was not "particularly interesting" to emphasize that

single image that riveted her attention. Her forceful rhythm perfectly repro-
duces the flapping motion that she apprehended visually. Initially the clarity
and precision of Dorothy Wordsworth's images may seem strictly pictorial,
but in fact they also derive from her expert control of sound and rhythm.

As we read from one day to another and one month to the next, heard
rhythms expand to felt rhythms. Changing phases of the moon and the
progression of the seasons mark off a slower, deeper, more encompassing
rhythm. Dorothy Wordsworth's prose creates an unpretentious sense of
continuity within flux, attuning us to that all-embracing, impersonal
rhythm of which she is a part. She never names it, never attempts to define
it, and yet it is steadily, palpably there, informing her writing with depth,
resonance, and wholeness.

Traveling through Westmorland in the summer of 1818, John Keats
wrote to his brother Tom from Windermere that the views of the lake "are
of the most noble tenderness—they can never fade away—they make one
forget the divisions of life; age, youth, poverty and riches. . . . I live in the
eye; and my imagination, surpassed, is at rest."[18] Although Dorothy
Wordsworth would never have written such words, they describe her mode
of seeing. Unlike her brother, Coleridge, Shelley, and sometimes Keats himself, she never depended on a fitful visionary gleam, never yearned toward a
distant glory or a dream. Nature sufficed.

In her journals Dorothy Wordsworth deliberately paints by the light of
common day. Her sketch of Berne, in 1820, conspicuously demonstrates
this:

> We ascended a hill till we came in view of as magnificent a prospect as
> can be conceived—the Jungfrau, the Finsteraar-horn, the Shreck-
> horn, the Wetter-horn, and many other famous mountains—their
> summits covered with snow. I sate upon one of the seats placed under
> shade of trees beside the broad high-way; and the party went further.
> . . . the city appeared to hang upon the half of a semi-circle of the
> near bank, crowned by the cathedral, and adorned by spires and tow-
> ers. . . . The green-tinted river flows below—wide, full, and impetu-
> ous. I saw the snows of the Alps burnished by the sun about half an
> hour before his setting. After that, they were left to their wintry,
> marble coldness, without a farewell gleam, yet suddenly the city, and
> the cathedral tower and trees were singled out for favour by the sun

among his glittering clouds, and gilded with the richest light—a few minutes and that glory vanished. I stayed till evening gloom was gathering over the city, and over hill and dale, while the snowy tops of the Alps were still visible.[19]

Dorothy Wordsworth does not speculate about what the prospect might have been from higher up the road or lament that her companions have proceeded on their excursion without her. What she saw before her was enough. She checked any impulse she might have had to regard such a scene as a type and symbol of eternity; she repudiated the obsessive *Sehnsucht* of the great Romantic poets, that aching toward some unchanging, imperishable perfection. Her goal was completeness rather than perfection, immanence rather than transcendence.

The unexpected sense of completeness that Dorothy Wordsworth's writing evokes resembles that of Keats's *To Autumn,* where the poet casts aside the persona of his earlier poems, which presses so anxiously toward the positive certainties of a less mutable world, to create an intense, impersonal moment of serene fulfillment and repose. In her work she also brings a "negative capability" into play. Her descriptions, like the lakeland landscape Keats admired, "make one forget the divisions of life," harmoniously merging discrete objects, blending what is near and far, high and low, into a solemn unity. Like the great Romantic poets who were her contemporaries, Dorothy Wordsworth was a visionary: "with an eye made quiet by the power / Of harmony, and the deep power of joy," she, too, could "see into the life of things." But where those poets struggled repeatedly to make that spirit within things explicit in their writing, Dorothy Wordsworth preferred to let it remain implicit, a mystery to be felt rather than disclosed. If some critics have taxed her heavily for her choice, other readers honor its fitness and find a quiet and abiding wisdom in her prose.

9

Wordsworth and Keats

JACK STILLINGER

John Keats's first meeting with Wordsworth, the occasion on which he recited the Hymn to Pan from his then unpublished *Endymion* and Wordsworth called it a "pretty piece of Paganism," is a famous anecdote in literary history. The meeting, arranged by a mutual friend, the historical painter Benjamin Robert Haydon, took place in the third week of December 1817 (around the sixteenth) at the house of Thomas Monkhouse, a cousin of Wordsworth's wife, in Queen Anne Street, Cavendish Square, London. Wordsworth, who was in town for several weeks on business, was forty-seven years old at the time and by far the most distinguished poet of his generation—author of ten volumes of verse, leading figure among the Lake school, and controversial proponent of widespread reform in the language and subject matter of poetry. Keats, at twenty-two, was nearly the *least* distinguished among living poets in Great Britain; he had published a single slim first volume, *Poems* (1817), which, as he said in a discarded preface to his next work, "was read by some dozen of my friends, who lik'd it, and some dozen whom I was unacquainted with, who did not."

We have six nineteenth-century accounts of this meeting: by Leigh Hunt (in a book about Byron published in 1828); Walter Savage Landor (in a letter of 1837); Haydon (in a letter of 1845); Richard Monckton Milnes (in his biography of Keats published in 1848); Charles Cowden Clarke (in a magazine article of 1861); and the painter Joseph Severn (in a manuscript autobiography written in the 1860s or 1870s). Five of the six accounts are reports at second (or third or fourth) hand, and they contain various mistakes and embroiderings concerning date, place, and the number and identities of those present; all, however, agree in condemning Wordsworth's bad behavior. Here is the version by Haydon, the only version by an actual witness, written twenty-eight years after the event:

> When Wordsworth came to Town, I brought Keats to him, by his Wordsworths desire— Keats expressed to me as we walked to Queen Anne St East where Mr Monkhouse Lodged, the greatest, the purest, the most unalloyed pleasure at the prospect. Wordsworth received him kindly, & after a few minutes, Wordsworth asked him what he had been lately doing, *I* said he has just finished an exquisite ode to Pan—and as he had not a copy I begged Keats to repeat it—which he did in his usual half chant, (most touching) walking up & down the room—when he had done I felt really, as if I had heard a young Apollo—Wordsworth drily said
> "a Very pretty piece of Paganism—
> This was unfeeling, & unworthy of his high Genius to a young Worshipper like Keats—& Keats felt it *deeply*—so that if Keats has said any thing severe about our Friend; it was because he was wounded— and though he dined with Wordsworth after at my table—he never forgave him.[1]

Keats's wounded feelings on the occasion, rather like his supposed faintness in reaction to the harsh reviews of the published *Endymion* several months later, were assumed to be fact through much of the second half of the nineteenth century and the first six decades of the twentieth; they appear as late as 1963 in the biography by Aileen Ward, who writes that "Keats was stunned. . . . He suddenly stopped seeing Wordsworth in the last week of January" (the latter statement is certainly true; Wordsworth left London on 19 January).[2] But the most recent full-length biographies of both Keats and Wordsworth—by W. J. Bate, Robert Gittings, and Mary Moorman— are more circumspect. Bate, for example, suggests that Keats "may have been more surprised than hurt" and "in retrospect may even have found [Wordsworth's] remark an amusing revelation of character."[3]

The fact is that Keats's letters and other biographical documents (many of which became available after—in some cases many decades after—the first published accounts of this meeting with Wordsworth) tell a different story. There is evidence of a genial and rapidly growing initial acquaintance between the two poets. Keats saw Wordsworth again on 28 December, at the so-called immortal dinner at Haydon's, when Wordsworth, Monkhouse, Keats, and Charles Lamb made up the party, with several others dropping in afterward—the occasion on which Keats and Lamb, agreeing that Newton had destroyed the poetry of the rainbow, drank "Newton's health, and confusion to mathematics!" Haydon's several-page record in his diary, written just after the event (and not, like his letter quoted above, nearly three decades later), describes a warm and festive affair, with lively conversation, uproarious jokes, and, for background, Haydon's huge painting *Christ's Entry into Jerusalem*, in which he had depicted both Wordsworth and Keats among the crowd of spectators. Haydon's conclusion gives no hint of unfriendly tension among the principals:

> There was something interesting in seeing Wordsworth sitting, & Keats & Lamb, & my Picture of Christ's entry towering up behind them, occasionally brightened by the gleams of flame that sparkled from the fire, & hearing the voice of Wordsworth repeating Milton with an intonation like the funeral bell of St. Paul's & the music of Handel mingled, & then Lamb's wit came sparkling in between, & Keats's rich fancy of Satyrs & Fauns & doves & white clouds, wound up the stream of conversation. I never passed a more delightful day, & I am convinced that nothing in Boswell is equal to what came out from these Poets. Indeed there were no such Poets in his time. It was an evening worthy of the Elizabethan age, and will long flash upon "that inward eye which is the bliss of Solitude." Hail & farewell!⁴

Three days after this dinner party, on 31 December, Keats met Wordsworth again while walking on Hampstead Heath. On 3 January he called on Wordsworth at his temporary lodgings in Mortimer Street (near Monkhouse's), and on the fifth he dined with him there. Perhaps he was with Wordsworth on other occasions too, for by the twenty-third (four days after the older poet had left town) he had, as he told his friend the theological student Benjamin Bailey, "seen a good deal of Wordsworth." The first note of disharmony in Keats's letters appears on 3 February, when, in an animated discussion of the egotism of modern poetry, he remarks to another friend,

John Hamilton Reynolds, "I will have no more of Wordsworth." But at this point, a month and a half after the "pretty piece of Paganism" incident, he is in the process of developing a theory of poetry in which the "wordsworthian or egotistical sublime" plays an important contrasting role. The earlier biographers were simplistic in seeing Keats's criticism of Wordsworth as a (delayed!) result of hurt feelings. Even at age twenty-two, Keats was very much his own person, and by 3 May, when he wrote down some of his most serious philosophical ideas in the "Mansion of Many Apartments" letter to Reynolds, with its extended comparison of Wordsworth and Milton, his stance toward Wordsworth had become that of a partner or fellow worker in the "grand march of intellect": "I will put down a simile of human life as far as I now perceive it; that is, to the point which . . . we both have arrived at. . . . To this point [a compound threshold of "dark passages"] was Wordsworth come. . . . Now if we live, and go on thinking, we too shall explore them."[5]

In his attitude toward the influences acting on him and helping to shape his career, Keats was one of the least anxious writers in English literature. He wanted to be a poet in part because he so much admired poetry, and poetry to him was what the individual poets who preceded him had accomplished. His earliest pieces on poetry—for example, *Imitation of Spenser, To Lord Byron, On Chatterton, Ode to Apollo*—are acutely aware of the presence and achievements of older poets and are congratulatory, openly admiring, and not in the least envious. When he sits down to compose, as he says in a poem on this very topic of relationship with his predecessors (the sonnet beginning "How many bards gild the lapses of time"), the sounds and images of previous writers intruding on his consciousness produce "no confusion, no disturbance rude" but instead make "a pleasing chime . . . pleasing music." Almost at the beginning of his career he arrived at an idea, really a mental picture, of "laurel'd peers" (as in *Ode to Apollo* and the sonnet *To My Brother George*), a masquelike array of "mighty Poets" initially as spectators to whatever subject he happens to have at hand, including his own attempts in rhyme, and then as a kind of distinguished academy that he will one day, if all goes well, be invited to join. His fellow feeling toward the three most major of his predecessors in English literature—Spenser, Shakespeare, and Milton—is thoroughly documented in his poems, letters, marginalia, and the reminiscences of his friends. His quietly confident prediction in a journal letter to his brother and sister-in-law on 14 October

1818, "I think I shall be among the English Poets after my death" (which is the more impressive for coming just *before* the year in which he produced, one after another in astonishing succession, all the works for which he is now most admired), is the best known of several passages assessing his strength in relation to the "peers" who had gone before.

Keats's remarkable independence does not, however, mean that he was uninfluenced by the poets with whom he enjoyed this congenial fellow feeling. On the contrary, as is well known, he was profoundly influenced by all the major authors whom he read. He first discovered Spenser around the age of sixteen, going through *The Faerie Queene,* in his friend Clarke's description, "as a young horse would through a spring meadow—ramping,"[6] and the effects on his poetic style, especially in the luxurious physicality of his imagery, show up all through his career; his earliest and two latest works are in the Spenserian stanza, as is the narrative poem with which he initiated his most fruitful period of productivity, *The Eve of St. Agnes.* The next significant beneficial influence (to speak only of the best known among English writers) was Shakespeare, who was pictured in profile on the title page of Keats's *Poems* of 1817 (along with an epigraph from Spenser) and then served as spiritual "Presider" over the composition of *Endymion* and in one way or another over much of the rest of Keats's poetry; as chief exemplar of nonegotistic artistic imagination, Shakespeare was Keats's theoretical as well as practical ideal. The third major influence was Milton, a principal inspiration for the Hyperion fragments and more generally for various elements of theme and technique in many of Keats's poems. The fourth major influence, and unquestionably the most important and pervasive among Keats's living contemporaries, was Wordsworth.

Keats's first references to Wordsworth in his extant letters come on 20 and 21 November 1816, when he sends Haydon the sonnet beginning "Great spirits now on earth are sojourning" (specifying Wordsworth, Leigh Hunt, and Haydon among the "spirits . . . standing apart / Upon the forehead of the age to come") and then, at Hunt's request, writes out a second copy for the painter to forward to Wordsworth ("The Idea of your sending it to Wordsworth put me out of breath—you know with what Reverence—I would send my Wellwishes to him"). There is another general mention (again in a letter to Haydon) on 11 May 1817, then a great many references to specific titles and passages by Wordsworth beginning in September, when Keats spent a month with Bailey at Oxford and the two men read and discussed Wordsworth almost daily. Probably *The Excursion* was the first of Wordsworth's works that Keats knew well; both Leigh Hunt and Keats's friend George Felton Mathew, in magazine reviews of Keats's *Poems* (1817), point to its influence on Keats's idea of the origin of myths in the opening poem of the volume, *I stood tip-toe,* written in December 1816, and there are many echoes of it in Keats's principal accomplishment of the following year, the four thousand-line *Endymion.* On 10 January 1818 (in writing to Haydon) and again on the thirteenth (to his brothers) Keats named *The Excursion* first among the three most considerable works of genius "in the modern world."

Other works that we can be sure he knew at least something about are Wordsworth's *Lyrical Ballads* (1798, 1800, 1802, 1805)—most notably *Tintern Abbey* and *The Idiot Boy,* first published in the original edition of 1798, and *The Old Cumberland Beggar,* the Lucy poems, and the Matthew poems, first published in the second edition (1800)—and *Poems in Two Volumes* (1807), containing, among other pieces, *Ode: Intimations of Immortality, Resolution and Independence, I wandered lonely as a Cloud, The Solitary Reaper,* and a number of sonnets that Keats mentions or echoes. The full contents of both *Lyrical Ballads* and *Poems in Two Volumes* were reprinted in Wordsworth's two-volume collected *Poems* of 1815. It is not certain which of these books Keats actually used; possibly he read, on different occasions, in all of them. There is no doubt, however, that he knew the works, especially those like *Tintern Abbey* and the *Intimations Ode* that he repeatedly alludes to in his letters and poems.

The most immediately obvious results of Wordsworth's influence are the two hundred or so echoes and borrowings that scholars have detected in Keats's poems (see, for the principal studies, the general note at the end of this chapter). A handful of random instances might include the brief description of "Startl[ing] the wild bee from the fox-glove bell" in Keats's first published poem, *O Solitude* (seeming to echo "bees . . . Will murmur by the hour in foxglove bells" in Wordsworth's sonnet beginning "Nuns fret not at their convent's narrow room"); the heart dancing with pleasure, "And always does my heart with pleasure dance," in *Specimen of an Induction to a Poem,* line 51 (compare Wordsworth's "And then my heart with pleasure fills, / And dances" in *I wandered lonely as a Cloud*); the wording to express uncertainty of origin in "many a verse from so strange influence / That we must ever wonder how, and whence, / It came" in *Sleep and Poetry,* lines 69–71 (echoing Wordsworth's "A happy, genial influence, / Coming one knows not how, or whence," in *To the Daisy* ["In youth from rock to rock I went"], lines 70–71); and both the ocean bosom image and the accompanying idea, "The blue / Bared its eternal bosom . . . But ye were dead," in *Sleep and Poetry*, 188–193 (echoing Wordsworth's "This Sea that bares her bosom to the moon . . . It moves us not" in the sonnet *The world is too much with us*).

Keats's first description of Glaucus in *Endymion* seems clearly indebted for several details to Wordsworth's first description of the Leech-Gatherer in *Resolution and Independence*. Here are some of Wordsworth's lines:

> I saw a Man before me unawares:
> The oldest man he seemed that ever wore grey hairs. . . .
> His body was bent double, feet and head
> Coming together in life's pilgrimage. . . .
> At length, himself unsettling, he the pond
> Stirred with his staff, and fixedly did look
> Upon the muddy water, which he conned,
> As if he had been reading in a book. . . .
>
> (lines 55–81)

Keats's description (drafted in September 1817, when he was visiting Bailey and reading Wordsworth at Oxford) similarly stresses the "unawares" character of the encounter and includes among other details the bodily feebleness of the old man, his gray / white hair, the presence of a staff / wand, and the conning of a hypothetical / real book:

> He [Endymion] saw . . .
> An old man sitting calm and peacefully.
> Upon a weeded rock this old man sat,
> And his white hair was awful, and a mat
> Of weeds were cold beneath his cold thin feet;
> And, ample as the largest winding-sheet,
> A cloak of blue wrapp'd up his aged bones. . . .
> Beside this old man lay a pearly wand,
> And in his lap a book, the which he conn'd
> So stedfastly, that the new denizen
> Had time to keep him in amazed ken,
> To mark these shadowings, and stand in awe.
>
> (bk. 3, lines 191–217)

Ode to a Nightingale has several Wordsworthian echoes in wording, image, tone, and cadence: for example, "The weariness, the fever, and the fret" (compare *Tintern Abbey*, lines 52–53: "the fretful stir / Unprofitable, and the fever of the world"); "Where youth grows pale, and spectre-thin, and dies" and "No hungry generations tread thee down" (compare *The Excursion*, bk. 4, lines 760–762: "While man grows old, and dwindles, and decays; / And countless generations of mankind / Depart; and leave no vestige where they trod"); "plaintive anthem" (compare *The Solitary Reaper*, line 18: "plaintive numbers"; Wordsworth's poem has a nightingale in the preceding stanza, and the solitary maiden working in the field is of course relatable to Keats's "sad heart of Ruth . . . amid the alien corn").

Individual connections and relations of this sort are easily displayed. Much more difficult, and impossible to document precisely, is Wordsworth's effect over the whole extent of Keats's art and thought: the subjects and themes Keats chose to write about, the forms and techniques he used, and his most serious ideas about poetry and human life. Influence study is by its very nature tentative, and it becomes more complicated when the two writers concerned are contemporaries—so many shared peculiarities can turn out to be the common product of an influence still earlier or elements of what William Hazlitt called "the spirit of the age." Nevertheless the traces of Wordsworth's presence are perceptible throughout Keats's work. In what follows I speculate about four areas in which Wordsworth's influence might be considered of first importance to the younger poet's career.

The *Lyrical Ballads* and *Isabella*

Keats's first complete narrative poem, *Endymion,* drafted in April–November 1817, tells the story of a shepherd prince who falls in love with a dream goddess, travels high and deep in search of her, and finally, after many speeches and complications of plot, is reunited with her, the two "vanish[ing] far away" into an eternity of bliss; it is a poem about love, dreaming, and the conflicting claims of human and immortal realms of existence. His next narrative poem, *Isabella,* drafted in February–April 1818, tells the story of a young woman whose lover is murdered by her brothers and who, when she learns of his fate, digs up his body, severs the head, carries it home to plant in a pot of basil, and goes mad and dies; this too is a poem about love, but also about betrayal, murder, madness, and death. It is not irrelevant to this difference that the interval between the two poems includes the several weeks in December–February during which Keats met Wordsworth and had the older poet's works and achievement as a modern writer frequently in his mind.

Scholars have long recognized, just as Keats did at the time, that the winter of 1817/1818 was a period of rapid growth and maturing for the young poet. Even before he finished the first draft of *Endymion* he was becoming weary of it, and his dissatisfaction grew as he revised and recopied the poem in January–March of the new year. One of the focuses of this dissatisfaction was the idea of "romance" (*Endymion* was subtitled "A Poetic Romance"), and a repeated motif in both his letters and his short poems of the time is the opposition between romance, visionary thinking, "skyey Knight errantry," on the one hand, and human suffering, evil, "disagreeables" in the real world, on the other. Serious conversations with his friend Bailey at Oxford along with deeper reading and thinking on his own after he returned to Hampstead combined to produce what he described in a letter to his brothers on 23 January: "I think a little change has taken place in my intellect lately." The consequent thematic maturity in his short poems this winter and early spring is noteworthy: there is a new focus on problems of human mortality (*In drear nighted December* and the sonnets *When I have fears* and *Four seasons fill the measure of the year*); the banishing of romance as "a barren dream" (the sonnet *On Sitting Down to Read* King Lear *Once Again*); differences between the complications of his own modern times and the simpler circumstances of the poets of old (*Lines on the Mermaid Tavern, Robin Hood,* the sonnet beginning "Spenser, a jealous honorer of thine"); the contrarieties of life (*Welcome joy, and welcome sorrow*).

One of the best of these short lyrics, *In drear nighted December,* composed in the month in which Keats became personally acquainted with Wordsworth, is quintessentially Wordsworthian in its emphasis on the difference between nature's unconsciousness of change and death and human consciousness of these same unhappy phenomena:

> In drear nighted December,
>   Too happy, happy tree,
> Thy branches ne'er remember
>   Their green felicity—

The north cannot undo them
With a sleety whistle through them,
Nor frozen thawings glue them
        From budding at the prime.

In drear nighted December,
        Too happy, happy brook,
Thy bubblings ne'er remember
        Apollo's summer look;
But with a sweet forgetting
They stay their crystal fretting,
Never, never petting
        About the frozen time.

Ah! would 'twere so with many
        A gentle girl and boy—
But were there ever any
        Writh'd not of passed joy?
The feel of not to feel it,
When there is none to heal it,
Nor numbed sense to steel it,
        Was never said in rhyme.

Keats's verse epistle beginning "Dear Reynolds, as last night I lay in bed," written some three months later, on 25 March 1818, treats a related Wordsworthian concern, the functioning and nonfunctioning of imagination. In combining images of a painting, a ship, and a castle (lines 23ff.) and concluding with a vision of cruelty in nature (86ff.), the epistle has elements in common with Wordsworth's *Elegiac Stanzas Suggested by a Picture of Peele Castle*; it breaks off with an allusion to one of Wordsworth's section headings ("Moods of My Own Mind") in his 1807 *Poems in Two Volumes*: "Away ye horrid moods, / Moods of one's mind!" (105–106).

These details are part of the recoverable context in which Keats composed his new romance ending, not in an eternity of bliss, but in madness and death. *Isabella* is a retelling in verse of a story in Boccaccio's *Decameron* (fifth "novel," fourth day), originally undertaken for a volume of verse narratives based on Boccaccio that Keats and Reynolds had planned to publish together. The project was abandoned after completion of this first story—by Reynolds probably because he knew he could not produce poems that would hold their own alongside Keats's (he was in any case mainly occupied in study of the law), and by Keats probably because he had already, in the single effort, accomplished most of what interested him in the project.

In recent decades, criticism of *Isabella* has focused on its realistic descriptions and the narrator's antiromantic stance as "modern" reteller of an old story whose simplicity and naiveté ("the gentleness of old Romance, / The simple plaining of a minstrel's song," lines 387–388) are no longer appropriate. Scholars comparing Keats's version with his source, the fifth edition (1684) of an English translation of 1620, have noted many changes by Keats that emphasize the gruesome aspects of the story—for example, the crude physical efforts involved in the exhumation of the dead lover Lorenzo (Isabella and her nurse "digged not far" in the original, but "Three hours they labour'd," clawing with knife and bare hands, in Keats's modernization); the rotting of the body (miraculously uncorrupted in the original); the suggestion of prolonged sawing or clumsy hacking in the removal of Lorenzo's head (neatly severed with "a keen Razor" in the original); the bizarre details of Isabella's care for the head (repeated kissing, combing its hair, pointing its eyelashes); her mental deterioration and separation from nature and reality. Scholars have also remarked on the narrator's self-presentation as modern reteller, including apologies both to Boccaccio and to the "Fair reader" for his grisly depiction of "wormy circumstance." The poem is generally viewed as transitional in Keats's career, anticipating further antiromantic developments in the narratives and lyrics of the following year, beginning with *The Eve of St. Agnes*.

The abundance of Wordsworthian elements in the poem, especially elements of the *Lyrical Ballads* and other poems that Wordsworth produced about the same time, suggests that Wordsworth may have played a significant role in the transition. Keats's basic story came from Boccaccio, of course, but Wordsworth wrote several narratives involving abandoned women, betrayal, and psychological deterioration, and Keats's elaboration of his given materials is certainly more Wordsworthian than Boccaccian. His characterizations of his principals are like Wordsworth's in (for example) *The Thorn, Michael,* and the story of Margaret in *The Ruined Cottage* (a poem of 1797–1798 that Keats read in its revised form in book 1 of

The Excursion). The combination of romantic pathos and exaggerated realism is another Wordsworthian feature, and Keats's "wormy circumstance" is relatable to the characteristic of Wordsworth's poetry that Coleridge had recently (in *Biographia Literaria,* published in July 1817) called "matter-of-factness." Above all, there is the Wordsworthian interest in psychology ("the primary laws of our nature," as Wordsworth wrote in the preface to *Lyrical Ballads,* "chiefly, as far as regards the manner in which we associate ideas in a state of excitement") that is the main concern in the second half of Keats's poem.

Isabella's "burthen" at the end—"O cruelty, / To steal my basil-pot away from me!"—is vaguely reminiscent of Martha Ray's refrain in *The Thorn*: "Oh misery! oh misery! / Oh woe is me! oh misery!" ("O misery!" itself occurs in line 235 of *Isabella*.) There are closer parallels (in imagery, tone, and general situation) between Keats's description of her alienation from the objective world—

> And she forgot the stars, the moon, and sun,
> And she forgot the blue above the trees,
> And she forgot the dells where waters run,
> And she forgot the chilly autumn breeze;
> She had no knowledge when the day was done,
> And the new morn she saw not: but in peace
> Hung over her sweet basil evermore,
> And moisten'd it with tears unto the core
>
> (417–424)

—and Martha Ray's similarly intense adherence to a special object (her thorn is Isabella's basil) in a natural setting of cosmic dimensions:

> And she is known to every star,
> And every wind that blows;
> And there, beside the Thorn, she sits
> When the blue daylight's in the skies,
> And when the whirlwind's on the hill,
> Or frosty air is keen and still. . . .
>
> (*The Thorn,* lines 69–74)

Isabella's wretched situation in the penultimate stanza of the poem, after her brothers steal away her basil pot—

Piteous she look'd on dead and senseless things,
   Asking for her lost basil amorously;
And with melodious chuckle in the strings
   Of her lorn voice, she oftentimes would cry
After the pilgrim in his wanderings,
   To ask him where her basil was . . .

                        (*Isabella* 489–494)

—again bears resemblance to some specific lines in Wordsworth, this time the description of Margaret in *The Excursion* when, near the end of her story, she frantically inquires of everyone after her missing husband:

          . . . and [she], in such piteous sort
That any heart had ached to hear her, begged
That, whereso'er I went, I still would ask
For him whom she had lost. . . .
. . . in yon arbour oftentimes she sate
Alone, through half the vacant sabbath day;
And, if a dog passed by, she still would quit
The shade, and look abroad. On this old bench
For hours she sate; and evermore her eye
Was busy in the distance, shaping things. . . .
. . . and she with faltering voice
Made many a fond inquiry. . . .

                        (1.865–892)

Such connections, supported by details of the biographical background, may be thought to constitute fairly impressive circumstantial evidence of Wordsworth's influence at an important turning point in Keats's career.

"Wordsworthian or Egotistical Sublime" and Negative Capability

"Negative Capability," the best known among the aesthetic and literary ideas in Keats's letters, may also be considered a development of the winter of 1817/1818, though the concept is discernible in his poetry earlier in 1817 (even if Keats himself was not fully conscious of it theoretically) and continues to be an explicit or hovering component of his critical thinking for the rest of his brief career. It first surfaces prominently in a handful of sentences in part of a letter written on 27 or 28 December 1817 in which he tells his brothers that a night or two earlier, when he went to the theater with his friends Charles Brown and C. W. Dilke and had "not a dispute but a disquisition with Dilke, on various subjects,"

> several things dovetailed in my mind, & at once it struck me, what quality went to form a Man of Achievement especially in Literature & which Shakespeare possessed so enormously—I mean *Negative Capability,* that is when man is capable of being in uncertainties, Mysteries, doubts, without any irritable reaching after fact & reason—Coleridge, for instance, would let go by a fine isolated verisimilitude caught from the Penetralium of mystery, from being incapable of remaining content with half knowledge. This pursued through Volumes would perhaps take us no further than this, that with a great poet the sense of Beauty overcomes every other consideration, or rather obliterates all consideration.

This passage is frequently related to Keats's remarks to his friend Richard Woodhouse ten months later (27 October 1818) on "the poetical Character":

> As to the poetical Character itself, (I mean that sort of which, if I am any thing, I am a Member; that sort distinguished from the wordsworthian or egotistical sublime; which is a thing per se and stands alone) it is not itself—it has no self—it is every thing and nothing—It has no character—it enjoys light and shade; it lives in gusto, be it foul or fair, high or low, rich or poor, mean or elevated—It has as much delight in conceiving as Iago as an Imogen. What shocks the virtuous philosop[h]er, delights the camelion Poet. It does no harm from its relish of the dark side of things any more than from its taste for the bright one; because they both end in speculation. A Poet is the most unpoetical of any thing in existence; because he has no Identity—he is continually . . . filling some other Body. . . .

Shakespeare, specifically named in the first passage and alluded to (as the conceiver of Iago and Imogen) in the second, is the prime exemplar of this power of sympathetic imagination, the poet's ability, as Woodhouse explained in a comment on the second passage, "to throw his own soul into any object he sees or imagines, so as to . . . speak out of that object—so that his own self will . . . be 'annihilated.' "[7] The opposite tendency, in which the writer's ego is central and all contraries must be resolved, is represented by Coleridge in the first passage (the Coleridge of *Biographia Literaria* rather than of *The Ancient Mariner, Kubla Khan,* and *Christabel*) and by Wordsworth ("the wordsworthian . . . sublime") in the second.

Scholars have long been interested in the source or sources of this basic idea. Hazlitt is the most frequently mentioned, especially for some remarks about Shakespeare that he delivered in a lecture of 27 January 1818 (a lecture that Keats probably attended and in any case certainly knew about):

> The striking peculiarity of Shakspeare's mind was its generic quality, its power of communication with all other minds—so that it contained a universe of thought and feeling within itself, and had no one peculiar bias, or exclusive excellence more than another. He was just like any other man, but that he was like all other men. He was the least of an egotist that it was possible to be. He was nothing in himself; but he was all that others were, or that they could become. . . . He had only to think of any thing in order to become that thing, with all the circumstances belonging to it. When he conceived of a character, whether real or imaginary, he not only entered into all its thoughts and feelings, but seemed instantly, and as if by touching a secret spring, to be surrounded with all the same objects . . . the same local, outward, and unforeseen accidents which would occur in reality.[8]

In a later lecture in the same series, on 3 March (the evening before Keats left Hampstead to go to Teignmouth), Hazlitt launched into a severe attack on the generalized type of the Wordsworth school, the Lake Poet:

> He [a "thorough adept in this school of poetry"] does not even like to share his reputation with his subject; for he would have it all proceed from his own power and originality of mind. Such a one is slow to ad-

mire any thing that is admirable; feels no interest in what is most interesting to others, no grandeur in any thing grand, no beauty in anything beautiful. He tolerates only what he himself creates. . . . He sees
nothing but himself and the universe. . . . His egotism is in some respects a madness. . . .[9]

Certainly these passages, implicitly contrasting Shakespeare and Wordsworth, have a bearing on Keats's "camelion Poet" letter to Woodhouse,
though they postdate the December 1817 statement on negative capability.

A passage in Haydon's diary for 22 December 1817 also compares
Wordsworth and Shakespeare: "Wordsworth's great power is an intense
perception of human feelings regarding the mystery of things by analyzing
his own, Shakespeare's an intense power of laying open the heart & mind of
man by analyzing the feelings of others acting on themselves. . . . Shakespeare has no moral code, and only leaves it at the option of all how to act
by shewing the consequence of such & such conduct in acting."[10] Since
Keats and Haydon were frequently together around this time, it seems likely
that Haydon's conversation was also among the immediate influences.
There has to have been some contribution by Dilke, of course, the friend
with whom a "disquisition" provoked the "dovetailing" that led to negative
capability in the letter. And there was also, much more generally and elu-
sively, some nonegotistic element in Keats's own personality acting as an
influence. In the December 1817 letter, Keats writes that "*at once* it struck
me. . . ," but he had dramatically portrayed Negative Capability in the
speeches and actions of *Endymion* during the preceding several months—
in the "fellowship with essence" passage of 1.777ff. ("blending pleasure-
able" in the original manuscript text), in various later comments in the
poem about identity and freeing oneself from "self-passion," and even in
much of the incidental language (for example, in verbs like "commune,"
"melt into," "blend," "mingle," "interknit," "commingle").

My point for the present occasion is simply that Wordsworth has to be
considered a prominent element in the development of negative capability.
Keats had firsthand evidence of Wordsworth's personal (as opposed to poetic) egotism from his meetings with the older poet in the winter of 1817/
1818 (Clarke's comment on the "pretty piece of Paganism" incident years
afterward sounds authoritative: "From Keats's description of his mentor's
[Wordsworth's] manner, as well as behaviour that evening, it would seem to

have been one of [his] usual ebullitions of egoism . . .").[11] And obviously there were complaints from others. "I am sorry," Keats writes to his brothers on 21 February 1818, "that Wordsworth has left a bad impression where-ever he visited in Town—by his egotism, Vanity and bigotry." Keats could set aside the personal egotism ("yet he is a great Poet," he adds in the letter just quoted), but *poetic* egotism was a more serious matter. Keats uses "Wordsworth &c" to exemplify the self-regarding stance of contemporary poetry in the important letter to Reynolds of 3 February 1818. "Poetry should be great & unobtrusive," Keats says there, "a thing which enters into one's soul, and does not startle it or amaze it with itself but with its subject." But Wordsworth is the leader among the egotists who "brood and peacock": "Old Matthew spoke to [Wordsworth] some years ago on some nothing, & because he happens in an Evening Walk to imagine the figure of the old man—he must stamp it down in black & white, and it is henceforth sacred." By October 1818, in the letter to Woodhouse, the antithesis of "camelion" poetry had become "wordsworthian or egotistical sublime," and Woodhouse saw in the letter "the distinction [Keats] draws between himself & those of the Wordsworth School."[12] Wordsworth is on the bad side in this opposition but plainly is a significant presence as Shakespeare's contrary. Both poets were essential to the formation of Keats's most famous critical idea.

Wordsworth's "Philosophy" and the Grand March of Keats's Intellect

Wordsworth is also a presence in several other important philosophical passages in Keats's letters. In the often-cited letter to Bailey on "the authenticity of the Imagination," 22 November 1817, at least half of the significant sentences embody Wordsworthian notions about the mind, the feelings, association of ideas, perceiving, creating, remembering—the substance especially of *Tintern Abbey*. Keats's phrase "the holiness of the Heart's affections," for example (in his affirmation of certainty concerning that and "the truth of Imagination"), contains three of Wordsworth's favorite words. Both his idea in the letter that "our Passions . . . [are] creative of essential Beauty" and the "little song" in *Endymion* that he refers to by way of illustration,

the Indian maiden's "O Sorrow" in 4.146–181, reflect the basic Wordsworthian doctrine of creative sensibility (Wordsworth's "strong creative
power / Of human passion" in *The Excursion*, 1.480–481, epitomizes a
main interest throughout his work). The opposition expressed in Keats's "O
for a Life of Sensations rather than of Thoughts" pointedly echoes the same
opposition running through both *Tintern Abbey* and the *Intimations Ode*.
When, in the process of winding up his topic, Keats makes a distinction between "the simple imaginative Mind" that he has been describing and "a
complex Mind—one that is imaginative and at the same time careful of its
fruits—who would exist partly on sensation partly on thought—to whom
it is necessary that years should bring the philosophic Mind," the concluding allusion to the *Intimations Ode* (line 186, "years that bring the philosophic mind") makes clear that Wordsworth is the model he is thinking of.

   Wordsworth is central to the "Mansion of Many Apartments" letter to
Reynolds, 3 May 1818, in which the main question is the extent to which
Wordsworth, Milton, and Keats himself have seen into the human heart and
the mystery of human life. "My Branchings out," Keats tells Reynolds,
"have been numerous: one of them is the consideration of Wordsworth's
genius and as a help . . . how he differs from Milton." Keats goes on to construct an elaborate simile of human life as "a large Mansion of Many Apartments, two of which I can only describe, the doors of the rest being as yet
shut upon me." The first is "the infant or thoughtless Chamber, in which we
remain as long as we do not think." "The awakening of the thinking principle" impels one on to the second, the "Chamber of Maiden-Thought,"
where among its effects is

> that tremendous one of sharpening one's vision into the heart and na-
> ture of Man—of convincing ones nerves that the World is full of Mis-
> ery and Heartbreak, Pain, Sickness and oppression—whereby This
> Chamber of Maiden Thought becomes gradually darken'd and at the
> same time on all sides of it many doors are set open—but all dark—
> all leading to dark passages—We see not the ballance of good and
> evil. We are in a Mist—*We* are now in that state—We feel the "bur-
> den of the Mystery," To this point was Wordsworth come, as far as I
> can conceive when he wrote "Tintern Abbey" and it seems to me that
> his Genius is explorative of those dark Passages. Now if we live, and
> go on thinking, we too shall explore them.

The fact that Wordsworth in this scheme advanced farther than Milton (whose "Philosophy, human and divine, may be tolerably understood by one not much advanced in years") Keats takes as proof that "there is really a grand march of intellect"; he himself, it is clear, intends to progress beyond Wordsworth by the same means. The whole (which has specific references to both *Tintern Abbey* and *The Excursion*) is presented to Reynolds "to show you how tall I stand by the giant"; it is an impressive assessment of the giant Wordsworth's genius and further testimony to the rapidity of Keats's own maturing.

The third of the best known philosophical passages, the several pages on the world as a "vale of Soul-making" in a late April section of Keats's longest journal letter to his brother and sister-in-law in America, 14 February–3 May 1819, again involves Wordsworthian progression:

> The common cognomen of this world among the misguided and superstitious is "a vale of tears" from which we are to be redeemed by a certain arbitrary interposition of God and taken to Heaven—What a little circumscribe[d] straightened notion! Call the world if you Please "The vale of Soul-making" . . . I say *"Soul making"* Soul as distinguished from an Intelligence—There may be intelligences or sparks of the divinity in millions—but they are not Souls till they acquire identities, till each one is personally itself. . . . I will call the *world* a School instituted for the purpose of teaching little children to read—I will call the *human heart* the *horn Book* used in that School—and I will call the *Child able to read, the Soul* made from that *school* and its *hornbook.* Do you not see how necessary a World of Pains and troubles is to school an Intelligence and make it a soul? . . . As various as the Lives of Men are—so various become their souls, and thus does God make individual beings, Souls, Identical Souls of the sparks of his own essence—This appears to me a faint sketch of a system of Salvation which does not affront our reason and humanity—I am convinced that many difficulties which christians labour under would vanish before it.

Wordsworth is not mentioned (or quoted or even verbally echoed) in the passage; yet commentators on it have referred to Wordsworth, especially to the ideas and images concerning the origin, development, and schooling of the human soul in the *Intimations Ode.* At the time, Keats had recently completed *The Eve of St. Agnes,* some 880 lines of *Hyperion,* and *La Belle Dame sans Merci* (among other works) and was about to begin writing his own great odes.

Peter Bell and the Genesis of Keats's Odes

A final speculation concerning the relationship of Wordsworth and Keats, this time an entirely novel one, is based on the unlikely juxtaposition of *Peter Bell,* Wordsworth's much-ridiculed tale of a lawless potter redeemed by an awakening of imagination, and Keats's great odes, the poems that, above all others, have secured him a place (along with Wordsworth) "among the English Poets." *Peter Bell* was first drafted in 1798, perhaps as a companion piece or counterpart to Coleridge's *The Ancient Mariner,* but it was revised several times in the next decade or so and remained in manuscript until 1819, when it was published on or about 22 April. Just before its appearance Keats mentions it twice in the spring 1819 journal letter to his brother and sister-in-law, first on 15 April—

> Wordsworth is going to publish a Poem called Peter Bell—what a perverses fellow it is! Why wilt he talk about Peter Bells—I was told not to tell—but to you it will not be tellings—Reynolds hearing that said Peter Bell was coming out, took it into his head to write a skit upon it call'd Peter Bell. He did it as soon as thought on it is to be published this morning, and comes out before the real Peter Bell, with this admirable motto from the "Bold stroke for a Wife" "I am the real Simon Pure"

—and then six days later, on the twenty-first, when he drafts (in the letter) a short review of Reynolds's work that he has agreed to do for Leigh Hunt's *Examiner* (where it appeared on the twenty-fifth). It was a clever project, and Reynolds's *Peter Bell,* published a week before Wordsworth's and causing a great deal of confusion in the press and at the booksellers, is in some parts (most notably the preface and the notes) a brilliant parody. Obviously, having gone to such lengths to make a good joke, Reynolds and Keats would be among the earliest readers of the real *Peter Bell* when it came out.

It was only about a week afterward that Keats wrote what we take to be the first of his great odes, the *Ode to Psyche.*

Peter Bell begins with a prologue intended (as Wordsworth makes clear in an accompanying dedicatory epistle to Robert Southey) to establish several ideas about the proper subject matter of poetry, the proper sphere of imagination, and the role of the supernatural. The narrator flies away from earth in a "little Boat," enjoys prying among the stars and planets for awhile, but soon becomes lost and homesick: "Then back to Earth, the dear green Earth . . . I've left my heart at home." The boat (a talking boat, modeled on Chaucer's talking eagle), who views the narrator's retreat with scorn, offers to take him to some equally remote places among the "nether precincts"—"Siberian snows," "a land / Where human foot did never stray . . . burning Africa," "the realm of Faery"—but these too are rejected by the narrator in a speech packed with significant Wordsworthian doctrine:

> "Temptation lurks among your words;
> But, while these pleasures you're pursuing
> Without impediment or let,
> No wonder if you quite forget
> What on earth is doing.

> "There was a time when all mankind
> Did listen with a faith sincere
> To tuneful tongues in mystery versed;
> *Then* Poets fearlessly rehearsed
> The wonders of a wild career.

> "Go— (but the world's a sleepy world,
> And 'tis, I fear, an age too late)
> Take with you some ambitious Youth!
> For, restless Wanderer! I, in truth,
> Am all unfit to be your mate.

> "Long have I loved what I behold,
> The night that calms, the day that cheers;
> The common growth of mother-earth
> Suffices me—her tears, her mirth,
> Her humblest mirth and tears.

"The dragon's wing, the magic ring,
I shall not covet for my dower,
If I along that lowly way
With sympathetic heart may stray,
And with a soul of power.

"These given, what more need I desire
To stir, to soothe, or elevate?
What nobler marvels than the mind
May in life's daily prospect find,
May find or there create? . . .

"But grant my wishes,—let us now
Descend from this ethereal height. . . ."
                              (lines 116–152)

The first point of interest relative to Keats is the modernist stance of Wordsworth's narrator. Keats had already, partly with Wordsworth's help, been self-consciously "modern" for a year or more (for example, in the view of Boccaccio's "old prose" taken in *Isabella*). There is nevertheless a fresh fervency about the situation in *Ode to Psyche*:

O brightest! though too late for antique vows,
    Too, too late for the fond believing lyre,
When holy were the haunted forest boughs,
    Holy the air, the water, and the fire;
Yet even in these days so far retir'd
    From happy pieties. . . .

Keats's lines echo both the idea and some of the language of the Wordsworth passage just quoted ("There was a time . . . faith sincere . . . an age too late").

The second point has to do with Wordsworth's emphasis on the supreme importance of the human mind ("What nobler marvels than the mind . . ."); the central subject of *Peter Bell* is what the narrator later invokes as "Spirits of the Mind," the working imagination of Peter's own mind. The obvious Keats connection here is the last stanza of *Ode to Psyche*, where the speaker offers his own mind as recompense for Psyche's lack of shrine, grove, oracle, and prophet: "a fane / In some untrodden region of my mind . . . branched thoughts . . . the wreath'd trellis of a working brain . . . shadowy thought."

The third point derives from the excursion–return structure of Wordsworth's prologue ("Up goes my Boat among the stars. . . . Then back to Earth . . . let us now / Descend from this ethereal height"). Such a structure appears only vestigially in *Ode to Psyche* (imaginative exploration of what Psyche *does not* have, followed by imaginative present remedy in the speaker's mind instead) but is central in two of the others, *Ode to a Nightingale* and *Ode on a Grecian Urn* (in each case an imaginative excursion to an ideal realm—the forest of the invisible bird, the art world of the urn—followed by a return to earthly reality), and is represented in what are usually taken to be the final two, *Ode on Melancholy* and *To Autumn,* by negative injunctions ("go not to Lethe," "Think not of them [the songs of spring]").

All five of Keats's great odes symbolize the working imagination; they are modern in stance and earthly (as opposed to ideal) in orientation, and they successively explore, and find impossible or unsatisfactory, such hypothetical alternatives to reality as religious ritual, mythology, fairy-tale romance, the past, the supernatural, the artificial. Rhetorically *Peter Bell* is nearly as unlike a Keats ode as it is possible for a poem to be, but its story and ideas could have helped point Keats in the direction he took in the famous series that he began so soon after its appearance.

There are biographical connections between Wordsworth and Keats; there are a great many Wordsworthian echoes in Keats's poetry and letters; there are general likenesses (as well as differences) between the two writers in subject matter, themes, attitudes, basic structures of thinking. Wordsworth was not the only influence on Keats's career, but he was undeniably an important one. It is probably only a coincidence that Haydon's *Christ's Entry into Jerusalem,* the painting displayed at his "immortal dinner" in late December 1817, has the portraits of Keats and Wordsworth, among the spectators, actually touching one another; Keats's head (in a two-dimensional view) just rests on the top of Wordsworth's. But perhaps Haydon was unconsciously prefiguring how tall Keats would "stand by the giant"—and at the same time showing Wordsworth as one of the bases that would help him stand so tall.

CHAPTER

10

Beyond the Imaginable
Wordsworth and Turner

KARL KROEBER

Most of us share the assumption that relations do exist between a poet and his age, but *proving* such relations is difficult. It is not even easy to connect the so-called sister arts of painting and poetry in the Romantic era. J.M.W. Turner (1775–1851), probably England's greatest painter, was almost an exact contemporary of Wordsworth (1770–1850), yet most observers are more impressed by differences between Turner's pictures and Wordsworth's poems than likenesses. Turner's *Hero and Leander,* for instance, seems about as un-Wordsworthian as a painting could be. Wordsworth seldom writes either of sexual passion or of classical myths, and when he does, as in *Laodamia,* he emphasizes stoic austerity: "the Gods approve the depth and not the tumult of the soul." Visually and narratively overwrought, *Hero and Leander* seems by comparison nothing but a tumult of foamy feelings.

Yet until we seek out what such disparate works may share, we cannot hope to say anything pertinent about the artists' age, about Romanticism. For the role of an individual artist in the history of art is definable only through linkages between his work and the necessarily different yet contemporaneous work of other artists, especially those practicing in other media. The paradox has been neatly summarized by Jean Laude: "Absolutely everything distinguishes a literary text from a painting or a drawing: its conception, its method of production, . . . its autonomous functioning. Nevertheless . . . a text and a painting cannot be disassociated from the synchronic

196

series to which they are linked."[1] To study one form of art in isolation from others is to deny oneself significant insight into the nature of that synchronic series that defines their "age." For practical reasons, of course, scholars often put aside art in media different from that on which they are at one moment focusing their attention. But institutionalizing this temporary practical necessity into a system, as universities do by dividing themselves into rigidly separate disciplines, cripples humanistic learning—not least by denying scholars diverse perspectives from which to evaluate their methods. The competing claims of traditional "historical" literary criticism and "postmodern" criticism may usefully be examined, for example, by analyzing their explanations of how works of art relate within what Laude calls "the synchronic series."

Historical criticism should keep us aware that works of art are human fabrications, not, therefore, usefully evaluated by methods developed for (or derived from) analyses of natural phenomena.[2] The beginning point in historical criticism, and the point to which it must ceaselessly return, is the *contingency* of art. Historical study is of something that happened once and that might have happened otherwise, including the possibility of not having happened at all. Only the most vulgar of Marxists and the very crudest of positivists any longer expect historical analysis to uncover "laws" equivalent to those sought in the natural sciences. Because art is the most gratuitous of human accomplishments, it most dramatically displays the history of culture as a story of contingencies. Henry VIII ordered his portrait from Holbein, and the citizens of Athens voted to rebuild their destroyed temple to Athena, but it was just the good fortune of King and citizens (and posterity) that their orders resulted in masterpieces. The citizens of Thebes paid for a large temple, and George I commissioned his portrait (several times), but who cares? This banal point bears repeating, because it reminds us that in describing the significance of "contemporaneous" successes in different arts, we do not describe causal sequences as we do when studying, say, simultaneous geologic phenomena.

A reminder is needed because literary history has too often during the past century treated art, implicitly or explicitly, as if it were explainable in terms of diachronic sequences of cause and effect. Many historical critics have engaged in futile elaborations of spurious genetic "sources." Since even the dullest academic perceives, eventually, that one cannot "prove" *The Faerie Queen* somehow caused *Paradise Lost* or that *Tristram Shandy* is responsible for *The Rime of the Ancient Mariner,* historical critics have sought for "causes" outside art to sustain the concept of prior-cause–subsequent-result. This begs the very question posed by art's "history," the puzzle of its contingency. Extrinsic events, of course, are not irrelevant: the development of music swerves when a great violinist loses an arm in a train wreck, as does the history of drama when Lorca is murdered by Fascists. But such events explain virtually nothing about the inner dynamics of art. A simple analogy from everyday life is good conversation, which depends less on where it occurs and what initiates it than on how it develops in itself. A primary thrust of so-called postmodern criticism has been to rectify the error of such simplistic historical analyses, to rescue the history of art from methods of crude causality, and to renew our awareness of the importance of lateral and associative affinities in art's exciting but frustrating synchronicities. Traditional academic historians, postmodernism in effect asserts, have been reluctant to confront the implications in art's creativity, its self-causative nature. And the unprofitable search for explanations outside the work of art's intrinsic dynamism has provoked postmodernism's insistence that we recognize art to be always "about itself."

If one visits with literature's sister, the visual arts (not to mention music), it is immediately plain that works of art are necessarily about themselves. Although painting and sculpture frequently—I would say usually—serve nonaesthetic purposes, serve, that is, practical physical, intellectual, spiritual, and ideological needs, they are also to a degree self-sufficient. This becomes obvious whenever a great work survives beyond knowledge of its original "place" and "practical" functions. *Beowulf* might be a case in point for literary critics, but more impressive are the extraordinary Greek bronzes, the Men of Riaci, recently recovered from the muddy floor of the Mediterranean, arguably the finest surviving works of ancient sculpture. What the Riaci bronzes "are," what they were made "for," even when they were cast, is unknown. But the statues speak eloquently for the preciousness of the human artifice they manifest. My observations of the visitors to the museum at Reggio di Calabria suggest that the bronzes impress all observers of every degree of sophistication with the care, skill, and imaginativeness that went into their making. By their mere being, the Riaci bronzes celebrate a possibility of human accomplishment.

Because of the accidents of time, one can only appreciate the Men of Riaci in themselves, as what they are now, since this is the only aspect of them that has so far survived. The careful precision by which a vision of the human form has been given such strong yet fluent embodiment in these bronzes, we examine with a pleased admiration paralleling our admiration for, say, Giotto's paintings in Padua of the stories of Christ and Mary, or Constable's *Haywain*, works about which we know infinitely more. Beyond any "reference," every piece of art manifests uniquely what a human being has done, might do, and, therefore, what one ought to spend time trying to do—or not to do.

Piles of rusting nails and randomly bent pipes on the floors of New York's Soho galleries, along with machine-polished metal and splattered canvases, accompanied by computer-originated magnifications of repetitious comic-book images, speak as loudly about themselves. This art announces its intrinsic worthlessness, advertises its value solely as commodity. Such works declare themselves to be junk, objects not worth the pain of loving craftsmanship—as the joke goes, how can you trash a contemporary art gallery?[3] The joke not merely condemns the artists' philistinism but also praises their integrity, since their art proclaims its meaninglessness, serving a need for conspicuous consumption by silicon-souled Yuppies and their paymasters, banks and corporate conglomerates.

Insofar as many artists in all media during recent decades have felt compelled to present their work as inherently transient, trivial, repetitive, boring, one is justified in categorizing this art under the heading of one of its substyles, "minimalist." Such a term does not, of course, exclude very large or very long works, like an Andy Warhol movie or a Philip Glass opera, but "minimalist" seems appropriate to describe the peculiar synchronic series of our age so far as it epitomizes its distinction from the art of other eras, from the earlier twentieth century back to those unidentified times in which the Men of Riaci were crafted.

Because art is always to a degree about itself, the diverse contingencies of individual works constitute, through simultaneous affiliations, a macrosystem, an understanding of which may deepen and enrich our appreciation of individual works composing it. Thus, to stay with my immediate example, recognizing a Glass opera as contributing to "minimalism" helps us to perceive that its length and repetitiveness are not failed attempts at development and complication (as we would judge these qualities in a work belonging to another highly formalistic series or macrosystem, such as Baroque music) but, instead, evidence of a deliberate reductiveness. Or, for a converse instance, in the searing self-criticism from which the assertive potency of Michelangelo's *Bound Slaves* seems to arise, one recognizes a force neither present in nor appropriate to either the Men of Riaci or the fiberglass dummies of 1980s superrealism, but a force whose diverse manifestations make up what we call the style of Mannerism.

Pursued rigorously and vigorously, postmodern methods enable us to solve Laude's paradox, for these methods direct our attention away from irrelevant matters of external causality. The historian of art seeks to describe affiliations among contemporaneously created artifacts that are markedly heterogeneous because each is self-caused. To put this complex matter too simply, the historicity of an artwork is to be apprehended only through exploration of all its specific contingencies. This is the only route to a true understanding of the "synchronic series" which each artwork helps to make appear. The series, in short, is not the cause of the individual works of art but the product of them and of responses to them by readers, viewers, listeners. If, then, we would understand Wordsworth's relation to his age, we must turn away from the invitingly broad but deceitful path that begins with a definition of his age. We must begin, instead, with particular works of art radically different from his but created by his contemporaries. Our aim must be to uncover hidden modes of parallelism linking authentically heterogeneous works.

As I have said, there does not appear to be much connection between many of Wordsworth's poems and Turner's paintings. But if we notice that Turner is a representational artist whose grandest canvases often mystify, obscure, and confuse their representations, it may occur to us that there is a parallel obfuscation in some of Wordsworth's poems, *The Thorn,* for instance. This lyric has provoked much controversy because it permits no assurance as to what exactly it represents. Wordsworth's manner of representing the thorn makes doubtful the processes of perception and conception through which the reader learns about the plant and the specific place and person associated with it. The poem consists entirely of the words of an unidentified speaker, apparently of somewhat limited intellectual abilities and of a superstitious cast of mind. The speaker recounts his observations of a stunted thorn by a small, moss-covered mound on the moor alongside a tiny pool, next to which a deranged woman often sits moaning, "O misery!" The speaker also reports what the local villagers have told him they believe about the woman and the spot, especially their conviction that she murdered her illegitimate baby and buried it in the mound by the thorn.

Wordsworth explained that this poem originated in his asking himself if he could invent a poem that would make "permanently impressive" for his readers a thorn he had often passed but never noticed until he happened upon it during a storm. Yet Wordsworth's "invention" seems to consist in surrounding the thorn with other features—pool, mound, destitute woman —that obscure it. Making the poem a dramatic monologue by someone such as a "retired sea captain" (as Wordsworth suggested we might think of the speaker) further "conceals" the thorn, for Wordsworth's narrator, whatever his profession, was deliberately chosen to be one to whom "readers . . . are not accustomed to sympathize in feeling . . . or in using such language."[4] The poet thus seems to put obstacles in the way of the success he desires, until we realize that one way to make the thorn "permanently impressive" for readers is to arouse in them an awareness of how such an object might be apprehended as impressive. Merely telling us that this thorn was of a striking shape, however accurately he might describe it, would be futile, since Wordsworth acknowledges that only the peculiar circumstances of a storm made *him* notice the plant. The poet's task is to create conditions of imagining the thorn that will permit readers to be impressed by it, make it worthy of wonder.

Readers of *The Thorn,* then, are brought to the plant through an unexpected and probably uncongenial mode of apprehension so that they may become conscious of inadequacies in it. They are thereby tempted into imagining a superior mode of apprehending the situation. The awakening of such imaginative effort is encouraged by the narrator's questioning of the villagers' perceptions and beliefs, a questioning that compels readers to reflect back on, to question, the narrator's way of judging and observing. I am not suggesting the poem is mistitled. It is not "about" the narrator, or the villagers, or the deserted woman per se. It is about how what each of these makes of the thorn—and makes of others' imaginings of the thorn's significance—may draw readers into exerting their imaginations. That Wordsworth's apparently perverse technique succeeds, that his "obscurantism" in fact enhances the thorn's impressiveness, is proved by the range of critical controversy his poem has provoked.

Wordsworth prevents the thorn from being subsumed within a single meaning, reduced to a conventionalized signification. He prevents the plant, one might say, from becoming merely the subject of a poem. Forced to have doubts about the villagers' and the narrator's impressions as they appear in the poem, we are led to try to comprehend how and why they might misinterpret. Our evaluating feeds back into intensified imagining of what thorn and pool could have represented for the woman, and her misery thereby may impress itself forcibly on our minds. The poem does not lead us to regress into a superstitious viewpoint; rather, it enables us to imagine for ourselves the elemental sufferings and uncertainties of human life from which can rise superstitious feelings capable of inspiring people to endow natural phenomena with qualities that can powerfully affect others' perceptions.

"There is a Thorn—it looks so old,
In truth, you'd find it hard to say
How it could ever have been young,
It looks so old and grey.
Not higher than a two years' child
It stands erect, this aged Thorn;
No leaves it has, no prickly points;
It is a mass of knotted joints,
A wretched thing forlorn.
It stands erect, and like a stone
With lichens is it overgrown.

"Like rock or stone, it is o'ergrown,
With lichens to the very top,
And hung with heavy tufts of moss,
A melancholy crop:
Up from the earth these mosses creep,
And this poor Thorn they clasp it round
So close, you'd say that they are bent
With plain and manifest intent
To drag it to the ground;
And all have joined in one endeavour
To bury this poor Thorn for ever.

(lines 1–22)

In these two opening stanzas there are several phrases—"looks so old," "looks so old and grey," "a wretched thing forlorn," "a melancholy crop," and the mosses' "manifest intent"—illustrating how the narrator's gropingly repetitive manner at once establishes that his "objective description" is in fact a construct of his mind, heavily loaded with emotional connotations imported by him. His repeated hesitant colloquialism "you'd say" tends to draw the reader in as a participant in this construction of the thorn's significance. But when a speaker such as this tells "us" what "we" would say, his assertion has the effect of stimulating us to imagine if we would, indeed, agree with him. Thus we are led to imagine how our judgment might differ from that attributed to us, and we have the beginning of the poem's interplaying of diverse impressions and judgments.

Even such a superficial consideration of some peculiarities in *The Thorn* may help us to understand why in one of his greatest paintings, *Snowstorm: Steamboat Off a Harbour's Mouth Making Signals in Shallow Water, and Going by the Lead,* Turner so efficiently obscures his very dramatic subject. The confusingness of the picture in good measure consists in Turner's abandoning representation by means of structures of geometric form, whose principal characteristics are visual distinctness and differentiation. One instantly perceives the difference between a cube and a cylinder, or between a pyramid and a sphere. But Turner's painting is structured primarily by colors, not shapes. Instead of portraying objects so that viewers may readily identify them by their differences from other objects, Turner sets us the problem of discerning his subject through modes of relationship and competing forces that are sometimes scarcely distinguishable. Wind-blown snow is different from the froth of ocean waves, but in Turner's picture we perceive both through similarities in the violence of their movements in a storm and through shifting complementarities of their colors—even through the actions of their meeting, conflicting, interpenetrating. The same is true of other elements in the scene, including the human artifacts, the ship, its smoke, the rockets it fires. The picture, in fact, is a multiplicity of interfaces of colors and movements that reflect, refract, and interfere with one another. In places, what is reflected or refracted is more vivid than its "original," leaving one often unsure what is original and what reflection, what "reality" and what "image."

Turner images an event, a complex event, the dynamism of which is represented through diverse and diversely interacting phenomena. Appropriate

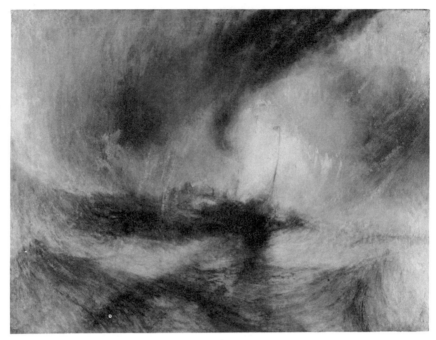

Snowstorm: Steamboat Off a Harbour's Mouth by J.M.W. Turner (N530). Courtesy of the Tate Gallery, London

to the ordering of such representation is the unstable kinesthesia provided by color, for, unlike shapes, colors not only keep changing but also determine, as they are determined by, shifts in associated colors. No color ever exists independent of its environment, its quality invariably being influenced by neighboring colors.[5] Turner exploits this fact to increase the self-destabilizing intrarelatedness of his painting. All its "confusions," resulting from its lack of simple geometric clarity, have the effect of encouraging viewers toward awareness of how they see, especially of how much of what they perceive is not distinctly registered optically. Thus, the observer's viewpoint for the scene is not immediately apparent; awareness of that uncertainty enhances one's sense of being *in* the storm oneself. Whether or not, as Turner claimed, he in truth made his observations for this canvas while lashed to the mast of another ship heaving in the tempest,[6] the effect of the picture is that of putting the viewer in hazard: "If one really allows one's eye to be absorbed into the forms and colors of the canvas, one begins to realize that, looking at it, one is in the centre of a maelstrom: . . . the lurch into the distance is not, as one would expect, *into* the picture, but out of it toward the right-hand edge. It is a picture which precludes the outsider spectator."[7]

Not only is Turner's subject an event, but his representation is itself an event, to be experienced by viewers as dubious in its significance exactly because it is a powerful action in process. The picture is visually baffling, as seeing in the midst of a storm at sea is baffling, so as to force us into perceiving imaginatively, not just registering sensations, but guessing what our fogged vision might reveal were it not obscured. This process compels us to recognize that valuable and meaningful perception requires an active mental shaping of possibilities presented by sensation in the very act of perceiving.

Most viewers say they are unsure of what they see in *Snowstorm* because the picture makes them aware that they may be seeing "inaccurately." This awareness, created by Turner's frustrating of easy perception, energizes a desire to see better, to discern through obscurity. Once we understand this aim in Romantic art, we will come to see that the external obscurities of a work such as *Snowstorm* are means also for bringing into the light of our awareness more subtle, inner, self-obfuscations. Through the experience of struggling to determine what we may be perceiving in Turner's disorienting stormscape, we may come to realize how much of what we normally see is determined not merely by exterior phenomena but also by the way we exert our psychic power upon our perceptions so as to construe ambiguous and transient visual clues. We may thus learn that we have the power to misconstrue, not least through lack of energy or audacity in construing. We remember simultaneously that a storm at sea is an ordinary occurrence, and a thorn an ordinary plant. It is easier to look at common things conventionally than to enter into the uncertainties of imaginative vision. We learn early in life the comfort of reducing the confusing forces of experience to an unambiguous and conclusive interpretation. What we perceive, therefore, is normally limited by our practice of letting perceptions fit our preestablished mental constructs. From such internally patterned limitations, Romantic works of art such as Turner's *Snowstorm* and Wordsworth's *The Thorn* seek to liberate us.

In their different arts Turner and Wordsworth are alike in creating a kind of doubly dramatic dialogue between perceptions and what both externally and internally shapes them. Turner and Wordsworth create art that represents, within their representations, difficulties in representing. This is why the doubt, "blurriness," unreliability, confusion in the work of both is regularly precipitated not by omission, not by cutting away, not by minimalizing, but by multiplyings, by overlayings, by additions of possibilities. Theirs is an art of maximizing. Dubieties provoked by their paintings and poems result not solely from actions represented but also from instabilities in acts of representation. Perhaps the simplest illustration of this trait appears in Wordsworth's famous lyric *The Tables Turned*, from which one learns by reading the poem in a book that it is wiser to enjoy nature than to seek wisdom reading books:

> Up! up! my friend, and clear your looks,
> Why all this toil and trouble!
> Up! up! my ftiend, and quit your books,
> Or surely you'll grow double.
>
> The sun above the mountain's head,
> A freshening lustre mellow,
> Through all the long green fields has spread,
> His first sweet evening yellow.
>
> Books! 'tis a dull and endless strife,
> Come, hear the woodland linnet,
> How sweet his music, on my life
> There's more of wisdom in it.
>
> And hark! how blithe the throstle sings!
> And he is no mean preacher,
> Come forth into the light of things,
> Let Nature be your teacher.
>
> She has a world of ready wealth,
> Our minds and hearts to bless—
> Spontaneous wisdom breathed by health,
> Truth breathed by cheerfulness.

One impulse from a vernal wood
May teach you more of man;
Of moral evil and of good,
Than all the sages can.

Sweet is the lore which nature brings;
Our meddling intellect
Misshapes the beauteous forms of things;
—We murder to dissect.

Enough of science and of art;
Close up those barren leaves,
Come forth, and bring with you a heart
That watches and receives.[8]

The self-destabilizing quality in Romantic art appears to originate in Romantic artists' awareness that art itself can pose a threat to the imaginative
potency giving rise to it. We see the most obvious form of this awareness in
Romantic artists' resistance to the deadening conventionality of mind they
thought the worst danger in a world of dawning industrial civilization.
Symptomatic of this mental passivity was the increasingly sensational and
hedonistic art that for Wordsworth revealed a psychic "torpor" against
which he inveighed in the preface to *Lyrical Ballads,* as, in more witty and
satirical fashions, did Jane Austen in *Northanger Abbey* and Thomas Love
Peacock in *Nightmare Abbey.* And in other works, both these novelists
present characters who are ridiculous because they adhere to novelistic conventions of behavior. Romantic art is shaped to free its audience from conventional, normalized patterns of perception and conception, not just of
other objects, but also of itself. Romantic art most frequently bewilders by
striving to provoke readers and viewers into expanding, extending, even
reconstituting what, unwittingly, they have come to accept as the limits of
the imaginable. Just as in Coleridge's words, the artist "dissolves, diffuses,
dissipates" what is given him in natural experience "in order to recreate"—
to disrupt in order to make anew—so the artist's re-creation—what we call
the "finished" work of art—should, the Romantics believed, encourage
readers and viewers into analogous half-perceiving, half-creating responses.
Turner's seemingly "unfinished" canvases of dynamic instability evidence

this Romantic commitment to arousing imaginative creativity in the audience. Contrary to what handbooks say, Romantic artists were not more imaginative than their predecessors, but they did more consistently strive to arouse imaginativeness in their readers and viewers. That this effort is as important in poetry as in painting can be demonstrated by brief attention to Wordsworth's *Resolution and Independence,* the poem Coleridge thought Wordsworth's most representative work, perhaps because the poem is about imagining.

Resolution and Independence begins with the poet enjoying the revivifying natural world on a brilliant morning succeeding a tempestuous night. The cheerfully self-satisfied poet then suddenly becomes despondent as his mind, from no external cause, plunges him from delight into dejection. Then, perhaps providentially but perhaps not, he happens upon an aged gatherer of leeches, whom he imagines as providing an example for buoying his spirits again. The poem thus presents the poet using the Leech-Gatherer to regain self-confidence.

The process by which the poet transforms images of the old man is introduced through the descriptive technique employed in the poem's opening, which modulates from the past tense in the first two lines into the present tense until the turn backward at the opening of the third stanza. This temporal sliding anticipates the later shifting back and forth between "is" and "seems," while tense and mode shiftings are complicated by typically sly Wordsworthian manipulations of prepositions. In line 1 the wind does not roar, but "there was a roaring *in* the wind," a slightly unusual phrasing, echoed in line 11 by the hare "running races in her mirth," a commoner usage whose oddity is emphasized by its parallel with the stranger, earlier line, so that we are tempted to "see" the joyousness attributed to the hare as embodied in the mist she kicks up from the "plashy earth." Such interplay unobtrusively attunes our mind to the poet both responding to and imposing upon externalities. The early lines, moreover, associate "in" with "all," the latter appearing in lines 1, 7, 8, 14, and 21. "All" is one of Wordsworth's favorite words, often, as here, employed to reinforce a sense both of the whole, the integral quality, of a situation and of the multiplicity of elements constituting that totality. Possibly because we are told "all the air is filled with pleasant noise of water," and "all things that love the sun" are abroad, it has seemed unsurprising to most readers that "the sky rejoices in the morning's birth," which is really quite an extraordinary phrase. The vital completeness of the scene, comprehending so many diverse elements, makes appropriate the unfolding of different moods within it. The buoyancy first evoked is dramatically changed by the poet's abrupt, unexternally motivated imagining of "another day" of "solitude, pain of heart, distress and poverty," so that one tends unthinkingly to accept his assertion that "gladness" *causes* "despondency and madness," however odd such logic might seem in another context, particularly one less superficially joyous.

Again unexpectedly and without discernible cause, the poet encounters in stanza 8 "a Man" who "seemed" the "oldest" of mankind. The remainder of the poem consists of superimposings of the poet's fantasies of the Leech-Gatherer upon his physical presence (rather as the poet had attributed feelings to the hare). The first superimpositions are similes, notably the doubled one of the rock that seems a sea beast:

> As a huge stone is sometimes seen to lie
> Couched on the bald top of an eminence;
> Wonder to all who do the same espy,
> By what means it could thither come, and whence;
> So that it seems a thing endued with sense:
> Like a sea-beast crawled forth, that on a shelf
> Of rock or sand reposeth, there to sun itself;
> ....
> Motionless as a cloud the old Man stood,
> That heareth not the loud winds when they call;
> And moveth all together, if it move at all.
>
> (lines 57–77)

This use of similes, and of similes on top of similes, characteristic of much Romantic lyricism, especially Shelley's, is a literary analogue to Turner's flooding our vision with transient and unstable details that defeat any reductive exactness of sight. Wordsworth compels his readers to see both the old man in his commonplace actuality (although to poet and reader *un*usual) and as a figure shaped and reshaped by the imagining poet—a figure the old man himself probably would not recognize. Reflexive doubling of vision is redoubled in the final stanzas, not merely by the dual possibility of stanza 16, one "in a dream" OR "a man from some far region," but also in the repetition of the poet's fantasy in stanza 19, a reiteration emphasized by the verbs "returned," "renew," "repeat," and "renewed" again. Nor are readers given any determinate relation of the vision in 19 to that in 16; they must imagine such connections as best they can. This reiterating has brought some readers to consider that resolution and independence are not, in fact, qualities instantaneously attained, that they are valuable, if difficult to achieve, attributes because they must be continuously reachieved.

Whatever one chooses to make of the situation, it has been created in a fashion designed to catch us up in the developing process of the poet's imagining. This is why we are jolted by the last stanza's final reversion into reflexive consciousness with the poet's remark, "I could have laughed myself to scorn." The phrase foregrounds a latent absurdity of the situation, an absurdity hinted at in the Leech-Gatherer's smile at the poet in line 120. There *is* something ridiculous in Wordsworth wandering about the moors imposing fantasies on an unpretentious old man. Because the human imagination is powerful, it can sometimes make an imaginer ridiculous. Imagination "distorts" what it works on—as we know that *Resolution and Independence* distorts the facts of the actual encounter that gave rise to the poem.[9] So it is necessary at the conclusion of a poem dealing with imaginative power and its joyous or gloomy consequences that Wordsworth gently shock readers back to awareness of the activity of their own minds responding to his poem. He does this by posing uncertainties about the poet's experience and, more significantly, about what he has *made* of the experience. The last two lines distance readers from the poet. The moral he draws, while comprehensible, is dubious enough and at least potentially so inadequate to what has gone before that we pause to question his summation, which means we withdraw from the poet, take a position from which we may reassess our interpreting experience throughout the preceding 138 lines. We thus become aware of our reading for our own purposes of the poet's "reading" for his purposes of the Leech-Gatherer.

Furthermore, if we recollect the emphasis early in the poem on the mind's self-generating polarities, the possibility of scornful laughter may alert us to darker implications in the uncertainty of the poem's conclusion. The last lines leave uncanceled Wordsworth's earlier vision of a fate of "despondency and madness," a destiny analogous to the grim one threatening in Turner's depiction of the distressed steamer laboring in a destructive vortex—a destiny frequently invoked by the painter under the rubric of "Fallacies of Hope." But hope can exist, one must remember, only in conditions of incertitude; hope does not pertain to situations of absolute assurance, for good or ill. So Wordsworth restoring his confidence to go forward does so in a fashion that may strike a reader as a misreading of the message embodied in the Leech-Gatherer's story. The undefinitive ending of *Resolution and Independence* is characteristic of Wordsworth's poetry, which is filled with conditional constructions, a grammatical equivalent to Turner's destablizing colors. And Wordsworth, contrary to his cultural reputation as a benignly optimistic nature poet, never flinches from the dark aspects of natural existence. He consistently recognizes death as the inevitable end for every mortal creature. Indeed, as more than one critic has observed, epitaphic forms and language are one of Wordsworth's favored means for displaying what he believes to be poetry's most significant functions. The aphoristic democraticness of his definition of the Poet in the preface to *Lyrical Ballads*, "a man speaking to men," for example, is sombrely elaborated in his later "Essay on Epitaphs":

> An epitaph is not a proud writing shut up for the studious; it is exposed to all—to the wise and the most ignorant; it is condescending, perspicuous, and lovingly solicits regard; its story and admonitions are brief, that the thoughtless, the busy, and indolent, may not be deterred, nor the impatient tired; the stooping old man cons the engraven record like a second horn-book;—the child is proud that he can read it;—and the stranger is introduced through its mediation to the company of a friend; it is concerning all, and for all;—in the churchyard it is open to the day; the sun looks down upon the stone, and the rains of heaven beat against it.[10]

Here the democratic idealism of language is situated literally in nature. The inscribed words are "subject to the soft handling of the elements" (to use Wordsworth's phrase from *The Excursion*) and illustrate concretely how the cultural is fitted to the natural. Human memorial stone and inscription belong in the world of sun and rain, the imaginative power there embodied appearing as a fulfillment of natural processes rather than as an assertion of the human against nature, or as an aspiration for what will transcend nature. By recording one human being's mortality, the epitaph

affirms humanity as significant to itself precisely because as individual beings each of us is transient. Hence the epitaph is "concerning all, and for
all," to be read, however, in diverse ways and for diverse purposes. The
unity of humankind is constituted of infinite differences. The epitaph "lov-
ingly solicits regard" because it appeals to what is most common, that is,
most elemental, in humanity, thereby linking together our diverseness.
Readings of the epitaph, therefore, are imaginative in the broadest sense,
readings onto, into, or over a text of elemental experience to recover some
of the awesomeness intrinsic to the brevity of individual human lives.

Two subsequent sentences clarify Wordsworth's sense of the importance of the epitaph as defining how and to what result we may read
imaginatively:

> In an obscure corner of a country church-yard I once espied, half-
> overgrown with hemlock and nettles, a very small stone laid upon the
> ground, bearing nothing more than the name of the deceased with the
> date of birth and death, importing that it was an infant which had
> been born one day and died the following. I know not how far the
> reader may be in sympathy with me; but more awful thoughts of
> rights conferred, of hopes awakened, of remembrances stealing away
> or vanishing, were imparted to my mind by that inscription there
> before my eyes than by any other that it has ever been my lot to meet
> with upon a tomb-stone.

The succinct anonymity of the inscription on the tiny, forgotten stone as-
sures that the significance of this simplest but most moving of epitaphs is
created by the imagining mind. The trivial memorial is the least sublime of
objects but profoundly evocative of "rights conferred . . . hopes awakened
. . . remembrances stealing away." These possibilities may come to us as startling, for we have taught ourselves not to believe that one can imagine so
much from so little. The poet's awareness of this difficulty emerges in his
doubt that his experience can be conveyed to others. As with the thorn and
the Leech-Gatherer, one notices here, too, that we are not allowed directly
to "see" or to "read" the tombstone ("there before *my* eyes"): we can only
read Wordsworth's reading of it. The slow-moving, monosyllabically ordered final phrase then makes us dwell on a comparison of experiences, subtly reminding us that none of our experiences, however unique, is isolated.

Our lives are fleeting because we live in time, but time alone makes possible the most humanly precious dimensions of comparison: remembrance and hope. The brevity of the infant's life memorialized thus may increase the magnitude of its implications for *our* lives. This can occur only because we can imagine—imagine more than we are usually taught we are able to. The unseen epitaph may deeply affect us because Wordsworth's reading of it encourages us to realize how awesome is the plainest, simplest, briefest human existence—if we will allow ourselves to endure imagining it.

11

Two Dark Interpreters
Wordsworth and De Quincey

JONATHAN WORDSWORTH

God smote Savannah-la-Mar, and in one night, by earthquake, removed her, with all her towers standing and population sleeping, from the steadfast foundations of the shore to the coral floors of ocean. And God said, "Pompeii did I bury and conceal from men through seventeen centuries; this city I will bury but not conceal. She shall be a monument to men of my mysterious anger, set in azure light through generations to come, for I will enshrine her in a crystal dome of my tropic seas." This city, therefore, like a mighty galleon with all her apparel mounted, streamers flying, and tackling perfect, seems floating along the noiseless depths of ocean; and oftentimes in glassy calms, through the translucid atmosphere of water that now stretches like an air-woven awning above the silent encampment, mariners from every clime look down into her courts and terraces, count her gates, and number the spires of her churches. . . .

Thither, lured by the loveliness of cerulean depths, by the peace of human dwellings privileged from molestation, by the gleam of marble altars sleeping in everlasting sanctity, oftentimes in dreams did I and the Dark Interpreter cleave the watery veil that divided us from her streets. We looked into the belfries, where the pendulous bells were waiting in vain for the summons which should awaken their marriage peals; together we touched the mighty organ keys that sang no *jubilates* for the ear of heaven, that sang no requiems for the ear of human sorrow; together we searched the silent nurseries, where the children were all asleep and *had* been asleep through five generations.

"They are waiting for the heavenly dawn," whispered the Interpreter to himself; "and when *that* comes, the bells and organs will utter a *jubilate* repeated by the echoes of Paradise." Then, turning to me, he said, "This is sad, this is piteous; but less would not have sufficed for the purpose of God."[1]

Savannah-la-Mar, De Quincey's version of the lost mythical city of Atlantis, has been overwhelmed in a moment, yet lives on, embalmed in the ocean depths as a monument of God's mysterious anger. The Dark Interpreter—not God, not De Quincey—sees hope in this situation: "They are waiting for the heavenly dawn." By implication, Atlantis may become the New Jerusalem: "This is sad, this is piteous; but less would not have sufficed for the purpose of God". In this aspect, the Dark Interpreter reminds one a little of the Pedlar at the end of Wordsworth's *Ruined Cottage,* as he too turns to his companion—the writer—to offer in the face of human suffering a wisdom that the writer himself cannot always feel:

> I well remember that those very plumes,
> Those weeds, and the high speargrass on that wall,
> By mists and silent raindrops silvered o'er,
> As once I passed did to my mind convey
> So still an image of tranquility,
> So calm and still, and looked so beautiful
> Amid the uneasy thoughts which filled my mind,
> That what we feel of sorrow and despair
> From ruin and from change, and all the grief
> The passing shews of being leave behind,
> Appeared an idle dream that could not live
> Where meditation was.
>
> (lines 513–524)[2]

Wordsworth of course has a variety of guides and second selves, some of them talkative and rather too explicit (if not the Pedlar, certainly the Wanderer whom he becomes in *The Excursion*); some of them more cryptic in their messages (Edward in *Anecdote for Fathers*, Johnny in *The Idiot Boy*); some with admonitions that are silent, or very nearly so—the Leech-Gatherer, whose speech is an irrelevance, and the London Beggar of the 1805 *Prelude,* book 7:

> And on the shape of this unmoving man,
> His fixed face and sightless eyes, I looked
> As if admonished from another world.
>
> (lines 621–623)

Wordsworth makes a specialty of the misunderstood and the incomprehensible, both of which have the effect of teaching us how to see. An uncharitable critic—the later Coleridge would do—might easily take the view that, as an interpreter, Wordsworth himself was *in* the dark. Certainly he valued darkness in an unusual way—and found it in unusual places:

> Visionary power
> Attends upon the motions of the winds
> Embodied in the mystery of words;
> There darkness makes abode, and all the host
> Of shadowy things do work their changes there
>
> (1805 *Prelude* 5.619–623)

As a child Wordsworth had seen "the hills / Grow larger *in the darkness*" (*Pedlar,* lines 21–22; emphasis added) and known what it was to suffer an invasion of his mind:

> In my thoughts
> There was a darkness—call it solitude
> Or blank desertion . . .
>
> (1805 *Prelude* 1.420–422)

As an adult he had claimed that "suffering is permanent, obscure and *dark*" and had come to hope very much that

> There is a dark
> Invisible workmanship that reconciles
> Discordant elements . . .
>
> (1805 *Prelude* 1.352–354)

in human existence.

"Suffering," De Quincey writes in *Suspiria de Profundis,* "is a mightier agency in the hands of Nature, as a Demiurgus creating the intellect, than most people are aware of." The statement is at once learned and casual. The Demiurge may be seen in Platonic thinking as the maker of the world, but in

Gnostic terms it is a power subordinate to the Supreme Being, directly responsible for the creation of evil. By analogy, suffering in the hands of Nature works through pain that is apparently evil. "The truth," De Quincey
continues, as casual as before, "I heard often in sleep from the lips of the
Dark Interpreter. Who is he? He is a shadow, reader, but a shadow with
whom you must suffer me to make you acquainted" (187). To some extent
we do indeed become acquainted with the Dark Interpreter. Through De
Quincey's image of the Alpine "Brocken Spectre," we learn that he is "originally a mere reflex of [the writer's] inner nature," "the dark symbolic mirror
for reflecting to the daylight what else must be hidden forever." And we
learn too of his ability to "swerve out of [the writer's] orbit, and"—in a
memorable phrase—"mix a little with alien natures" (182). Like the "plas-
tic," or creative, power of the 1799 *Prelude* that is "at times / Rebellious,
acting in a devious mood" (2.411–413), the Interpreter is not always willing to be subject to the conscious mind. He exists in dreams, and in reverie,
because "there is in the dark places of the human spirit—in grief, in fear, in
vindictive wrath—a power of self-projection . . ." (188). He may "assume
new features or strange features, as in dreams always there is a power not
contented with reproduction, but which absolutely creates or transforms"
(183).

To return to De Quincey's teasing question, What, then, is the Dark Interpreter? Depending on whether one prefers to speak German, or Latin, or
Greek, he is a doppelgänger, an alter ego, a parhelion (De Quincey's own
word). Clearly he is allied to the imagination and is in some sense a recognition of the existence (and the strangeness) of the unconscious. It is worth insisting, however, that he is a literary creation and that although he is defined
by De Quincey in terms of dreams, he is seldom in fact shown to be part of
one. Despite the whimsical side to his nature, it may be that he is best
thought of as a prophet. He lives in the darkness that is associated with
revelation—the darkness of Tiresias, of Milton, of Wordsworth's London
Beggar. Behind him is the traditional paradox that darkness equals light
(Gloucester's "I stumbled when I saw" [*King Lear,* act 4, sc. 1, line 21]),
and it is appropriate that his name can on second thoughts be read in two
different ways. He is not just mysterious, powerful (with "Dark" as an adjective), but one who interprets the darkness (with "Dark" as a noun). This,
I suspect, was to have been his role in the larger scheme for *Suspiria* that
was never completed;[3] and I believe that even in the fragmentary work that

has come down to us, he is both far more important, and far less capricious, than is commonly assumed. The chief problem for the reader is to see how De Quincey's perception of suffering reconciles the Interpreter's association with both darkness as horror and darkness as wisdom.

The *Confessions* move from autobiography—fictionalized no doubt, but still largely mundane—into the re-creation of dream; *Suspiria de Profundis* (Breathings from the Depths), as the title suggests, moves into a world even less concerned with actualities. Dreams are still central, still the source of power and information, because, "in alliance with the mystery of darkness," dreaming "is the one great tube through which man communicates with the shadowy," because the capacity for dreaming "forces the infinite into the chambers of a human brain and throws dark reflections from eternities below all life upon the mirrors of the sleeping mind" (114). But in *Suspiria,* dream itself—that is, the attempted re-creation of actual dream—merges into a world of myth-making imagination that is the sublime of De Quincey's achievement. As he becomes further and further dissociated from actualities, more and more able to move in the Wordsworthian inner space of the mind ("eternities below all life"), he creates the appropriate second self: the darker, more mysterious interpreter of the dark messages of the unconscious.

As one would expect from a close reader of *The Prelude,* De Quincey's work (the single, larger prose poem that is *Confessions* and *Suspiria*) is a version of *Paradise Lost:* a myth of the Fall and a quest for higher understanding. As one easily might not expect, it is curiously coherent. Part 1, *Confessions,* offers false paradises and delusive hopes; it is a prolonged and dreadful Fall, on which the writer comments as his own Dark Interpreter. Part 2, *Suspiria,* goes back into childhood experience to seek the origins and nature—and finally the purpose—of suffering, discovering, as it does so, that other self who can say to us convincingly: "This is sad, this is piteous; but less would not have sufficed for the purpose of God."

The outset of *Confessions,* the start of the journey that is De Quincey's adult life, is very important. He is leaving behind youth and Manchester Grammar School, stealing away in the dawn after a moment of tragicomedy as his trunk bounds down the stairs past the sleeping headmaster's door:

Gathering courage from the silence, the groom hoisted his burden again [a touch of Milton's *Lycidas* and Wordsworth's *The Ruined Cottage* that signals new beginnings][4] and accomplished the remainder of his descent without accident. I waited until I saw the trunk placed on a wheelbarrow and on its road to the carrier's; then, "with Providence my guide," I set off on foot, carrying a small parcel, with some articles of dress under my arm, a favorite English poet in one pocket and a small (12 mo) volume, containing about nine plays of Euripides, in the other. (33)

The allusions, dense and meaningful, offer us (a little darkly) the terms in which later events are to be interpreted. It is Milton who goes into quotation marks:

> The world was all before them, where to choose
> Their place of rest, and Providence their guide;
> They hand in hand, with wandering steps and slow,
> Through Eden took their solitary way.
> *(Paradise Lost*, bk. 12, lines 646–649)

But the end of *Paradise Lost,* as De Quincey well knew, is the beginning of *The Prelude:*

> The earth is all before me—with a heart
> Joyous, nor scared at its own liberty,
> I look about, and should the guide I chuse
> Be nothing better than a wandering cloud,
> I cannot miss my way.
> (1805 *Prelude* 1.15–19)

Wordsworth is the "favorite English poet," qualifying the presence of Milton, emphasizing the sense of a new beginning, yet tacitly pointing to the contrast of De Quincey's own situation. "It had been my intention originally," he writes, "to proceed to Westmoreland, both from the love I bore to that county and on other personal accounts. Accident, however, gave a different direction to my wanderings, and I bent my steps toward North Wales" (*Confessions* 33). His language poignantly echoes Wordsworth's in *The Brothers* ("the love / which to an only brother he has borne," lines 68–69), and his situation resembles the poem's plot: De Quincey at this stage dared not go to see Wordsworth in Westmorland, just as the character Leonard does not dare make himself known, or even inquire for his brother. Unlike the joyous, confident Wordsworth, De Quincey shares with Adam and Eve the "wandering steps and slow." He is subject to accident, and though he may choose Providence as his guide, he can, and does, miss his way. The final touch is that although he has *Lyrical Ballads* in one pocket, standing for all sorts of future hopes, in the other he has a volume of Greek tragedy, suggesting quite another view of the world.

Though the reader cannot know it at this point in the *Confessions,* in retrospect it is the lack of a companion that stands out above all from De Quincey's references to *Paradise Lost* and *The Prelude.* Adam and Eve may be said to take "their solitary way" out of Eden, but they go hand-in-hand, their love apparently strengthened by the experience of pain and normality. Wordsworth of course speaks much of solitude, and in the *Prelude* quotation his pronouns are all in the first person ("The earth is all before me . . . the guide I chuse"); but he is just off to Dove Cottage to live with Dorothy, the "dear, dear sister" of *Tintern Abbey.* "Where'er my footsteps turned," he was to write after three months together in the wet and windy Paradise of Grasmere,

> Her voice was like a hidden bird that sang;
> The thought of her was like a flash of light,
> Or an unseen companionship, a breath
> Or fragrance independent of the mind
> (*Home at Grasmere,* lines 110–113)

Solitude for De Quincey was not so privileged. He was truly alone, and despite the later devotion of Peggy Simpson (his wife), there is a sense in which he continued to be so. He too had had a sister, but we do not learn of her hold over his imagination until we have watched, and shared in, the pain of his search for her. *Suspiria,* darker and deeper in its interpretations, later restores to Elizabeth De Quincey the central position which in fact she always held; the *Confessions* meanwhile gives pride of place to her surrogate.

Ann of Oxford Street is fifteen and an orphan. A "brutal ruffian" has "plundered her little property" (De Quincey speaks of gaining redress from a magistrate, so perhaps we should take the words literally), and she has been forced to become a prostitute. So much for the bare facts. If we wish to know of the life she led, we shall get a far better idea from Henry Mayhew's

London Labour and the London Poor or from the squalid reminiscences of Boswell, who congratulates himself on shouting at a prostitute in the Strand and demanding that an officer on half pay should be allowed to "roger for sixpence" and who disports himself wearing a device, designed not to save the girls from pregnancy, but to save him from the pox.⁵ We no more hear of such details from De Quincey than we hear from Wordsworth what Martha Ray in *The Thorn* had for breakfast. Can it, one wonders, have helped Ann to earn her living that she and De Quincey should pace together night after night along Oxford Street? Was he so young and so small (about five feet, according to Carlyle) that men who accosted her took no notice of his presence? What in any case did he feel when they did so? No answers are likely to emerge. Like *The Ruined Cottage* or *Michael,* this is a story of loss. All that truly matters takes place in the mind of the survivor. There is the brief moment of sharing that heightens the poignancy; there is the quite arbitrary separation; and there are the years that follow: "Then it was, at this crisis of my fate, that my poor orphan companion, who had herself met with little but injuries in this world, stretched out a saving hand to me" (*Confessions* 43−44). The echoes now are from the address to Dorothy at the crisis of Wordsworth's fate in the 1805 *Prelude,* book 10:

> And then it was
> That the beloved woman in whose sight
> Those days were passed . . .
> Companion never lost through many a league—
> Maintained for me a saving intercourse
> With my true self . . .
>
> (907−915)

De Quincey and Ann are seated on the steps of a house in Soho Square; De Quincey has fainted from hunger:

Uttering a cry of terror, but without a moment's delay, she ran off into Oxford Street, and in less time than could be imagined, returned to me with a glass of port wine and spices that acted upon my empty stomach . . . with an instantaneous power of restoration; and for this glass the generous girl, without a murmur, paid out of her own humble purse, at a time, be it remembered, when she had scarcely wherewithal to purchase the bare necessaries of life, and when she could have no reason to expect that I should ever be able to reimburse her. (44)

"O youthful benefactress!" De Quincey continues, heightening his style, and recollecting *Tintern Abbey*—

> How oft in spirit have I turned to thee
> O sylvan Wye—thou wanderer through the woods—
> How often has my spirit turned to thee!
>
> (lines 56–58)

—as his thoughts turn to the future implications of that moment: "How often, in succeeding years, standing in solitary places and thinking of thee with grief of heart and perfect love—how often have I wished that, as in ancient times. . . ." (The train of thought seems to waver at this point, but to dark interpretation, the analogy that follows is very important.)

> have I wished that, as in ancient times the curse of a father was believed to have a supernatural power and to pursue its object with a fatal necessity of self-fulfillment, even so the benediction of a heart oppressed with gratitude might have . . . power . . . to waylay, to overtake, to pursue thee into the central darkness of a London brothel or (if it were possible) into the darkness of the grave, there to awaken thee with an authentic message of peace and forgiveness and of final reconciliation! (44)

The incident offers De Quincey no "life and food for future years." Insofar as it is a "spot of time,"[6] it contains no "renovating virtue"—just pain, and a terrible sense of the "impotence of grief." In a moment of apocalyptic insight, the Pedlar of *The Ruined Cottage* had

> . . . muse[d] on one
> By sorrow laid asleep or borne away,
> A human being destined to awake
> To human life, or something very near
> To human life, when he [should] come again
> For whom she suffered.
>
> (370–375)

But this fantasy of the quickening power of love has the air of one who has come out on the far side of grief, having made an interpretation of the darkness that De Quincey is still seeking impotently to penetrate.

To find a Wordsworth comparably baffled, comparably turning to the myths of antiquity in desperate wish fulfillment, one has to go right back to the schoolboy *Vale of Esthwaite* of 1787, with its spooky Gothic version of that central *topos* of classical literature, the visit to the Underworld:

> On tiptoe as I leaned aghast
> Listening the hollow-howling blast,
> I started back—when at my hand
> A tall thin spectre seemed to stand
> . . . on one bended arm he bore
> What seemed the poet's harp of yore;
> One hand he waved, and would have spoke,
> But from his trembling shadow broke
> Faint murmuring—sad and hollow moans
> As if the wind sighed through his bones.[7]

Many of these details will be applied in 1798 to *The Discharged Soldier* (later incorporated in *Prelude*, book 4), who looks like a ghost but is perfectly human; but the Spectre of *The Vale of Esthwaite* lives on the other side of the border; he *is* a ghost, but like Hamlet's father, whom he frequently recalls, he is a troubled one. It is easy to laugh at the poetry—especially when the Gates of Hades turn out to be at the foot of Helm Crag ("facilis discensus Averno"!)—but within the Gothic idiom Wordsworth, only three-and-a-half years after his father's death, is playing over traumatic material that will return in the *Hamlet* references of *The Prelude* and the *Intimations Ode*.[8] In De Quincey's words, he is surely seeking "some tranquillizing belief as to the future balances and the hieroglyphic meanings of human sufferings" (*Confessions* 44):

> He waved again, we entered slow
> A passage narrow, damp and low;
> I heard the mountain heave a sigh
> Nodding its rocky helm on high,
> And on we journeyed many a mile . . .
> Now as we wandered through the gloom
> In black Helvelyn's inmost womb
> The Spectre made a solemn stand,
> Slow round my head thrice waved his hand,
> And cleaved mine ear—then swept his lyre

That shrieked terrific, shrill and dire.
Shuddered the fiend: the vault along
Echoed the loud and dismal song.
'Twas done!—the scene of woe was o'er;
My breaking soul could bear no more.

(Vale of Esthwaite)

Continuous drafts in the manuscript break down at this point as Wordsworth strives to bring the Underworld visit, and the personal wish fulfillment, to a climax. A thunderous sound is heard, a "massy door" flies open,
and it becomes clear that some kind of initiation ceremony is taking place
that leaves the poet each night in the power of the forces of darkness. "Together we are hurled," the sequence concludes,

Far, far amid the shadowy world;
And since that hour the world unknown—
The world of shades—is all my own.

Aeneas in the Underworld of Virgil had learned from his father Anchises
of the future of their race; what Wordsworth learns is far less certain. Taking possession of "the world of shades," however, he surely becomes a Dark
Interpreter in his own right; and as the Spectre is himself a minstrel, it is
tempting to see the experience as comparable to the 1805 *Prelude* moment
of consecration to poetry:

I made no vows, but vows
Were then made for me: bond unknown to me
Was given, that I should be—else sinning greatly—
A dedicated spirit.

(4.341–344)

In addition, one wonders whether the poet has not at some unconscious
level penetrated into the darkness of his father's grave, carrying with him De
Quincey's "authentic message of peace and forgiveness, and of final reconciliation." Such a view would certainly be borne out by the version of the
Prelude "spot of time" that is contained in *The Vale of Esthwaite*:

One evening, when the wintery blast
Through the sharp hawthorn whistling passed
And the poor flocks, all pinched with cold,

Sad-drooping sought the mountain fold,
Long, long, upon yon steepy rock
Alone I bore the bitter shock—
Long, my swimming eyes did roam
For little horse to take me home,
To bear me (what avails my tear?)
To sorrow o'er a father's bier.

"Flow on," the poet continues, addressing himself a little comically to the unavailing tear,

... in vain thou hast not flowed,
But eased me of a heavy load,
For much it gives my heart relief
To pay the mighty debt of grief—
With sighs repeated o'er and o'er
I mourn because I mourned no more.

The sense of grief as a "mighty debt" owed to his father surely carries some of the resentment felt by Satan when faced with "The debt immense of end-less gratitude" he owed to God (*Paradise Lost* 4.52). And, given the extent to which all the spots of time depend upon guilt, it is interesting to learn from this earliest version that Wordsworth had not at first been able to mourn.

De Quincey's curious fantasy that "a heart oppressed with gratitude" (oppressed, that is, with not having the chance to express its gratitude) might be given a supernatural power comparable to that of the father's curse, shows a way of thinking that is very important to the *Confessions* and perfectly reflected in his escaping from school with *Lyrical Ballads* in one pocket, Euripides in the other. Searching for Ann "through the mighty labyrinths of London," he looks toward the woods and fields that lie past Marylebone (now Regent's Park) and says in his mind, "*That* is the road to the north, and, therefore, to [Grasmere], and if I had the wings of a dove, *that* way I would fly for comfort." To which he adds in 1821, "Thus I said, and thus I wished in my blindness" (57). Grasmere had come to be associated with "the second birth of [his] sufferings," the opium dreams that reenact the loss of Ann: "There it was that for years I was persecuted by visions as ugly, and as ghastly phantoms, as ever haunted the couch of an Orestes"

(57). Most appalling of these visions are those in which the Dark Interpreter shows his power to "swerve out of . . . orbit, and mix a little with alien natures." The phrase is echoed by De Quincey in 1849 in a passage from *The English Mail Coach* that is still more appalling in its implications.. "The dreamer finds housed within himself—occupying, as it were, some separate chamber in his brain—holding, perhaps, from that station a secret and detestable commerce with his own heart, some horrid alien nature" (*English Mail Coach* 243). As the horrors increase, the parhelion is capable, not just of changing shape, but of multiplying: "not one alien nature, but two, but three, but four, but five, are introduced within what once he thought the inviolable sanctuary of himself" (244). De Quincey at Dove Cottage is hunted down, "the inviolable sanctuary" of his mind invaded, by furies who are products of his own inner darkness, versions of himself. By a powerful illogic it comes to seem that he is being tormented (turned into the fated tragic hero of Euripides) for making the assumption that Wordsworth's Paradise of Grasmere could be Paradise for him—in effect, one might say, for assuming that life could be lived on the level of his pleasure in *Lyrical Ballads*. Like the opium with which it is so closely linked, Grasmere can only *seem* to bring comfort, "an assuaging balm" for "the wounds that will never heal." The famous address to opium has its strange and earnest eloquence because even as he writes, having suffered all the tortures of constant attempts at withdrawal, De Quincey goes back into the hopes the drug will always *promise*—and sometimes *appear*—to fulfill:

> Thou buildest upon the bosom of darkness, out of the fantastic imagery of the brain, cities and temples, beyond the art of Phidias and Praxiteles—beyond the splendor of Babylon and Hekatompylos; and, "from the anarchy of dreaming sleep," callest into sunny light the faces of long-buried beauties and the blessed household countenances, cleansed from the "dishonours of the grave." Thou only givest these gifts to man, and thou hast the keys of Paradise, O just, subtle, and mighty opium!
>
> (*Confessions* 71)

What the opium dreams *truly* do, of course, is to show that in human life "years . . . far asunder [are] bound together by subtle links of suffering derived from a common root." The *Confessions*, however, is an evasive work.

There are many dark hints that can be interpreted with the aid of the *Suspiria*—Ann is loved as a sister, Margaret De Quincey plays Electra to her husband's Orestes, the Wordsworth allusions take us very frequently to Dorothy—but we are never told directly that the suffering the dreams induce or reveal is linked back beyond the loss of Ann to its root in the death of the loved and admired seven-year-old elder sister, Elizabeth. Why the final link in the chain was not revealed we cannot know; perhaps there was no deliberate intention to leave it out. The *Confessions* finally is huddled together, given an entirely bogus rationale—"Not the opium-eater, but the opium, is the true hero of the tale, and the legitimate center on which the interest revolves" (100)—and a falsely triumphant conclusion. De Quincey's claim in the final pages to have conquered the addiction is both untrue and irrelevant. The brief last paragraph, however, takes us back to Milton (and therefore to Wordsworth) in a way that is immensely revealing:

One memorial of my former condition still remains; my dreams are not yet perfectly calm; the dread swell and agitation of the storm have not wholly subsided; the legions that encamped in them are drawing off, but not all departed; my sleep is tumultuous, and like the Gates of Paradise to our first parents when looking back from afar, it is still (in the tremendous line of Milton):

With dreadful faces thronged and fiery arms. (102)

The mood in which De Quincey had set out from Manchester, taking Providence as his guide and heading (if indirectly) for Grasmere and Dove Cottage, had been inappropriate. He had not understood that for him Paradise was behind, not before—that its gates were barred against reentry. The *Confessions* has its brief moments of light (notably as De Quincey rouses himself from the horrors of his crocodile dreams to kiss the faces of his children standing by the bed), but for the most part it is a very dark interpretation. No lasting hope is offered of any kind. We see the tragedy of one who is fated to suffer as surely as if the father's curse—the blood-guilt of the House of Atreus—were upon him. In *Suspiria*, De Quincey will go back to the root of his suffering, seek to understand why "less would not have sufficed for the purpose of God"; but he does not do so in the *Confessions*.

Grevel Lindop in a recent essay draws attention to the evangelicalism of

De Quincey's mother and quotes John Foster making play with the expected moral connotations of darkness: "After having explored many a cavern or dark ruinous avenue, [the sophisticated traveller] may have left undetected a darker recess in his [own] character."⁹ Few writers have been more preoccupied by the inner depths of the mind than De Quincey and Wordsworth, but for all De Quincey's evangelical upbringing—and despite the fact that both might seem to be writing in a confessional mode—neither of them seems ever to think of darkness as sin. This is particularly striking since both to some extent structure their work on *Paradise Lost* and the concept of a personal Fall, and both take (in general terms) a moral view of life. Looking back into the darkness of their past, they see things that went wrong, not things they did that were wrong.

The big difference between them, of course, is that where De Quincey spends a lifetime trying to see the fated tragedy of his experience in terms of a larger Christian vision, Wordsworth has almost from the first the power to "make / Our noisy years seem moments in the being / Of the eternal silence" (*Intimations Ode,* lines 156–158). He is the child of his own ode, possessing as an instinct the truths that De Quincey is toiling all his years to find. As a Dark Interpreter Wordsworth has a unique central insight into the nature of mental process and human development that enables him to transform guilt and discomfiture—

> Fallings from us, vanishings
> Blank misgivings of a creature
> Moving about in worlds not realized
> (*Intimations Ode* 146–148)

—and not only to transform them, but to turn the energies that are released into a source of creative strength. If he did not think in terms of sin, he was nonetheless fascinated by the workings of guilt. In rather crude forms one sees this in *Salisbury Plain, The Borderers,* or *Peter Bell,* but the key text is *The Prelude* version of the Waiting for the Horses. Returning to this episode early in 1799, eleven-and-a-half years after *The Vale of Esthwaite,* Wordsworth tells us not of "the mighty debt of grief" that he has been unable to pay, but of a stronger, stranger guilt felt at the original moment:

> Ere I to school returned
> That dreary time, ere I had been ten days

> A dweller in my father's house, he died,
> And I and my two brothers, orphans then,
> Followed his body to the grave.
>
> (1.349–353)

"A dweller in my father's house" has an allegorical ring—one kind of father so easily slips into the other—and introduces the suggestion of human impermanence, but on the whole the verse up to this point has a grave matter-of-factness. We enter now into the confusion of the child's mind:

> The event,
> With all the sorrow which it brought, appeared
> A chastisement; and when I called to mind
> That day so lately passed, when from the crag
> I looked in such anxiety of hope,
> With trite reflections of morality,
> Yet with the deepest passion, I bowed low
> To God who thus corrected my desires.
>
> (1799 *Prelude* 1.353–360)

The logic of guilt is so compelling that for a moment, despite the phrase "trite reflections," placed there to warn us of the child's terrible wrongness, we almost accept the vengeful God who punishes hope and has to be bought off in desperate appeasement. On second thoughts, however, it is the passion that should stand out—"For the reader cannot be too often reminded that poetry is passion; it is the history or science of feelings" (Wordsworth's note to *The Thorn*). In this case, perhaps "science" is the better word. Wordsworth as interpreter is analyzing the passion—watching it make a series of chemical changes. Hope turns to guilt and misplaced moral fervor, which send the mind back to the scene of the crime, charging the details of a wholly uninteresting landscape with the power and significance that create a spot of time:

> And afterwards the wind and sleety rain,
> And all the business of the elements,
> The single sheep, and the one blasted tree,
> And the bleak music of that old stone wall,
> The noise of wood and water, and the mist
> Which on the line of each of those two roads

> Advanced in such indisputable shapes—
> All these were spectacles and sounds to which
> I often would repair, and thence would drink
> As at a fountain.
>
> (1799 *Prelude* 1.361–370)

It is a very odd claim. The mind, going back to a past landscape highlighted by guilt, comes instead to value that landscape for its intensity. Imperceptibly the motive for revisiting the past turns from guilt to pleasure, from pleasure to admiration, as the mind wonders at its former powers, taking them, in Geoffrey Hartman's phrase, as "evidences of election."[10] In the final stage of transformation, the past, by virtue solely of qualities conferred upon it by the mind itself, becomes the source of renewed creativity, that is, both of imaginative material and of new creative energies.

Though associated with the *Prelude* spots of time, this process had already been isolated by Wordsworth in a draft conclusion to *The Ruined Cottage* of March 1798, not only before the "spots" had been conceived, but before the *Lyrical Ballads*:

> He had discoursed
> Like one who in the slow and silent works,
> The manifold conclusions of his thought,
> Had brooded till Imagination's power
> Condensed them to a passion whence she drew
> Herself new energies, resistless force.[11]

Having drafted part 1 of the 1799 *Prelude*, Wordsworth felt so confident that the mind could indeed generate its own creative power that he was able to conclude the Waiting for the Horses section with the magnificent assertion:

> And I do not doubt
> That in this later time, when storm and rain
> Beat on my roof at midnight, or by day
> When I am in the woods, unknown to me
> The workings of my spirit thence are brought.
>
> (1.370–374)

By whom, one might ask. What slave is it that goes back to the fountain of the past to bring the poet his elixir? The answer, of course, is the silent, unconscious, beneficent power of association. Wordsworth and De Quincey are both associationists, and both would agree that the power was dark, unaccountable in its workings. Wordsworth does not have to say consciously to himself "Ah! it's raining on my roof at midnight—that reminds me of the sleety rain and business of the elements on 19 December 1783!" And De Quincey knows that "the subtle links of suffering" revealed to him in dreams as the result of opium are present, though uncomprehended, in *all* human experience. Both have the wish to track the power of association back to its source. Wordsworth, with astonishing intuition, relates it in the Infant Babe section of the 1799 *Prelude* to "the discipline of love"—the original experience of relationship in the arms of the mother, which gives to a child imaginative strength, and with it the confidence to build up an awareness of the external world (2.267–310). De Quincey does not go back so far. Building rather on the *Intimations Ode* than on *The Prelude*, he sees childhood as innocence—in his case the innocence of the nursery, and sisters, and warm fires, and picture-book illustrations of the Bible—and adulthood as suffering (not always felt, but always there as the condition of experience). He would not deny that childhood associations persist, but they are important as the vision of what is lost, as a contrast that brightens our sense of the darkness that closed forever around the growing boy.

It is possible, of course, to take the view that just as the dreams of Kate Wordsworth, and Ann, and Fanny of the Bath Road point back to the death of his sister, Elizabeth, so her loss, which seemed to De Quincey himself to be the root of his sufferings, in fact merely screened from his sight the earlier deprivation of his mother's love. But there is far less invitation in De Quincey's work to think in such terms than there is, for instance, to think that mountains chasing Wordsworth across a lake have something to do with a punishing father. Wordsworth takes into account the importance to his imagination of things that he cannot understand—experiences

> Which, be they what they may,
> Are yet the fountain light of all our day,
> Are yet the master light of all our seeing
> (*Intimations Ode* 153–155)

—and within his conscious memory he seems to prize no one incident especially. De Quincey is more categorical, and of course also more boastful. He is dealing in terms of revelation—one that took years to decipher but that nevertheless leaves him asserting that he is in possession of a truth gained in a single moment of inspiration: "O flight of the solitary child to the solitary God—flight from the ruined corpse to the throne that could not be ruined! —how rich wert thou in truth for after years!" (*Suspira* 132). (Again the poignancy of a quotation—this time a repetition—from *Tintern Abbey*.) "Rapture of grief that, being too mighty for a child to sustain, foundest a happy oblivion in a heaven-born dream . . . whose meaning, in after years, when slowly I deciphered, suddenly there flashed upon me new light; and even by the grief of a child, as I will show you, reader, hereafter, were confounded the falsehoods of philosophers" (132). "I, the child, had the feelings," De Quincey writes a few pages later in *Suspiria*, beautifully expanding upon the Wordsworthian two consciousnesses, "I, the man, decipher them. In the child lay the handwriting mysterious to *him*, in me the interpretation and the comment." (139).

What, then, of De Quincey's darkest interpretation, his taking leave of Elizabeth? In construction the passage is a Wordsworthian spot of time, adopting at first the quiet narrative tones of the Waiting for the Horses: "The house was large; there were two staircases, and by one of these I knew that about noon, when all would be quiet, I could steal up into her chamber" (129). In the background one might well be hearing:

> There was a crag,
> An eminence, which from the meeting-point
> Of two highways ascending overlooked
> At least a long half-mile of those two roads
> (1799 *Prelude* 1.335–338)

Characteristic too is the stealth ("I could steal up into her chamber") and the disappointment of expectations—or perhaps, one should say, the replacement (as on Mount Snowdon) of one kind of fulfillment with another far more rich. De Quincey in fact heightens his narrative by incorporating two successive disappointments: the locked door and the moving of the bed. As a further Wordsworthian strategy, there is the moment when the writer (as in the Waiting for the Horses section) steps back to comment on the nature and effect of his own writing ("Let me pause an instant") before returning us with heightened awareness to the central focus of his narrative. On this occasion he has two things in mind. He tells us of his theory of *involutes* (the "perplexed combinations of concrete objects"—like Wordsworth's single sheep, stone walls, and hawthorn bushes—that stand, in our associative memory, for the feelings and thoughts of the past[12]), and he reminds us in his flattest of tones "why death, *caeteris paribus*, is more profoundly affecting in summer than in other parts of the year": "the reason, as I [have] suggested, lies in the antagonism between the tropical redundancy of life in summer and the dark sterilities of the grave" (*Suspiria* 129). The tones and style have changed again, as they so frequently change in De Quincey, and give place to a use of balanced antiphony that recalls in its deliberately nonmetrical cadence the intonation of the Psalms: "The summer we see, the grave we haunt with our thoughts; the glory is around us, the darkness is within us" (129).

Perhaps one may be allowed to take these thoughts back into the central narrative: "I imagine that it was exactly high noon when I reached the chamber door"—"high noon" in anticipation of summer's tropical redundancy and "I imagine" as a gentle reminder of the controlling presence of the writer—

I imagine that it was exactly high noon when I reached the chamber door; it was locked, but the key was not taken away. Entering, I closed the door so softly that, although it opened upon a hall which ascended through all the stories, no echo ran along the silent walls. Then turning round, I sought my sister's face. But the bed had been moved, and the back was now turned. Nothing met my eyes but one large window wide open, through which the sun of midsummer at noonday was showering down torrents of splendor. The weather was dry, the sky was cloudless, the blue depths seemed the express types of infinity; and it was not possible for eye to behold or for heart to conceive any symbols more pathetic of life and the glory of life. (129)

In Wordsworth's great study of light and dark, the moon falls like a flash upon the slopes of Mount Snowdon (1805 *Prelude* 13.1–65); De Quincey here is less dramatic but no less impressive, closer perhaps to the brilliant handling of anticlimax in the Crossing of the Alps section of *The Prelude* (6.452–456). Imagination comes athwart the writer not as an unfathered vapor but as a torrent of sunlight shooting from a clear blue sky. The "types and symbols" of Wordsworthian eternity (6.571) are echoed and carefully *adapted* to admit not just of the glory, but the pathos, of life.

It is the pathos above all that we remember as De Quincey the writer turns back to his sister and, standing beside her body, hears the "wind that [has] swept the fields of mortality for a hundred centuries," the "hollow, solemn, Memnonian, but saintly swell" that "is in this world the one sole *audible* symbol of eternity." The thought seems infinitely consoling, yet it cannot assuage the physical loss, annul the detail, for instance, of Elizabeth's "frozen eyelids, [and] the darkness that seemed to steal from beneath them." De Quincey's tones in this later paragraph have changed from the tenderness of "I sought my sister's face" to a self-wounding sense of antagonism ("From the gorgeous sunlight I turned round to the corpse"); now in this beautiful, appalling fantasy, we have darkness stealing from the eyes that had once been the source of light. It will take a powerful vision to reconcile such pain.

The vision of *Suspiria,* lacking in the *Confessions* written twenty-five years earlier, is of education through suffering; at its center are Levana and Our Ladies of Sorrow. Levana is to De Quincey very much what Nature is to the child Wordsworth: an influence, or amalgam of influences, personified as a goddess:

> By the education of Levana . . . is meant not the poor machinery that moves by spelling books and grammars, but by that mighty system of central forces hidden in the deep bosom of human life, which by passion, by strife, by temptation, by the energies of resistance, works forever upon children, resting not day or night, any more than the mighty wheel of day and night themselves, whose moments, like restless spokes, are glimmering forever as they revolve. (173)

De Quincey's footnote to this passage refers the image of glimmering spokes to Wordsworth, but one suspects that (like Coleridge who so often seems to pay back only to withhold) he is not unaware of a deeper debt. As in *Prelude,* book 5—centering on *There Was a Boy,* about which De Quincey elsewhere writes so well[13]—there is the opposition between formal education and the unruly actualities of a child's existence. And in each case there is the insistent need to believe that behind these actualities lies a controlling power, uncomprehended yet beneficent. De Quincey, as always, is both more knowing and more demonstrative—he will claim the power for himself, by creating its agents a part of his own myth:

I want a term expressing the mighty abstractions that incarnate themselves in all individual sufferings of man's heart; and I wish to have
these abstractions presented as impersonations. . . . Let us call them,
therefore, *Our Ladies of Sorrow*. I know them thoroughly and have
walked in all their kingdoms. Three sisters they are, of one mysterious
household; and their paths are wide apart; but of their dominion there
is no end. Them I saw often conversing with Levana, and sometimes
about myself. Do they talk, then? Oh, no! Mighty phantoms like these
disdain the infirmities of language. (174)

The mention of incarnations, followed so soon by the reference to "infirmities of language," shows that the Wordsworth whom De Quincey now
has in mind is the writer of the "Essays upon Epitaphs";[14] but there are
other echoes too in this densely allusive prose. The "phantoms" especially
are important, taking us back to the couch of Orestes and to the second
birth of De Quincey's sufferings in the opium dreams at Dove Cottage, yet
at the same time hinting at the new understanding, the new vision, of *Suspiria*. In the *Confessions* De Quincey had been hunted down by nameless
and numberless furies; his vision had been of Hell. Now, he can name his
Eumenides, propitiate them as the agents of God, and turn his Hell to
Purgatory. "See that thy sceptre lie heavy on his head," says Our Lady of
Tears, consigning him to her dark sister, the Mater Tenebrarum: "Suffer not
woman and her tenderness to sit near him in his darkness. Banish the frail-
ties of hope, wither the relenting of love, scorch the fountain of tears, curse
him as only thou canst curse. So shall he be accomplished in the furnace"
(178). The tones and associations have changed abruptly from Lear cursing
Goneril ("Dry up in her the organs of increase," *King Lear* 1.4.279) to those
of the Old Testament or the apocalyptic Blake. What follows is like a
strange inversion—a curse that is yet a blessing—of Coleridge's prayer for
his son Hartley at the end of *Frost at Midnight*:

So shall he be accomplished in the furnace, so shall he see the things
that ought *not* to be seen, sights that are abominable, and secrets that
are unutterable. So shall he read elder truths, sad truths, grand truths,
fearful truths. So shall he rise again *before* he dies. And so shall our
commission be accomplished which from God we had—to plague his
heart until he had unfolded the capacities of his spirit. (178)

The Sisters of Sorrow exist to accomplish God's purpose, perhaps should be seen as aspects of God himself ("and of their dominion there is no end"), and De Quincey in this final passage claims for himself, not just the position of the Wordsworthian chosen son, but a more than Christ-like role: "so shall he rise again *before* he dies." For a moment the writing takes on a blasphemous confidence. But it is not one that is easily, or long, sustained. The different fragments, episodes, myths of *Suspiria* enact again and again the death of Elizabeth, seek again and again to assuage the loss, in creating a God who could let it happen. The pain is willed and dwelt upon as if its very intensity were a guarantee that somewhere, somehow, the divine plan *must* exist. Understanding is fashioned out of need. The apocalyptic triumph of *The English Mail Coach,* in which God finally stretches forth his hand to save, is the product of the most bizarre dwelling on the horror of a God who does not care. The image of darkness stealing from beneath the eyelids of Elizabeth finds a parallel in the living marble of the arm that sinks imploring, disembodied, and betrayed, into the dark grave of the quicksands.

We are placed, as always, in a dream or reverie. There is a girl dressed in white, running through the dawn along a beach, chased by the writer, who, in trying to help, is the cause of her death:

Round a promontory of rocks she wheeled out of sight; in an instant I also wheeled round it, but only to see the treacherous sands gathering above her head. . . . last of all, was visible one white marble arm. I saw by the early twilight this fair young head, as it was sinking down to darkness—saw this marble arm, as it rose above her head and her treacherous grave, tossing, faltering, rising, clutching, as at some false deceiving hand stretched out from the clouds—saw this marble arm uttering her dying hope, and then uttering her dying despair.

(*English Mail Coach* 270)

The arm that is symbolic of hope and despair reaches out to a God who is treacherous as the sands themselves, treacherous as time and death and darkness that overwhelm the child in her beauty and promise. As the end of *The Mail Coach* makes clear, and *Savannah-la-Mar* makes far clearer, he is the God to whom we pray—whom we falsely create—in the hope of being relieved of suffering that is finally beneficial.

The nurseries of Savannah-la-Mar lie beneath the waves "waiting for the heavenly dawn": "This is sad," says the Dark Interpreter, "this is piteous; but less would not have sufficed for the purpose of God." God, we recall, "smote Savannah-la-Mar," not as he smote Sodom and Gomorrah, in an act of righteous vengeance, but "as a monument to men of his mysterious anger"—the anger of a beneficient God who yet inflicts pain, who yet is the source of human grief. Embalmed by the imagination like the child of the 1805 *Prelude,* book 7, who is

> destined to live,
> To be, to have been, come and go, a child,
> And nothing more . . .
>
> (402–404)

the city lies on the ocean floor in a strange reconciliation of opposites and antagonisms. "Set in azure light through generations to come," she has at once the tropical redundancy of summer and "the dark sterility of the grave." She is "one ample cemetery," and yet fascinates the eye with semblance "of human life still subsisting" outside time and "sacred from the storms that torment our upper air" (*Suspiria* 197–198). Ultimately it is a prophetic vision, as Wordworth's never is. The sunken city, so tangible, so beautiful, and capable even of carrying a message of hope, is reduced in the Dark Interpreter's bizarre image of the water drops into a mathematical point so infinitessimal that it, and the human presence that it has seemed to embody, quite simply disappear:

> For again subdivide that solitary drop, which only was found to represent the present into a lower series of similar fractions, and the actual present which you arrest measures now but the thirty-sixth millionth of an hour; and so by infinite declensions the true and very present, in which only we live and enjoy, will vanish into a mote of a mote, distinguishable only by a heavenly vision. (199)

By destroying utterly "the true and very present, in which only we live and enjoy"—what Wordsworth clung to, and indeed celebrated, as

> the very world which is the world
> Of all of us, the place in which, in the end,
> We find our happiness, or not at all
> (1805 *Prelude* 10.725–727)

—De Quincey can finally be reconciled to his original loss, and to the tragic reenactments of that loss, of which his life and dreams have consisted. We are presented with the infinite spot of time, time reduced to so small a spot ("a mote of a mote") that it and suffering together disappear into the eternity that alone can assuage. And yet, the sunken city is standing still and waiting. Suffering has earned the future hope. Man as in Blake is trampled in the winepresses, subjected to "the agriculture of God" so that he may learn acceptance of the divine purpose: "Upon the sorrow of an infant he raises oftentimes from human intellects glorious vintages that could not else have been. Less than these fierce plowshares would not have stirred the stubborn soil" (199). Finally it is a quite traditional, and quite a dark, interpretation.

12

Wordsworth's Hedgerows
The Infrastructure of the Longer Romantic Lyric

THOMAS MCFARLAND

In his *History of the Synoptic Tradition,* Rudolf Bultmann, in speaking of similitudes, observes, of one of the strands of language in the gospels, that "ideas and conditions, characters and commands are given expression in immense concreteness." For instance, notes Bultmann:

> In Matt. 5.45 the goodness of God is pictured by saying he makes his sun to shine on the evil and the good, and sends his rain on the just and the unjust. Anxious folk are depicted in Matt. 6.25, 31 by their own questions: "What shall we eat? What shall we drink? and Wherewithal shall we be clothed?". . . . The son's request to the father in Matt. 7.9f. is concretely expressed as asking for fish or bread. . . . Evil desire must be exterminated, even to plucking out the eye or cutting off the hand (Matt. 5.29f.). The right hand must not know what the left hand does (Matt. 5.3). . . . A camel goes more easily through a needle's eye, than a rich man enters the kingdom of God (Mk. 10.25). The Pharisees strain at gnats and swallow camels (Matt. 23.24).[1]

Of special interest is that this "immense concreteness" accompanies the movement of thought into the most abstract regions of spiritual concern.

The texts identified by Bultmann, indeed, seem primordial localizations

of what Heidegger calls, in *Was heisst Denken?*, a "totally specific interpretation of 'Being'—Being as being present." This, he insists, is an

> interpretation of Being [that] has been current so long that we regard
> it as self-evident.
>
> Since in all metaphysics from the beginning of Western thought, Be-
> ing means being present, Being, if it is to be thought in the highest in-
> stance, must be thought as pure presence, that is, as the presence that
> persists, the abiding present, the steadily standing "now."[2]

Anwesenheit, or "presence," for Heidegger, arose as the chief characteristic
of Western thought by the early identification of two Greek words, *physis*
and *idea* ("for two thousand years, these ties between *logos, alētheia,
physis, noein,* and *idea* have remained hidden in unintelligibility"). As he
discusses the interrelations of the words in his *Einführung in die Metaphysik,* Heidegger concludes that "in the end the word *idea, eidon,* 'idea,'
came to the fore as the decisive and predominant name for being (*physis*).
. . . The word *idea* means that which is seen in the visible, the aspect it
offers."[3]

The abstract insistence of Heidegger combines with the concrete examples of Bultmann to suggest important truths for the study of poetry.
Though a poem is a concretion, the idea of a poem, obviously, is an abstraction. But this abstraction, I suggest, following the derivation by which "*idea*
means that which is seen in the visible," is inextricably bound up with a
form of *Anwesenheit.* In this presence, the "idea" is not formally given as
object of inspection but, for all that, is ineluctably constituted as something
that potentially could be "seen in the visible." It is "seen," however, by
poets, readers, and critics only by implication, as the inexplicit and unconscious substratum of the poem. But this substratum—or better, because it
takes a definite form as something that might be "seen in the visible," even
though it is not consciously so seen in the surface attendings of the poem,
this infrastructure—nevertheless exerts a decisive control on our expectations of what is fitting in the poem's language and organization.

The infrastructure in the longer Romantic lyric assumes particular importance, for it differs from that of other kinds of poetry. It dictates, in fact, the
decorum of such a lyric, and a false mental picture of what it is can likewise
result in a false criticism of the poem, for critics, no less than poets, proceed

from subliminal awareness of concrete shapes underlying the abstract wordage of the poem. Although the concept of *decorum* is usually associated with neoclassic poetry, one of my purposes here is to suggest that it should also be associated, though in a different way, with Romantic poetry. George Puttenham, in *The Arte of English Poesie,* devotes considerable discussion to the conception of what is fitting to a poem:

> The Greekes call this good grace of euery thing in his kinde *to prepon,* the Latines *decorum;* we in our vulgar call it by a scholasticall terme *decencie;* our owne Saxon English terme is *seemelynesse,* that is to say, for his good shape and vtter appearance well pleasing the eye; we call it also *comelynesse,* for the delight it bringeth comming towardes vs, and to that purpose may be called *pleasant approche.* So as euery way seeking to express this *prepon* of the Greekes and *decorum* of the Latines, we are faine in our vulgar toung to borrow the term which our eye only for his noble prerogatiue ouer all the rest of the sences doth vsurpe, and to apply the same to all good, comely, pleasant, and honest things, even to the spiritual objectes of the mynde.[4]

Notable in Puttenham's statement is the insistence that what is fitting refers to a "spiritual object" of the mind, which in turn possesses a "good shape and vtter appearance well pleasing the eye." *Decorum, prepon,* decencie, seemelynesse, comelynesse, are all governed by the visually objective: "to borrow the term which our eye only for his noble prerogatiue ouer all the rest of the sences doth vsurpe." Puttenham's exaltation of sight over all the rest of the senses resumes a long tradition signalized by Aristotle's insistence that the desire of humans to know makes them prefer sight to all other senses (*Metaphysics* 980ª22−28). In the eighteenth century, again, Joseph Addison inaugurates his series of papers on the imagination by saying that "our sight is the most perfect and most delightful of all our Senses." "It is this sense," he continues, "which furnishes the Imagination with its Ideas; so that by the Pleasures of the Imagination or Fancy (which I shall use promiscuously) I here mean such as arise from visible Objects."[5]

Puttenham's emphasis coincides too with the biblical characteristics noted by Bultmann, as well as with the theoretical insistences of Heidegger. The "spiritual objects of the mynde" comprised by great poetry are made up not only of the words and meanings of the poem but also by a visually concrete, if submerged, image, which can be "seen in the visible." This is the truth celebrated in a different terminology by R. P. Blackmur's conception of "language as gesture."

It is the violation of the sense of what is fitting that generates most judgments as to what constitutes a fault in a poem. Horace, indeed, in his *Ars Poetica*, builds his main argument around the necessity of knowing what is fitting in poetry. In the neoclassic period, this usually referred to the decorum of occasions, of materials, of expectations, and of genre, much as in Horace himself. But in Romantic times, the matrix changed because of definitive pronouncements on the freedom and unboundedness of the poet with regard to subject matter, occasion, content, and form. Romantic poetry, said Friedrich Schlegel in his famous definition, was a "progressive universal poetry" that took up everything into its movement; "the bounded is loathed by its possessor," concurred Blake. The movement of poetry was conceived as a flow. Good poetry, as Wordsworth defined it, was "the spontaneous overflow of powerful feelings." "Shelley," wrote Mary Shelley, ". . . was thrown on his own resources, and on the inspiration of his own soul; and wrote because his mind overflowed." "The poem entitled *Mont Blanc*," confirmed Shelley himself, was "an undisciplined overflowing of the soul." Romanticism, said Kierkegaard in synopsis, "implies overflowing all boundaries."[6]

The ideas of progression, of unboundedness, and of flow combined to produce the subliminally visual infrastructure of the longer Romantic lyric. That infrastructure—or "spiritual object of the mynde"—was not an entity compressed, stressed, and demarcated, but an entity unbounded, progressive, and flowing. The visual infrastructure, in short, was a stream. And the importance of this visual infrastructure, found in the world of nature, was augmented by a special urgency of the Romantic agenda, one that, under the general aegis of pantheism, of "the one Life within us and abroad," sought to conceive mind and nature as a single entity. Friedrich Hölderlin, for only one of innumerable examples, declared that to heal the split between self and world, "to unite ourselves with nature in one infinite entity, is the aim of all our aspirations." The Romantic philosopher Friedrich Schelling, again, said that nature was visible mind, and mind was invisible nature.[7] It is not merely a Wordsworthian, but a Romantic, merging of human being and nature that is signalized by Wordsworth's question:

Was it for this
That one, the fairest of all rivers, loved
To blend his murmurs with my nurse's song,

....

For this didst thou
O Derwent! winding among grassy holms
Where I was looking on, a babe in arms
Make ceaseless music that composed my thoughts?
(*Prelude* 1.269−271, 274−277)

To look at a stream, however, is not only to be aware of water moving by but also to be aware that neither beginning nor end can be seen; and this characteristic dictates the nature of those poems of which I speak. For the longer Romantic lyric must be a poem that cannot be taken in at a single intuition of two open pages. The reader in his progress must at some point lose to view, physically and with regard to meaning as well, both the beginning and the ending of the poem. The aesthetic tension of beginning, middle, and end is accordingly radically redistributed. "O stream!" says Shelley in *Alastor*, "Whose source is inaccessibly profound, / Whither do thy mysterious waters tend? / Thou imagest my life." It images his poem, too, as it does all the longer Romantic lyrics, for *Alastor* streams on for 720 lines, *Epipsychidion* for 604, *Lines Written among the Euganean Hills* for 373, *The Witch of Atlas* for 672, and so on. Even *Mont Blanc* is a longer Romantic lyric, for it extends to more than 140 lines and cannot physically be surveyed at a single glance.

Shelley's commitment to the streaming infrastructure is apparent too in his curious challenge to Keats to see which poet could first compose a poem of four thousand lines. It is true, of course, that Keats's product in the competition, *Endymion*, showed that he did not at that time manage the streaming mode very well, and some of his greatest poems, such as *To Autumn* or *Ode on a Grecian Urn*, clearly do not overlay a streaming infrastructure. His more mature *Hyperion* does follow the streaming course, however (Shelley, significantly, regarded it as Keats's best poem), and such marvels as *The Eve of St. Agnes* and even *Ode to a Nightingale* do as well.

Similar observations could be made about all the Romantic poets. Not only do Wordsworth's greatest statements—*Tintern Abbey, The Immortality Ode, The Ruined Cottage, Michael*, the first two books of *The Pre-*

lude—all overlay a streaming infrastructure, but Wordsworth, like the other Romantics, seemed virtually hypnotized by the idea of running water (Mary Moorman's biography, indeed, on its very first page says: "The first object which attracted him as he gazed into the past was a river. He beheld it as a source of beneficence and peace, and hailed it as an influence stretching back even beyond the gates of conscious memory. . . . The sound of running water was always among the most precious to him of all the multitudinous sounds which reached his sensitive ears from the mysterious universe. He often felt it almost as part of his own being").[8]

Wordsworth, indeed, though he sometimes bemoaned a certain propensity for short forms such as sonnets and was rebuked by Coleridge for indulging that propensity, could set even the sonnets to streaming, as in his *The River Duddon: A Series of Sonnets*, where the 14-line unit, under the visual impact of the river, is multiplied by thirty-four to produce a longer Romantic lyric of 476 lines. The sense of the river as physical object is unmistakably correlated with the actual composition of the verse. In Sonnet 12, for instance, Wordsworth exhorts his muse to stream: "On, loitering Muse—the swift stream chides us—on," and further down in the same sonnet he refers to "The Bard who walks with Duddon for his guide."

But to bypass other familiar examples, we may look at a typical though virtually unknown poem. In a longer Romantic lyric of 204 lines, written during the desiccated 1820s and called, with lurching clumsiness, *Composed When a Probability Existed of Our Being Obliged to Quit Rydal Mount as a Residence,* Wordsworth not only streams in writing but writes about streams. Thus, after a perfunctory look at "Sky-piercing Hills" and "familiar trees" as objects to which he might have to bid farewell, he settles down to the "pellucid Spring" (line 8), which henceforth becomes the chief topic of his poem. He hails it as "translucent Spring" (30), detects its "dimpling stir of life" (38), hails it again as "Thou, clear Spring" (84), and speaks of its "rippling airs / Concealed" (95–96). He then begins to take in other flowings, noting bizarrely that

> Millions of kneeling Hindoos at this day
> Bow to the watery Element, adored
> In their vast Stream, and if an age hath been
> (As Books and haply votive Altars vouch)
> When British floods were worshipped, some faint trace

Of that idolatry, through monkish rites
Transmitted far as living memory,
Might wait on Thee, a silent Monitor,
On thee, bright Spring, a bashful little-one,
Yet to the measure of thy promises
True, as the mightiest

(120–130)

Later he says—interestingly enough for this argument about the visual infrastructure of poetry—that "new-born waters" are "deemed the happiest
source / Of Inspiration for the conscious lyre" (163–164). He concludes the
poem with a tribute "To thee, dear Spring, and all-sustaining Heaven!"
(204). A great Wordsworthian poem, no less than this banal effort, is also to
the measure of its promises true in that it too takes its course from the
streaming infrastructure. *Tintern Abbey,* with its length of 159 lines, represents a choice example of the longer Romantic lyric, one whose strength
allows it to serve, as the poem just noted cannot, as basis for a fairly convo-
luted argument about poetic quality and the criteria for judging it.

Now it was notoriously the case that the New Criticism, which promul-
gated the techniques for reading poetry that still reign in our educational
systems, did not particularly care for Romantic poetry, especially the
streamlike poetry of the longer Romantic lyric. "The literary critic," said
John Crowe Ransom, for instance, in *The World's Body,* "also has something to say about romanticism, and it might come to something like this:
that romantic literature is imperfect in objectivity, or 'aesthetic distance,'
and that out of this imperfection comes its weakness of structure; that the
romantic poet does not quite realize the aesthetic attitude, and is not the
pure artist." In *The New Criticism,* again, he speaks of "the shoddy resonances like those of the romantic Wordsworth." In that same volume, referring to Wordsworth's *Prelude,* he writes:

The poet became a little paralyzed, we may imagine, when he took pen
in hand to write a poem; or got that way after going a certain distance
in the writing of a long one. I go beyond the direct evidence here, but I
assume that making distinguished metrical discourse was such a job,
and consisted in his own mind with so much corruption of the sense at
best, that he fell into the habit of choosing the most resounding words,

and stringing them together as the meter dictated. This is not unusual in Romantic poetry. The point to make about Romantic poetry now is not the one about its noble words, but a negative and nasty one: the noble words are almost absurdly incoherent.[9]

It is interesting to note that Ransom here attacks not the usual New Critical victim, Shelley, but Wordsworth, whose prestige in general was somewhat less eroded than that of other Romantics. Indeed, Cleanth Brooks, in *The Well Wrought Urn,* makes the *Intimations Ode* one of the ten poems discussed in detail. To be sure, Brooks seems to find the ode considerably flawed ("The 'Ode' for all its fine passages, is not entirely successful as a poem"). And his animadversions could be supplemented by more severe ones from Yvor Winters and F. R. Leavis, who, though not New Critics narrowly defined, were in sympathy with the larger trends of that school.[10]

The concept of "weakness of structure" is at the forefront of Ransom's animus against Romantic poetry in general. The phrase readily lends itself to describing a dissatisfaction with the streaming infrastructure of the longer Romantic lyric. For Ransom, as Brooks says, "insists on a rather tight and systematic structure of the images of a poem," and that in itself militates against the very idea of "going a certain distance in the writing of a long one." One is accordingly not surprised to find that the New Critics thought well of the compact paradoxes and ironies of Blake's gnomic verses—which were all they seemed to know of Blake; it remained for Northrop Frye, with theoretical categories suited to longer, flowing poems such as *The Faerie Queene* and *Paradise Lost* (which the New Critics almost unanimously denigrated) to point to the power of the lengthy prophetic books. By the same token, none of the New Critics was very enthusiastic about Wordsworth's *Prelude,* which seems to us now almost unarguably the greatest poem of the nineteenth century, but Brooks and Robert Penn Warren in their highly influential textbook, *Understanding Poetry,* admired the intensely compacted *A Slumber Did My Spirit Seal.*[11]

It seems clear, in brief, that the New Critics, when they inspected a poem, were as much involved with a subliminally visible infrastructure as were the Romantics when they generated their longer lyrics. But the infrastructures in the two instances were entirely different. The New Critics actually wanted a "tight and systematic structure" in their field of view, even though such a structure is not favored in nature over streaming structures. "The first law to be prescribed to criticism," said Ransom in *The World's Body*, ". . . is that it shall be objective, shall cite the nature of the object rather than its effects upon the subject." To stand by a stream, aware neither of a beginning nor of an end, is not to cognize the "object" Ransom had in mind; indeed, it is precisely the lack of an intensive object ("romantic literature is imperfect in objectivity") that he pairs with "weakness of structure" in his general indictment of Romantic poetry. Simply stated, what the New Critics wanted to see was an object hard, compact, demarcated, not an object extended and streaming. Still more specifically, where the Romantics actually saw the visual idea of a stream in their mind's eye, the New Critics, to accept the phrase proffered by Brooks, actually saw a well-wrought urn (Brooks even says that "the poem, if it be a true poem is a simulacrum of reality," and the statement seems to refer less to reality as such, which is a very large and diffuse conception, than to the idea of a concrete visual object).[12] Such an infrastructure is not congruent with most Romantic poetry; it pertains perhaps to Keats's *Ode on a Grecian Urn,* to his *To Autumn,* to a few shorter poems by Blake and Wordsworth, and to very little else.

That the urn was actually a visual object, an infrastructure that the poem had to overlay, rather than a mere trope, is crucial to an understanding of New Critical theory. Brooks, indeed, readily admits that he and his fellow critics conceive Donne's phrase as actually constituting the structure they want to see:

> The urn to which we are summoned, the urn which holds the ashes of the phoenix, is like the well-wrought urn of Donne's "Canonization" which holds the phoenix-lovers' ashes: it is the poem itself. One is reminded of another urn, Keats's Grecian urn, which contained for Keats, Truth and Beauty, as Shakespeare's urn contains the ashes of a Phoenix. The urns are not meant for memorial purposes only, though that often seems to be their chief significance to the professors of literature. . . . We must be prepared to accept the paradox of the imagination itself; else "Beautie, Truth and Raritie" remain enclosed in their cinders and we shall end with essential cinders, for all our pains.[13]

To "accept the paradox of the imagination itself" is, for the New Critics, to engage in the judgments on coherence of their kind of approach, with its emphasis on a texture of tensions: paradox, ambiguity, and irony ("there is

irony of a very powerful sort in Wordsworth's 'Intimations Ode,'" says
Brooks approvingly).[14] To them the phoenix of meaning arises, as it were,
only when the ashes are stirred by close critical reading. To that end, and especially to illustrate the way in which the differing infrastructures dictate
different aesthetic expectations, let us inspect the opening of *Tintern Abbey*,
which we shall follow until the first sharp divergence from the New Critical
infrastructure occurs:

> Five years have past; five summers, with the length
> Of five long winters! and again I hear these
> Waters, rolling from their mountain-springs
> With a soft inland murmur.—Once again
> Do I behold these steep and lofty cliffs,
> That on a wild secluded scene impress
> Thoughts of more deep seclusion; and connect
> The landscape with the quiet of the sky.
> The day is come when I again repose
> Here, under this dark sycamore, and view
> These plots of cottage-ground, these orchard-tufts,
> Which at this season, with their unripe fruits,
> Are clad in one green hue, and lose themselves
> 'Mid groves and copses. Once again I see
> These hedge-rows, hardly hedge-rows, little lines
> Of sportive wood run wild: these pastoral farms
> Green to the very door; and wreaths of smoke
> Sent up, in silence, from among the trees!

There is, one thinks, nothing until the line about the hedgerows that New
Criticism would find at fault. The opening, indeed, is memorable and arche-
typally poetic. In a discussion called "Poetry and the Poem: The Structure of
Poetic Content," I have argued that two depth features, which are called
essentia and *ens,* are necessary to all true poetry. Poetic *ens* is the intermin-
gling of the sense of human life with the awareness of the concrete outer
world, of subject with object. As Robert Langbaum has said of the Romantic lyric in general, "The poet talks about himself by talking about an object; and he talks about an object by talking about himself." One applauds
the insight at the same time one insists that it is not a characteristic restricted to the Romantic lyric but one defining of poetry as such. So, too,

Coleridge recognizes that "in every work of art there is a reconcilement of the external with the internal." When Wordsworth says that "there is not a single image from Nature in the whole body" of Dryden's verse, he is recognizing that poet's radical deficiency in *ens,* and Leavis is recognizing the same deficiency when he describes Shelley's peculiar fault as a "weak grasp upon the actual." Again, the early poetry of Yeats is insipid mainly because of a Shelleyan lack of *ens*. The Imagist Manifesto in modern British and American poetry was actually a declaration of the necessity of *ens* in the complete poetic act, and Pound's instructive criticisms of Yeats were largely a rectification of that poet's tendency toward weak realization of *ens*.[15]

The second feature that true poetry must exhibit is *essentia*. The *essentia* of a poetic act consists in the invocation of time's flow past a framed now. The lyric instant, or essence of poetry, consists in summoning an awareness intrinsic to the human situation but one that can be indicated neither by philosophy nor by any other discursive form: that is, it presents the peculiarly human mode of existence in its eternally dual form as the simultaneity of nowness and passing away, or, in Jasperian terms, as a tension of *Dasein* and *Existenz*.

In the lines that begin *Tintern Abbey*, the *essentia* is profound and insistent, engaging in a direct, simple, and extraordinarily powerful way the being of the observer and the flow of time past him: "Five years have past"; and then the time is hammered home: "five summers"; and hammered again: "five long winters." The powerful strokes of time's passage are matched with equally powerful repetitions that recall it to nowness: "again I hear"; "Once again do I behold"; "The day is come when I again repose / Here, under this dark sycamore"; "Once again I see / These hedge-rows." *Ens* supervenes upon this establishment of *essentia*, and intertwines with it, as the mood of the observer fuses with the perspective of the eternal world: "and again I hear / These waters, rolling from their mountain-spring / With a soft inland murmur.—Once again / Do I behold these steep and lofty cliffs." The structure of entic perspective is here particularly intriguing. First, the poet hails the streaming infrastructure: "again I hear / These waters, rolling from their mountain-spring / With a soft inland murmur." The evocation, however, is auditory and symbolic rather than visual, and it thereby serves to deflect emphasis, which is rebestowed upon the overtly visual beholding of "these steep and lofty cliffs"; for the poem will not actually deal with flowings of water but will instead constitute the flow itself.

The power, directness, and harmonic simplicity of the opening are virtually Handelian in their majesty. There is no muting or finesse but everywhere power and insistence. Following this organ prelude, as it were, the
connections with external nature become more particularized and delicate.
The generality by which "thoughts of more deep seclusion" are said to be
parallel to a connection of "the landscape with the quiet of the sky" gives
way to the specific and immediate: "Here, under this dark sycamore";
"These plots of cottage-ground, these orchard tufts." The specifications
lead to the famous hedgerows: "Once again I see / These hedge-rows,
hardly hedge-rows, little lines / Of sportive wood run wild."

But here, from the expectations of New Critical structure, a flaw ob-
trudes. Since the progression has been from the generality of "mountain-
springs" and "steep and lofty cliffs" — indeed, from "landscape" and "sky"
— to specific objects like "this dark sycamore," one would expect any appo-
sitional structure for hedgerows to specify in still more precise detail.
Instead, the passage runs off into fanciful imprecision: "These hedge-rows,
hardly hedge-rows, little lines / Of sportive wood run wild." The sense of
the poetic eye of decorum wavering from the object is then strengthened by
"these pastoral farms, / Green to the very door." Pastoral farms, presumably farms for sheep rather than for grain or cattle, nevertheless invoke by
the actual word "pastoral" a tradition of imitation and a tradition of artificiality, neither of which seems to fit very well with the sublime directness
and simplicity of the opening.

One can almost imagine a severe critic such as Winters or Leavis saying
brusquely: "Make up your mind, are they hedgerows or are they not?" Certainly in this tradition of insistence on clear articulation of images, which is
heir to the criticisms of Pope and Dr. Johnson, precise delineation is valued.
But in "hedge-rows, hardly hedge-rows," imagistic reference begins to eddy,
as though there has been a slackening in the poet's attention. The New Critics looked upon T. S. Eliot as "one of the most important sources of a new
criticism," felt that "it is likely that we have no better critic than Eliot"
(both statements occur in Ransom's *The New Criticism*). But Eliot himself
was heir to Pound's insistence on precision and compression in imagery;
and the Imagist Manifesto, which expresses concerns close to both Eliot
and Pound, exhorts the poet, in its fourth statement, "To present an image
(hence the name imagist). We are not a school of painters, but we believe
that poetry should render particulars exactly and not deal in vague generali-

ties. . . ." The fifth statement in the manifesto urges a "poetry that is hard and clear, never blurred nor indefinite," and the sixth says that "concentration is of the very essence of poetry." *Tintern Abbey* in the hedgerow passage does not seem to be rendering particulars exactly, nor does the verse here seem to be "hard and clear"; it seems, on the contrary, "blurred and indefinite." And the "hedge-rows, hardly hedge-rows" equivocation does not seem to show much of the desiderated concentration.

If it be interposed in defense of "hedge-rows, hardly hedge-rows" that Wordsworth did not subscribe to Imagist tenets, the counter would be that he did not do so historically, but he did so virtually. Indeed, the first item in the Imagist Manifesto accords absolutely with Wordsworth's own prescription (in the preface to *Lyrical Ballads*) of the language really used by men, for it bids us "to use the language of common speech, but to employ always the *exact* word, not the nearly-exact, nor the merely decorative word." Richard Aldington, in fact, pointed out, in the preface to the imagist credo, that "these principles are not new; they have fallen into desuetude. They are the essentials of all great poetry."

How much Wordsworth himself concurred in these views might be gauged from his criticism of James Macpherson's *Ossian:* "In nature everything is distinct, yet nothing defined into absolute independent singleness. In Macpherson's work it is exactly the reverse; everything . . . is . . . defined, insulated, dislocated, deadened,—yet nothing distinct." Again, he said that "in his [Dryden's] translations from Vergil, whenever Vergil can be fairly said to have had his *eye* upon his object, Dryden always spoils the passage."[16]

If Wordsworth does not quite seem to keep his own eye upon the object in the equivocation about the hedgerows, it would accordingly appear that by theories to which he himself subscribed, he would here be open to Winters's fierce denunciation (expressed with regard to the *Immortality Ode*): "Wordsworth gives us bad oratory about his own clumsy emotions and a landscape that he has never fully realized."[17] One does not need to accept Winters's customary rhetorical exaggeration to see that the charge about "a landscape that he has never fully realized" is a duplicate of Wordsworth's own judgment of Macpherson. Furthermore, it is apparent to any close reader of Wordsworth that the great poet is not usually very specific in his invocation of nature.

This claim about Wordsworth's lack of visual particularity in the rendering of nature will seem outrageous only to the uninitiated. It has, in fact, been made repeatedly by those who pay close attention to poetry. For a single instance, Donald Davie, in *Articulate Energy: An Inquiry into the Syntax of English Poetry*, speaking of the blank verse of *The Prelude,* says:

> We can make a start by pointing out that Wordsworth's world is not pre-eminently a world of "things". His language. . . . is not concrete. Because in the Preface to *Lyrical Ballads* Wordsworth castigated some earlier poets for giving no proof that they had ever truly *looked* at natural phenomena, it is often supposed that his own verse is full of such phenomena rendered in all their quiddity and concreteness. But this is a sort of optical illusion. What Wordsworth renders is not the natural world but (with masterly fidelity) the effect that world has upon him. . . . As Lionel Trilling remarks:
>
>> . . . . His finest passages are moral, emotional, subjective; whatever visual intensity they have comes from his response to the object, not from his close observation of it.[18]

To this last, one would only urge the amendment that Wordsworth's response was not characteristically to "the object" as such, New Critical bias notwithstanding, but to the streaming connection he saw in the natural scene.

For example, consider the supreme lines in *Tintern Abbey* that run this way:

>   And I have felt
>   A presence that disturbs me with the joy
>   Of elevated thoughts; a sense sublime
>   Of something far more deeply interfused,
>   Whose dwelling is the light of setting suns,
>   And the round ocean and the living air,
>   And the blue sky, and in the mind of man:
>   A motion and a spirit, that impels
>   All thinking things, all objects of all thought,
>   And rolls through all things.
>
>   (lines 93–102)

The passage is remarkable for its nonspecific generality as it hails nature, from the unspecified "presence" and the unspecified "elevated thoughts" at the beginning, to the unspecified "objects of all thought" and the unspecified "all things" at the end. In between, the nominations of nature are hugely unspecific. The "setting suns" here have none of the particularized glory of the orange sky of evening in *The Prelude*'s skating scene, the "blue sky" is about as general a description as one can imagine—so general as to be almost banal—and the imagistic precision or particularization of "round ocean" and "living air" is virtually nil.

And yet, despite its radical failure to measure up to the criteria of the Imagist Manifesto or the New Criticism, the passage is enormously powerful, a true apex of poetry. In what does its power consist? Perhaps as good an answer as any is that it consists in the sense of inevitability. The movement of the passage is so sure and deep that its statement seems ineluctable; it seems, that is, to constitute a steady current of certainty, an irresistible flow of feeling. The flow exists in the ordering of the words themselves. Thus the first and second lines are powerfully enjambed, the second and third are enjambed as well, as are the third and fourth. The sixth line flows from the fifth also, not by enjambment but by the variant efficacy of the conjunction "And," and the seventh line maintains the flow from the sixth by a second use of "And," and further impels it by a third "and" immediately afterward. The eighth and ninth lines again flow by enjambment, which is reinforced by the apposition in the ninth line, while the tenth line begins with yet a fourth "And."

Though these lines viewed as overlaying a well-wrought urn as infrastructure might be criticized for lacking a desired distinctness and particularity of imagery, viewed in terms of a different awareness of infrastructure, they incur no such judgment. When one sees a streaming infrastructure, the passage exhibits an exquisite decorum, for just as the particularized stones in a dry stream bed are more clearly delineated because there is no flow, so the presence of flow make their precise outline less prominent. And just as the streaming infrastructure is hailed at the poem's outset by the assurance that "again I hear these / Waters, rolling from their mountain-spring," so does the verb "roll" in that passage, which augments the sense of flow, govern and conclude the movement of the "sense sublime" passage:

> A motion and a spirit, that impels
> All thinking things, all objects of all thought,
> And rolls through all things.

At least part of the grandeur of the whole passage, indeed, stems precisely from the onomatopoeic triumph that all ten lines "roll through" our poetic ear just as the motion and spirit "rolls through" all things. The passage is a miracle of cadence, a living embodiment of the movement of a stream.

Just as what seems flawed when taken to overlay the infrastructure of a sharply delimited object seems correct when referred to the streaming infrastructure, so too does the equivocation about the hedgerows no longer seem a poetic flaw when adjusted to the proper infrastructure. The imagery of *Tintern Abbey,* in fact, begins to stream before the "hedge-rows, hardly hedge-rows" passage, which thereby reveals itself as continuing the flow already set in motion:

> these orchard-tufts,
> Which at this season, with their unripe fruits,
> Are clad in one green hue, and lose themselves
> 'Mid groves and copses. Once again I see
> These hedge-rows, hardly hedge-rows, little lines
> Of sportive wood run wild:
>
> (11–16)

The image of the "orchard-tufts," instead of remaining static and precise, streams to the vision of "one green hue" and streams further to "groves and copses." Immediately following, the "hedge-rows" stream to "hardly hedge-rows" and stream further to "little lines of sportive wood run wild."

But the second streaming of imagery is different in structure from the first. The "orchard-tufts" stream by a movement of the eye: they "lose themselves / 'Mid groves and copses." The "hedge-rows," however, stream not by a movement of the eye but by a movement of the imagination. If one looks long enough at "orchard-tufts," they can in fact merge into "one green hue"; yet no matter how long one looks at "hedge-rows," they never in fact become "little lines of sportive wood run wild." Though one "should gaze for ever," he "may not hope from outward forms to win / The passion and the life, whose fountains are within." One can move from "hedge-rows" to "little lines of sportive wood run wild" only by an act of imagination, and the act in this instance is that eddy of mind known as reverie. Indeed, the mental possibility called reverie was one of the treasured hallmarks of the Romantic sensibility, and by its agency the distinctness and

sharpness treasured by the Imagist Manifesto give way to unwilled merg-
ings. Both the high Romantic credentials of reverie and its unbidden merg-
ings are indicated by Rousseau's *Rêveries d'un promeneur solitaire:*

> Coming out of a long and sweet reverie, seeing myself surrounded by
> greenery, flowers, and birds, and letting my eyes wander in the dis-
> tance over the Romantic banks that bordered a vast expanse of clear
> and crystalline water, I assimilated to my fictions all these amiable ob-
> jects, and finding myself at last brought back by degrees to myself and
> my surroundings, I could not mark the point of separation between
> fictions and realities, so much did everything collaborate equally in en-
> dearing to me the reflective and solitary life that I led in this lovely
> place.[19]

It is almost as though Wordsworth's "hedge-rows, hardly hedge-rows,
little lines / Of sportive wood run wild" were produced exactly to illustrate
Rousseau's reveristic annulment of "the point of separation between fictions
and realities." The "hedge-rows" are realities of present vision, the "little
lines of sportive wood run wild" are fictions arising from the reality, and the
equivocating word "hardly" bridges the line of separation between the two.
The merging from reality to fiction is, moreover, precisely an instance of
flow.

Indeed, the idea of flow is as intrinsic to reverie as it is to the infrastructure of the longer Romantic lyric. Rousseau explicitly links his apotheosis of
reverie with the movement of water, for reverie must be a current, or to use
a later phrase, a stream of consciousness:

> I let myself go and drifted slowly as the water moved me [writes Rous-
> seau], sometimes for several hours, absorbed in a thousand confused
> but delicious reveries which, without having any well-defined or con-
> stant object, were nonetheless to my taste. . . . The flux and reflux of
> that water, its sound, continuous but swelling at intervals, striking
> continually my ear and my eyes, supplanted the internal movements
> that the reverie extinguished in me and sufficed to make me feel my ex-
> istence with pleasure, without taking the trouble to think. From time

to time arose a feeble and short reflection on the instability of the things of this world of which the surface of the waters offered me the image; but soon these weak impressions died out in the continuous movement that rocked me, and which, without any active participation of my mind, did not fail to take hold of me. (1:1044–1045)

If the progression of "hedge-rows, hardly hedge-rows" may be seen as according with the flux and drifting of reverie as well as with the decorum of a streaming infrastructure, its relationship with its antecedent passage nevertheless seems, with regard to decorum, more problematic. For the relation of the "orchard-tufts" losing themselves "'Mid groves and copses" and of the "hedge-rows" merging into the reveristic fiction of "little lines of sportive wood run wild" is not precisely parallel; from the expectations of a wellwrought urn, indeed, the relationship is flawed. Both passages flow; but they are asymmetrical in that one represents a movement of the eye and the other a movement of imagination.

Yet from the perspective of the streaming infrastructure, that asymmetry is not a flaw. Not only did the Romantics in general theoretically prefer the unboundedness of the asymmetrical to the restriction of symmetry—prefer the unfinished Gothic cathedral to the symmetrical Greek temple—but such preference for the asymmetrical characterized their taste in streamings. They looked not toward the placidity of an Afton flowing gently between placid green banks; rather, they looked toward the image of the mountain torrent, rushing now fiercely, now gently, in windings and turnings, sometimes as a cataract, against boulders, outcroppings of land, and other asymmetrical features that emphasized the strength and wildness of the flow. The sounding cataract haunted the Romantics like a passion. "The little boat," says Shelley in *Alastor,* "Still fled before the storm, still fled, like foam / Down the steep cataract of a wintry river." Keats, again, in *Hyperion* evokes "the solid roar / Of thunderous waterfalls and torrents hoarse."

Such a streaming was in marked contrast to the movement of water that the neoclassic sensibility could on occasion assert as its own poetic ideal. Sir John Denham's famous wish that his verse might be like the Thames envisions a flow quite unlike that of a boulder-strewn mountain torrent:

> O could I flow like thee, and make thy stream
> My great example, as it is my theme!

Though deep, yet clear, though gentle, yet not dull,
Strong without rage, without o'er-flowing full.

(*Cooper's Hill*)

As Dr. Johnson said, "almost every writer for a century past has imitated" Denham's lines, following upon Dryden's commendation of them. Yet though the image of their flow constitutes an ideal for the neoclassic sensibility, it does not refer to the streaming that makes up the infrastructure of the longer Romantic lyric.

That infrastructure is as replete with boulders as the lyrics themselves are full of asymmetries. Certain modes of critical assumption tend to stigmatize such asymmetries as faults. Some asymmetries, of course, might indeed eventually be seen as faults. Others, however, like the image of the hedgerows, exactly fit the decorum of the flowing infrastructure of the longer Romantic lyric. (Even those that are faults can be allowed in a longer poem, according to Horace's own definition of decorum: "there are faults we should be ready to forgive. . . . When there are plenty of fine passages in a poem, I shall not take exception to occasional flaws that the poet has carelessly let slip, or that his fallible humanity has not guarded against. . . . I am put out when . . . Homer nods, although it is natural that slumber should occasionally creep over a long poem"). Nor is it easy in every circumstance to define what constitutes a fault in a poem. To speak with assurance, one may not rely on unexamined assumptions but must rather be aware of the decorum of the whole poem, the decorum of its tradition, and lastly, the decorum of the literally visual concretion that underlies its poetic form.

A final point. When the "hedge-rows" stream over into "little lines of sportive wood run wild," they actually are not in violation of Wordsworth's own views of the relation of an image to the natural object. Earlier, I adduced his comments on Macpherson as tantamount to the tenets of the Imagist Manifesto. In one important respect, however, Wordsworth's emphasis is unique. He argues that in Macpherson everything is "defined, insulated, dislocated, deadened,—yet nothing distinct." But "in nature everything is distinct, yet nothing defined into absolute independent singleness." The red wheel-barrow of the Imagists is, as it were, defined "into absolute independent singleness." But for Wordsworth the image is not to be thus torn from the matrix of awareness. To have the "orchard-tufts" lose themselves "'Mid groves and copses" precisely illustrates the "distinctness" of the natural object at the same time that it denies its "singleness" by relating it to the natural matrix. So, too, the "hedge-rows" are cognized distinctly; but they are not "defined, insulated, dislocated, deadened." And they are not "defined into absolute independent singleness." Rather, quite in keeping with Wordsworth's own visualization of the natural image, no less than with the infrastructure of the poem as a whole, their distinct cognizance is linked and related to the fanciful cognizance of "little lines of sportive wood run wild."

The Heritage of the Age of Wordsworth

13

Wordsworth and the Victorians

CARL WOODRING

To the Victorians generally, Wordsworth was the restorer of emotion and the redeemer of childhood. After Wordsworth's insistence that pursuit of the true, the good, and the beautiful required thought imbued with emotion, Dryden and Pope became, for Victorian poets and critics, "classics of our prose" rather than classical poets.[1] Charlotte Brontë's Jane Eyre and Dickens's David Copperfield would probably have been nearer to the miniature adults of Elizabethan drama or to the wicked little vipers of Scottish Calvinism had Wordsworth's *Intimations Ode* been less well known. Jane Austen would have thought herself mad had she devoted half a novel to the early childhood of a heroine. The Victorian novelists had the precedent of Wordsworth in "discovering" the fascinating intricacies of childhood.

It is usually said that Oliver Twist, a penniless orphan among thieves, speaks in a cultivated way because Dickens was a vain snob, but readers could more readily accept such speech because Wordsworth, as Milton's heir in giving doctrine to a nation, taught that the child is a prince from heaven "trailing clouds of glory." The ode represented mother earth as a "homely Nurse" and foster-mother to the princeling child; why not a Fagin as her more sinister urban deputy diverting the child from its divine origin? The more orthodox, including John Henry Newman, complained that the ode trampled a belief basic to Christianity: the divinity of an infant is incomplete until baptism. To put the matter crudely, Wordsworth helped less theologically minded Victorian Christians turn from attention to the Cross toward affection for baby Jesus.

Wordsworth was Victoria's poet Laureate from 1843 until his death in 1850; Tennyson, as his successor, declared him "such a poet as kings should honour," a poet able to make a reign famous by "the utterance of memorable words concerning that period."[2] It became a common refrain for major Victorians that Wordsworth was a noble, morally pure priest of a natural religion. In 1879 Matthew Arnold declared him third only to Shakespeare and Milton among the great English poets. "But this is not enough to say," Arnold continued, because Wordsworth also excelled all poets of Europe after Molière except Goethe.[3] Charles Kingsley in 1844 called Wordsworth "poet, but preacher and prophet of God's new and divine philosophy, a man raised up as light in a dark time."[4] One reviewer of *The Prelude* (1850) spoke for many; Wordsworth had "an intense realization that the earth is adorned with beauty to win man to good."[5]

In *The Youth of Nature* (1852), Arnold anointed him prophet, "sacred poet," and "priest to us all."[6] Writers who acknowledged a frequent drabness called him nevertheless "nature's priest," "Priest of Nature," the "high priest of pure Nature-Worship." Harriet Martineau, in her *Ode to Religious Liberty* published in the Unitarian *Monthly Repository* for January, 1829 (3:43), had hailed this "great High-Priest" specifically as "the Prophet" of religious freedom. Most, however, located his priesthood among the hills and streams. Elizabeth Barrett declared in a sonnet *On Mr. Haydon's Portrait of Mr. Wordsworth on Helvellyn* that the poet "Takes here his rightful place as poet-priest."[7] The "here" points simultaneously to the mountain and to Haydon's success in positioning Wordsworth at the appropriate height. The designation as priest was brought to earth by Dante Gabriel Rossetti, who said that Wordsworth "was too much the High Priest of Nature to be her lover."[8] The Honorable Roden Noel, nevertheless, a poet and formerly groom of the privy chamber to Queen Victoria, began his celebratory address of 1884, recorded soon after in the *Transactions of the Wordsworth Society,* in defense of "that Poetry of Nature of which Wordsworth was High Priest" (6:24).

John Stuart Mill's *Autobiography* tells how his utilitarian education had brought him to a dull despair, his feelings corroded by rational analysis, until an encounter with Wordsworth's two-volume edition of 1815 brought him "thought coloured by feeling, under the excitement of beauty," a "source of inward joy, of sympathetic and imaginative pleasure, which could be shared in by all human beings."[9] Charles Darwin's conversion went in the opposite direction; he read *The Excursion* "twice through" in

1828, but in the intensity of biologic search he lost—"wholly lost," he says, perhaps slyly, "to my great regret"—"all pleasure from poetry of any kind."[10]

Scientists who could lose all feeling for poetry were greatly outnumbered by readers who pressed leaves or flowers between pages containing the poems *To the Daisy* or *The Small Celandine.* Such feeling was not confined to mute, inglorious readers. Of those who envisioned the poet as rising sublimely above his mountains, Arnold was the most persistent in high praise. He had a closer knowledge than other writers of the *person,* for his father, the headmaster of Rugby, had built a house in the Lake country near the Wordsworths, so that from age twelve Arnold spent his summers near a poetic eminence aged sixty-four and older. He lamented Wordsworth's death promptly in *Memorial Verses:* Byron, who died in 1824, had been a seductive spectacle of passion at strife with law; the death of Goethe in 1832 had meant the loss of a diagnostic physician able to say where a sick age was hurting. And now Wordsworth was gone:

> He found us when the age had bound
> Our souls in its benumbing round;
> He spoke, and loosed our heart in tears.
> He laid us as we lay at birth
> On the cool flowery lap of earth,
> Smiles broke from us and we had ease. . . .[11]

In editing his selection of Wordsworth's poems in 1879, Arnold paid tribute to "the great body of good work which he has left to us," but he wished to disengage from this large body the best poems and to separate himself from the "Wordsworthians"—he used the term as one might call inadequate readers of Jane Austen "Janeites." Among those who admired Wordsworth "for the wrong things" Arnold specified Leslie Stephen, who, finding in Wordsworth's poetry a distinctive ethical system, believed the poetry precious "because his philosophy is sound."[12] Stephen therefore, like Keats, admired *The Excursion.* Arnold did not.

Concerning praise and blame of Wordsworth by major Victorian writers, certain generalizations are possible. About 1829 the Apostles club, including Tennyson, Arthur Henry Hallam, John Sterling, R. C. Trench, Frederick Dension Maurice, and Richard Monckton Milnes, introduced at Cambridge the taste for moral elevation that made Wordsworth their poet. His austerity, even his frugality, seemed admirable to earnest Victorians of that generation. Milnes, as Lord Houghton and no longer dead serious, was president of the Wordsworth Society in 1885. Purity remained the watchword. Personal encounters with Wordsworth were almost always troubling. Many contemporaries of the Apostles saw the poet plain; whether at Rydal Mount or in London or in Cambridge (where his brother Christopher was master of Trinity College from 1820 to 1841), few liked what they saw or heard. For once, the dyspeptic Carlyle, in 1835, is typical: "I did not expect much; but got mostly what I expected. . . . [One finds] a kind of *sincerity* in his speech: but for prolixity, thinness, endless dilution it excells all the other speech I had heard from mortal. A genuine man (which is much) but also essentially a *small* genuine man."[13]

In *The Poetry of Experience* Robert Langbaum traced the development of the dramatic monologue, as practiced by Browning, Tennyson, and Pound, from the early lyrics of Wordsworth. For the poets who came after Wordsworth, nothing in his practice of verse had as much influence as his insistence in 1800 and again in 1815 that the artificiality of poetic diction should be avoided because the language of poetry could and should be the language spoken in "real life"; the poet, a man speaking to men. (He means to include women, but perhaps just barely.) From this insistence on the language of conversation came George Meredith's freedom to twist language into knots tighter than John Donne's, and Browning's freedom to have the soliloquizer in a Spanish cloister begin with the lines, "Gr-r-r—there go, my heart's abhorrence! Water your damned flower-pots, do!"[14] Ordinary diction as well as common subject, but both in descent from Wordsworth, led to Kipling's tribute to steam:

> "Goodbye, Romance" . . .
> . . . and all unseen
> Romance brought up the nine-fifteen.[15]

Major poets incorporated Wordsworthian phrases and devices, often deliberately. A passage from *Tintern Abbey,*

> Not for this
> Faint I, nor mourn nor murmur; other gifts
> Have followed; for such loss, I would believe,
> Abundant recompense,

and one from the *Intimations Ode,*

> Not for these I raise
> The songs of thanks and praise;
> But for those obstinate questionings
> Of sense and outward things,

join in Robert Browning's *Rabbi Ben Ezra:*

> Not for such hopes and fears
> Annulling youth's brief years,
> Do I remonstrate: folly wide the mark!
> Rather do I prize the doubt
> Low kinds exist without,
> Finished and finite clods, untroubled by a spark.[16]

Admiration from other great writers resulted in less direct imitation. On her twentieth birthday Mary Anne Evans wrote of Wordsworth's poems: "I never before met with so many of my own feelings, expressed just as I could like them."[17] Later, as George Eliot, she drew sustenance from Wordsworth for all her fiction and only too identifiably for her dramatic poem *The Spanish Gypsy.* She reread poems by him, including *The Excursion,* with both her common-law husband and, near the end, her legal husband. The "One great society alone on earth; / The noble living and the noble dead," from *The Prelude* (bk. 10, lines 394–395), reappears in Eliot's hymn O *May I Join the Choir Invisible,* as "those immortal dead who lived again / In minds made better by their presence."[18] When she finished her rustic parable *Silas Marner* in 1861, she wrote to her publisher: "I should not have believed that any one would have been interested in it but myself (since William Wordsworth is dead) if Mr. Lewes had not been strongly arrested by it."[19] She took her epigraph for the book from Wordsworth's *Michael.* To emulate *Michael* was a noble aspiration, but Eliot found no place in *Silas Marner* or elsewhere for the self-ironic comedy of Wordsworth's *Peter Bell, The Waggoner, The Farmer of Tilsbury Vale,* or *The Idiot Boy.* Perhaps even more indicative is her epigraph to chapter 80 of *Middlemarch,* from *Ode to Duty:* "Stern Lawgiver! . . . / Thou dost preserve the Stars from wrong." For all her interest in civilization and social consequences, she continued to accept Wordsworth's doctrine of nature as healing balm. It took the oblique, indefinite perspective of Walter Pater, in an essay of 1874 for the *Fortnightly Review,* to describe Wordsworth's poetry as bold and passionate, distinguished by "impassioned contemplation."

In the decades immediately before and after the Reform Bill of 1832, Wordsworth's conversion to the conservatism of Edmund Burke was deplored by many of the young. That he had accepted from a reactionary government the distributorship of stamps for Westmorland and part of Cumberland fueled Browning's poem *The Lost Leader:* "Just for a handful of silver he left us." In May 1850 the *Democratic Review of British and Foreign Politics* shed no tears over the death of the Laureate, "the salaried slave of Aristocracy and pensioned parasite of Monarchy." Although Browning and others pronounced Wordsworth a leader lost to the liberal cause, some found the case more complicated. Edward Caird, called in the *Dictionary of National Biography* "a 'radical' in politics, religion, and philosophy," a specialist in Kant and Hegel as professor of moral philosophy in Glasgow University and, later, as master of Balliol College, radical enough to urge upon Oxford degrees for women and education for working men, might seem an unlikely promotor of the "lost leader." Like other liberal or radical Wordsworthians, however, from Henry Crabb Robinson to E. P. Thompson, Caird acknowledged Wordsworth's own claim to be democratic in outlook. In *Fraser's Magazine* for February 1880, Caird counted Wordsworth with Rousseau as an upholder of the dignity of agricultural labor: "Wordsworth is Rousseau moralised, Christianised, and, as it were, transfigured by the light of imagination." Rousseau's and Wordsworth's "return to Nature," according to Caird, meant "a return by each man upon himself, an awakening in him of a consciousness of his capacities, his rights, and his duties" (21:214, 215).

Carlyle stirred his contemporaries; Wordsworth, as Arnold and others noted, calmed them. Or so they thought. Wordsworth was in fact too successful in convincing several generations that Nature never did betray the heart that loved her, with the corollary that one impulse from the vernal wood is better than all the books that teach anything to the contrary. To the deistic argument of the eighteenth century that the Creator designed the mechanism of our universe as a magnificent watch that will tick forever in Newtonian perfection, Wordsworth added a sense of divine underpresence in every hill, vale, and butterfly. Nature and the human mind are gloriously married. When lamentable geologic discoveries and other evidence made it clear that nature, careless of the individual and even of the type, was red in tooth and claw from ignorance of any law except survival of the fittest, the pain of Victorian doubt was blamed on the inadequacy of the Bible to meet the challenge. The blame was misdirected. Christianity, including the Wesleyan revival of passionate belief, had represented earth as eternally at war with soul. It was Wordsworth who taught persuasively that humanity and nature are gloriously married. It was Wordsworth's persuasiveness, repeated by his many imitators and disciples, that made necessary the explanation in Mill's essay "Nature" that no ethical lessons can be drived from the study of natural process, for nature teaches that the murderous strong will survive and the rest go down. The correction did not prevent Stopford A. Brooke from devoting half of his *Theology in the English Poets* to an affirmative presentation of Wordsworth's doctrine: "He does possess a philosophy, and its range is wide as the universe."[20]

Perhaps the last of the devout Wordsworthians of Victoria's reign was William Hale White. In *The Autobiography of Mark Rutherford* (1881), White's fictional persona is transformed by discovering the *Lyrical Ballads:*

God is nowhere formally deposed, and Wordsworth would have been the last man to say that he had lost his faith in the God of his fathers. But his real God is not the God of the Church, but the God of the hills, the abstraction Nature, and to this my reverence was transferred. . . . Wordsworth unconsciously did for me what every religious reformer has done,—he re-created my Supreme Divinity; substituting a new and living spirit for the old deity, once alive, but gradually hardened into an idol. (19)

A year after he published an account of Wordsworth and Coleridge manuscripts (and two years after the last of his novels under the pseudonym Mark Rutherford, Wordsworthian in their sincerity, Orwellian in their flatness), White published *An Examination of the Charge of Apostasy against Wordsworth* (1898), an attempt to renew Wordsworth's reputation as an advocate of social justice.

Wordsworth's poems were readily available to ordinary readers. During his lifetime, his latest work might appear in an expensive quarto, as *The White*

Doe of Rylstone did. But inexpensive editions, ranging from selections for the pocket to double-columned collective editions, appeared at the statistical average of two a year until the end of the nineteenth century. If White was the most devout disciple near the end of the era, the most industriously dedicated was William Knight, who edited the poems in eight volumes (1882–1886), with additional volumes later, including a *Life* (vols. 9–11). Edward Dowden reviewed Knight's edition with an eye jaundiced enough to make predictable his own edition of 1892–1893. A. B. Grosart's three-volume edition of Wordsworth's prose in 1876 remained the standard, in default of a better, until the edition by W. J. B. Owen and Jane Worthington Smyser in 1974, almost a round century later.

As soon as the circumstances of copyright made *The Excursion* freely available, three editions of book 1 were issued as school texts. Two appeared in 1863, one edited by the Reverend Derwent Coleridge and published by Moxon, the second edited by the Reverend Hugh George Robinson, published in Edinburgh and London. The third, in 1864, was edited by the Reverend Charles Henry Bromley and published by Longmans. These three began the tradition of including in anthologies for school use book 1 of *The Excursion* (or selections from it), which lasted until Jonathan Wordsworth, in *The Music of Humanity* (1969), urged instead the choice of the earlier version, *The Ruined Cottage,* which lacks the Pedlar's consolations. We cannot know what the Victorians of 1863 would have chosen had the earlier manuscript been available to them, but we can guess. The Victorian Wordsworth offered clear consolation, clearest of all, perhaps, to strict Anglicans like Derwent Coleridge.

Although Wordsworth had not entirely resisted the temptingly remunerative annuals, with steel engravings to illustrate their poems (and prose sketches), bound in satin or gold-stamped leather to serve as Christmas gifts, and observed in all the best parlors, he was not in general a table-book poet. But after the success in 1857 of Moxon's illustrated Tennyson and *The Poets of the Nineteenth Century,* edited by Robert Aris Willmott and published by Routledge, Willmott followed with *The Deserted Cottage* (books 1 and 2 of *The Excursion*) in 1859, with engravings that inspired an illustrated Wordsworth for sitting rooms in 1866.[21] This table book was reprinted later in a cheaper edition. With Birket Foster as the chief illustrator, the wood engravings were mostly picturesque scenes derived from the text, with a few domestic activities specified by Wordsworth depicted always as out of doors. Everything is sweet. The boy who commits ravage in the poem *Nutting* gazes naively in the engraving toward a picturesque tree. Poor Susan is an innocent maid safe in the rural enclosure that she envisions in the poem as she stands in a notorious London street at early morn. For *We Are Seven* a plump little girl with an armful of firewood addresses a comfortably agreeable listener: everything is left for Max Beerbohm's caricature in *The Poets' Corner*, "Wordsworth in the Lake District, at cross purposes." For page after page, nothing looms except two of the several hares that have multiplied from the single hare of *Resolution and Independence*.

The opinion is often expressed that Pre-Raphaelite attention to detail derived from Wordsworth, and there seems to have been a vague sense that genuine landscape painting could not be imagined without him. Yet the chief visual image called up by mention of him must have been the picturesque vignettes of ruined Tintern Abbey that accompanied most printings of his "Lines Composed . . . on Revisiting the Banks of the Wye. . . ." Some of the many appearances of that poem were owed to the popularity of the ruined abbey among picturesque painters and engravers.

Periodicals of various kinds kept Wordsworth's name before a large audience. The chief exception might be *Blackwood's Magazine*. John Wilson had seen to it that *Blackwood's* alternately praised and reviled his eminent neighbor from 1817 to 1835; when Chauncey Hare Townshend exercised the same extremes, in February 1830, Wordsworth purported to restrain his daughter's fiancé from answering: "Who that ever felt a line of my poetry would trouble himself to crush a miserable maggot crawled out of the dead carcass of the Edinburgh review."[22] In later years *Blackwood's* took a much greater interest in current fiction and current problems. Reviewers in the influential, weekly *Athenaeum*, including Macaulay, Elizabeth Barrett, and the broad-churchman F. D. Maurice, tended to offer Wordsworth as the model "poet-hero" and "poet-prophet," although Tennyson gradually replaced him in that office.[23] The *Saturday Review*, which began its long life as a weekly newspaper in 1855, took up at once the new taste for Tennyson, who had succeeded Wordsworth as a more active Laureate.[24] *Fraser's Magazine*, known for its rambunctiousness in earlier years as "Rebellious Fraser's," published frequent parodies, with *We Are Seven* a favorite (as it was of parodists generally), but retained Wordsworth as the standard by which other poets were to be judged; the Rossettis' friend William Allingham was editor from 1874 to 1879.

Wordsworth's influence extended well beyond parlors, libraries, and nurseries. William Howitt, an avid Wordsworthian until he and the Laureate got to know one another better, noted wryly in *Homes and Haunts of the Most Eminent British Poets* (1847) that Wordsworth had done much more than any other single figure to bring not only "tourists and hunters of the picturesque" to the Lake country but also railroads and steamboats to transport them. The Wordsworth Heritage, as Howitt would be aware, now attempts to preserve both the beauty that Wordsworth inherited and the historical effects of his presence in the Lakes.

There were more serious objections than Howitt's. The more adherents Wordsworth's philosophy of nature won, the louder the protestations from those who found repose in nature unacceptable. Even Matthew Arnold, the year before *Memorial Verses,* had renounced Nature as an ethical model for man in a sonnet then called *To an Independent Preacher Who Preached That We Should Be "in Harmony with Nature":* "Nature is cruel, man is sick of blood."[25] In asserting again and again that Wordsworth was to be valued for his criticism of life rather than for his philosophy, Arnold was not elevating poetic technique above philosophy but rejecting Wordsworth's belief in nature as moral and curative. It is not curative nature that is praised in *Memorial Verses,* but the soothing effect of Wordsworth's humanistic moral vision. For John Ruskin, Wordsworth's expressions of thought about nature made him not wrong so much as dull. Wordsworth thought about nature when he should have demonstrated praise by describing it in close detail. If one preached detail, why not practice it? In a set of *The Poetical Works of William Wordsworth in Five Volumes* (1827), now in the library of the University of Wisconsin at Madison, Ruskin made notes from 1879 to 1889 for the purpose of countering Arnold's edition of selections from Wordsworth with one of his own.[26] In addition to indications of his favorites, he wrote in the margins such remarks as "Not so good as I used to think it," "Rubbish," and "Twaddle waddle." Although much has been erased, a full scholarly account of this set would further our understanding of Ruskin's attitudes toward Wordsworth.

Swinburne had none of Arnold's or even Ruskin's inhibitions. In an essay on Byron used as preface to his selection of Byron's poems in 1866, Swinburne declared Arnold wrong to elevate Byron above Shelley but right at least in rejecting the philosophy of Wordsworth, who used nature "as a vegetable fit to shred into his pot and pare down like the outer leaves of a lettuce for didactic and culinary purposes." In *Essays and Studies* (1875) he added a footnote to defend this objection to Wordsworth's "philosophic or theological cookery."[27] Rejection is evident even in his choice of time and place for poems: *Tenebrae* begins "At the chill high tide of the night"; *By the North Sea* describes a coast where "Doubt and death pervade her clouded spaces"; several poems describe with masochistic joy the fierce waves that lash bathers in the sea. Wordsworth lingers in the shadows of *The Poet and the Woodlouse*. If Wordsworth was a pantheist, as some Victorian critics assert, it was a school of pantheism different from Swinburne's. Even Swinburne's babies, as in the poems *Babyhood* and *In a Garden*, have a softness to the touch from which Wordsworth would have recoiled.[28]

Thomas Hardy, in various ways a disciple of Swinburne, set his novels in a pastoral tradition that had wandered and stumbled a great deal since its revival by Wordsworth. If his settings were Wordworthian, his gloomy reflections on fossils and on degenerate forms of nature were not. Only in his penultimate novel, *Tess of the d'Urbervilles* (1891), however, did Hardy begin overtly to throw acid. In the opening chapter, with reference to Wordsworth's *Lines Written in Early Spring*, the novelist remarks sardonically: "Some people would like to know whence the poet whose philosophy is in these days deemed as profound and trustworthy as his song is breezy and pure, gets his authority for speaking of 'Nature's holy plan.'" In chapter 41, he quotes the lines about "trailing clouds of glory" as an example of "ghastly satire" and answers them with his Father Time, the child who kills himself and siblings. Darwin conquers Wordsworth in Hardy and Conrad. It did not occur to Hardy any more than to earlier Victorians that Wordsworth might be a poet of doubt.

Objections to the unevenness of Wordsworth's style, which had begun with the first appearance of *Lyrical Ballads*, continued in the Victorian period. Expert opinion agreed that when he was good, he was very, very good but that he was sometimes deplorably unpoetic. He seemed not to be able to distinguish shots that hit the center of the target from those that fell among tares or parched soil. Tennyson detected a sufficient number of "flat and essentially prosaic phrases" in *The Excursion, The Prelude,* and even in *Tintern Abbey* to suggest "a want of literary instinct."[29] Mill, implying that he knew personally poets more skilled than Wordsworth, was yet perceptive enough to see that he had been fittingly rescued by this "poet of unpoetical natures."[30] Several critics satisfied readers' sense of Wordsworth's dullness by noting that, unlike Keats and Byron, he had no sense of smell. Even in the *Transactions of the Wordsworth Society*, R. H. Hutton was able to speak of the poet's "two styles," the buoyant and energetic style of his youth and that of his age, with its economy of description, direct expression of thought, and visionary, meditative joy.[31] James Kenneth Stephen spoke for a larger number in his parody of *Thought of a Briton on the Subjugation of Switzerland* (despite that title, a fine sonnet) beginning "Two Voices are there; one is of the sea":

> Two voices are there: one is of the deep;
> It learns the storm-cloud's thunderous melody,
> Now roars, now murmurs with the changing sea,
> Now bird-like pipes, now closes soft in sleep:
> And one is of an old half-witted sheep
> Which bleats articulate monotony,
> And indicates that two and one are three,
> That grass is green, lakes damp, and mountains steep:
> And, Wordsworth, both are thine: at certain times
> Forth from the heart of thy melodious rhymes,
> The form and pressure of high thoughts will burst:
> At other times—good Lord! I'd rather be
> Quite unacquainted with the ABC
> Than write such hopeless rubbish as thy worst.[32]

Parodies had followed immediately upon *Lyrical Ballads*, before Shelley's *Peter Bell the Third* and Hartley Coleridge's piercing laughter in *He lived admist th'untrodden Ways*, ending on *The White Doe of Rylstone*, unread: "It's still in Longman's shop, and oh! The difference to him!"[33] Periodicals and pamphlets of verse had been peppered with travesties, but none gave a keener thrust than Stephen's.

When the Wordsworth Society ceased to be in 1888, Professor Knight declared that it had been successful beyond all hope. Yet irreverence reached its fullest intensity in July of that year when Samuel Butler argued in the *University Review* that Wordsworth must have meant by "the difference to me" that he had got Lucy into the kind of trouble that had led him to promise imprudently to marry her. He would not have said "few could know when Lucy ceased to be" unless "he was aware of circumstances that precluded all but those implicated in the crime of her death from knowing the precise moment of its occurrence." An otherwise unintelligible poem made sense if he had cut Lucy's throat or smothered her "in concert, perhaps, with his friends Southey and Coleridge"—the few who could know.[34] Butler's *Notebooks* include several attempts to deflate Wordsworth's self-importance and prudery, for example in the suggestion that Canon Ainger was the sort who would expurgate even Wordsworth, and how thankful we should feel that Wordsworth was not a musician: fancy having to sit out a symphony by the author of *The Excursion*.

As the Victorians knew nothing about Annette Vallon, the mother of Wordsworth's French daughter, biographers and reviewers told of his morally pure life as a recluse in the Lakes, but Thomas De Quincey, Walter Savage Landor, and Leigh Hunt reminded readers anecdotally that Wordsworth was an ordinary mortal, unusual largely in being more self-centered than the average. *Fraser's Magazine* republished in June 1846 James Hogg's bitter memory of an occasion when Hogg and John Wilson, along with De Quincey and Dorothy Wordsworth, were not enough to dislodge William's conviction that only one poet was present. Yet the complainers never said of Wordsworth what Auden was to write of Yeats, "You were silly like us," but always that he had a unique way of being silly, a way that some of them called "babyism."

The Reverend H. D. Rawnsley, a devoted Wordsworthian but one with "a certain love of the humorous," went among the peasants of Westmorland and Cumberland to learn if any of them were as deep as the poet's Michael and Matthew and to discover whether any remembered the Laureate. He found that they remembered "Wudsworth," all right, but that, unlike Coleridge's son Hartley, he never talked with poor folk or children. And unlike Hartley, he was not a philosophical poet, or one you wanted to read. "He wozn't a man as said a deal to common folk." Rawnsley's first witness was a woman who had once been in service at Rydal Mount: " 'Well you know,' were her words, 'Mr. Wordsworth went humming and booing about, and, she, Miss Dorothy, kept close behind him, and she picked up the bits as he let 'em fall, and tak 'em down, and put 'em together on paper for him.'"[35] It was her opinion that neither Dorothy nor the poet could "make sense out of 'em." "You must love Wordsworth," said Tennyson, "ere he will seem worthy of your love."[36]

A tour through N. Stephen Bauer's critical bibliography of Victorian references to Wordsworth can throw doubt on any generalizations ever made, including all those in the present essay and any that could have been made instead, concerning Wordsworth among the Victorians.[37] The contradictions recorded by Bauer are sufficiently rife to raise questions about any expression of critical assurance at any time. One Victorian critic or another declared one position and the next denied it: Wordsworth (a) wrote simply, (b) preached simplicity, but did not practice it; (a) his importance is in theory, (b) his prefaces are stupidly wrong, but he is important for *The Excursion*—no, says another, for small lyrics; (a) he improved steadily, (b) he worsened precipitously; (a) he never forgets man, (b) he always forgets man; (a) he revolutionized the lyric, the ode, the sonnet, or philosophical poetry, (b) he introduced nothing new; any given poem is (a) magnificent, (b) an example of his "babyism" or his prosaic flaccidity. Margaret Oliphant preferred *The Excursion* to the self-important *Prelude*—but she excepted the story of Margaret as a failure.[38] Our chief advantage over the Victorians is that they have no opportunity to point out our absurdities. Only the language of assessment has changed.

Without going on to Oscar Wilde—who was, paradoxically, respectful —we can let Henry James attempt a summary. In his review for the *Nation* of Stopford Brooke's *Theology of the English Poets*, on 21 January 1875, James referred with awe to Wordsworth's "almost fathomless intimacy with Nature": "Nature, as we look at her nowadays, did not really receive anything like her dues until Wordsworth began to set the chords a-murmuring." Yet it was lax of Brooke to be even more leisurely than the "inordinately diffuse" Wordsworth, with a vexing quotation of passages from this "most prosaic of poets as well as the most poetic—in which the moral flavor has apparently reconciled him to the flatness of the form more effectually than it will do most readers."[39]

Affirming human nature, Wordsworth was content to rest his case on the average rural English child. He required no reader to believe in the nobility of a savage or the decency of a Frenchman. He left it to the novels of Dickens to argue that the goodness of an English child could overcome urban temptations and heaped-up filth. Wordsworth's view satisfied the needs, answered the request, of most Victorian readers. Until the end of the century, most of those readers took for granted something like the Ruskinian view that art, including poetry, should uphold normative moral standards in worshipful praise of natural law and human aspiration. They were not wrong in believing that Wordsworth, with some such purpose in mind, created a body of poetry tending in its content to look in hope upon human purpose.[40]

14

Wordsworth in America

DAVID SIMPSON

The pace at which the United States of America came into being as an independent political entity was truly breathtaking. A declaration in 1776, a successful war, and a constitution in 1787 created the technical foundations of nationhood. Life as a whole was of course more complicated than life on paper, and the early years of the new republic were turbulent ones, most obviously so in the bitterly contested transition from Federalist to Jeffersonian administrations around 1800. Political and ideological affiliations to Great Britain did not disappear overnight, and the course of the French Revolution was monitored with some concern by those who feared the possibility of a similar upheaval within the new nation. By 1815 America had in many ways "won," and had definitely not lost, another war against the parent state, ruled over by the same aging and increasingly erratic parent figure of George III, and national self-confidence was beginning to consolidate and to look to its own western horizons. James Fenimore Cooper, with the luxury of hindsight, was able to affirm that the War of 1812 had been the real war of *mental* independence. Cadwallader, the main character in Cooper's *Notions of the Americans,* declares that the United States subsisted in a state of "mental bondage" until 1812, after which it emerged into true nationhood. Thus, while the events of 1776 belong to the *revolutionary* war, those of 1812 are "emphatically termed the war of independence."[1]

Cooper's account suggests that the achievement of independence was by no means as simple as the bare recitation of dates and events might imply. In the realm of literature and the literary culture, the process was especially complex and lasted for many decades beyond even 1815. Of course, there is no simple, progressive evolution. British reputation mattered far less to Whitman and to Thoreau in the mid-nineteenth century than it did to James and Eliot in the early twentieth century. But in the early national period, it proved much easier for most Americans to deny the claims of the King and his ministers than to cut themselves off from the legacies of Shakespeare and Milton. Joel Barlow tried, in *The Columbiad,* but was taken to task even more roundly by the conservative critics in his own country than by the British reviewers; Noah Webster's early efforts at reforming the language met with similar responses. Correspondingly, the early reputation of Washington Irving, who was widely admired on both sides of the Atlantic, had to do not only with his undoubted qualities as a writer but also with his ability to project fairy-tale solutions to or representations of the contemporary political and cultural tensions between the two nations. Both British and American readers were made to feel that fantasy and good humor could still overcome the intensity of their differences; the Revolutionary War is not the least important event slumbered through by Rip Van Winkle.

The conditions for the reception of British writers in early nineteenth-century America were thus somewhat complicated and ambivalent. As native writers tried to create a truly independent national literature, they were always obliged to recognize a common language and an inherited literary culture. This culture was of course itself far from monolithic: Milton's republicanism must have seemed far more conformable to an American literature than, say, Dryden's celebrations of royal authority. But even Milton was not an American, however congenial his principles might have seemed. Many writers and critics therefore felt a strongly expressed sense of inferiority or belatedness. Some felt that a democracy, with its unstable and quixotic public life, did not provide the proper ambience for the development of a great literature; other felt that the society of the new republic was not yet complex and mature enough to provide the raw materials for sophisticated transcriptions of human life and manners; still others lamented that America was a nation of traders and jobbers, with no respect for the life of the mind. Some of these concerns began to be assuaged with the rise of "Indian" tales and historical novels in the 1820s, but they took many years to disappear completely. Moreover, along with all these imagined cultural deficiencies—real enough to the writers of the times—American authors were also faced with a distinct economic disadvantage in having to compete with cheaply reprinted pirated editions of the established British writers, which proliferated owing to the absence of a proper copyright law. The works of Scott and Byron not only arrived with the imprimatur of a highly developed literary culture; they tended to cost considerably less than the first efforts of the native muse.

The modern reader who recognizes in Wordsworth one of the greatest of British poets and who is acquainted with the state of affairs in America just described might be led to expect a deluge of pirated editions, accompanied by careful estimates of their aesthetic and political qualities by an eager critical press. This was far from what happened, mostly because through much of his early career Wordsworth was a relatively minor poet in Britian itself. Among the writers we may still commonly remember, Scott, Byron and George Crabbe were far more popular than Wordsworth; Francis Jeffrey's infamously negative reviews were probably less to blame for this than the intrinsic difficulty of Wordsworth's "simple" poetry. Given these factors, the first American notices of that poetry came rather quickly—from Joseph Dennie, the conservative, Federalist editor of the *Port Folio*. Between 1801 and 1804 Dennie published samples from *Lyrical Ballads,* with favorable remarks about their quality and originality.[2] Since Wordsworth's poems were obviously not written in opposition to the war with France, or to slavery, or to the government's policy in Ireland, nor were they an explicit response to any of the other political crises of the times, Dennie seems not to have picked up any radical or Jacobin signals from them. No more did he sense a major challenge to contemporary ideas of decorum in this collection of abandoned women, dispossessed families, and idiot boys. Indeed, even the British *Anti-Jacobin Review,* which brought itself into being to combat the "torrent of licentiousness" apparent in British public life, published a short notice of *Lyrical Ballads* pronouncing it to be a volume of "no ordinary merit".[3]

Critics continue to debate the political affiliations of Wordsworth's poetry in general and of *Lyrical Ballads* in particular. Closet conservatism, or sophisticated "radical" alternative? A break with, or just another version of, the established conventions? Without seeking to decide this question here, it is clear that neither Dennie nor the editors of the *Anti-Jacobin* who were so often his mentors found any cause for disapproval, at least upon first inspection. An American reprint of the second edition appeared in

Philadelphia in 1802 and was welcomed by the *Port Folio.* But by 1807, when Wordsworth's two-volume *Poems* appeared in Britain, the mood had changed. Dennie then began to find something disturbing in Wordsworth's commitment to simplicity of style and subject. In this, he was again following his British mentors, for whom the question of decorum was to be the central problem with Wordsworth for the next fifteen years, and beyond.

In the years following the 1807 *Poems,* Wordsworth published his Cintra pamphlet and the *Guide to the Lakes,* as well as *The Excursion;* the collected *Poems* of 1815, with their new editorial categories; and various other poems and collections between 1815 and 1822. None of these writings seems to have registered as a major publishing event in America, and it was not until 1824 that a four-volume *Poetical Works* appeared from Cummings, Hilliard and Company in Boston. By that time, the ground had been somewhat prepared by Richard Henry Dana, Sr.'s favorable estimate in the *North-American Review* (8[1819]). The 1824 edition occasioned a very careful and well-informed review in the *Atlantic Magazine* (2[1825]: 334–348, 419–435), in which the question of decorum was brought to the fore. The article had high praise for Wordsworth, especially for *The Excursion, Tintern Abbey,* and *Laodamia,* the last being described as a "short but conclusive specimen of what he can accomplish, when emancipated from the tyranny of system" (433). The "system" was of course Wordsworth's declared loyalty to the language and characters of ordinary life, as first set forth in the preface to the 1800 edition of *Lyrical Ballads.* For this reviewer, the "true" Wordsworth was to be found in those poems where the system was ignored—poems written in complex blank verse and conventional "poetic diction," in which the poet does not seem to aspire to be "a man speaking to men" (as Wordsworth had claimed to be in his preface of 1800).

Thus began, for American criticism, the selection and constitution of a canon of "essential" poems, of the kind that has marked almost all subsequent versions of Wordsworth. Selection is indeed almost inevitable, given the range, variety and sheer volume of Wordsworth's writings in prose and verse. One should not sneer at those who have made the canons, nor self-righteously chastise them for leaving things out; it is more helpful to speculate about why some poems have been constantly in the forefront of attention and why others might have been ignored. This is not just a matter of self-evident aesthetic quality, though that is the vocabulary that critics and editors have tended to use. For all kinds of reasons, it is clear that some generations have had different priorities from others and have selected their "Wordsworth" accordingly. Within the same generations, different factions have also argued their cases.

Looking at Wordsworth's reception in nineteenth-century America, we can see clear patterns of consensus emerging, but we must also recognize a high degree of diversity. The reviewer for the *Atlantic Magazine* mentioned and discussed a range of poems that might put many modern professional critics to shame. We can often see an agreement among the reviewers about what will be argued about, even when the conclusions are different. For Wordsworth has always been a contested rather than a universally accepted author. Looking at the terms of these arguments can tell us much about Wordsworth today, but also a great deal about the priorities, certain and uncertain, of American literary culture.

F.W.P. Greenwood reviewed the 1820 London edition of the *Miscellaneous Poems* for the *North-American Review* (18 [1824]: 356–371). He admired the commitment to our "one common nature" (362), to simple language, and to the representations of external nature and of childhood. But he too favored *Tintern Abbey* over some of the "simpler" poems (in fact not at all simple) and accused Wordsworth of using "many words and phrases, to which custom has annexed low and comic associations" (358). For Greenwood, Wordsworth also wrote too much—a view with which many have since agreed—so that "his beauties are to be dug up from the midst of worthlessness" (359).

This response is in many ways typical of what was to follow throughout the century. It would be hard to overestimate the continuing shock that readers seem to have felt at the language and events of "low life" being offered in entire seriousness as the matter for poetry. Nonetheless, Greenwood is a positive critic, and in deriving from Wordsworth's descriptions of nature the conviction that "there is more mind, more soul about us, wherever we look, and wherever we move" than was apparent before reading them (367), he sounded a prophetic note. These must have seemed arresting words to the young men and women who were to mature into the luminaries of what we have come to recognize as Transcendentalism.

Through the 1830s, American interest in Wordsworth picked up and developed, as so often in these matters of reputation, in directions very little under the author's own control. In 1837, in Philadelphia, the first distinctly American edition of the *Complete Poetical Works* was published by Henry

Reed (the 1836 New Haven edition had been a reprint of the 1832 London edition). This edition is significant because Reed found himself moved to expand the category of "Poems of the Imagination" that had figured in Wordsworth's editorial classifications in the various editions since 1815. Because Reed was working with the 1832 edition and had not seen the 1836 volumes over which Wordsworth took much trouble, he had to make his own decisions in anticipating Wordsworth's own "unexecuted intention" of assigning the poems of *Yarrow Revisited* (1835) to the various editorial categories in the complete works.[4] This he did following an "attentive study" of the 1815 principles of classification. As it happened, Reed added only four poems from *Yarrow Revisited* into Wordsworth's own 1832 table of contents, but they are four important ones: *Gold and Silver Fishes in a Vase, Liberty, The Egyptian Maid,* and *Stanzas on the Power of Sound.* This is hardly evidence of any massive rearrangement of the canon, nor does it suggest to the uninitiated reader that the "Poems of the Imagination" are the primary part of it. But Reed's decisions made an important impression on Wordsworth himself, who approved, in the 1845 correspondence between the two men, the expansion of that category. Reed may thus be said to have achieved the distinction of assisting Wordsworth in editing himself and to have contributed to the incremental centrality of the idea of the Romantic imagination for the readers of the mid-nineteenth century.

Letters between Reed and Wordsworth were relatively frequent during the 1840s, largely motivated on Wordsworth's part by a lively concern for the security of his financial investments, and those of his friends, in American stock. On his side, Reed was constantly inviting Wordsworth to visit America, or at least to write something about the "great *moral* ties between the two nations, which you more than any other man could draw closer."[5] The poet's response was modest—three sonnets on Christianity in America —and somewhat qualified by his fears for the future of a "tumultuo[u]s democracy" (56). One or two of Wordsworth's opinions are worth noting. In 1839 he declared that "German transcendentalism . . . would be a woeful visitation for the world were it not destined to be as transitory as it is pernicious" (14); and he had no more patience with its American successor, asking, "Where is the thing which now passes for philosophy at Boston to stop?" (57).

Not, to be sure, at any point amenable to the aging poet. It was inevitable that a body of poetry such as Wordsworth's would make an important contribution to the genesis of American Transcendentalism. At the same time, the relation between them was far from simple. Emerson remained hostile to Wordsworth for a long time and never expressed an unqualified admiration. On the other side, Wordsworth's poems, and his explanations of them, could not but have contributed to the vitalist doctrines of those Boston philosophers. He admitted to Reed, in a letter of 1845, that he had tried to invest "the material Universe" with "spirituality" (144). Such statements as this, taken together with his explicit concern for nature, with the religiosity for such poems as *The Excursion* (open to a variety of readings, to be sure), and with his declared antimaterialism (as that doctrine was commonly understood), demanded attention for their "transcendentalist" potential. The *New York Review*'s essay on Reed's 1837 edition (4 [Jan. 1839]: 1–70), a highly favorable one ranking Wordsworth with Shakespeare and Milton, exploited the intuitionist, antianalytic strand in his writings, seen as entirely free from the "faithless spirit of inquiry" (7). The imagination is the central poetic faculty, and it is akin to "revealed truth," for philosophy can tell "not one syllable respecting the history of the human soul" (13). The reviewer approved the way in which "the sensuous and the spiritual are blended into one" (50) but was emphatic in freeing the imagination from any determining empirical constituent and from the contagion of the principles of scientific exposition. What was suggestive but always ambivalent for Wordsworth himself was here rendered didactic and unambiguous.

Even more rhapsodic in his appreciation of Reed's 1837 edition was E. P. Whipple, writing for the Boston *North-American Review* (59 [1844]: 352–384). This article is an eloquent celebration of Wordsworth's "spiritualism," which is one of the two great tendencies of the age, the other being the French Revolution and its ongoing effects. Despite certain ambiguities, Wordsworth's poems are also "in the highest degree democratic" (383). The striking feature of Whipple's argument is its continual redefinition of the Wordsworthian balance of mind-in-nature into a model of mind *over* nature. This is, to be sure, one part of what is in Wordsworth a continuous and unstable spectrum of mind–world relations, wherein no single or final moment is properly typical of any other. But Wordsworth was interested in the continuity of the process rather than in the isolation of a fixed and universal formula. Whipple, on the other hand, wanted to put the case that spiritualism makes "the inner world of the mind paramount to the external world of matter" so that "in the hands of the imagination, nature is a huge plaything, to be tossed about, and forced into whatever shape, and made to symbolize whatever sentiment, the sovereign faculty may impose. . . . Thus all poetry must, to a great extent, be transcendental" (356–357).

Wordsworth's is especially so, and in this above all he is the true prophet of the new age. The reader of today is likely to find it hard to ignore the degree of anxiety or guilt that often informs Wordsworth's transcriptions of the mind treating nature as a plaything. In poems like *Nutting,* and in many passages of *The Prelude* (which Whipple of course could not have seen), Wordsworth examines the delusions and transgressions that may result when man forgets his place, and the rights of others to their places. Whipple registered none of this anxiety and made Wordsworth the exponent of that emphasis on the ideal, mental control of experience that was so convenient an ideology for westward expansion and the doctrine of manifest destiny. We may find it written large in Whitman's poetry and, more ambivalently, in Emerson's writings; it speaks for a confidence in the indestructability of nature that few British poets, confined to the threatened corners of a smaller world, could hope to maintain, unless they transposed their optimism to the colonies—as Wordsworth, mostly, did not.

Whipple further developed the interpretation of Wordsworth's poems as in some sense anti-intellectual, a legacy that has persisted until the present day and has moreover formed many people's notions of what "Romanticism" is. Where Wordsworth both describes and displays a careful integration of thought and feeling, neither excluding the other, Whipple projected a poet of indescribable intuitions. Thus Wordsworth's best poetry has "the vagueness and indistinctness of music": "His description of indefinite emotions as subtile ideas is so expressed as to be heard by the soul, rather than seen by the mental vision. It awakens a certain mysterious and unspeakable delight" (365). Whipple's Wordsworth, like those judged to be good poets by the New Critics of the 1930s and after, has the gift of "abstracting the sentiment from the circumstances which surround it, and making it stand out in the pure light of its own nature" (373). Coleridge, in *Biographia Literaria* (1817), had complained of Wordsworth's *failure* to do exactly this, noting his habit of filling in the empirical and circumstantial details that Coleridge himself wished to regard as irrelevent. Where Whipple saw a fortunate "absence of dramatic power" and a disregard for the "accidents" of "situation" (374), Coleridge had found exactly these things, and disapproved. Both critics wanted to create a Wordsworth who projects a mind out of, or over, nature, rather than a mind in constant interaction with a shifting environment whose details are always important and sometimes even determining. Coleridge did see the evidence in Wordsworth's writing that counted against him and called it bad poetry; Whipple did not see it at all.

The mention of Coleridge, who was of course a very important figure for many American critics, especially in Boston, should serve as notice that the "transcendentalizing" of Wordsworth was not a purely American phenomenon. John Stuart Mill's *Autobiography,* published posthumously in 1873, made the point even more clearly. Recounting his own childhood and early education, lived out within the narrow confines of a utilitarian, scientific household, Mill described the revolutionary effects upon him of reading Wordsworth seriously for the first time. Brought up to regard feelings as imprecise and irrelevant obstacles to the pursuit of rational understanding, Mill lost his capacity for pleasure. Jean François Marmontel woke him up to the need for "the internal culture of the individual,"[6] but Wordsworth's poems, first studied in 1828, did far more. They proved, he said, a "medicine for my state of mind" and a true "culture of the feelings"; they revealed that "there was real, permanent happiness in tranquil contemplation" (89).

Mill in fact went on to argue for a balance or synthesis of thought and feeling in the ideal personality, but we can still sense the degree to which he experienced poetry as a *relief* from an otherwise overpowering utilitarian culture. It is thus understandably simplified as having "no connexion with struggle or imperfection" (89), a notion that any student of Wordsworth would now regard as having little to do either with the themes of the poet's writings or with his experiences in composing them. But Mill's version of Wordsworth has proved highly enduring, and it is symmetrical with the "transcendental" poet of Whipple and others. Both Mill and the American critics were clearly reacting against what they saw as the hegemony of scientific culture, and the same concern was to carry through into the later thoughts of I. A. Richards and F. R. Leavis. If they shared this reaction, a tentative distinction may yet be suggested: the American image of Wordsworth tended much more to stress the vitality and energy of nature and the natural feeling, while Mill projected a poet of retirement, peaceful contemplation and soliloquy. It is tempting to relate this difference, once again, to the exuberant and expansive nationalism of the American scene, whose energies the Boston sages imbibed even as they deplored, as they sometimes did, its excesses.

The "transcendental" Wordsworth was then a familiar figure in mid-century America. Orville Dewey, visiting Grasmere in the 1830s (as many nineteenth-century American intellectuals did), was at first disappointed at the physical presence of the bard himself—so much so that he thought he might have come to the wrong house![7] But the raw edges that were left after a long conversation about politics were soothed by an evening vigil on the shores of Grasmere Lake—almost a living out of the final scenes of *The Excursion*—during which Dewey gave over "all thoughts but of religion and poetry" (1:94). Richard Henry Dana, Sr. had been one of the earliest exponents of a poet who showed that our heartstrings "run upon and connect themselves with every thing in nature".[8] Perhaps the most extreme expression of the divinely vital Wordsworth comes later, in Henry Hudson's (1884) image of the poet as God's chosen messenger, one of the "translators and interpreters" who can, "as it were, touch and elicit the Divine meanings embodied in the forms of sense."[9] Not only is Wordsworth a countervoice to the prevailing analytic and scientific culture: he has been "specially, providentially, raised up and sent forth to that end" (8).

But this is only part of the story of what happened to Wordsworth in nineteenth-century America. Various interpretations of American culture and of the American identity have so privileged the role of New England and of Transcendentalism that we tend to forget that the profile of the times was more complicated, as were many of the so-called Transcendentalists themselves. As I have said, Wordsworth seems to have been almost always a contested poet. R. H. Dana, Jr., introduced to his work by E. T. Channing while still a student, was surely typical of his kind of spending "nearly a whole day" reading the *Intimations Ode,* over and over again, and becoming "infatuated with its spirit."[10] But Dana was a Harvard student, growing up in spiritual Boston. For those of his generation and specific disposition, this was perhaps the most formative of all of Wordsworth's poems, and it is constantly cited as such. But at the same time, others were attacking the whole tenor of Wordsworthianism. In so doing, they were not simply following in the steps of their British counterparts who happened to be engaged in the same task. For, by about 1830, there were enough American poets who claimed or seemed to be writing in the manner of Wordsworth to

inspire a strong division of loyalties among their peers. Reviewing William
Cullen Bryant's 1831 volume, along with the latest from N. P. Willis, James
McHenry spoke out strongly against those he termed the "American Lakers."[11] The English poets of the same school—oddly including Keats and
Shelley—were an "ill-judged model," with their "heaviness of thought, . . .
slovenliness of diction . . . and abstruse dulness" (154, 161). Among their
American followers, Willis was the worst offender, with his "whining puer-
ilities" and "unintelligible jargon" (157). This essay has its place in the battle between wordly Philadelphia and spiritual Boston, its real target being
the "New-England school" (162); but McHenry did place some blame on
the paradigm of the "dull and drawling *Excursion*" (174). Boston itself was
far from unanimous in its response: in the same year that McHenry's essay
appeared, the *North-American Review* (35 [1832]: 165–194), while praising Wordsworth himself, ascribed the fact that there were "few who read,
and fewer still who relish him" not only to his own theoretical assertiveness
but also to the "sickly race of versifiers" who have followed him, turning
simplicity into "infantine inanity" (174–175).

Throughout the 1830s and beyond, readers found it hard to distinguish
Wordsworth from the "school" of Wordsworth. The poet became part of
the debate about Transcendentalism. Just four years after McHenry's negative review, the *American Quarterly Review* (20 [1836]: 66–68), ostensibly
responding to *Yarrow Revisited,* printed an elaborate recantation regretting
its previous insensitivity to the "calm voice of a solitary and tranquil spirit"
(66) and praising Wordsworth's consistent courage and dedication in the
face of years of misunderstanding and hostility. Philadelphia now seems to
have been won over to the cause of intellectual idealism: "It is a mistake to
suppose that it is the men of action who govern the world, for they are only
the agents of the men of thought, and forward the views and carry out the
impulses these superior spirits give to the course of things" (81). Transcendentalism seems here to have conquered the field.

But a decade later, the *North-American Review* (54 [1847]: 402–435),
was still negatively identifying—of course with *some* justice—Wordsworth
with his American admirers. In a review of nine American poets, headed by
Emerson and William Ellery Channing, their "exaggerated and fantastic
manner" was attributed to Wordsworth's example, as was their tendency to
fall into raptures over "low and disgusting objects, which no poetry can elevate above their intrinsic meanness and vulgarity" (420). While the best of

Wordsworth may be free from this taint, his "servile imitators" offered only "mystic ravings and transcendental silliness" (421).

There is no doubt that in the division between the followers of the "line of wit" and the new Romantics typified first by Bryant and then by Emerson, the obvious affiliation of Wordsworth's writings is with the second. Bryant seems to have admired Wordsworth greatly, though seldom without qualification. G. C. Verplanck remarked on the similarities between the two as early as 1821, the year of Bryant's first major volume, and in 1827 the American poet praised Wordsworth's "spirituality" and his "vein of lofty and profound meditation."[12] In 1845 he was able to visit the seventy-five-year-old poet, and the two apparently enjoyed each other despite their superficial differences of opinion. Wordsworth's reception by Emerson—specified by the 1847 reviewer as the leader of the "servile imitators"—is rather more complicated. Emerson's estimations of his peers and predecessors are frequently embedded in an irony that can prove hard to unravel precisely. He began life by admiring the Byronic rather than the Wordsworthian model. In 1832 he described Wordsworth as a "genius that hath epilepsy, a deranged archangel." Meeting him in 1833 Emerson found a "narrow and very English mind" and a "general tameness and conformity" of thought on questions that did not pertain to poetry. By 1840 he was allowing Wordsworth a "wisdom of humanity," but one based on "limited poetic talents." Even when he held up the British poet as having done "more for the sanity of this generation than any other writer," and as the corrective voice for a "worldly and ambitious age," he never allowed himself to omit references to his limitations.[13] This is not just a constitutional aggressivity on Emerson's part; he recognized that his own poems were less akin to Wordsworth's than his hostile critics were claiming.

A complete assessment of Wordsworth's reputation in nineteenth-century America—which this essay does not of course aspire to be—would then be likely to confirm that he did *not* take America by storm, even as he impressed some important factions, notably the Transcendentalists. Even here, we find that the rank-and-file members of the movement were more rhapsodic in their enthusiasm than major figures like Emerson. Various versions of Wordsworth appealed to various critics. Generally, the complex poems like the great *Intimations Ode* and *Tintern Abbey* appealed more than the apparently "simple" poems which seemed to be contaminated by associations of the vulgar or the grotesque. The complexity of these simple

poems was almost never perceived or argued, even where they were appreci-
ated. Ironically, and with the luxury of hindsight, it might seem to us now
that the complex poems were popular largely because they defied a certain
kind of understanding; they were to be "felt" or intuited rather than explained or argued. Generations of sensitive readers have continued to enjoy,
for example, the great Ode, without being able to explain what some of its
notorious passages might actually *mean*. The nineteenth-century critics did
much to put in place that Wordsworth who is the transcriber of vague but
somehow important feelings and the enemy of analytic thought. At the same
time, there was a considerable diversity to the critical response. The *Southern Literary Messenger,* for example, found cause to celebrate the *Sonnets
Dedicated to Liberty* (3[1837]: 705−711, 721) as expressions of a serious
and admirable republicanism and, some years later, to write approvingly of
"Wordsworth's Portraiture of Woman" (21 [1855]: 686−688). Many readers, like Emerson, maintained a general response somewhere between approval and disapproval. The material I have presented does not seem to me
to support James Russell Lowell's claim that Wordsworth "found (as other
original minds have since done) a hearing in America sooner than in England."[14] The Wordsworth "controversy" was at first much more vigorous
in Britain, and when his reputation did begin to rise in America, most dramatically in proto-Transcendentalist circles, it was not uncontested. Lowell
himself had much to say that was negative. He found Wordsworth's genius
to be naturally prosaic rather than poetic, so that he was at best "a poet of
passages." When inspiration failed, as it often did, the verse was "leaden."
The poet's self-imposed isolation and self-preoccupation had also been dis-
abling. As the "historian of Wordsworthshire" he manifested a "dry and
juiceless quality" and an "absolute want of humor." He was a poet completely lacking in that "urbanity of mind" that can only come from commerce with one's kind (242, 243, 240, 241).

    This verdict, published quite close in time to Henry Hudson's case for the
same poet as the messenger of God, shows the continuing diversity of American responses to Wordsworth. Henry T. Tuckerman was a typical reader
when he declared that "the quantity of his verse is wholly out of proportion
to its quality."[15] Much of the explanation for this mixture of praise and
blame must lie in the sheer size and variety of the Wordsworth canon. We
have still not found, and perhaps never will find, a way of writing about all
of the poetry in any single critical vocabulary or approach. Matthew Ar-

nold, faced in 1879 with the task of editing a Wordsworth still not "fully recognised" either at home or abroad, was quite clear about the need to select the best out of a canon that the poet himself never seems to have censored. We tend not to be quite as confident as Arnold was in doing away with "a great deal of the poetical baggage" that comes along with Wordsworth's best work.[16] But we have not really moved beyond the predicament of this eminent Victorian. The most persuasive and powerful readings of Wordsworth by twentieth-century critics have all been based on a very small proportion of the total body of poetry. To give only the most formative example, Geoffrey Hartman's interpretation is based on a selection both historical and thematic. It deals only with the poetry up to 1814 and privileges therein the passages of visionary or apocalyptic import.[17] At the time of this writing, we have still to find a satisfactory way of "reading" most of the later poetry, and quite a bit of the earlier poetry, too.

Earnest concern for this task is probably to be limited to a very small group of professional critics. Meanwhile, readers will continue to feel free to pick and choose as they wish, as the creative writers themselves so often have. The crisis in self-confidence felt by so many of the authors of the early republic had largely passed by the 1850s, though it would return again for some anxiously transatlantic spirits. Those whom one might expect to have been most open to a Wordsworthian influence seem to have been relatively indifferent to his presence, whatever they might have imbibed from their sense of the spirit of the age. The preface to Whitman's *Leaves of Grass* does have something, on the grand scale, of the democratic initiative that is at the heart of Wordsworth's preface to *Lyrical Ballads*. And Thoreau has an affinity for lakes. But neither writer is in any thorough or conscious way a disciple of Wordsworth, or of Wordsworthianism. Moving west, the literature of prairies and mountains would perhaps inevitably have found Wordsworth too tame for adaptation into the American landscape. But his example has continued to preoccupy or inspire later writers, or at least to assist them toward their own self-definitions. Ezra Pound, awkwardly American at the best of times, was a typical Modernist in his disdain for Wordsworth's "slobber" and "endless maunderings." For Pound, Wordsworth's best moments were "Imagist" moments, capturing the essential object in a moment of time, but they were always buried "in a desert of bleatings."[18] Like Coleridge and Whipple, albeit for quite different reasons, Pound could see no way of accepting those "accidental" details that Wordsworth so frequently insisted on putting into poetry. Pound spoke his mind; others, one suspects, have more often proven Wordsworth, or some appealing version of him, upon their creative pulses. As a dedicated Wordsworthian, I see his legacy in the plain-speaking complexity of Robert Frost, in the natural eye of Theodore Roethke, in the self/other paradoxes of Wallace Stevens; also, perhaps, in the "egotistical sublime" of a Charles Olson, and in the urgent but unstable public address to God and the state of a Robert Lowell. Few if any of these poets are to be called *followers* of Wordsworth, but they have all, I think, found something in him, or produced something that bears comparison with his work. For there are many Wordsworths. Harsher critics have complained that he wrote too much and that he displays the arrogant conviction that everything he wrote is important. But behind the occasionally strident public voice, there is much of the blessed innocent who is able, in a way that few other poets can match, to publish the poetry that will embarrass him and result in the loss of "reputation," while hoping all the time for future restoration, or for the approval of a few natural hearts. Who but Wordsworth could have published *Gipsies,* a poem that has so discomforted most Wordsworthians that they have ignored it completely? There are many other examples of poems that we still have to understand, before we can assume the right of judgment. If such longevity be the fate of our species, there is here much of life and thought for future years.

15

1800 and the Future of the Novel
William Wordsworth, Maria Edgeworth, and the Vagaries of Literary History

GENE W. RUOFF

Although literary manifestos know no particular season, the turns of centuries offer strong inducements for declaring the end of old ways and the beginning of new. The year 1800 saw the publication of two critical documents which attempted to reshape both the ends and the means of literature and which continue, acknowledged or not, to bear heavily on our conceptions of modernity in the arts.

The second of these documents to appear, William Wordsworth's preface to his and Samuel Taylor Coleridge's second edition of *Lyrical Ballads*, has become a canonical text of modern criticism, reprinted in whole or in part in every historical anthology of English literature, found in every substantial compendium of world criticism. It has been made indispensable to an understanding of modern culture, a watershed in the history of both aesthetic taste and artistic practice. In his magisterial study of Romantic aesthetic theory, *The Mirror and the Lamp*, M. H. Abrams claims that Wordsworth, "the first great romantic poet, may also be accounted the critic whose highly influential writings, by making the feelings of the poet the center of critical reference, mark a turning-point in English literary theory."[1]

The other critical manifesto has been less celebrated, for a variety of reasons, few of which redound to the credit of historians of literature. In January of 1800 a slender anonymous volume appeared in London entitled

Castle Rackrent: An Hibernian Tale Taken from the Facts, and from the Manners of the Irish Squires, before the Year 1782. The book was a great and immediate popular success. Its third London edition in 1801 revealed its author to be Maria Edgeworth, an Anglo-Irishwoman whose prior literary fame had rested primarily on a collection of children's stories and a treatise on education. *Castle Rackrent* also has a preface, a modest declaration of a new kind of fiction as admirably pointed and brief as Wordsworth's, love it as we might, is not.

In the sections which follow I juxtapose the works of Wordsworth and Edgeworth, exploring the tasks for poetry and fiction which two remarkable and original writers foresaw at the beginning of their century. I move from their preface-manifestos to a comparison of *Castle Rackrent* and one of Wordsworth's major narratives of 1800. My concluding section sketches a possible literary history capable of honoring the achievement of Edgeworth in *Castle Rackrent* as fully as that of Wordsworth in *Lyrical Ballads* has been. Both writers saw literature as a powerful force for human understanding and social betterment. Neither wished for a moment to disengage the writer from the social complexities of the age or to produce an art safe for sanitary aesthetic contemplation. The abiding irony is that Wordsworth's achievement, for which he is renowned, came in a form which has lost most of its societal force. Those of us who teach poetry for a living know that our hardest task is to re-create a sense of how very much poetry mattered in Wordsworth's day, when the form had a true public audience. Wordsworth reformed a literary kind which within a century of his death would be consigned to the caretakership of universities. Edgeworth, only a woman, only a provincial, writing what Jane Austen would wryly term "only a novel," created a kind of fiction which continues to play a vital role in the world at large.

A Tale of Two Manifestos

M. H. Abrams's discussion of Wordsworth's preface to *Lyrical Ballads* treats the work as a triumphant codification of an expressive poetics: "The year 1800 is a good round number, ... and Wordsworth's Preface a convenient document, by which to signalize the displacement of the mimetic and pragmatic by the expressive view of art in English criticism" (22). Certainly an artist-centered aesthetic is easily deducible from Wordsworth's preface and forms a central part of Wordsworth's contribution to modern culture. The battle of expressive poetics is refought annually (or semesterly, or quarterly) in every poetry-writing class in the land. But, as Abrams himself acknowledges, there is much more in Wordsworth's preface than the poet's joy in the activities of his own mind.

Recent critics have been especially attentive to a polar counterthrust of the preface, its emphasis on the dramatic or dialogic properties of poetry, its subordination of the poet's voice to what Wordsworth calls "the real language of men in a state of vivid sensation" or "the very language of men."[2] In the 1800 Preface, Wordsworth contents himself with debunking the artificial elevation of "poetic diction" (251), castigating the stale "phrases and figures of speech which from father to son have long been regarded as the common inheritance of Poets" (251) and, most notoriously, denying any "essential difference between the language of prose and metrical composition" (253). He concludes: "Poetry sheds no tears 'such as Angels weep,' but natural and human tears; she can boast of no celestial Ichor that distinguishes her vital juices from those of prose; the same human blood circulates through the veins of them both" (254). But the full extent of Wordsworth's revaluation of the language of poetry becomes clear in an important passage added to the preface in 1802. Wordsworth has been speaking of the poet's powers of sympathetic imagination, through which he can enter into situations and feelings alien to his own:

> But, whatever portion of this faculty we may suppose even the greatest poet to possess, there cannot be a doubt but that the language which it will suggest to him, must, in liveliness and truth, fall far short of that which is uttered by men in real life, under the pressure of those passions, certain shadows of which the Poet produces, or feels to be produced, in himself. However exalted a notion we would wish to cherish of the character of a Poet, it is obvious, that while he describes and imitates passions, his situation is altogether slavish and mechanical, compared with the freedom and power of real and substantial action and suffering. So that it will be the wish of the Poet to bring his feelings near to those persons whose feelings he describes, nay, for short spaces of time perhaps, to let himself slip into an entire delusion, and even

confound and identify his own feelings with theirs; . . . he will feel that there is no need to trick out or elevate nature: and the more industriously he applies this principle, the deeper will be his faith that no words, which his fancy or imagination can suggest, will be to be compared with those which are the emanations of reality and truth.

(1802 Preface, 256–257)

Wordsworth's program calls for poetry to rediscover its roots in spoken language and aspire to the expressiveness of language as it is uttered in real situations, under the pressure of immediate emotion. His claim that such vernacular utterances are "emanations of reality and truth" could hardly be made more strongly.

Edgeworth's preface to *Castle Rackrent* puts forward similar claims for vernacular truth. She begins with a defense of the widely ridiculed "taste of the public for anecdote" as "an incontestable proof of the good sense and profoundly philosophic temper of the present times."[3] Her statement will remind readers of *Lyrical Ballads* of the number of its poems which consist entirely of accounts of verbal encounters with a motley assortment of children, old men, and wandering women. Poems like *Anecdote for Fathers, We Are Seven, The Last of the Flock,* and *Simon Lee* have invariably been the most disputed and scorned of Wordsworth's canon, as their matter has often seemed too mundane and trivial for memorialization in verse. Wordsworth's aesthetic motives are clear from his 1800 preface: he is countering the literary excesses of his age—"frantic novels, sickly and stupid German Tragedies, and deluges of idle and extravagant stories in verse" (249)— in order to demonstrate that "the human mind is capable of excitement without the application of gross and violent stimulants" (249). Like Wordsworth, Edgeworth sets her celebration of anecdote against dominant literary practices of her day, not in the belles lettres, but in the writing of history:

> The heroes of history are so decked out in the fine fancy of the professional historian; they talk in such measured prose, and act from such wicked and diabolical motives, that few have sufficient taste, wickedness or heroism, to sympathize with their fate. Besides, there is much uncertainty even in the best authenticated ancient or modern histories; and that love of truth, which in some minds is innate and

immutable, necessarily leads to a love of secret memoirs and private anecdotes. (1)

Edgeworth particularly objects to the literariness of monumental histories, their sublimity and diabolism which are roughly equivalent to Wordsworth's "gross and violent stimulants" and do equal damage to something both writers insist is *truth*.

Edgeworth insists that truth can only be caught off guard: "We cannot judge either of the feelings or of the characters of men from their actions or their appearance in public; it is only from their careless conversations, their half finished sentences, that we may hope with the greatest probability of success to discover their real characters" (1). For Edgeworth, rhetorical finish can be as destructive of truth as poetic diction is for Wordsworth. Her preface revels in paradox, as she goes on to proclaim that

> the merits of a biographer are inversely as the extent of his intellectual powers and talents. A plain unvarnished tale is preferable to the most highly ornamented narrative. Where we see that a man has the power, we may naturally suspect that he has the will to deceive us, and those who are used to literary manufacture know how much is often sacrificed to the rounding of a period or the pointing of an antithesis. (2–3)

Both Wordsworth's and Edgeworth's uses of the term *truth* bear examination. It is clear that neither is claiming anything like objective or even referential truth for vernacular utterances. They are jointly interested in truth which resides in and derives from scrupulous attention to an individual's perception and construction of events. Wordsworth's claims for the higher truth of poetry can sometimes be extravagant. But his poet reaches universality through particularity, not generality; and he conveys it through the language of men rather than the family language of poets. He will not "break in upon the sanctity and truth of his pictures by transitory and accidental ornaments, and endeavour to excite admiration of himself by arts, the necessity of which must necessarily depend upon the assumed meanness of his subject" (1802 Preface, 260). Both Wordsworth and Edgeworth equate truth with immediacy and spontaneity, with language which arises directly from feeling without rhetorical intention. Pursuing her contention that the "talents of a biographer are often fatal to his reader," Edgeworth observes the justice in attending to "those, who without sagacity to discriminate character, without elegance of style to relieve the tediousness of narrative, without enlargement of mind to draw any conclusions from the facts they relate, simply pour forth anecdotes and retail conversations, with all the minute prolixity of a gossip in a country town" (3).

Where Wordsworth and Edgeworth differ most markedly is on a principle that Wordsworth calls "selection." He rejects the notion that the poet should serve as a "translator, who deems himself justified when he substitutes excellences of another kind for those which are unobtainable by him; and endeavours occasionally to surpass his original, in order to make some amends for the general inferiority to which he feels he must submit" (1802 Preface, 257). Still, the poet must adopt language "purified indeed from what appear to be its real defects, from all lasting and rational causes of dislike or disgust" (1800 Preface, 245), to the end of "removing what would otherwise be painful or disgusting in the passion" (1802 Preface, 256–257). Whatever other "selections" he may have made, Wordsworth clearly chose to remove the regionalisms and verbal idiosyncrasies from the speech of his characters, perhaps in the interest of avoiding quaintness and condescension. In her role as editor of her narrator's supposed verbatim account, Edgeworth reports that she "had it once in contemplation to translate the language of Thady into plain English" (4). She abandoned the notion for two reasons: "Thady's idiom is incapable of translation, and besides, the authenticity of his story would have been more exposed to doubt if it were not told in his own characteristic manner" (4).

Coleridge, we remember, objected strongly to Wordsworth's highly particularized narrators, as well as to his general proclivities for dramatic form. In the *Biographia Literaria* he calls special attention to Wordsworth's note to *The Thorn*, which confessed the need for an introductory poem to establish fully the character of its narrator:

The Reader will perhaps have a general notion of it, if he has ever known a man, a Captain of a small trading vessel, for example, who being past the middle age of life, had retired upon an annuity or small independent income to some village or country town of which he was not a native, or in which he had not been accustomed to live. Such men having little to do become credulous and talkative from indolence; and from the same cause, and other predisposing causes by which it is probable that such men may have been affected, they are prone to superstition.[4]

In lyric poetry, Coleridge comments, "it is not possible to imitate a truly dull and garrulous discourser, without repeating the effects of dullness and garrulity" (289). We can only wonder what Coleridge might have said of Edgeworth's description of Thady Quirk's "claims to the public favor and attention": "he was an old illiterate steward, whose partiality to *the family* in which he was bred and born must be obvious to the reader. He tells the history of the Rackrent family in his vernacular idiom, and in the full confidence that Sir Patrick, Sir Murtagh, Sir Kit, and Sir Condy Rackrent's affairs, will be as interesting to all the world as they were to himself" (4). If garrulity and dullness are not virtues in a narrator, what about illiteracy, partiality, dialectal interference, and complacency? In keeping with her more radical exploration of the potential of vernacular literature, Edgeworth's Thady Quirk makes Wordsworth's eccentric old sea captain seem a member of the mainstream of society.

   If the program sketched so briefly in Edgeworth's preface is more daring than Wordsworth's, how can we account for her work's having led to her immediate lionization while Wordsworth's sparked continuing attacks from critics like Coleridge and Francis Jeffrey and satirists like Lord Byron? The core of the answer probably derives from the relative prestige of their chosen forms. In declaring an urgency for the reform of poetry, Wordsworth attacked a venerated institution reinforced by all the high solemnity an accepted classical canon can provide. In creating an altogether new form for fiction—*Castle Rackrent* was the first family saga novel, the first novel written wholly in dialect, and the first novel written in a largely realistic mode to employ ironically limited narration[5]—Edgeworth had a free hand because prose fiction had so little prestige. In his disregard for the novel, Wordsworth shared the attitudes of his age. As late as 1834, he agreed that Jane Austen's novels "were an admirable copy of life," only to add that "he could not be interested in productions of that kind." In 1842 he lamented the rage for Charles Dickens's works among Dr. Arnold's schoolboys and the following year described Dickens (upon whom Wordsworth was a massive influence) as "a very talkative, vulgar young person—but I daresay he may be clever. . . . I have never read a line he has written."[6] The novel as a form was not sacred enough for sacrilege. Further, both *Castle Rackrent*'s Irish subject matter and its "foreign" idiom could insulate the English reader from any possible discomfort that his own tastes, behavior, prejudices, or politics were being called into question (which they were), whereas Wordsworth's scorn for the pretentiously elevated tastes of his age is evident throughout his preface. Finally, while Wordsworth persevered in reprinting both his preface and his notorious experimental poems in all collected editions throughout his lifetime, Edgeworth silently abandoned the brilliantly innovative form she had created. Her subsequent Irish novels, *Ennui* (1809), *The Absentee* (1812), and *Ormond* (1817), are enlivened by authentic voices, but those voices are contained within and subordinated to an omniscient narrative voice which is careful to explain, to weigh, and to judge. To an extent, her own growing talents as a fictive biographer—and *Ormond* especially is a splendid novel—are allowed to become fatal to *her* readers. The reasons for her retreat, I suspect, may be found in the greatest virtues of *Castle Rackrent*.

Two Plain Unvarnished Tales

Comparing across genres is risky business. However concrete and detailed a poet may intend to be, for example, his form will tolerate a much higher level of abstraction than novels ordinarily can. Further, poetry's use of the vernacular will entail both selection and some degree of syntactic manipulation, not only for propriety, as Wordsworth claimed, but simply to satisfy the demands of lineation and meter. Byron's example in *Don Juan* suggests that the closer a poem approaches vernacular utterance in lexicon and syntax, the more shocking and potentially comical will be its play against the genre's commitments to formal regularity. Nevertheless, cross-genre comparisons are crucial to any synchronic literary study, especially in the Romantic period, when the novel is developing a momentum which will make it the commanding form of the coming century and when excluding it from our understanding is tantamount to ignoring many of the most distinguished contributions of women to literature written in English.

One work from the *Lyrical Ballads* of 1800, *Michael: A Pastoral Poem*, especially recommends itself for discussion alongside Edgeworth's "plain unvarnished tale." It is, says Wordsworth, a story "ungarnish'd with events, / Yet not unfit, I deem, for the fireside, / Or for the summer shade" (lines 19–21). The tale will be "a history / Homely and rude," related for "the delight of a few natural hearts" (34–36). Wordsworth's recommendations for his tale, its simplicity, homeliness, rudeness, and even its unbookish orality suggest an aesthetic strategy of artlessness comparable to that of Edgeworth. In addition, both works have as their theme a dominant issue of their decade, the passage of landed property out of its hereditary line of descent, which is taken as a sign of tremendous economic, social, and cultural change. In the writings of Edmund Burke and Thomas Paine, the entailed estate had come to stand, respectively, for the glories and abuses of the English system of government. The crucial issue in their debate was whether any generation or any number of generations could, like a legator, bind in perpetuity the mode of governance of generations to come.[7] Wordsworth tells the story of the shepherd Michael, "An old man, stout of heart, and strong of limb" (42); his wife Ruth, "a comely Matron, old / Though younger than himself full twenty years" (81–82); and Luke, the son of their old age and hope for the continuity of the life of "their Forefathers" (388). Edgeworth tells through Thady Quirk of the dispossession of the house of Rackrent, an Anglo-Irish estate which at the end of four generations of assorted and inventive improvidence passes from the hands of the family Thady has served.

Both writers were aware of the potential political significance of their tales, although in Edgeworth's case *afraid* might be the better word. Her preface takes considerable pains, in this year of impending "union" with Great Britain, to disengage her account from contemporary relevance:

> The Editor hopes his readers will observe, that these are 'tales of other times;' that the manners depicted in the following pages are not those of the present age: the race of Rackrents has long since been extinct in Ireland, and the drunken Sir Patrick, the litigious Sir Murtagh, the fighting Sir Kit, and the slovenly Sir Condy, are characters who could no more be met with at present in Ireland, than Squire Western or Parson Trulliber in England. (5)

The work's title page points to events "before the year 1782," which was the date both of Edgeworth's own arrival in Ireland as a fourteen-year-old

girl and of the birth of the short-lived Irish Nation, which survived a
hopeful, complacent childhood and tumultuous adolescence only to die in-
gloriously in the Act of Union of 1800. Few readers have been taken in by
the transparent evasions of this part of the preface, nor have social historians documented any radical improvement in the attitudes and manners of
the post-Ascendancy Anglo-Irish gentry, whose conduct became increasingly defensive and repressive through the next two decades of escalating
demands for Roman Catholic emancipation, radical intellectual militancy
inspired by the successes of the French Revolution, and finally an abortive
armed rebellion in 1798, which tried in vain to combine the passions underlying the two causes to bring about a united and independent nation.[8]

Wordsworth's political claims for *Michael* are expressed most clearly in
a letter written to the English liberal leader Charles James Fox in January
1801, accompanying a complimentary copy of *Lyrical Ballads*. One of a series of letters and presentation copies to notables suggested by Coleridge, it
is the only one Coleridge did not also compose. Wordsworth warms to his
task when he reaches the reason he has been "emboldened to take this liberty" of addressing Fox: the poems *The Brothers* and *Michael*.[9] Wordsworth sees about him "a rapid decay of the domestic affections among the
lower orders of society." This disease, which he finds widespread in Europe,
has recently been hastened in England "by the spreading of manufactures
through every part of the country, by the heavy taxes upon postage, by
workhouses, Houses of Industry, and the invention of Soup-shops &c. &c.
super-added to the increasing disproportion between the price of labour and
that of the necessities of life." After offering anecdotal evidence of the rural
poor's "sublime conviction of the blessing of independent domestic life," he
adds: "If it is true, as I believe, that this spirit is rapidly disappearing, no
greater curse can befal a land." Both *Michael* and *The Brothers* eulogize
"small independent *proprietors* of land, . . . men of respectable education
who daily labour on their own little properties. . . . Their little tract of land
serves as a kind of permanent rallying point for their domestic feelings, as a
tablet upon which they are written which makes them objects of memory in
a thousand instances when they would otherwise be forgotten." The passage of Michael's estate "into a Stranger's hand" (line 475) is nothing less
than a chapter in the death of English independence, English domestic love,
and—the inference is obvious—England itself.

One can no more doubt the seriousness of Wordsworth's social concerns than the greatness of the poem in which he attempted to express them. (*Michael* is more immediately apposite to his remarks to Fox than *The Brothers*.) What is worth examination is how effectively Wordsworth's poetic strategies in *Michael* manage to reinforce his political agenda, broadly construed. The first strategy appears in his subtitle itself, "A Pastoral Poem." Wordsworth's invocation of the pastoral calls forth two traditions in English verse which coexist as uneasily as they did in Theocritus, who is widely blamed for having started it all: the erotic and the elegiac. Erotic pastoral is a line of courtly wit in which amorous young shepherds woo cruel and reluctant virgins to a life of rural ease and natural (that is, carnal) pleasure, while the maidens bemoan the lies of overheated shepherds. Elegiac pastoral is a more serious matter altogether. Still, more than one reader has agreed with Samuel Johnson, who found in John Milton's *Lycidas* that the fancy dress of the form worked against its purposes: "passion runs not after remote allusions and obscure opinions. Passion plucks no berries from the myrtle and the ivy, nor calls upon Arethuse and Mincius, nor tells of rough *satyrs* and *fawns with cloven heel*. Where there is leisure for fiction there is little grief."[10] Whatever the validity of Johnson's strictures, it is plain that in both its primary incarnations pastoral is deeply implicated in that family language of poets from which Wordsworth distances himself in his preface. Pastoral elegy may indeed be the acid test of a reader's tolerance for literary artifice. In calling *Michael* a pastoral, Wordsworth works against the grain of his readers' expectations. If they come expecting the literary shepherds of Arcadian lore, he will give them a genuine shepherd, whose life is strict and toilsome:

> . . . the storm, that drives
> The Traveller to a shelter, summon'd him
> Up to the mountains; he had been alone
> Amid the heart of many thousand mists,
> That came to him, and left him, on the heights.
>
> (56–60)

If readers come expecting amorous play, Wordsworth will give them a different kind of love story, the love of an aged man for his wife and the son of their declining years and for the fields which are his patrimony. If readers come expecting the tale of a miraculously gifted youth cut off before his prime, Wordsworth will tell a more moving story, of a man who outlives

any rational hopes for the future of his son and his land, and of the death of
an entire way of life.

The first of Wordsworth's strategies in *Michael* is to displace the concerns of an artificial convention by those of ordinary life. The second is to
reinvent a pastoral tradition, or at least to readjust its emphases. Michael
is presented as more than an eighteenth-century shepherd whose story
Wordsworth heard in, say, 1782. He is simultaneously a biblical shepherd
whose life is a reenactment of the lives of the patriarchs of the Old Testament. Wordsworth strips pastoral of its elaborate accretions by returning it
to other roots in Judaic lore. If the biblical resonances of characters' names
suggest such a reading (Michael, Luke), the ritualistic nature of Michael's
language in the poem's central episode confirms it. After deciding that Luke
must leave the land for the city in order to earn money to free it from an
unanticipated debt, Michael takes his son to the place where they have
planned to build a sheepfold:

> Lay now the corner-stone,
> As I requested, and hereafter, Luke
> When thou art gone away, should evil men
> Be thy companions, let this Sheep-fold be
> Thy anchor and thy shield; amid all fear
> And all temptation, let it be to thee
> An emblem of the life thy Fathers liv'd,
> Who, being innocent, did for that cause
> Bestir them in good deeds. Now fare thee well—
> When thou return'st, thou in this place wilt see
> A work which is not here, a covenant
> 'Twill be between us; but whatever fate
> Befall thee, I shall love thee to the last,
> And bear thy memory with me to the grave.
>
> (414–427)

Enormously powerful, Michael's speech is heart wrenching in the light of
Luke's rapid degeneration. But it is not the language spoken by men, unless
those men have learned their pronominal and preterit formations from the
King James Bible and their syntax from Milton.

In his efforts to enhance the significance of Michael's character, Wordsworth creates for him here a language which is almost timeless. Although

the slightest push would send it skidding into Hollywood Amish, it still succeeds because the actions of the story are equally timeless. This one speech of Michael's is redolent of Abraham and Isaac, of God and Noah, of Christ and Peter. Throughout the poem biblical cadences and narrative parallels clearly but unobtrusively create a Michael of mythical stature whose defeat is a matter of more than historical, more even than national, importance. It is a wonderful poem, and it works. But the *way* in which Wordsworth makes it work militates against a full realization of the polemical intentions expressed in the letter to Fox.

What Wordsworth has learned from biblical narrative is that things happen. Although events follow one another sequentially, their causation is obscure, and close examination of motives is, at best, frustrating. Wordsworth enhances Michael's stature by making him live outside time, but at the cost of making it difficult to locate within time and historical contingency the causes of the ills that overset him. Take the problem which creates the threat to his estate. Michael has been a model of industry and stewardship. As he tells his son,

> These fields were burthen'd when they came to me;
> 'Till I was forty years of age, not more
> Than half of my inheritance was mine.
> I toil'd and toil'd; God bless'd me in my work,
> And 'till these three weeks past the land was free.
>
> (384–388)

The new encumbrance arises from his having pledged his land as security for a loan to his brother's son, "a man / Of an industrious life, and ample means" (221–222). The poem is all but silent on the circumstances and causes of the nephew's failure:

> But unforeseen misfortunes suddenly
> Had press'd upon him; and old Michael now
> Was summon'd to discharge the forfeiture,
> A grievous penalty, but little less
> Than half his substance.
>
> (223–227)

In *The Making of a Tory Humanist,* Michael Friedman remarks that "as Social history 'Michael' is relatively accurate."[11] The climate of speculation of eighteenth-century England, leading to rapid fortunes and sudden reverses which created unpredictable booms and busts in the general econo-my, reached well into Wordsworth's sacred precincts of the North: "many people in the Lake District were involved directly or indirectly in commer-cial ventures, often at great risk," especially overseas trading (187). Words-worth certainly knew this from personal experience, but his poem does not. The events of his story are datable only to the extent that the poet claims to have talked with "more than one who well / Remember the Old Man" (460–461). No particular events or policies are seen to have shaped Mi-chael's destiny, and the poem seems to have in mind no offending law or de-structive social practice other than the pledging of land as security for the use of money, a foundation stone of capitalism and hardly a recent innova-tion. Without an example of malfeasance by any individual or institution, the poem appears simply to maintain that things like this should not happen.

Wordsworth's lack of interest in problems of agency is shown even in his abrupt summary of Luke's fall:

> Meantime Luke began
> To slacken in his duty, and at length,
> He in the dissolute city gave himself
> To evil courses: ignominy an shame
> Fell on him, so that he was driven at last
> To seek a hiding-place behind the seas.
>
> (451–456)

Whatever Wordsworth may think, the "dissolute city" is a place, not a cause. Nothing explains why Luke went wrong there while Richard Bate-man, a parentless "parish-boy," was able to turn a basket of "pedlar's wares" taken with him to London into a fortune: "he grew wondrous rich, / And left estates and monies to the poor" (268–278). I am not sug-gesting that *Michael* suffers as a poem from its lack of historical, social, and economic detail or that Wordsworth should have dragged in the work-houses and postal rates he cited to Fox. I would not trade it for Thomas Malthus's *Essay on the Principles of Population* or all of William Cobbett's broadsides, and I would give a wide berth to anyone who would.

Wordsworth was torn between two desires, to do justice to the character of his hero and to depict the problems of his age. Few readers have regretted that he chose the former, or that he chose to develop the aged shepherd as a mythical figure, inevitably diminishing his representative utility as a victim of historical social ills. The more fully Michael assumes the characteristics of an Abraham or a Job, the less clearly he can be seen as a victim of specific, and correctable, abuses. The more Luke is called upon to serve as a mix of an unredeemed Prodigal Son and Joseph, sold unto Pharaoh, the less useful it is to inquire into the causes, motives, and stages of his corruption. The fate of Michael's land itself increases the poem's obscurities. Michael's wife Isabel survives her husband by three years:

> . . . at her death the estate
> Was sold, and went into a Stranger's hand.
> The cottage which was named The Evening Star
> Is gone, the ploughshare has been through the ground
> On which it stood; great changes have been wrought
> In all the neighbourhood.
>
> (483–488)

Wordsworth suggests an economic shift from herding to tillage which makes little sense in the the terrain of the Lake country, ideally suited only to sheep and tourists. Michael's "hidden valley" (8) may always be an exception, but because the poem describes no current cultivation or habitation ("It is in truth an utter solitude" [13]), its altered use appears to have been short-lived. In the end the fate of the land seems as mythically rooted as its inhabitants: it falls from herdsmen to agriculturalists, just as Abel fell to Cain. In the Golden Age, as we know from Genesis, from Hesiod, and from Ovid, man did not till the ground.

Castle Rackrent is also the story of a Golden Age and a Fall, as these notions are registered through the language and consciousness of Thady Quirk, the masterless but still faithful servant of a family which is "one of the most ancient in the kingdom" (8). Edgeworth's novel is so little known to the general reader that a close examination of its first few pages may be in order. Thady begins:

Having out of friendship for the family, upon whose estate, praised be Heaven! I and mine have lived rent free time out of mind, voluntarily undertaken to publish the Memoirs of the Rackrent Family, I think it my duty to say a few words, in the first place, concerning myself.

—My real name is Thady Quirk, though in the family I have always
been known by no other than *"honest Thady"*—afterwards, in the
time of Sir Murtagh, deceased, I remember to hear them calling me
"old Thady;" and now I'm come to "poor Thady"—for I wear a long
great coat winter and summer, which is very handy, as I never put my
arms into the sleeves (they are as good as new,) though come Holan-
tide next, I've had it these seven years; it holds on by a single button
round my neck, cloak fashion—to look at me, you would hardly
think "poor Thady" was the father of attorney Quirk; he is a high
gentleman, and never minds what poor Thady says, and having better
than 1500 a-year, landed estate, looks down upon honest Thady, but I
wash my hands of his doings, and as I have lived so will I die, true and
loyal to the family. (7–8)

Thady displays, as Edgeworth's preface suggested, "all the minute prolixity
of a gossip in a country town," particularly unable to distinguish his narrative line from incidental details about himself. His intention to relate the history of "the family" quickly segues into an account of his own origins and
name, and then into a detailed description of the cloak which represents his
current state in life. The cloak receives closer attention than his son, who is
at this point given a profession and income but no name.

Few forms present a greater challenge to the reader than those which employ the voices of naive first-person narrators. If the fictionalized teller cannot discriminate significance, what is to guide the reader to the significance
of the tale? Generations of critical controversy surround the question of
properly reading such narrators as Daniel Defoe's Moll Flanders, Jonathan
Swift's Lemuel Gulliver, Wordsworth's old sea-captain in *The Thorn*, Emily
Brontë's Nellie Dean, and Mark Twain's Huck Finn. Thomas Flanagan
claims that "every line" of Thady's account "requires either a gloss or a
challenge." For example, Flanagan says, " 'Rent-free' sounds pleasant
enough, but was the technical term for a special kind of slavery."[12] Flanagan's brief chapter in his *Irish Novelists* remains the best introduction
to *Castle Rackrent* for the general reader, and his chapters on the social,
economic, and political backgrounds of Irish fiction are recommended to
anyone prone to bouts of unexamined Anglophilia. In what follows I will
attempt to fill in some of Flanagan's analysis and extend its implications,
perhaps in ways he would not warrant.

Let me begin with the business of Thady's cloak, both because it seems at first blush an intrusion of pure zaniness and because it points to the way politics works in the novel. Thady himself is as innocent of political ideas as a Chicago ward heeler. Both know the mechanisms of politicking—of lobbying, wining, dining, even of outright buying of votes—but neither has any sense of an agenda, of a goal for the political process. Thady does not feel himself oppressed. He has been the top boy through a series of masters and, through flattering, cajoling, and otherwise acting the wily slave, has done all right by his lights. He has managed to help his son Jason to an education and to put him in the way of some good things. His current quarrel with Jason is that he has broken the rules of the system and risen above himself. Thady is too busy identifying with the Rackrents to see himself as a member of a subjected group, whether that group is defined by nationality, economic status, or religious persuasion.[13] In her role as editor, it is Edgeworth herself who makes a political reading of Thady's tale inescapable. Thady's discussion of his "long great coat" occasions a digressive footnote on its "high antiquity" *(Castle Rackrent*, 7). The editor cites as authority Edmund Spenser's *View of the State of Ireland,* beginning with a denial of the cloak's Scythian origins and learnedly tracing its use among the Jews, the Chaldees, the Egyptians, the Greeks, and the Romans. At first this seems to be mere antiquarian foolery, and indeed the editor plays the fool on a number of occasions. Finally, though, the editor turns to her source's views on the use of the Irish mantle as "housing, bedding, and clothing." Spenser felt that the use of the cloak should be banned by law, because

> it is a fit house for an outlaw, a meet bed for a rebel, and an apt cloak for a thief.—First, the outlaw . . . maketh his mantle his house, and under it covereth himself from the wrath of Heaven, from the offence of the earth, and from the sight of men. . . . Likewise for a rebel it is as serviceable; for in this war that he maketh (if at least it deserve the name of war), when he still flieth from his foe, and lurketh in the *thick woods, (this should be black bogs,)* and straight passages waiting for advantages; it is his bed, yea, and almost his household-stuff. (8)

Edgeworth's passage from Spenser (the black bogs are her interpolation) provides ample testimony to her source's attitudes toward the people he helped Lord Grey to rule. It is overstating the case only slightly to say that

Spenser thought it would be a wonderful country if only the indigenous inhabitants were all exterminated. By inserting this note in this place, Edgeworth insinuates a political frame of reference for Thady's apolitical tale,
because the Irish cloak is a memento of Ireland's rebellious past. What
Thady understands only as a sign of his poverty takes on broader and
threatening meanings.

More than anything else, the opening pages of *Castle Rackrent* present
for scrutiny an ideology of family, of "the" family, which for Thady is the
Rackrent family. Within such a context Thady Quirk gives his "real" name
only to bury it in the series of honorifics, *honest Thady, old Thady,* and
poor Thady, through which he has been conditioned to think of himself.
Denial of the patronymic is of course a tool of social oppression, a transparent part of a ruling class's attempt to suppress loyalties and ties other than
those which serve its ends, which are to itself. When we read stories of the
antebellum American South which feature "Tennie's Jim" and "Tomey's
Turl," we recognize the device at work. Thady has wholly accepted the constructions of his masters. In his loyalty to "the family" he has denied all
other identity. He warms to Sir Kit, the most morally repugnant of his succession of owners, in a pathetic scene: "one morning my new master caught
a glimpse of me as I was looking at his horse's heels, in hopes of a word
from him — and is that old Thady! says he, as he got into his gig — I loved
him from that day to this, his voice was so like the family" (19). Thady has
disowned his son, "attorney Quirk," in order to remain "true and loyal" to
his former owners, whose line is now most deservedly defunct.

Thady's loyalty to "the family" suggests that an examintion of its gene-
alogy would be in order, especially since Burke, the most famous Anglo-
Irishman of the age, constantly warned of the dangers of holding in disdain
such honored and honorable feudal ties. Thady stresses the antiquity of the
Rackrents, only to allow that "this is not the old family name, which was
O'Shaughlin, related to the Kings of Ireland — but that was before my time"
(9). Upon the death of Sir Tallyhoo Rackrent, who "lost a fine hunter and
his life, at last, by it, all in one day's hunt . . . the estate came straight into
the family, upon one condition, which Sir Patrick O'Shaughlin at the time
took sadly to heart, they say, but thought better of it afterwards, seeing how
large a stake depended upon it, that he should, by Act of Parliament, take
and bear the sirname and arms of Rackrent" (9). Flanagan speculates that it
is "likely that Patrick had had to change not merely his name but his creed"

(70), from Catholic to Protestant. From the outset of the story, the price of becoming one of "the family" is repudiation of family in its natural sense.

The line of Rackrent carries many burdens, but fertility and family feeling are not among them. Thady never mentions a wife or child of Sir Patrick, who entertains on a lavish scale and dies one night after several days of celebrating his birthday: "Just as the company rose to drink his health with three cheers, he fell down in a sort of fit, and was carried off— they sat it out, and were surprised, on enquiry, in the morning, to find it was all over with poor Sir Patrick" (11). The lineage of Sir Murtagh, the next Rackrent, reveals in its cloudiness the uneasy shifting of Thady's idea of family. He is first mentioned only as "the heir who attended the funeral," whose first act is to stop the outraged celebrants at the wake when they offer to rescue the body of Sir Patrick, which has been seized for debt. We are then told that "the new heir" refuses to pay any of the debts of the deceased because of the affront to his honor. Only then is Sir Patrick referred to as Sir Murtagh's "father," by which time the reader must wonder whether the term has any base in biologic reality. Subsequent rumors that the seizure of the body was a sham, planned as a ruse to free Sir Murtagh of those bothersome "debts of honor," further undercut any notions of filial devotion. Issues of relationship are further muddied when Castle Rackrent becomes known as Castle Stopgap during Sir Murtagh's parsimonious reign, of which Thady is deeply ashamed. Sir Murtagh expires in midst of a raging argument with his pinchpenny wife, and as he dies without issue, the estate goes to his younger brother, Sir Kit Stopgap, the first Rackrent to become an absentee landlord, squeezing his tenantry through a middleman to support his gambling debts in Bath— "but that was the only fault he had, God bless him!" (32). Sir Kit marries a Jewish wife for her money. Shortly after bringing her to Ireland, he locks her in her room for seven years because she will not surrender her jewels to him. Following Sir Kit's death in a duel, the estate comes to Sir Connolly, "by the Grace of God heir at law," of "a remote branch of the family" (38). Edgeworth's ironic play is evident here, because the new inheritor is only biologically remote: he has grown up in the village itself. The pathetic life and death of Sir Condy, as he is known, occupy more than half the novel.

The generations of Rackrent do not need generation to propagate themselves. Thady's first and last masters appear from outside any direct family line, their claims traced along precarious routes of male Protestant descent.

Edgeworth could not make it clearer that Thady's understanding of "the family" is wholly unnatural, a cultural construct which exists only in and through the language of legal fiction, with no relationship to lived experience. Flanagan remarks that Thady himself "creates the illusion of family, out of the feudal retainer's pride in the house which he serves" (77). It might be more accurate to say that he embraces uncritically an illusion of family which has another creator, the body of English inheritance law, modified to fit the peculiar necessity of keeping Irish lands safely in Protestant ownership. The few remaining Catholic properties in Ireland in the eighteenth century fell under different laws. According to Flanagan, "at the death of a Catholic landowner, . . . his property was broken up and distributed equally among his children. To this there was one exception. Any son, if he conformed to the [Protestant] Church of Ireland was permitted to dispossess his father and come into full possession" (11). Here was a law that might hasten the decay of Wordsworth's "domestic affections" among the upper classes as well. Thady has been sold, and has cheerfully and earnestly bought, an idea of family devoid of content, a meaningless label of identity. To be "true and loyal to the family" is to have no identity at all.

It would be nice to find a hero in this tale. One could wax sentimental with Thady about Sir Condy, the last Rackrent, who is at least good-hearted as he drunkenly pursues a ruinously expensive political career and allows his wife's extravagance to lead him to bankruptcy. But haplessness is finally not a winning character trait. It might be even nicer to read the tale's resolution as comic and to see in Jason Quirk's dispossession of Sir Condy some version of poetic justice, the lands passing at last into native Irish hands and Thady himself becoming the sacred progenitor of the new "family." That view will not wash either. Jason becomes a man of the law, which in this novel as in so many others is something considerably more frightening than Spenser's outlaws, thieves, and rebels. In the great scene in which Jason confronts Sir Condy with the mountain of bills and accounts he owes and announces that he has a purchaser of the Rackrent lands ready for him, Jason has become little more than a human calculating machine, blithely profiting from human disaster. Thady attempts to intervene on behalf of his master:

> "Look at him (says I, pointing to Sir Condy, who was just leaning
> back in his arm chair, with his arms falling beside him, like one stu-

pified) is it you, Jason, that can stand in his presence and recollect all that he has been to us, and all we have been to him, and yet use him so at the last?" — "Who will he find to use him better, I ask you? (said Jason) — If he can get a better purchaser, I'm content; I only offer to purchase to make things easy and oblige him — though I don't see what compliment I am under, if you come to that; I have never had, asked, or charged more than sixpence in the pound receiver's fees, and where would he have got an agent for a penny less?" (76–77)

Thady is all emotion in the service of a meaningless loyalty; Jason has reduced all emotion to a commercial transaction. Jason has gone to school to the Rackrent landlords, and he has surpassed them all in his understanding of the convertibility of land and money. They have successively bled the estate to feed their vices and their vanities. Jason will continue to bleed the estate, but in the pure and disinterested pursuit of money itself. He has no inconvenient vanities and vices, as well as no affections, no family, and no nation. He is the ultimate, and wholly credible, stranger into whose hands the land has passed.

Edgeworth's knowledge of and interest in the ways of inheritance would have come naturally to her. She had an active managerial role in her father's estate, helping Richard Lovell Edgeworth to run it almost from the day of her arrival in Ireland until his death thirty-five years later. She was then his oldest surviving child, but of course the estate did not descend to her. It went to Lovell Edgeworth, the eldest surviving son, eight years her junior and the issue of her father's second wife. Lovell's qualifications for his inheritance included a history of disputes over money with both father and sister, and twelve years of imprisonment in France during the Napoleonic wars, which, if they were hardly his fault, did little to hone his skills as a manager. In eight trying years Lovell ran the estate into debts totaling £26,000 and turned its affairs over to his novel-writing sister in 1826. She held things together until 1833, when the revelation of more secret debts led to Lovell's selling the estate and his debts to his younger half-brother Sneyd, in return for an annuity of £250. Maria continued as agent for the absentee Sneyd until she was seventy-one years old.[14] Ah, patriarchy!

Edgeworth's preface ends with a prophecy. It may be her own entirely, or it may reflect the views of her distinguished and energetic father: "When Ireland loses her identity by a union with Great Britain, she will look back with a smile of good-humoured complacency on the Sir Kits and Sir Condys of her former existence" (5). The reader can only wonder if that warm generosity of spirit will extend to the Jason Quirks of her present existence. Both the novel's preface and postscript try to put a progressive face on the story that has been told. Thady's tale knows better—not only better than its teller but also better than its editor. The tale looks directly at the land, the law, the government, and the people of Ireland and finds the future hopeless. Edgeworth's later Irish novels are hopeful—they argue for the progress possible through enlightened landlords like her father, for gradual education of the populace, for tolerance and understanding between Catholic and Protestant, Irishman and Englishman. Her future writings confirm that she was Ireland's first great, as well as its first, novelist. But Thady Quirk would remain Ireland's prophet. Wordsworth's *Michael* created a mythically charged, honorable past to pit against the "utter solitude" of its present. The land remains, even the unfinished sheepfold, always ready to be put to use. *Castle Rackrent* has destroyed its past in the act of retelling it; its present is empty; its future is only too imaginable.

The Heirs of *Castle Rackrent*

Imagine a land. It will not be a nation, because it will be occupied, perhaps through conquest, through purchase, through military alliance for purposes of "protection," or through simple economic domination. All are just names for the right of power. The land will have several classes: a ruling elite not native to it; a political structure which may have native elements but will nonetheless be the tool of the ruling elite; finally, a much larger indigenous population, differing from its ruling elite in history, language, religion, and customs.

The ruling class of the land will not be homogeneous. Some of its masters will be enlightened and well meaning; others will be brutes. Some will come as light bringers and end as brutes. Its natives will be equally diverse. The vast majority will be the faceless oppressed, wretchedly poor and comically ignorant of the "gifts" of civilization. Others will rise within the ruling establishment, becoming petty managers and factotums. They will not be worth much, but they will not cost much either. Some will prove intelligent and capable, will receive educations modeled after those of their rulers, and will be rewarded by positions of power and influence. Their success will entail some small sacrifices, such as total deracination and the suppression of all their ties of kinship, and the most pressing desire of their lives will be the most impossible: assimilation. They will be disdained by the rulers and feared by the ruled. Rulers and ruled will share one thing equally: they will be degraded by their experience.

Such a land may be least interesting at the point of initial conquest, when pillage of natural resources and theft of cultural artifacts is the major thrust of the occupying power. The most interesting times occur when its occupying rulers try to make something of the land, to change its indigenous economy in ways which make it produce something of greater commercial value to themselves. Disruptions in the economy of the ruling nation may dictate more efficient or altogether new uses for its possessions, territories, or protectorates. At such a time, ways of life must change. Hunters must become herdsmen, herdsmen farmers, or farmers factory workers. Women who have spent their lives grinding corn into meal may find themselves on an assembly line, soldering printed circuit boards. Economic evolution, which would have been imperceptibly gradual without foreign influence, is suddenly forced overnight, and the old ways are brought into sharp juxtaposition with the new.

The land we have been imagining has also been imagined over the past two centuries by many of the greatest writers in the world, and in their greatest works. It was the chosen land of Sir Walter Scott, who proclaimed straightforwardly that he learned from Edgeworth how to create it. It was the land of Ivan Turgenev, who showed that cultural hegemony could be as quietly disruptive a force as political occupation, when progressive Westernized landlords come into conflict both with feudalists and with the serfs whose lots they wish to alleviate. There is even an obscure claim that Turgenev was directly influenced by Edgeworth (see George Watson's appendix to *Castle Rackrent*, 115–117). Joseph Conrad explored this land most thoroughly in *Nostromo*, a searing indictment of imperialism in his fictive Costaguana. His *Heart of Darkness* has probed the motives, means, and ends of the earliest stages of colonial exploitation for virtually everyone who reads. William Faulkner mined this land as thoroughly as Scott and Turgenev, tracing in *Go Down, Moses,* perhaps his most compelling work, eighty years of social evolution from hunting culture through the ravages of commercial agriculture, with each generation cursed by its belief that the land (and its inhabitants) can be bought and sold.[15] E. M. Forster con-

ducted one brief and enigmatic tour in *A Passage to India*. The land continues to live in the works of Gabriel García Marquez, Patrick White, Nadine
Gordimer, Carlos Fuentes, Alejo Carpentier, Chinua Achebe, and hundreds
of other writers of empire, known and unknown. The land is vast, always
the same, and always different. It is worth knowing that it first existed in
1800 in the Ireland created by Edgeworth, where England had long been
practicing for India.

One often hears writers like Edgeworth and Scott described as "re-
gional" novelists, a label suggesting circumscription and a degree of provin-
ciality which somehow keeps them outside the Great Tradition. In fact, they
are more nearly *international* novelists whose works treat cultural, political,
and economic conflicts riddled with implications that have grown more
rather than less crucial with the passage of time. Those of us who have centered our study of Romanticism on Wordsworth are occasionally disturbed
that he has not traveled well. Indeed, outside English-speaking cultures he
has traveled hardly at all, while Scott and Byron have had massive impact
on world culture. In a notorious essay, "Wordsworth in the Tropics," Aldous Huxley claimed that Wordsworth's conception of Nature would melt
in the equatorial sun: "Wandering in the hothouse darkness of the jungle,
he would not have felt so serenely certain of those 'Presences of Nature,'
those 'Souls of Lonely Places,' which he was in the habit of worshipping on
the shores of Windermere and Rydal."[16] Anthropologists would tell us that
Huxley is wrong here, that worship of Nature can adapt itself to the most
hostile climates. What has not been so readily transplantable is Wordsworth's social thought, the intense Englishness of which is so apparent in a
work like *Michael*. Even Wordsworth's great international poem, *The Prelude*, is, in the end, a thoroughgoing repudiation of alien influences. Its story
of an ingenuous youth, who is willingly seduced by a foreign ideology but
returns both to his native land and his senses, is a powerful one. But that
story has not loomed so large in history as another which has been infinitely
repeated—the story of a land oppressed by a foreign ideology, bereft of a
meaningful sense of nationhood, looking toward a future as problematic as
its past and present. For that story we must reluctantly leave the greatest
English poet of his age and turn to his Anglo-Irish contemporary, whom literary history has treated less kindly. Rediscovery of Edgeworth diminishes
Wordsworth not a jot, and it helps to reassert both the fertile diversity of the
age of Romanticism and its importance for our own.

16

"The Very Culture of the Feelings"
Wordsworth and Solitude

MORRIS DICKSTEIN

Ploughing indiscriminately through the shelves of the local public library, I first came upon Wordsworth's poetry in one of those tasteful, decorous anthologies that had descended (in every sense) from Francis Turner Palgrave's *Golden Treasury*. Such samplers encouraged a reader to admire the isolated "gems" of lyric poetry without confronting the ache and grit of any single poet's struggle with language. (At least they were not weighed down with the kind of textbook apparatus that distances poems into unresisting objects of study.) The poems I read were all short ones—*She was a phantom of delight* and *The Solitary Reaper* are the two I remember—and they left me with a sense of Wordsworth as a chaste and conventional poet who made simple celebratory lyrics out of momentary impressions—a poet of nature and married love. This was the Victorian Wordsworth, or one of them: fervent yet detached, perfectly moral, as passionless as an old gray stone. Without the zest of a Cavalier poet or the gusto of a Byron, this was a writer I felt I could easily pass up.

A few years later, in college it must have been, I discovered the *Intimations Ode,* which, for ten years—until I heartlessly dissected it to teach it for the first time—never failed to bring tears to my eyes. I remember reading it aloud through clouded eyes to the girl I planned to marry, as if it could tell her something irreplaceably intimate about *me*, tell her who I really was. Perhaps it was the unusual richness of language ("not wholly free from something declamatory," said Matthew Arnold [see Notes to Chapter 16]), or my own ambivalence about the losses and gains of growing up. The celebrated rhetoric, with its use of Platonic myth, gave the poem a certain opacity to which I could attach my own feelings, as if to confirm Coleridge's remark that "poetry gives most pleasure when only generally and not perfectly understood." Once dispelled, this feelingful obscurity could never be restored—a loss not so different from the one Wordsworth describes in the poem. But by then, other poems of Wordsworth, more transparent pieces like the Lucy poems, the Matthew poems, and *Resolution and Independence,* had begun to stir me even more deeply. Earlier I had imported a note of self-pity into my reading of Wordsworth, but now I caught glimpses of his "calm and terrible strength." This was a Victorian Wordsworth I had not grasped through the anthology—not the poet of duty and domestic affection, certainly not the handmaiden of Nature who numbered the petals of the daisy, but a poet who tapped the mainsprings of feeling in life's early joys as in its later losses.

This is not exactly the poet featured in the remarkable Wordsworth revival that began in the 1950s. In an essay written for the centenary of Wordsworth's death in 1950, Lionel Trilling tried to account for the neglect and even ridicule this once-loved poet had suffered. He attributed it to a strain of passivity and even quietism in Wordsworth, a quality "very close to the Stoic *apatheia,* to not-feeling," which was so much at variance with the modern predilection for "the powerful, the fierce, the assertive, the personally militant." Yet Trilling recalled that a hundred years earlier, on the occasion of Wordsworth's death, Matthew Arnold had paid tribute to precisely the opposite quality, his ability to *feel,* his "healing power" that revived the wounded capacity for feeling in his contemporaries.

This seems strange to us today. We have come to see the nineteenth century as a period of grand operatic passions, from the career of Napoleon to the canvases of Delacroix and Turner, from the novels of Dickens, Melville, and Dostoevski to the music dramas of Verdi and Wagner. But to Arnold it was an "iron time / Of doubts, disputes, distractions, fears," haunted by all the cerebral, mechanistic, desacralizing influences that seemed to have dried up the elemental emotions. In this pass, the more titanic, Promethean figures could provide no guidance:

> Others will teach us how to dare,
> And against fear our breast to steel:

> Others will strengthen us to bear—
> But who, ah who, will make us feel?
> (*Memorial Verses,* lines 64–67)

Though Arnold explicitly rejects the stoic reading of Wordsworth, it may well be that stoicism and depth of feeling are two sides of the same coin: not a coin many modern critics have seen fit to wager. Perhaps the crisis of feeling described by so many writers in the nineteenth century is something we no longer experience in any significant way. Yet a crisis of feeling is a persistent, unrecognized symptom of criticism itself. As our critical vocabularies have flourished on the analytic side, they have atrophied on the affective side. We have no accepted language in which to examine what really moves us in a writer—a question we have relegated to an older, impressionistic belles lettres. The question of feeling embarrasses most contemporary critics. Even the so-called reader-response methods going back to I. A. Richards almost always concern how we *interpret* poetry, not how we respond to it. The much-debated problem of "indeterminacy" belongs to the domain of meaning, not feeling; the rest we leave to the effusions of the book reviewers.

Yet Wordsworth himself ascribed "all good poetry" to "the spontaneous overflow of powerful feelings." All through the nineteenth century he was read as the embodiment of what John Stuart Mill called the "culture of the feelings." Invoking the same therapeutic metaphor Arnold had used, Mill described how Wordsworth had gone beyond scenic pictures to create landscapes of feeling: "What made Wordsworth's poems a medicine for my state of mind, was that they expressed, not mere outward beauty, but states of feeling, and of thought coloured by feeling, under the excitement of beauty. They seemed to be the very culture of the feelings, which I was in quest of" (Mill, *Autobiography* 89). By his own account Mill had been raised virtually as a thinking machine, until he suffered a nervous breakdown in early adulthood. The first relief came in a moment of intense emotional empathy as he was reading the memoirs of Jean François Marmontel: "From this moment my burthen grew lighter. The oppression of the thought that all feeling was dead within me, was gone. I was no longer hopeless: I was not a stock or a stone" (85).

Mill's and Arnold's difficulties were partly their own, but their way of reading was also of their age. To both of them the more obviously emotional poetry of Byron, with its theatrical gloom and introspection, was part of the problem, not any kind of solution. (Of Byron, "whose peculiar department was supposed to be that of the intenser feelings," Mill writes: "The poet's state of mind was too like my own. . . . His Harold and Manfred had the same burthen on them which I had" (88). The failure of feeling, after all, was Byron's first serious theme.) Without undue anachronism, though at some risk of doing violence to the current concerns of criticism, it should be possible to explore what moves us in Wordsworth's poetry, as Mill and Arnold did.

There is something paradoxical about taking Wordsworth as the epitome of the Man of Feeling, for in many obvious ways his writing is less "romantic" than that of Shelley, Byron, or even Coleridge. If he rejects the poetic decorum of elevated subjects and generalized sentiments, he more than sustains a strict moral decorum, never tantilizing the reader with jarring revelations. His bottomless self-regard, his inexhaustible attention to the movements of his mind, helped make Byron and Shelley possible, but they recoiled from his chaste English reserve. Their style of confiding in the reader was more urbane and cosmopolitan—Byron's continental fame was no accident—yet also more ejaculatory and self-dramatizing. The confidence fostered by their class origins made them less wary of self-exposure: they were largely exempt from the middle-class proprieties. Wordsworth could never have written a line like Shelley's "I fall upon the thorns of life! I bleed!" (*Ode to the West Wind*, l. 154). He seems not to have considered publishing *The Prelude* in his lifetime, for he found it "a thing unprecedented in literary history that a man should talk so much about himself" (letter to Sir George Beaumont, 1 May 1805). In the same letter he attributes this dubious project not to "self-conceit" but to a "real humility." Baffled in his literary course, he needed a subject that was simply given to him: "Here, at least, I hoped that to a certain degree I should be sure of succeeding, as I had nothing to do but describe what I had felt and thought; therefore could not easily be bewildered."

Wordsworth had his own way, so different from Shelley's, of evoking pain and pathos; it was oblique and understated, free of all self-pity, darkly suggestive rather than frontally direct. A great moment in Wordsworth that still moves me to tears comes near the end of *Michael*, where no emotion at all is made explicit. Everyone who has read the poem remembers the resonant biblical restraint with which the story is told, yet also the timeless, patient way it works up Michael's relation to the land, the sheer isolation of a

rural family living in tune with the rhythms of nature, and Michael's anxious love for Luke, the child of his old age. But the conclusion of the "plot,"
Luke's descent into dissipation and debt in the big city, is sketched in
offhandedly with brutal speed in less than six lines, as if plot itself were a
cumbersome device, a mere afterthought. Yet Luke's decline is full of rever-
berations, for it shatters the covenant he made with his father, disrupts the
continuity of life on the land, and almost destroys his father's reason for
living.

At this point, in a quintessential Wordsworthian gesture, instead of
showing us Michael's reaction, the camera-eye shifts over to reassuring gen-
eralities about human nature, endurance, and love:

> There is a comfort in the strength of love:
> 'Twill make a thing endurable, which, else
> Would overset the brain, or break the heart.
>   (lines 448–450)

These lines, like Michael's very temperament, are all the more heartbreak-
ing for what they suppress, for the way they avoid any overt show of grief.
As Wordsworth characteristically averts his eyes, he gives all the more
weight to what we do not see, to all the contained emotions in Michael and
in *Michael*, which almost fail to come to the surface.

In the next line, Wordsworth retreats into local legend, distancing the
story into a past we know only from oral witness and communal memory.
We circle back to where we began—to the unfinished sheepfold, the "strag-
gling heap of unhewn stones" that the poem set out to decipher by attaching
a story to it. These stones are the traces of a life lived and griefs borne,
which the poet will translate into an intelligible legacy to future generations
("for the sake / Of youthful Poets, who among these hills / Will be my second self when I am gone," 38–40). The stones are an emblem of Michael
himself, mute, stoic, indestructible, whose only expression of grief is a not-
doing, a repeated act of omission we hear of only by rumor:

> —and 'tis believed by all
> That many and many a day he thither went,
> And never lifted up a single stone.
>   (464–466)

The peculiar narrative proportions of *Michael* are best explained by a comment Wordsworth himself made in the preface to the *Lyrical Ballads*. Compared to the popular literature he saw around him, with its pandering to a "degrading thirst after outrageous stimulation," in his work "the feeling . . . gives importance to the action and situation, not the action and situation to the feeling." Wordsworth attacked "the gaudiness and inane phraseology of many modern writers" and set out to show that "the human mind is capable of being excited without the application of gross and violent stimulants," such as he found in "frantic novels, sickly and stupid German tragedies, and deluges of idle and extravagant stories in verse."

Of *Michael* and *The Brothers*, the center pieces of the second (1800) volume of the *Lyrical Ballads*, one could almost say what Dr. Johnson says of *Clarissa*: to read them for the story alone would be maddening. Wordsworth was trying to distinguish between feeling and mere sensation, which could be better supplied by Gothic novels, supernatural ballads, and the daily cataclysms of urban journalism. He was one of the first to grasp the social and psychological conditions of modern life that demanded the constant stimulation of popular culture and mass journalism, which he took as evidence of mental "torpor" rather than liveliness of feeling. When Walter Benjamin wrote in his great essay on storytelling that "every morning brings us news of the globe, and yet we are poor in noteworthy stories" he was developing an insight first articulated by Wordsworth:

> A multitude of causes, unknown to former times, are now acting with a combined force to blunt the discriminating powers of the mind, and, unfitting it for all voluntary exertion, to reduce it to a state of almost savage torpor. The most effective of these causes are the great national events to which are daily taking place, and the increasing accumulation of men in cities, where the uniformity of their occupations produces a craving for extraordinary incident, which the rapid communication of intelligence hourly gratifies.[1]

Wordsworth tried to counter this by looking for deeper, more authentic sources of feeling, either in his own mind or in the unlikely human material around him. He centered on rustic life because it seemed little touched by the modern world but also because he saw it in the process of going under, buried by the social changes he keenly perceived.[2] The healing, prescriptive metaphors of Arnold and Mill are not Victorian additions, for they are already implied by Wordsworth's own diagnosis of the modern world.

In trying to evoke genuine feelings, Wordsworth is not always as oblique as he is in *Michael*. Trilling in his centenary essay calls attention to Wordsworth's way of giving unexpected epiphanies to characters, especially very old men, to whom we usually attribute something less than a full identity. The words that escape from Matthew, the old schoolmaster, at the end of *The Two April Mornings* and *The Fountain* are only two of the most poignant examples, all the more effective because they are directed at a well-meaning companion, the poet himself, who is as yet too young to understand them. (We are given to feel that he will make sense of them only much later, perhaps in writing the poem itself, after he too has learned a few of life's difficult lessons.) Wordsworth's other method of conveying emotion is more simple and direct, but still far from the breast-baring tone of Shelley's anguished appeals to the reader. The endings of the Lucy poems diminish in emotional expression as they increase in a hopeless intensity of feeling, as the speaker's idle fears in the first poem give way to tight-lipped grief in those that follow.

Wordsworth's great simplicity is rarely more powerful than in the final stanza of *She dwelt among the untrodden ways,* which is entirely free of the elevated language that Wordsworth calls "poetic diction":

> She lived unknown, and few could know
> 　　When Lucy ceased to be;
> But she is in her grave, and, oh,
> 　　The difference to me!
>
> 　　　　　　　　　(lines 9–12)

The mainsprings of emotion here lie partly in what is not said, the depth of reaction implied rather than described. They are there in the very clumsiness of the words used, such as the slightly gauche repetition of "unknown" and "know" in the first line and the need to draw out "difference" into a full three-syllable word. They lie in the flat impersonality and sonorous vagueness of such phrases as "ceased to be" and "in her grave," as if, in the wake of death, the exact circumstances could be of no conceivable interest. They can be found minutely in the punctuation itself, such as the three halting commas at the end of the third line which resolve themselves into a powerful exclamation point in the line that follows. Above all, with the precision of a Dutch miniature, they rest in the blurted "oh"—an unlikely rhyme-word that gives the impression of being outside the planned words of the poem, of having escaped from the poet involuntarily, like the things Michael does *not* do around the unfinished sheepfold.

The same terrifying simplicity seals Lucy's death and the poet's loss in *Three years she grew in sun and shower* and *A slumber did my spirit seal*:

> Thus Nature spake—The work was done—
> How soon my Lucy's race was run!
> She died, and left to me
> This heath, this calm, and quiet scene;
> The memory of what has been,
> And never more will be.
>
> (*Three Years*, lines 37–42)

These lines would be ridiculously simple if they were not profoundly moving. If they tell us nothing and everything of what Wordsworth is feeling, it is because, to his mind, what he is feeling *personally* is of no import. The austere generality of the language ("what has been / And never more will be") clangs with the chords of fatality, like the arrival of the stone guest at the end of *Don Giovanni*, or Poe's variations on "nevermore" in *The Raven*. This is death without the trimmings of poetic sentiment or religious consolation. The poem is less about personal loss than about the irretrievable character of death itself and the abstract, almost cosmic aloneness of the bereaved.

The poem rests on the truism that the dead do not suffer, only the survivors, and Wordsworth is a survivor who in some ways envies the dead. Lucy will die into nature, perpetually young and unchanged, beyond all the pains of growth, loss, and individuation. Her state will be blessed—by its permanent vitality and also its sheer insensibility:

> "She shall be sportive as the fawn
> That wild with glee across the lawn
> Or up the mountain springs;
> And hers shall be the breathing balm
> And hers the silence and the calm
> Of mute insensate things."
>
> (13–18)

The poet envies the sublime continuity of the dead. He imagines Lucy's integration into a larger order of things, her freedom from the flux of consciousness and change: dead, she is beyond dying; still, she is beyond stirring; lost, she is beyond losing. Wordsworth's most explicit statement of his own deep longing for stasis comes a few years later in the *Ode to Duty* of 1804:

> Me this unchartered freedom tires;
> I feel the weight of chance-desires:
> My hopes no more must change their name,
> I long for a repose that ever is the same.
>
> (lines 37–40)

In *Three years she grew in sun and shower,* the quiescence of death remains something more cheerful: a permanent childhood in the bosom of nature, with all the vital animal energies intact—in short, the earlier days of Wordsworth himself (as recalled in *Tintern Abbey*), "when like a roe / I bounded o'er the mountains, by the sides / Of the deep rivers, and the lonely streams, / Wherever nature led" (lines 67–70).

What comes out in the Lucy poems, as in his many sketches of decrepit old men, is that Wordsworth is the man of feeling who desperately longs for the condition of not-feeling, the insensibility that might free him from the distinctly human trials which are his great subject. Though Wordsworth made less of his own suffering than any other Romantic writer, his acute self-awareness rendered even the physical act of writing a burden to him. At the peak of his great decade, he wrote to Sir George Beaumont that "I do not know from what cause it is, but during the last three years I have never had a pen in my hand for five minutes, before my whole frame becomes one bundle of uneasiness; a perspiration starts out all over me, and my chest is oppressed in a manner which I cannot describe" (14 October 1803).

In the Lucy poems Wordsworth conveys what he feels without describing it directly. He movingly objectifies his sense of loneliness and loss, the pains of memory, which Lucy herself will never experience. What happens to Lucy? To Wordsworth this is beside the point. His narrative reticence is so great that in *A slumber did my spirit seal* her death occurs, as it were, offstage, in the white space between the two stanzas:

> A slumber did my spirit seal;
> I had no human fears:

> She seemed a thing that could not feel
> The touch of earthly years.
>
> No motion has she now, no force;
> She neither hears nor sees;
> Rolled round in earth's diurnal course,
> With rocks, and stones, and trees.

The most eerie feature of this poem is the striking resemblance between "life" in the first stanza and "death" in the second. The speaker's lack of apprehension and Lucy's seeming invulnerability are both reproduced in the muted description of the insensibility of death. Lucy in death repeats in a more sublime key the young man's ignorance of life, while he, living with the burden of all he has learned, imagines her now as an orbiting "thing," in touch with larger forces, rolling with the motions of the planet, saved from this hard-won knowledge. Lucy will never become fully human, will never know tragedy; she has withdrawn into the life of objects, alive only in the poet's grieving.

This poem is one of the enigmatic marvels of English literature, probably inexhaustible, saying so much by saying very little. The second stanza tells us even less of the speaker's feelings than the two preceding poems. In much the way the English conduct their social life through coded signals that outsiders rarely can penetrate, here Wordsworth tactically reveals himself by suggestion, indirection, the imagination of opposites. We locate Wordsworth by what he projects upon Lucy, and by imagining him bereft of Lucy—not from what he tells us in the first person. Wordsworth's "sincerity" is his technique of being true to his feelings without being explicit about them.

This style of indirection enabled Wordsworth to appeal strongly to the twentieth century, while Shelley and Swinburne have grown less attractive even to perfervid adolescents, who used to chant their verses as gestures of generational rebellion. The New Critics and their English allies, such as F. R. Leavis, spoke for a large part of twentieth-century taste in their preference for objectified emotion over naked emotional display. Deflationary understatement and symbolic indirection are key features of the tonality of modernism. On the other hand, over the last twenty years, poets recoiling from the ironies of modernism have found in Wordsworth a rich meditative quality that has given them a technique of inwardness, a different way of tapping their emotions, that inevitably recalls the kind of strength Arnold and Mill drew from his poetry.

Meanwhile, scholars and critics approaching Wordsworth from another angle have laid bare a phenomenological complexity that makes the difficult poems of Blake seem pat by comparison. Proust's art of memory and Freud's scientific validation of the unconscious mind have highlighted qualities in Wordsworth which the nineteenth century could not fully apprehend, features which have made *The Prelude* virtually a modern discovery. The ever-increasing analytic subtlety of Wordsworth criticism has left the Victorian Wordsworth looking dated and simplistic, but it has not often brought us much closer to what moves us in Wordsworth's verse. Perhaps we can no longer say, as Matthew Arnold did in a more innocent time, that "nature herself seems . . . to take the pen out of his hand, and to write for him with her own bare, sheer, penetrating power." This begs the question of what makes one style or subject more "natural" than another, and it even misstates Wordsworth's relation to the natural world. But at least we can look for the sources of that power, as the Victorians invariably did, since they felt it.

Were I to choose one theme that best crystallizes Wordsworth's emotional style, I would focus on Wordsworth as a poet of solitude. Solitude is the ground for Wordsworth's initial imaginative links with nature, as it also marks his later experiences of time, loss, and separation. Solitude—as in "emotion recollected in tranquillity"—is the condition for Wordsworthian sincerity and self-exploration, yet it is also the condition he devotes himself most to overcoming. This is the paradox: solitude enables man to commune with himself, to tap the springs of personal power, yet it also cuts him off from other men, who may be trapped in their own forms of isolation. How Wordsworth resolves this conflict is one of the essential threads in his poetic development.

By temperament, it seems, Wordsworth was an immensely solitary man, though he spent most of his life surrounded by a large, devoted family, including a wife and children he loved and a sister who was virtually his alter ego. He needed adoring women around him. Yet he had little of Keats's "negative capability," little novelistic feelings for the inner lives of others. His sister, who was closest to him, he treated in *Tintern Abbey* as a kind of Lucy who survives, static and unchanging in her intimacy with nature—less an autonomous being than a reflection of his former self. In his late note on the *Intimations Ode*, he describes the solipsism he experienced as a child: "I was often unable to think of external things as having external existence, and I communed with all I saw as something not apart from, but inherent in, my own immaterial nature. Many times while going to school have I grasped at a wall or tree to recall myself from this abyss of idealism to the reality." This is consistent with the powerful childhood memories recorded in the first *Prelude* of 1798–1799, which either take place alone, in terrible communion with the power of nature, such as the boat-stealing or nest-robbing episodes, or *seem* to take place alone despite the presence of others, such as the skating scene, where the inner experience is equally solitary. Wordsworth's guarded comment on these memories seems definitive: "And I was taught to feel—perhaps too much— / The self-sufficing power of solitude" (1799 *Prelude*, bk. 2, lines 76–77).

One need not look too far to find solitude inscribed everywhere in Wordsworth's poetry, for there is hardly a word that appears more frequently, in more pregnant contexts. Compared to nature, the city is a soulless, leveling solitude, though it is also the place where the young Coleridge kept himself apart and "sought / The truth in solitude" (1799 *Prelude* 2.505–506). A protagonist of *The Excursion* is called the Solitary, and *Lucy Gray, or Solitude* is a ballad version of the Lucy themes of death and transfiguration. Wordsworth wrote innumerable poems about blighted, solitary men, such as *The Old Cumberland Beggar* and the account of the Discharged Soldier, both written early in 1798. The latter, never published by Wordsworth in its original form, was finally integrated into the fourth book of *The Prelude*, where, in one of the poem's late additions, it was preceded by a long, artificial tribute to Solitude, full of literary touches, as if Wordsworth, like the poor soldier himself, still remembered *what* he felt but not how.[3] Solitude belongs to an essential complex of ideas in Wordsworth that includes nature and the authenticity of personal experience (what Keats calls "the holiness of the heart's affections"). As a boy it was a condition of his imaginative formation yet also something he needed to outgrow; as a grown man and a poet, it is a condition of memory and creative flow yet also something to which—unlike other Romantic poets from William Collins onward—he refuses to attribute any ultimate value. Probably the most famous reference to solitude comes in *I wandered lonely as a Cloud,* a poem almost too familiar to analyze in detail yet too essential to pass over.

In the *Golden Treasury* era this was thought of as the poem about the daffodils, but during our Wordsworth revival it has been recognized as one of Wordsworth's most complex lyrics. In a centenary essay of 1951, Frederick Pottle showed how Wordsworth had selected and heightened details from Dorothy's journal to create something newly imagined, something quite different from a minute transcription of the natural world.[4] With the critical tools we have learned to bring to bear on lyric poetry, we can easily see that it is less about daffodils than about perception. The fine concluding stanza recalls the relations of memory and imagination to nature in *Tintern Abbey* and *The Prelude*:

> For oft, when on my couch I lie
> In vacant or in pensive mood,
> They flash upon that inward eye
> Which is the bliss of solitude;
> And then my heart with pleasure fills,
> And dances with the daffodils.
>
> (lines 19–24)

Yet something else occurs here aside from a rhymed statement about emotion recollected in tranquillity, for this poem is about the difference between loneliness and solitude, about all the ways of being alone and being together.

Paradoxically, with Dorothy at his side, Wordsworth was by no means alone when he saw the flowers, yet he makes himself a paradigm of the isolated man, the detached poetic observer who sees everything but belongs to nothing:

> I wandered lonely as a cloud
> That floats on high o'er vales and hills . . .
>
> (1–2)

There is something not altogether unpleasant about this footloose detachment, especially as compared with the undifferentiated togetherness he projects on the scene before him:

When all at once I saw a crowd,
A host, of golden daffodils;
Beside the lake, beneath the trees,
Fluttering and dancing in the breeze.

Continuous as the stars that shine
And twinkle on the milky way,
They stretched in never-ending line
Along the margin of a bay:
Ten thousand saw I at a glance,
Tossing their heads in sprightly dance.

(3–12)

Wordsworth highlights the almost infinite number of the flowers, their merger into a larger mass—a "crowd," a "host," a kind of flower phalanx—and their reciprocal interchange with the "dancing" waves beside them:

The waves beside them danced; but they
Out-did the sparkling waves in glee.

(13–14)

To emphasize this idea, Wordsworth omits several of Dorothy's images for the flowers, as when she compares the "long belt of them" to a "turnpike" or "busy highway," or describes too cutely how "some rested their heads upon these stones as on a pillow for weariness."

Wordsworth's daffodils in their frenzy of ecstatic interaction can no more grow weary than the lovers on Keats's urn. Lined up alongside the lake, tossing their heads in time with the waves and the breeze, they have submerged their "identity" as surely as Lucy has been assimilated into nature. Only the poet stands apart, unable to tune his mood fully to the joy before him.

A poet could not but be gay,
In such a jocund company:
I gazed—and gazed—but little thought
What wealth the show to me had brought.

(15–18)

The double negative of line 15 and the repeated verb of line 17 point up the recalcitrance of the poet's mood, yet the final stanza (lines 19–24) shows how much more than mood was involved. To gaze and gaze is to try to *will* participation, to dictate self-surrender to the tyranny of the eye, the mere fact of physical presence.

His poetic calling urges joy, *demands* that he appreciate the scene before him, but his heart is not in it. He is a pensive, perhaps gloomy man, given to the fits of depression described in *Tintern Abbey* and *Resolution and Independence*. Yet in solitude, with his will and determination relaxed, the scene takes him unawares, as by an unforced access of grace, providing him with emotional capital for difficult times to come. The poem shifts at this point from the anecdotal past to the actively recurring present. What did not happen then is now endlessly reenacted.

Time and absence have brought the scene inwardly alive for him. "The bliss of solitude" is the opposite of the detached loneliness described in the opening lines. It is almost an oxymoron—a synthesis of being alone and being together, transcending both the isolation of the observer and the impersonal merging of the daffodils (which he compares to the "milky way"). Like the many solitary childhood experiences early in *The Prelude*—whose purpose became clear to him only much later, perhaps only as he was sketching the theodicy of the poem itself—the encounter with the daffodils is portrayed as a kind of education by solitude, in which the isolated self is sounded almost to the depths of its being. If loneliness detaches us from experience, solitude connects us to it. Loneliness is keen sighted but deadening. For the inner, meditative self, phenomenal experience can block perception but absence can become a heightened form of presence. A "vacant" or a "pensive" mood—with all the Miltonic associations of pensiveness—can prove a better ground for feeling than the active life, the immediate promptings of the natural world, or the sheer will to feel.

If Shelley and Swinburne in their very rhythms are poets of liquid self-surrender, Wordsworth is the contemplative poet who stands apart, not yielding to the world but slowly assimilating it to himself. What Keats described with mocking respect as the "wordsworthian or egotistical sublime," Wordsworth himself saw as a resistance which the imagination demanded, a detachment whose temporal dimension is called "emotion recollected in tranquillity." Wordsworth's impulse to solitude was so great that his first important poem was a sternly worded warning against its attractions. The full topographical title of this poem in the *Lyrical Ballads* of

1798 was "Lines left upon a Seat in a Yew-tree which stands near the Lake of Esthwaite, on a desolate Part of the Shore, yet commanding a beautiful Prospect." Part of the importance of this poem was formal, since here Wordsworth developed the style of blank-verse meditation that Coleridge needed for his conversation poems and he himself would use in *Tintern Abbey* and *The Prelude*. Coleridge may even have contributed to the moralistic conclusion of the poem, whose tone and message bring to mind the last section of *The Eolian Harp*, with its warning against "these shapings of the unregenerate mind."

Yet the substance of Wordsworth's poem is as significant as its new style. Like so many of Wordsworth's most moving works—*The Ruined Cottage*, for example, and *Michael*—this poem is a meditation on a place, the reading of a landscape to recover its almost lost human meaning. Wordsworth adapts the locodescriptive poem of the eighteenth century into a proleptic attack on Byronic solitude, visionary pride, and self-cultivation. Yet this peculiarly ambiguous attack is also a tribute to the recluse whose "unfruitful life" it describes, whose pleasure in nature is very much like Wordsworth's own, whose disappointed idealism, now turned inward, resembles the archetypal story of the young men of the 1790s.

In fact the disheartened man on whom Wordsworth modeled his poem, the Rev. Mr. Brathwaite, seems to have been less solitary and saturnine than we would guess from Wordsworth's account. According to a standard local guidebook that Wordsworth mentioned that this man "purchased the ground including this station, and erected an elegant and commodious building thereon, for the entertainment of his friends, called *Belle-Vieu*." Wordsworth makes him a complete solitary, whose philanthropic hopes have been soured by frustration, pride, and worldly neglect. Like *I wandered lonely as a Cloud*, the poem stresses the conjunction of loneliness with natural beauty. Even the title emphasizes this paradox, for it describes the scene as "a *desolate* part of the shore, yet commanding a *beautiful prospect*." The sublime visual prospect substitutes for the broken worldly prospects of this embittered man, who takes "a morbid pleasure" in the barrenness and desolation of the spot yet somehow transcends himself by contemplating the beauty of the distant scene:

> How lovely 'tis
> Thou seest, and he would gaze till it became

> Far lovelier, and his heart could not sustain
> The beauty still more beauteous.
>> (1798 version, lines 31–34)

Wordsworth's doublings of "lovely" and "beauty" convey the transition to another order of experience. With these lines a poem about a man who "with the food of pride sustained his soul / In solitude" turns into a poem about the bliss of solitude, as his almost involuntary immersion in nature draws him away from a lonely self-contemplation. This leads in turn to a partially renewed feeling for those he left behind:

>   Nor, that time,
> Would he forget those beings, to whose minds,
> Warm from the labours of benevolence,
> The world, and man himself, appeared a scene
> Of kindred loveliness: then he would sigh
> With mournful joy, to think that others felt
> What he must never feel: and so, lost man!
> On visionary views would fancy feed,
> Till his eyes streamed with tears. In this deep vale
> He died, this seat his only monument.
>> (1798 version, 34–43)

Here, with little inner logic, Wordsworth introduces the counterpoint to solitude that would occupy him all his life: the sympathetic imagination that arises paradoxically from the solitary experience of nature. The recluse goes from a morbid pleasure in mere desolation to the appreciation of beauty at a safe distance and, finally, to being overpowered by natural influences which, for the moment at least, transform him. Exactly how and why this progress occurs is not explained here, but an older Wordsworth tried to explain it when, in his final revision of this passage, he added an additional line: "Nor, that time, / When nature had subdued him to herself, / Would he forget those beings. . . ."

Wordsworth appears to have sensed the inner contradictions that enrich and complicate the poem, which is at once a memorial to this man and a denunciation of his pride and self-involvement, a sermon against solitude and a vivid celebration of its pleasures. There is even a pun, perhaps intentional, on "visionary views," which refers to both the landscape (the prospect) and the man's altruistic social ideals. The moral side of Wordsworth's mind praises the active life, full of the "labours of benevolence," but his imagination is irresistibly drawn to this setting of luxurious self-indulgence. (The same ambivalence impales Coleridge in *The Eolian Harp* and other early conversation poems.) This leads to the forced insistence "that true knowledge leads to love" (56), that solitude need not be misanthropic, for surrender to nature can somehow lead to fellow feeling by some chemistry Wordsworth needed to affirm. He would devote much of *The Prelude* to proving that love of nature leads to love of man, an idea that haunted him in proportion to his own impulse to solitude.

Wordsworth's whole body of work can be seen as an effort to reconcile nature with community, solitary introspection with human sympathy. In the annus mirabilis of 1798 this profound ambivalence leads him to take his treatment of solitude in two entirely different directions. On the one hand he begins writing the autobiographical poetry of *The Pedlar, Tintern Abbey,* and above all the two-part *Prelude* of 1798–1799, in which solitude and nature are necessary elements of all deep personal formation. On the other hand he writes about characters like the Discharged Soldier, the Old Cumberland Beggar, the old man in *Old Man Travelling,* and Margaret in *The Ruined Cottage,* for whom being alone is neither formative nor creative, whose experiences of loss, bereavement, and terrible isolation enable Wordsworth to touch the very bedrock of human endurance.

If the poetry of childhood memories can be described as "education by solitude," the other poetry can be said to depict the *blight* of solitude, the afflictions of extreme poverty or old age, of terrible losses that begin to affect the mind—a solitude of dwindling rather than growth, the reduction to a hard shell of diminished selfhood that verges on nonbeing. The Matthew poems, and later *Resolution and Independence,* say it all: these old men have experienced what the young can scarcely comprehend, though it is almost a full education for them to try.

I cannot here explore the many examples of either kind of poetry. Sometimes they spring up in the same poem, as the autobiographical elements in *The Pedlar* accrete around the story of Margaret in *The Ruined Cottage,* and Wordsworth is at a temporary loss about how to combine them (as he will eventually do in the first book of *The Excursion*). A text like *The Discharged Soldier* may remain unpublished because Wordsworth is not yet sure whether he is telling his own story or that of the blighted veteran whom he approaches with so much hesitancy and repulsion.

In *The Pedlar* and the two-part *Prelude*, Wordsworth describes how his early apprenticeship to nature had schooled him in the life of feeling—a tutelage that somehow grounded him in morality and instilled in him "the sentiment of being"—something far more than an appreciation of landscape, "for in all things / He saw one life, and felt that it was joy" (*The Pedlar*, lines 217–218).[5] At the beginning of the same passage, Wordsworth writes: "From nature and her overflowing soul / He had received so much that all his thoughts / Were steeped in feeling" (204–206). To Wordsworth the corollary of this "feeling" is a growth of human sympathy that vitalizes even the inanimate:

> To every natural form, rock, fruit, and flower,
> Even the loose stones that cover the highway,
> He gave a moral life; he saw them feel,
> Or linked them to some feeling.
>
> (332–335)

This kind of sentiment used to be written off as Wordsworth's nature mysticism, though in the preceding lines he carefully ascribes it to the mind's powers of analogy or intuition. (Such perception arises, he says, "From deep analogies by thought supplied, / Or consciousnesses not to be subdued.") In an earlier passage he had described nature as an actualization of scripture, a totality of feeling that confirms the written promise:

> But in the mountains did he FEEL his faith. . . .
> There littleness was not, the least of things
> Seemed infinite, and there his spirit shaped
> Her prospects—nor did he *believe*; he saw.
>
> (122, 126–128)

These solitary experiences give the Pedlar a steady equilibrium, an emotional openness and depth beyond that of a social being wrapped up in the trivial concerns of self and other, the false needs imposed by social forms:

> In his steady course
> No piteous revolutions had he felt,
> Unoccupied by sorrow of its own
> His heart lay open. . . .
> He had no painful pressure from within
> Which made him turn aside from wretchedness
> With coward fears. He could afford to suffer
> With those whom he saw suffer. Hence it was
> That in our best experience he was rich,
> And in the wisdom of our daily life
>   (271–275, 281–285)

Wordsworth takes the Pedlar on a breathtaking trajectory from the solitary encounter with nature to the daily round of common experience, the Wordsworthian hallowing of the ordinary.

This was not a journey easily taken, certainly not by Wordsworth himself. Despite the autobiographical elements that went into him, the Pedlar is an idealized figure whose role was to guide the poet toward a wise understanding of the grim decline of Margaret and her family. In *The Ruined Cottage* he berates his younger, less philosophical friend for his gloomy reaction to this shatteringly poignant tale. With his perfect equanimity, to which the poet could only aspire, *he* "could afford to suffer / With those whom he saw suffer," to see their lives as something to celebrate, as part of a longer human rhythm, a redemptive pattern. Wordsworth's way of dealing with suffering is to put a frame around it, to bend it away from tragedy toward consolation, to avoid the kind of naked, unmediated approach that could prove merely shocking or depressing. That is why he often presents himself as a young man taking instruction from an older man, getting a glimpse of the human depths but also learning at the same time how to read them aright. This secular theodicy sustains Wordsworth's treatment of human suffering. He needs to cushion its meaning without recourse to any divine purpose.

But when Wordsworth in the first books of *The Prelude* describes his formative experiences in the first person, they certainly include those "wild varieties of joy or grief" which the Pedlar was spared. His is instructed by nature through a ministry of fear that often leaves him shaken and terrified. Yet these experiences are just the ones nature uses to build up his capacity for deep feeling, to shape him as a man and as a poet:

> Thus, from my first dawn
> Of childhood, did ye love to intertwine
> The passions that build up our human soul
> Not with the mean and vulgar works of man,
> But with high objects, with eternal things.
> (1799 *Prelude* 1.132–136)

This is one of Wordsworth's most deeply felt arguments for education by solitude and by nature. Social man and all his works are tainted, and the knowledge they offer is emotionally shallow, even perverse. They muffle the shocks of existence, stunt the elemental passions. Wordsworth's education was more fearsome. By his own account he became what he was by confronting forms and powers that could seem blank, inhuman, and pitiless. After the boat-stealing episode, when the craggy cliffs around the lake seem to be looming up over him, stalking him,

> . . . for many days my brain
> Worked with a dim and undetermined sense
> Of unknown modes of being. In my thoughts
> There was a darkness—call it solitude
> Or blank desertion—no familiar shapes
> Of hourly objects, images of trees,
> Of sea or sky, no colours of green fields,
> But huge and mighty forms that do not live
> Like living men moved slowly through my mind
> By day, and were the trouble of my dreams.
> (1799 *Prelude* 1.120–129)

There is nothing casual, benign, or picturesque about this picture of nature working through his mind, nothing animistic or quasi-human. This is a terrible confrontation with inhuman power, an emptying out of himself, a fierce emotional education he could not have gotten from being apprenticed to the familiar in nature or in man.

Even when no fear is involved, when his contact with nature is with a vast calm vacancy, this education by solitude gives him access to something unique and powerful. Simply by stepping out onto a hill before the first birdsong of morning, the boy experiences a cosmic rush that echoes within his own inner being. He recalls peering out

> At the first hour of morning, when the vale
> Lay quiet in an utter solitude.
> How shall I trace the history, where seek
> The origin of what I then have felt?
> Oft in those moments such a holy calm
> Did overspread my soul that I forgot
> The agency of sight, and what I saw
> Appeared like something in myself, a dream,
> A prospect in my mind.
>   (1799 *Prelude* 2.393−401)

As with the "beautiful prospect" and "visionary views" of the yew-tree lines, Wordsworth is toying with the notions of sight and insight, adapting the idea of landscape to a mental space of self-reflection. The silent prospect turns him inward, toward a dreamlike, fugue state that signals the access of unconscious knowledge. The external solitude leads to a deeper solitude, a profound calm in which the agency of sight gives way to an inner landscape —an "inscape" of the mind.

During this period Wordsworth also began writing that other poetry in which solitude is anything but benign, in which blank desertion takes on quite a different meaning, and solitary characters, though irreducibly real in themselves, also become quasi-mythical emblems of the human condition. (In the seventh book of *The Prelude,* Wordsworth describes a blind beggar with a sign across his chest as "a type / Or emblem, of the utmost that we know, / Both of ourselves and of the universe" [1805 *Prelude* 7.617−619].) Though the *Lyrical Ballads* is full of stricken, infirm, or abandoned figures who live harsh lives, Wordsworth only gradually learns to give their suffering and endurance a symbolic character. The prototype for this kind of poem is probably *The Old Cumberland Beggar,* together with other poems of 1798 I have already mentioned. These portraits reach their culmination in the figure of the Leech-Gatherer four years later in *Resolution and Independence.* As critics like Geoffrey Hartman have acutely observed, these are borderline characters, "boundary beings" at one extreme of life;[6] as such they are closely related to Wordsworth's perpetual children like Lucy, Lucy Gray, or the Danish Boy, who are arrested at the other extreme.

Trilling once remarked that Wordsworth "was haunted by the mysterious fact that he existed," and I imagine this led him to test the limits of life with creatures who are not quite human, though subjected to the worst of human ills. The proportion of realism differs greatly from poem to poem. The schoolmaster Matthew, though old, is far from decrepit or simply emblematic, hiding his disappointments under the mask of the man of mirth, while figures like the Leech-Gatherer or the blind beggar make Wordsworth feel "as if admonish'd from another world" (1805 *Prelude* 7.622).

Sometimes Wordsworth oscillated wildly within the same poem. Attacked in his own day for weighing down his poetry with pedestrian detail, Wordsworth revised experimental poems like *The Thorn* and turned *Old Man Travelling* (a poem about a specific person) into *Animal Tranquillity and Decay* (a poem about a mythical emblem) simply by removing the matter-of-fact lines in which the old man actually speaks. Despite their similarity, the two versions can be said to touch the opposite extremes of Wordsworth's imagination, the literal and the mythical, both equally essential to the poet he was. The real old man, we note, is not so solitary: dialogue personalizes him, makes him a more definite presence. He is traveling to visit his dying son in a hospital. The literal facts may make for one of the "sudden and unpleasant sinkings" that Coleridge disliked in Wordsworth's poetry; but in this pedestrian incarnation he remains our best poet of the humble joys and duties of everyday life.

Something of the same division can be found in *The Old Cumberland Beggar,* the poem from which *Old Man Travelling* first originated. I had always thought of it as badly split between the first sixty-six lines, which give us an effective portrait of the aged beggar on his rounds, and a ponderous epilogue twice that length, where a moralizing Wordsworth turns to special pleading in a style he would soon outgrow. The tone of the poem does shift at line 67 when Wordsworth turns to direct address and somewhat preachy argumentation ("But deem not this Man useless. Statesmen! ye / Who are so restless in your wisdom"). But the first sixty-six lines would not, by Wordsworth's standard, really be a poem. The structure of the poem, as is so often the case in Wordsworth, is one of text-and-commentary. Though it is somewhat clumsily executed here, this structure perfectly mirrors the poem's overall theme, which is how we relate to the old man, what we make him signify to us, not what he is *en soi*. (Wordsworth was not George Crabbe: his goal was never simply to leave us with a realistic slice of rural life, but to turn fragments of recollection into metaphor and meaning.) Wordsworth "reads" the old beggar for us the way he reads the ruins of Margaret's cottage or the pile of stones in *Michael*.

I do not propose to recast all of Wordsworth's best known lyrics into meditations on solitude, but the word recurs at significant turns throughout *The Old Cumberland Beggar*. "He travels on, a solitary Man" is used twice as a refrain. This man has reached an age when there is no more aging, no more lessness or diminution:

> Him from my childhood have I known; and then
> He was so old, he seems not older now.
>
> (lines 22–23)

Though these lines establish a link between the boy growing up and the man who seems forever old, this is not something the man himself can perceive. The fields and hills and sky that fed the boy's love of solitude and helped to form him are no longer present for this man who, deeply bent, sees only the grave-sized patch of earth beneath his feet, his only "prospect":

> On the ground
> His eyes are turned, and, as he moves along,
> *They* move along the ground; and, evermore,
> Instead of common and habitual sight
> Of fields with rural works, of hill and dale,
> And the blue sky, one little span of earth
> Is all his prospect.
>
> (45–51)

He is almost beyond being—"scarcely do his feet / Disturb the summer dust" (59–60). Yet for all this evocation of an almost metaphysical isolation ("His age has no companion," 45), Wordsworth's commentary awkwardly nudges the poem toward the opposite point, that the beggar has an integral place in the community, as a figure who elicits charity and sympathy from everyone who sees him on his rounds.

Here the poem's structure nicely duplicates its theme. Wordsworth's aim in all the poems of this kind—in *The Old Cumberland Beggar*, in *The Ruined Cottage*, in the lines on the Discharged Soldier—is not simply to display heartrending examples of solitude, poverty, and human blight. This would be just the kind of social tourism he avoids in *Michael* and dislikes in the popular verse of the period, when the magazines were full of poems about mad mothers, idiot children, crippled veterans, and forsaken Indians. Wordsworth dipped into this material for the *Lyrical Ballads,* but his own aims soon outgrew this fashion.

Primitivism and mere pathos had little appeal for him. What Wordsworth does, as I have suggested, is to build a frame around the emblem of the Solitary Man. He wants us to see this figure through the eyes of an observer who will be pressed, almost against his will, to assimilate such a wrenching spectacle, to make it part of his own deeper consciousness of humanity. For this purpose, a narrator like the small-town gossip in *The Thorn,* full of local lore and superstition, was no longer adequate. His own character and limitations got in the way. The limits of his speech were also the limits of his mind. He could serve as chorus but not as protagonist. He had no capacity to grow and change. Only the poet himself could fully play the part.

In *The Old Cumberland Beggar* Wordsworth does not yet understand the direction he is taking. This poem too may be seen as an oblique chapter of his autobiography, but the frame, somewhat ponderously, embraces the whole community, all who give alms to the beggar on his rounds. He is a living lesson in organic community. In him his neighbors behold "a record which together binds / Past deeds and offices of charity" (89–90), as well as a "silent monitor" who reminds them of "want and sorrow" and of their own quiet blessings. Though solitary, he does not really live alone: "While in that vast solitude to which / The tide of things has borne him, he appears / To breathe and live but for himself alone" (163–165), he serves in fact to teach all around him "that we have all of us one human heart" (153).[7] Since the poem is about how the community responds to the beggar, it is structured as a commentary on the opening portrait of him. Wordsworth first brings the beggar himself into focus, then "reads" his relation to the surrounding community—the people who themselves draw meaning from the beggar's presence in their lives.

When he writes *Tintern Abbey* and *The Prelude* Wordsworth will learn to avoid this awkward separation. In part by making himself the observing subject, he will interweave narrative, discursive, and meditative passages far more seamlessly. In *The Ruined Cottage,* in the lines on the Discharged Soldier, in other texts that feed into *The Prelude* such as the Boy of Winander, in the Lucy and Matthew poems, and finally in *Resolution and Indepen-*

dence, Wordsworth constantly improves the frame by developing the auto-biographical point of view. An intricate poem like *The Two April Mornings* contains wheels within wheels, different layers of time that give us the impression of an almost infinite regress. *The Ruined Cottage* surrounds the story of Margaret with a double frame: the pedlar who actually knew Margaret—saw her, as it were, in different "takes" at each stage of her decline—and the young man for whom he constructs and interprets the tale.

The lines on the Discharged Soldier, also written in the early months of 1798, were Wordsworth's first attempt to weave together the two kinds of discourse on solitude we have been considering here. The frame is in the first thirty-five lines about the poet himself, which precede the shocking appearance of the ravaged veteran. The first part of the poem is a happy conjuring of the restorative powers of an evening walk, with

> My body from the stillness drinking in
> A restoration like the calm of sleep
> But sweeter far. Above, before, behind,
> Around me all was peace and solitude:
> I looked not round, nor did the solitude
> Speak to my eye, but it was heard and felt.
>
> (lines 22–27)

Soon afterward, however, the speaker must confront a figure who represents solitude as desolation, who, unlike the Cumberland Beggar, has been uprooted from his native place, not even willing to ask for alms to allay the wretchedness of his travels:

> His face was turned
> Towards the road, yet not as if he sought
> For any living thing. He appeared
> Forlorn and desolate, a man cut off
> From all his kind, and more than half detached
> From his own nature.
>
> He was alone;
> Had no attendant, neither dog, nor staff,
> Nor knapsack—in his very dress appeared

A desolation, a simplicity
That appertained to solitude.

(55–65)

After watching him for a long time, the narrator subdues his "heart's specious cowardice" (85), approaches the man to elicit his story, and finally ar-
ranges for his food and shelter for the night. He has passed from his own
self-delighted state, alone with himself and nature, into a condition of kinship with another—the very link the poor veteran has lost. The man has
appeared before him as the craggy mountains loomed over him as a boy,
giving a tincture of terror to a setting of tranquil beauty, drawing out his capacity to feel, respond, identify. Here, too, Wordsworth has been "fostered
alike by beauty and by fear," by the "impressive discipline of fear" he
evoked in the early books of *The Prelude* (1850, 1.302, 603).

The figure of the Discharged Soldier is an early sketch for the remarkable
apparition of the Leech-Gatherer. When he speaks he gives an impression
quite different from his frightful appearance, for he is "neither slow nor eager, but unmoved, / And with a quiet uncomplaining voice, / A stately air of
mild indifference" (96–98). Indifferent himself, he makes some unstated
difference to the young man who encounters him and takes momentary
responsibility for him. The poem itself is a rehearsal for what *Resolution
and Independence* fully achieves, a merger between the two kinds of poetry
Wordsworth had been writing in 1798, the autobiographical poetry of education and growth and the emblematic poetry of suffering and sympathy.

As Jared R. Curtis has shown in *Wordsworth's Experiments with Tradition,* the 1802 poem was still embryonically a "lyrical ballad." Under
the presumed title of *The Leech-Gatherer,* it included a long speech, now
largely lost, in which the old man told his own story, with many details
of family history we can find in Dorothy's journal. Though Wordsworth
warmly defended this speech when Sara and Mary Hutchinson (his future
wife) found it "tedious," he soon removed the offending passage, substituting a few lines of indirect discourse, and gave the poem its more general
title. Mythicizing and distancing the old man while amplifying his own reaction to him, he shifted the center of interest from the Leech-Gatherer to
the growth of a poet's mind.

Here at last the frame becomes the story, for Wordsworth has interwoven his own life with this stirring image of blight and fortitude and

made the encounter a turning point in his personal crisis. Only partly human himself, "not all alive nor dead, / Nor all asleep" (64–65), the Leech-Gatherer enables Wordsworth to test the limits of life and death, emboldens him to go beyond fear to a renewed though stoic self-confidence, enlarging his range of sympathy while tempting him with the very emblem of *apatheia,* not-feeling. The meeting is not only a way out of his moment of crisis but also a significant stage in his understanding of humanity.

Here is one key to the "culture of the feelings" which Arnold and Mill found in Wordsworth. If Wordsworth moves us deeply, it cannot simply be for the way he attended to the moods and associations of his own mind. Wordsworth's poetry conveys the drama of the solitary man who was able to integrate his feeling for himself with his feeling for others, to move on, as he always insisted, from love of nature to love of man. Wordsworth progressed from a cultivation of his own feelings in solitude to an understanding of the solitude, pain, and loss of others—moved from pure inwardness to mutual sympathy. He built a bridge from the sublime to the ordinary and taught the visionary moods of his youth to speak the language of the common life.

When Wordsworth's brother John drowned at sea in 1805, it confirmed something the poet had always known yet kept from himself—a sense of the ambiguity of nature's providential care, an awareness that the sum of our joys was interwoven with the sum of our losses. He wrote several letters vowing to keep the bond with his brother in death as he had in life. In his *Elegiac Stanzas* he promised again to turn from solitude to sympathy, as he had in every major poem since *Tintern Abbey*:

> Farewell, farewell the heart that lives alone,
> Housed in a dream, at distance from the Kind!
>
> (lines 53–54)

In the course of this transition, never wholly completed, Wordsworth wrote all the poetry we still value today. Yet he also cut himself off from the freshest shoots of his own imagination, which had grown up in a soil of dreamy solitude. He still had too much spirit to devolve into a poet of stoic endurance, yet too much egotism to immolate himself on the altar of the community. While it lasted this tension proved invaluable to him.

The moral dimension of Wordsworth's poetry was perhaps what enabled John Stuart Mill to assimilate Wordsworth's self-cultivation to his own commitment to social reform and progress. Mill had already rejected Byron's "culture of the feelings" because it merely fed his own depression, spiraling inward without issuing in mental relief or empathy for the plight of others. Wordsworth, finally, was not a tragic poet but one whose consoling ideas could help his readers live with tragedy. He showed them how to expand their range of feeling without falling into gloom or desperation. Along with Byron and Rousseau, Wordsworth helped establish the individual human subject as the measure of authenticity and truth. But he went beyond his own inward turning to demonstrate that the poetry of solitude, if it closely examined the meaning of that solitude, was also a poetry of basic human connections, the kind he found it hard to believe in when he was growing up. In confronting the death or loneliness or seemingly diminished humanity of others, Wordsworth was better able to gain access to his own buried life.

Notes

Chapter 1. The Dawn of Universal Patriotism

1. For a fuller account of the matters presented briefly here, see my *Commerce des Lumières: John Oswald and the British in Paris, 1790–93* (Columbia, Mo., 1986).

2. *The Letters of William and Dorothy Wordsworth: The Early Years, 1787–1805*, ed. Ernest de Selincourt, 2d ed. rev. Chester L. Shaver (Oxford, 1967), 66. Cited hereafter as *Letters: Early Years*.

3. Mary Moorman, *William Wordsworth: A Biography, the Early Years* (London, 1957), 44. Moorman (63) notes that while the poet wrote his *Happy Warrior* poem in response to news of the death of his brother John and of Lord Nelson, "the reader feels bound to add" that the character depicted largely represents Wordsworth's own character—and Beaupuy's. Oddly enough, the poet was quite aware and critical of the moral flaw in Nelson's character: he had precisely *not* kept the law, having breached faith after a truce with the Neapolitans. (Moorman also quotes the remark by Wordsworth to the effect that the best thing Nelson did for his country was to die! Nor was this an uncommon judgment at the time.)

4 See, however, Robert Gordon, "Wordsworth and the Domestic Roots of Power," *Bulletin of Research in the Humanities* 81(1978): 90–102.

5. The inhibiting qualifier is that he considers himself "little graced with power / Of eloquence"—and then the double bind: "even in my native speech" (*Prelude* 10.131–132).

6. Gwynn Williams, *Artisans and Sans-culottes: Popular Movements in France and Britain during the French Revolution* (New York, 1968).

7. *Parliamentary History* 30:553.

8. Another British contributor of direct military assistance was "Captain Wilson, a half-pay officer, perhaps the Scotchman who ultimately married Wolfe Tone's widow." He "offered a seven-barrelled gun, all the barrels of which could be discharged simultaneously." John Goldsworth Alger, *Englishmen in the French Revolution* (London, 1889), 51.

9. John Goldsworth Alger, *Paris in 1789–1794: Farewell Letters of Victims of the Guillotine* (New York, 1902), 300.

10. Alger, *Paris,* 330.

11. William Eden, Baron Auckland, *The Journal and Correspondence of William, Lord Auckland,* ed. G. Hogge (London, 1860–1862), 2: 207–208.

12. Alger, *Paris,* 326, translated from *Patriote français,* 21 Nov. 1792.

13. François Furet, *Interpreting the French Revolution* (Cambridge, 1981), 125–126.

14. Modern British historians still misinform us about this maneuver, but see two chapters in Lucyle Werkmeister's *A Newspaper History of England 1792–1793* (Lincoln, Neb., 1967): "The Insurrection Which Wasn't" and "The Convocation of Parliament."

Chapter 2. Wordsworth as Satirist of His Age

1. He was writing to Francis Wrangham on 7 November. Wordsworth's letters are quoted from Ernest de Selincourt, ed., *The Letters of William and Dorothy Wordsworth,* 6 vols. (1935–1939), rev. Chester Shaver, Mary Moorman, and Alan Hill (Oxford, 1967).

2. "My First Acquaintance with Poets", William Hazlitt, *Complete Works,* ed. P. P. Howe (London, 1931), 17:118.

3. The others were Spenser, Shakespeare, and Milton.

4. The Juvenal "imitations" are included among Wordsworth's "Juvenilia," in Ernest de Selincourt and Helen Darbishire, eds., *The Poetical Works of William Wordsworth,* rev. ed., vol. 1 (Oxford, 1952).

5. Coleridge's *Table Talk* for 21 July 1832.

6. Averill's text of 1794 can be found in his *Cornell Wordsworth* (Ithaca, N.Y., 1984) edition of the poem.

7. Quotations are from the text established by Stephen Gill in his *Cornell Wordsworth* edition of *The Salisbury Plain Poems,* published in 1975.

8. 8 June 1794.

9. Quoted from the text in W. J. B. Owen and Jane W. Smyser, eds., *The Prose Works of William Wordsworth,* 3 vols. (Oxford, 1974).

10. Quoted from Owen and Smyser, *Prose Works.*

11. Quoted from the Owen and Smyser, *Prose Works.*

12. 14 Jan. 1801.

13. Coleridge's letter is printed in *The Letters of William and Dorothy Wordsworth: The Early Years, 1787–1805,* ed. Ernest de Selincourt, 2d ed., rev. Chester L. Shaver (Oxford, 1967), app. 6.

14. The sonnet was published at the front of a pamphlet, *Kendal and Windermere Railway* (1845).

15. Throughout, the 1805 text of *The Prelude* is quoted from de Selincourt's edition, revised by Helen Darbishire.

16. Alfred North Whitehead, *Science and the Modern World* (New York, 1925).

17. Quoted from the text established by Stephen Parrish in the *Cornell Wordsworth,* (1977).

18. In the *Essay, Supplementary to the Preface.*

19. Ford Swetnam, "The Satiric Voices of *The Prelude,*" in *Bicentenary Wordsworth Studies,* ed. Jonathan Wordsworth and Beth Darlington (Ithaca, N.Y. and London, 1970).

20. In the preface to Matthew Arnold's 1879 selection of Wordsworth's *Poems.*

Chapter 3. "The Work of Man's Redemption"

I owe large debts to Shirley Strum Kenny for a provost's fellowship and to the Graduate Research Board of the University of Maryland. The perspective on Romantic prophecy afforded here is complementary to the ones provided by M. H. Abrams, *Natural Supernaturalism: Tradition and Revolution in Romantic Literature* (New York, 1971); idem, "English Romanticism: The Spirit of the Age," in *Romanticism Reconsidered,* ed. Northrop Frye 26–72 (New York, 1963); idem, "Apocalypse: Theme and Variations," in *The Apocalypse in English Renaissance Thought and Literature,* ed. C. A. Patrides and Joseph Wittreich, 342–368 (Manchester and Ithaca, N.Y., 1984); and by Geoffrey Hartman, "The Poetics of Prophecy," in *High Romantic Argument: Essays for M. H. Abrams,* ed. Lawrence Lipking (Ithaca, N.Y., 1981). For a selective, but ample, listing of commentaries on prophecy and apocalypse in the Romantic period, see Joseph Wittreich, "The Apocalypse: A Bibliography," in *Apocalypse in English Renaissance Thought and Literature,* esp. 414–420.

1. C. S. Lewis, *The Literary Impact of the Authorized Version* (London, 1950), 21.

2. *Correspondence of Robert Southey with Caroline Bowles,* ed. Edward Dowden (Dublin, 1881), 52.

3. Jerome McGann, *The Romantic Ideology: A Critical Investigation* (Chicago, 1983), 2.

4. Vasily Rozanov, *The Apocalypse of Our Time and Other Writings,* ed. Robert Payne (New York, 1977), 236.

5. Jacques Derrida, "Of an Apocalyptic Tone Recently Adopted in Philosophy," *Oxford Literary Review* 6 (1984): 22.

6. See the unsigned review in the *Literary Gazette* reprinted in *Coleridge: The Critical Heritage,* ed. J. R. de J. Jackson (London, 1970), 388–389; and see, too, the unsigned reviews, 394, 401.

7. E. S. Shaffer, *"Kubla Khan" and the Fall of Jerusalem: The Mythological School of Criticism and Secular Literature 1770–1880* (Cambridge, 1975), 90.

8. Christopher Small, *Mary Shelley's "Frankenstein": Tracing the Myth* (Pittsburgh, 1973), 29.

9. Abrams, *Natural Supernaturalism*, 13.

10. Hazlitt's unsigned review from *Yellow Dwarf* and John Wilson's from *Edinburgh Review* are both reprinted in *Byron: The Critical Heritage*, ed. Andrew Rutherford (London and New York, 1970), 133, 154.

11. See both the unsigned review in *Literary Gazette* and the review by W. S. Walker in *Quarterly Review*, both reprinted in *Shelley: The Critical Heritage*, ed. James E. Barcus (London and Boston, 1975), 236, 262.

12. See Harold Bloom, *Shelley's Mythmaking* (1959; reprint, Ithaca, N.Y., 1969), 95; and Earl Wasserman, *Shelley: A Critical Reading* (Baltimore, 1971), 373.

13. F. R. Leavis, *Revaluation: Tradition and Development in English Poetry* (London, 1936), 6.

14. Howard Nemerov, *Reflexions on Poetry and Poetics* (New Brunswick, N.J., 1972), 111, 218.

15. Jonathan Wordsworth, *William Wordsworth: The Borders of Vision* (Oxford, 1982), 114.

16. Carl Jung, *Psychology and Religion*, trans. R. F. C. Hull (New York, 1958), 453.

17. Carl Becker, *The Heavenly City of the Eighteenth-Century Philosophers* (New Haven, Conn., 1932), 139.

18. Abrams, *Natural Supernaturalism*, esp. pp. 325–372.

19. David Roskies, *Against the Apocalypse: Responses to Catastrophe in Modern Jewish Culture* (Cambridge, Mass., 1984).

20. See Bernard McGinn, "Early Apocalypticism: The Ongoing Debate," in *The Apocalypse in English Renaissance Thought and Literature*, 2–39.

21. Roskies, *Against the Apocalypse*, 310.

Chapter 4. Pleasure and Play

1. Meanwhile, paradoxically, the attempt by American primary and secondary education to make teaching itself nothing but pleasure has further lowered its standing.

2. *The Notebooks of Samuel Taylor Coleridge*, vol. 3, *1808–1819*, ed. Kathleen Coburn (Princeton, N.J., 1973), entry 3615.

3. Lionel Trilling, *Beyond Culture: Essays on Literature and Learning* (New York, 1965), esp. 57–64.

4. Vladimir Sergeyevich Solovyov, *The Justification of the Good: An Essay in Moral Philosophy,* trans. Natalie A. Duddington (London, 1918).

5. In *"Dionysus in Lyrical Ballads,"* Donald Davie nominates "glee" as the hallmark of the poet's work and associates this glee with Nietzsche's portrayal of the Dionysiac spirit and also with *admiratio* as Aristotle defines it. Davie's is an especially important insight, which may be susceptible of modification, mainly in the respect that Wordsworth is set on *domesticating* glee, breaking down its private character, and giving it a social foundation. (*Wordsworth's Mind and Art,* ed. A. W. Thomson (Edinburgh, 1969), 110–139.)

6. *The Letters of William and Dorothy Wordsworth: The Middle Years, 1811–1820,* ed. Ernest de Selincourt (Oxford, 1937), hereafter cited as *Middle Years.*

7. James A. W. Heffernan, *Wordsworth's Theory of Poetry: The Transforming Imagination* (Ithaca, N.Y., 1969), esp. 81–86. John Dennis (1657–1734) was a dramatist and critic whose work was subjected to attack by Pope and to neglect by posterity. Heffernan, via Wordsworth, has given him a new lease on life.

8. Michael G. Cooke, *The Romantic Will* (New Haven, Conn., 1976), 179.

9. Many of the poems deal with the aftermath of this material pleasure. *The Thorn* recalls such pleasure while moving us to a higher order of pleasure. The work may at times be cool, perhaps, but it is misleading to say, as Ferry and Perkins do, that the writer lacks human sympathy and is almost a despiser of humankind (see David Ferry, *The Limits of Mortality* (Middletown, Conn., 1959), 51f., and David Perkins, *Wordsworth and the Poetry of Sincerity* (Cambridge, Mass., 1964), 4f.).

10. Ernest de Selincourt and Helen Darbishire, eds., *The Poetical Works of William Wordsworth,* rev. ed. vol. 2 (Oxford, 1957).

11. Friedrich Schiller, *On the Aesthetic Education of Man, in a Series of Letters,* ed. and trans. with an intro., commentary, and glossary of terms by Elizabeth M. Wilkinson and L. A. Willoughby (Oxford, 1967).

12. *The Early Letters of William and Dorothy Wordsworth* (1787–1805), ed. Ernest de Selincourt (Oxford, 1935).

13. William Barrett and Henry D. Aiken, eds., *Philosophy in the Twentieth Century: An Anthology* (New York, 1962), 4:457–458.

14. Emmett Grogan, *Ringolevio: A Life Played for Keeps* (Boston, 1972).

15. Ernst Kris, *Psychoanalytic Explorations of Art* (New York, 1952), 39f.

16. Meredith Anne Skura, *The Literary Use of the Psychoanalytical Process* (New Haven, 1981), 185f.

17. D. W. Winnicott, "Transitional Objects and Transitional Phenomena," *International Journal of Psychoanalysis* 34 (1953): 89–97.

18. Peter Berger and Thomas Luckman, *The Social Construction of Reality: A Treatise in the Sociology of Knowledge* (New York, 1966).

19. Quoted by Kenneth R. Johnston, *Wordsworth and The Recluse* (New Haven, Conn., 1984), 388 n. 7.

20. Arthur Schopenhauer (1788–1860) usually, and probably unjustly, placed among the pessimists in philosophy, is best known for his anti-Kantian *The World as Will and Representation*; he also wrote "lighter" or more "topical" essays of considerable astuteness.

Chapter 5. "Wordsworth" after Waterloo

1. *Democratic Review,* May 1850, 473. My thanks to John Birtwhistle for this reference and for much else in the way of bibliography and comment on the matters taken up here.

2. Robert Browning, *Poems,* ed. John Pettigrew, 2 vols. (New Haven and London, 1981), 1:410.

3. Robert Browning, *Letters,* ed. Thurman L. Hood (London, 1933), 166–167.

4. William Hazlitt, *Collected Works,* ed. P. P. Howe, 21 vols. (London and Toronto, 1931), 17:22–34 (cited hereafter in the text).

5. On Byron as an alternative to the Lake Poets, Browning wrote to Elizabeth Barrett soon after *The Lost Leader,* "I would at any time have gone to Finchley to see a curl of his [Byron's] hair or one of his gloves, I am sure—while Heaven knows that I could not get up enthusiasm enough to cross the room if at the other end of it all Wordsworth, Coleridge, and Southey were condensed into the little China bottle yonder." Letter of 22 August 1846, cited in William Clyde De Vane, *A Browning Handbook* (New York, 1955), 160–161.

6. George Gordon Byron, *Letters and Journals,* ed. Leslie Marchand, 12 vols. (Cambridge, Mass., 1973–1982), 7:253; *Don Juan,* ed. Truman Guy Steffan and Willis W. Pratt, 4 vols. (Austin, Tex., 1957), 2: Dedication, st. 1 (this edition cited hereafter in the text). For other references to the Lake Poets as "renegadoes," see *Don Juan,* canto 4, st. 115, and canto 10, st. 13.

7. Byron does most of the damage in a footnote: "Wordsworth's place may be in the Customs—it is, I think, in that or the excise—besides another at Lord Lonsdale's table, where this poetical charlatan and political parasite licks up the crumbs with a hardened alacrity; the converted Jacobin having long subsided into the clownish sycophant of the worst prejudices of the aristocracy" (*Don Juan* 4.10–11). Byron may well have seen Peacock's letter to Shelley; see n. 11 below.

8. While Wordsworth, Coleridge, and Southey are attacked together in the first cantos, Wordsworth comes in for the brunt of the criticism in later cantos, beginning with the three satiric stanzas on *Peter Bell* and *The Waggoner* in 3.98–100.

9. *Shelley's Poetry and Prose,* ed. Donald H. Reiman and Sharon B. Powers (New

York, 1977), 323 (unless otherwise indicated, all text citations from Shelley's poetry are to this edition).

10. The two standard articles are John Edwin Wells, "Wordsworth and De Quincey in Westmorland Politics, 1818," *PMLA* 55 (1940): 1080–1128 and Wallace Douglas, "Wordsworth in Politics: The Westmorland Election of 1818," *MLN* 54 (Nov. 1948): 437–449. Peter Manning returns us to this campaign to show its abiding effects on Wordsworth's subsequent writings in "Wordsworth at St. Bees: Scandals, Sisterhoods, and Wordsworth's Later Poetry," *ELH* 52 (1985): 33–58.

11. G. T. Garratt, *Lord Brougham* (London, 1935), 109–110. One observer of the election was Thomas Love Peacock, who sent word of it to Shelley in Italy: "Brougham is contesting Westmorland against the Lowthers. Wordsworth has published an *Address to the Freeholders*, in which he says they ought not to choose so poor a man as Brougham, riches being the only guarantees of political integrity. . . . Of course, during the election, Wordsworth dines every day at Lord Lonsdale's" (*Works*, edited by H. F. B. Brett-Smith and C. E. Jones, 10 vols. [London, 1924–1934], 8:199).

12. Dorothy Wordsworth, who attended Brougham's speech, wrote William a long report the next day on Brougham's comments, *The Letters of William and Dorothy Wordsworth*, ed. Ernest de Selincourt, 2d ed. rev. Chester L. Shaver, vol. 2, *The Middle Years*, pt. 2, 1812–1820 (Oxford, 1970), 442–444, 448–449 (cited hereafter in the text); for De Quincey's published defense of Wordsworth against Brougham's remarks see Wells, "Wordsworth in Politics," 1098–1010.

13. The most detailed account of the affair is given by Frank Taliaferro Hoadley, "The Controversy over Southey's *Wat Tyler*," *Studies in Philology* 38 (1941): 81–96. For Hazlitt's and Francis Jeffrey's influential articles, see, respectively, *Examiner*, 9 Mar. 1817, 157–159, and *Edinburgh Review* 20 (Mar. 1817): 151–174.

14. T. C. Hansard, *The Parliamentary Debates* (London, 1817), 35:1090.

15. Writing to Benjamin Robert Haydon about Smith's attack, Wordsworth expressed his dismay at the question: "How came he to use that word Renegado?" *Middle Years*, 393; Coleridge published an essay entitled "Apostacy and Renegado" in the *Courier* on 2 April—see *Essays on His Times*, ed. David V. Erdman, 3 vols. (London and Princeton, N.J., 1978), 2:473–478. For Southey's response to the term, see below.

16. The fact that the radicals who published *Wat Tyler* were out to embarrass Southey in 1817 suggests that the *Wat Tyler* affair was not the first charge of renegadism to be brought against him. Even before the publication of *Wat Tyler*, they knew from *Joan of Arc*, a radical publication of 1794, what Southey's politics had been, and his acceptance of the laureateship in 1813 was already a clear indication to them that his views had fundamentally changed. It was not just Southey's acceptance of the laureateship that offended, however, but what he wrote in that capacity. Haz-

litt's 1816 *Examiner* review of *The Lay of the Laureate, Carmen Nuptiale,* attacked not only Southey's vanity but also his political sincerity when it took up Southey's comparison of his position with Spenser's. "Poets were not wanted in those days," wrote Hazlitt, "to celebrate the triumphs of Princes over the People." As for Southey's decision to accept the post: "Mr. Southey ought not to have received what would not have been offered to the author of Joan of Arc" (Hazlitt, *Collected Works,* 7:89).

17. *Thanksgiving Ode* (London: Longman, 1816), 17.

18. And Shelley again uses the ode as a framework for his critique of a poet he now thinks dead to the needs and purposes of the greater social world. Unlike Browning, Shelley does not suggest that Wordsworth's desertion was motivated by greed or money. The Poet is rather portrayed as a victim of a kind of poetic solipsism, a willingness to confuse his own impulses with the life of the world around him until, staring into the diminishing peaks of a horned moon that reflect his own weary eyes, he seems to melt away into the image of himself that he has projected into the landscape.

19. See n. 6 for edition cited.

20. This is the place to take up the one potential exception to Shelley's claim to priority in this matter: the *in*decisive early judgment of Leigh Hunt. Hunt's 1814 edition of *The Feast of the Poets* characterizes the Lake Poets, led by Southey, but including Wordsworth, as political turncoats. This critique elaborates politically what was said of them in the 1811 version of the poem in Hunt's *Reflector,* where the attack is along the (unpolitical) lines of Jeffrey's ongoing campaign against the perversion of taste and talent by poetic system. In 1814 this same line of criticism is extended, and joined to a comment about Wordsworth's having accepted the stamp distributorship for Westmorland. But Hunt later admitted he had not even read Wordsworth at the time of his early attacks, and he withdrew most of his criticisms when he again revised the *Feast* for the edition of 1815. In the 1815 verses, Hunt's Apollo, host of the poets' feast, tells Wordsworth that he has "the key to my heart," and in the accompanying notes Hunt pronounces Wordsworth the greatest poet of the age. It was a matter of some embarrassment to Hunt that on the day Wordsworth visited Hunt in London to acknowledge the compliment, Hunt's *Examiner* ran an article on Milton's *Comus* by Hazlitt that, as an afterthought, criticized Wordsworth's sonnet *Royal fortitude* on the Stuarts in the 1815 *Poems* (11 June 1815, 382). As if by way of compensation the *Examiner* went on to publish three of Wordsworth's (nonpolitical) sonnets in 1816. And when Hunt reviewed Wordsworth's apparently Legitimist Waterloo sonnets that same year, he seems to struggle not to come to terms with their political content: "It would be monstrous, in our opinion, if a Poet like Mr. Wordsworth . . . *could* accompany such men as the Allied Sovereigns and their Ministers in all their destitutions of faith and even com-

mon intellect; and what we quarrel with him for in the present instance is, first, that while he is understood not to do so . . . , he leaves it to be supposed by his readers that the case is otherwise" (18 Feb. 1816, 97). Three years later, however, in his review of *Peter Bell* Hunt desists from special pleading: Wordsworth had become simply a "soi-disant philosopher" and a "ci-devant patriot" (*Examiner*, 2 May 1819, 271). I wish to thank Charles Robinson and Timothy Webb for valuable references on Hunt's series of responses.

21. *Edinburgh Review* 1(Oct. 1802): 70–71.

22. *Edinburgh Review* 24 (Nov. 1814): 4.

23. *Edinburgh Review* 37 (Nov. 1822): 449.

24. See n. 4.

25. Hazlitt elaborates some of these ideas in his pointed essay "On the Character of Country People," *Collected Works* 17:66–71. For a reading of Hazlitt's review that weighs these emphases very differently, see B. Bernard Cohen, "William Hazlitt: Bonapartist Critic of *The Excursion*," *Modern Language Quarterly* 10 (1949): 158–167.

26. Cited by Reiman and Powers, *Shelley's Poetry and Prose*, 88.

27. *Prose Works*, ed. W. J. B. Owen and Jane Worthington Smyser, 3 vols. (Oxford, 1974), 3:166 (cited hereafter in the text).

28. See n. 9.

29. See Kenneth R. Johnston, *Wordsworth and the Recluse* (New Haven, Conn., 1984).

30. Certainly Jeffrey and other reviewers picked up on Wordsworth's claims that the present work represented a fuller articulation of an ongoing project—or "system," they called it—than he had yet offered. See, for example, John Herman Merivale in the *Monthly Review* 66 (Feb. 1815): 124.

31. John Jordan showed this in "The Hewing of Peter Bell," *Review of English Studies* 7 (1967): 559–603, and has now been able to give all the textual evidence in his edition of the poem in Stephen Parrish, gen. ed., *The Cornell Wordsworth, Peter Bell* (Ithaca, N.Y., and London, 1984).

32. *Letter to William Smith*, 2d ed. (London: John Murray, 1817), 27–28.

33. See Georg Lukács, *The Historical Novel*, trans. Hannah and Stanley Mitchell (London, 1962), 172–183; cf. "Narrate or Describe," in *Writer and Critic* (New York, 1971), 110–148.

34. James K. Chandler, *Wordsworth's Second Nature* (Chicago, 1984).

35. E. P. Thompson, *The Making of the English Working Class* (New York, 1966), 603.

36. R. J. White, *Waterloo to Peterloo* (London, 1957), 20 (cited hereafter in the text).

37. Place Collection, British Museum, 39, vol. 4, p. 85.

38. *The Letters*, ed. Hyder E. Rollins, 2 vols. (Cambridge, Mass., 1958), 2:194.

39. *Scotsman* 14 (19 Aug. 1820): 45.

40. See, for example, *Middle Years*, 393–394.

41. The difference between Hunt's reviews of 1816 and 1819, though even in the former one can see the incipient radical fear of Holy Leaguism, epitomizes what happens to nuances in the post-Waterloo period; see note 20 above.

42. *Yellow Dwarf* 3 Jan. 1818: 4–5.

43. Roger Ingpen and Walter E. Peck, eds., *The Complete Works of Percy Bysshe Shelley*, 10 vols. (London, 1926–1930), 6:196.

Chapter 7. The Triumphs of Failure

1. Cited by Stephen Gill in his edition, *William Wordsworth*, in the Oxford Authors series (London, 1984), 379.

2. John Jordan, *Why the "Lyrical Ballads"?* (Berkeley and Los Angeles, 1976).

3. Mary Moorman, *William Wordsworth, a Biography: The Early Years, 1770–1803* (Oxford, 1957); Mark L. Reed, *Wordsworth: The Chronology of the Early Years, 1770–1799* (Cambridge, Mass., 1967), 25–34.

4. Mark Reed, "Wordsworth, Coleridge, and the 'Plan' of the *Lyrical Ballads*," *University of Toronto Quarterly* 34 (1965): 238–253. Other critics have defended the organization of the *Lyrical Ballads* of 1798, with or without reference to Wordsworth's preface; cf. Stephen Prickett, *Wordsworth and Coleridge: The Lyrical Ballads* (London, 1975), and John Beer, *Wordsworth and the Human Heart* (New York, 1978). James H. Averill has made a persuasive case for the volume's "workmanlike" degree of internal coherence, without claiming a "seamless" organic unity ("The Shape of 'Lyrical Ballads' (1798)," *Philological Quarterly* 60 [1981]: 387–407). Averill bases his case on Coleridge's claim that the poems in the volume are related to each other like the parts of an ode. He discusses the thematic importance of the opening and closing poems, isolates an opening sequence or movement of four poems, points to the function of certain obvious pairings like *The Tables Turned* and *Expostulation and Reply*, and identifies a central section of "poems whose topics . . . are particular instances of personal and institutional inhumanity: 'The Thorn,' 'The Last of the Flock,' 'The Dungeon,' and 'The Mad Mother'" (402).

5. I refer to the volumes in the continuing *Cornell Wordsworth* series published by Cornell University Press, particularly those edited by James Butler (*The Ruined Cottage and the Pedlar* [Ithaca, N.Y., 1979]), Stephen M. Parrish (*The Prelude, 1798–1799* [1977]), Beth Darlington (*Home at Grasmere* [1977]), and Joseph Kishel (*"The Tuft of Primroses," with Other Late Poems for "The Recluse"* [1986]).

6. Helen Darbishire, *The Poet Wordsworth* (Oxford, 1950), 90; Emile Legouis,

The Early Life of William Wordsworth, 1770–1798 (London, 1897); John Alban Finch, "Wordsworth, Coleridge, and *The Recluse, 1798–1814*" (Ph.D. diss., Cornell University, 1964); Jonathan Wordsworth, *William Wordsworth: The Borders of Vision* (Oxford, 1982); Kenneth R. Johnston, *Wordsworth and "The Recluse"* (New Haven, Conn., 1984).

7. All quotations from Wordsworth's poems are from *William Wordsworth: The Poems,* vol. 1, ed. John O. Hayden (New Haven, Conn., 1981), to which I am also indebted for information on the chronology and composition of *Lyrical Ballads.*

8. Moorman, *William Wordsworth: Early Years,* sees two separate streams of composition coming together in January–February of 1798, those of *The Ruined Cottage* and the *Prospectus* lines, which then break off when Wordsworth turns to the *Lyrical Ballads* project (355–363). Most scholars would now regard these two streams as essentially one—*The Recluse.* Stephen M. Parrish, in *The Art of the Lyrical Ballads* (Cambridge, Mass., 1973), the best comprehensive study of the poems in both volumes, also draws the relation between *Lyrical Ballads* and *The Recluse* in negative terms: *The Recluse* project was bad for Wordsworth's poetic development because it encouraged his natural egotism into abstract philosophical conceptions that led ultimately to his creative decline, diverting him from his best voice of "lyrical, narrative, and dramatic utterance" (59). Mary Jacobus does not directly mention *The Recluse,* but the entire two-part division of her book, between introspective lyrics and tragic ballads, corresponds to the division I am proposing—which has of course always been the most popular way of discriminating among Wordsworth's contributions (*Tradition and Experiment in Wordsworth's Lyrical Ballads (1798),* Oxford, 1976). She shows very clearly how *The Pedlar* (a separate version of *The Ruined Cottage*) stands behind the early spring lyrics of 1798, as an abstract presence—and thus, in her estimation, a less successfully poetic one. Don H. Bialostosky makes no reference to *The Recluse* in *Making Tales: The Poetics of Wordsworth's Narrative Experiments* (Chicago, 1984), but his conclusions and mine about *Lyrical Ballads* are in general congenial, despite some differences in our ways of categorizing its poems.

9. Wordsworth's radical surgery on his compositions of 1798, dividing their interpretive burden away from their sociological thrust, goes directly opposite to his impulse in revising *An Evening Walk* in 1793. There, he nearly doubled the length of the poem by adding contemporary sociopolitical comments which lie heavily on the conventionally descriptive lines of the published version, though these revisions were never adopted in subsequent printings (James H. Averill, ed., *An Evening Walk* Ithaca, N.Y., 1984). These two contrasting actions, inserting sociological commentary in 1793 and carefully separating it out in 1798, may thus be seen to demarcate in compositional terms the beginning and end of Wordsworth's most intense commitment to political activism. Alan Bewell has recently proposed another dual aspect

for some of the poems in *Lyrical Ballads*, viewing narratives like *Goody Blake and Harry Gill* as "case histories" in eighteenth-century psychopathology, cut off from the systematic and theoretical contexts which supported them in Wordsworth's sources, such as Erasmus Darwin's *Zoonomia* ("A 'Word Scarce Said': Hysteria and Witchcraft in Wordsworth's 'Experimental' Poetry of 1797–1798," *ELH* 53 [Summer 1982]: 370–371). More generally, the division I am discussing could be related to the dialectical thrust of many Romantic works on the relation of natural (or imaginative) beauty to social responsibility, especially Blake's *Songs of Innocence and of Experience: Showing the Two Contrary States of the Human Soul* (1789–1794).

Chapter 8. Reclaiming Dorothy Wordsworth's Legacy

1. *Journals of Dorothy Wordsworth,* ed. William Knight (reprint in 1 vol., London, 1924), vii–viii.

2. Thomas De Quincey, "William Wordsworth," *Recollections of the Lakes and the Lake Poets,* ed. David Wright (Harmondsworth, 1970), 131–132.

3. De Quincey, "William Wordsworth," 204–205.

4. Joanna Russ, *How to Suppress Women's Writing* (Austin, Tex., 1983).

5. Selections from Dorothy Wordsworth's Grasmere Journal and one of her poems have, however, been included in Sandra Gilbert's and Susan Gubar's *Norton Anthology of Literature by Women: The Tradition in English* (New York, 1985), 196–206.

6. *The Poetry of Dorothy Wordsworth, Edited from the Journals,* ed. Hyman Eigerman (1940; reprint, Westport, Conn., 1970).

7. Elizabeth Hardwick, *Seduction and Betrayal: Women and Literature* (New York, 1974), 143. The chapter on Dorothy Wordsworth first appeared in idem, "Amateurs: Dorothy Wordsworth and Jane Carlyle," *New York Review of Books,* 30 Nov. 1972, 3–4.

8. Margaret Homans, *Women Writers and Poetic Identity: Dorothy Wordsworth, Emily Brontë, and Emily Dickinson* (Princeton, N.J., 1980), 3.

9. *Letters of William and Dorothy Wordsworth: The Middle Years,* pt. 1, 1806–1811, ed. Ernest de Selincourt, 2d ed. rev. Mary Moorman (Oxford, 1969), 24–25.

10. Quoted from Susan Levin and Robert Ready, "Unpublished Poems from Dorothy Wordsworth's Commonplace Book," *Wordsworth Circle* 9 (1978): 37.

11. The letter, dated 30 July 1891, is quoted by Jean Strouse, in *Alice James: A Biography* (New York, 1982), 338.

12. *Letters of William and Dorothy Wordsworth: The Middle Years,* 454. Dorothy Wordsworth's published journals include the Alfoxden Journal (1798), Journal of

Visit to Hamburgh and of Journey from Hamburgh to Goslar (1798), The Grasmere Journal (1800–1803), Recollections of a Tour Made in Scotland (1803), Excursion on the Banks of Ullswater (1805), Excursion up Scawfell Pike (1818), Journal of a Tour on the Continent (1820), Journal of My Second Tour in Scotland (1822), and Journal of a Tour in the Isle of Man (1828). Unpublished journals at the Wordsworth Library at Dove Cottage, Grasmere, include a fragment from 1821 and entries between 1824 and 1835.

13. Mary Jane Moffat and Charlotte Painter, eds., *Revelations: Diaries of Women* (New York, 1975), 5.

14. Thomas Mallon, *A Book of One's Own: People and Their Diaries* (New York, 1984).

15. Virginia Woolf, "Dorothy Wordsworth," in "Four Figures," *The Second Common Reader* (1932; reprint, New York, 1960), 155.

16. Unless otherwise noted, passages from Dorothy Wordsworth's journals are quoted from *The Journals of Dorothy Wordsworth,* 2d ed., ed. Mary Moorman (Oxford, 1971).

17. Robert Gittings and Jo Manton, *Dorothy Wordsworth* (Oxford, 1985), 77.

18. *Letters of John Keats,* ed. Robert Gittings (London, 1970), 101, 103.

19. "Journal of a Tour on the Continent," *Journals of Dorothy Wordsworth,* ed. Ernest de Selincourt, 2 vols. (1941; reprint, London, 1959), 2:101–102.

Chapter 9. Wordsworth and Keats

The number of scholarly works centering on Wordsworth and Keats together is surprisingly small in view of the importance of the relationship. The principal items are Clarence D. Thorpe, "Wordsworth and Keats—A Study in Personal and Critical Impression," *PMLA* 42 (1927): 1010–1026, mainly biographical information; John Middleton Murry, *Keats* (London, 1955), chap. 11, "Keats and Wordsworth," 269–291 (first published in Murry's *Studies in Keats New and Old,* 1939), biographical anecdotes plus scattered impressions concerning Wordsworth's influence; Thora Balslev, *Keats and Wordsworth: A Comparative Study* (Copenhagen, 1962), an undiscriminating collection and survey of verbal similarities; Jack Stillinger, *The Hoodwinking of Madeline and Other Essays on Keats's Poems* (Urbana, Ill., 1971), especially the essay "Keats, Wordsworth, and 'Romanticism,'" 120–149, mainly on the two poets' theories of imagination; Miriam Allott, "Keats and Wordsworth," *Keats-Shelley Memorial Bulletin* 22 (1971): 28–43, on the older poet's influence on Keats's style as well as ideas; and Mario L. D'Avanzo, "'Ode on a Grecian Urn' and *The Excursion,*" *Keats-Shelley Journal* 23 (1974): 95–105, on specific connections between the Grecian passages of Wordsworth's poem and the subject and "character" of Keats's ode. The one major book-length study, a splendid work received just in time for inclusion in this note, is Susan J. Wolfson's *The Questioning Presence: Wordsworth, Keats, and the Interrogative Mode in Romantic Poetry* (Ithaca, N.Y., 1986). The biographies by Walter Jackson Bate, *John Keats* (Cambridge, Mass., 1963), and Robert Gittings, *John Keats* (Boston, 1968), contain extensive commentary on the relationship. A great many "echoes and borrowings" from Wordsworth are cited in the annotated editions by Douglas Bush, *John Keats: Selected Poems and Letters* (Boston, 1959); Miriam Allott, *The Poems of John Keats* (London, 1970; 3d impression, with corrections, 1975); and John Barnard, *John Keats: The Complete Poems* (Harmondsworth, 1973; 2d ed., 1976). The most comprehensive and useful collection of Wordsworthian echoes is a recently completed work by Beth Lau, "Keats's Reading of Wordsworth: An Essay and Checklist," *Studies in Romanticism,* forthcoming.

1. *The Keats Circle: Letters and Papers, 1816–1878,* ed. Hyder Edward Rollins (Cambridge, Mass., 1948), 2:143–144.

2. Aileen Ward, *John Keats: The Making of a Poet* (New York, 1963), 157.

3. See Bate, *John Keats,* 264–268; Gittings, *John Keats,* 167–168; and Mary Moorman, *William Wordsworth: A Biography,* vol. 2, *The Later Years, 1803–1850* (Oxford, 1965), 316–318.

4. *The Diary of Benjamin Robert Haydon,* ed. Willard Bissell Pope (Cambridge, Mass., 1960–63), 2:173–176.

5. Throughout this essay, Keats's letters are quoted from *The Letters of John Keats,* ed. Hyder Edward Rollins (Cambridge, Mass., 1958).

6. Charles Clarke and Mary Cowden Clarke, *Recollections of Writers* (London, 1878), 126.

7. For Woodhouse's comment, see Keats's *Letters,* 1:389.

8. *The Complete Works of William Hazlitt,* ed. P. P. Howe (London, 1930–34), 5:47–48.

9. Ibid., 5:163.

10. Haydon's *Diary,* 2:171.

11. Clarke and Clarke, *Recollections,* 149.

12. See Keats's *Letters,* 1:388.

Chapter 10. Beyond the Imaginable

1. Jean Laude, "On the Analysis of Poems and Paintings," *New Literary History* 3 (1972): 471.

2. This point is cogently asserted by Christine Brooke-Rose, *A Rhetoric of the Un-*

real (Cambridge, 1981), 15. The most thoughtful discussion of the larger issues involved in the difference between humanistic and scientific scholarship with which I am acquainted is provided by Marshall G. S. Hodgson, *The Venture of Islam*, 2 vols. (Chicago, 1961), especially the introduction to vol. 1.

3. A moderate example: In *New York Times*, 25 February 1985, p. C 20, there was a favorable notice of the work of John Armleder, "who converts ratty old furniture into sculpture by dashing paint across it and . . . hanging it askew."

4. *The Poetical Works of William Wordsworth*, ed. Ernest de Selincourt and Helen Darbishire, rev. ed., 5 vols. (Oxford, 1952–1959), 2:512, where de Selincourt is citing from Wordsworth's preface to *Lyrical Ballads*. The preceding quotation, from the aging poet's many comments dictated to Isabella Fenwick, appears on 511 of this standard edition, from which all my citations from *The Thorn* (2:240–248) and *Resolution and Independence* (2:235–240) are taken.

5. Julia Kristeva has called attention to studies proving that "all colors . . . have a noncentered or decentering effect, lessening both object identification and phenomenal fixation." "Giotto's Joy," in *Desire in Language,* ed. Leon S. Roudiez, trans. Thomas Gora, Alice Jardine, and Leon S. Roudiez (New York, 1980), 225. Rudolph Arnheim, *Art and Visual Perception: The New Version* (Berkeley and Los Angeles, 1974), 235, observes that "in no reliable sense can we speak of color 'as it really is'; it is always determined by its context."

6. Recent scholarship makes it appear that the sensational story is probably apocryphal; see Luke Herrmann, *Turner* (Boston, 1975), 234.

7. John Berger, *About Looking* (New York, 1980), 147–148.

8. I cite here the version from the 1798 *Lyrical Ballads,* as reprinted by R. L. Brett and A. R. Jones in their edition (London, 1963), 105–106, so as to call attention to the importance of different versions of Wordsworth's shorter poems as well as his longer ones. De Selincourt's edition, of course, uses for its texts the poet's final versions.

9. De Selincourt and Darbishire, *Poetical Works,* 510–511, cites Dorothy's account in her Journal (3 Oct. 1800) of the meeting in which she notes that the man lived by begging.

10. "Essay upon Epitaphs, I," in *The Prose Works of William Wordsworth,* ed. W. J. B. Owen and Jane Worthington Smyser, 3 vols. (Oxford, 1974), 2:59; the subsequent quotation is from "Essay upon Epitaphs, III," 2:93.

Chapter 11. Two Dark Interpreters

1. Thomas De Quincey, *Suspiria de Profundis, 'Confessions of an English Opium-Easter' and Other Writings by Thomas De Quincey,* ed. Aileen Ward (New York

and London, 1966), 197–198. All De Quincey quotations are cited by page number from this edition.

2. Wordsworth quotations are from texts prepared for the forthcoming *Cambridge Wordsworth* but, unless noted to the contrary, may be found in either Stephen Gill's *William Wordsworth*, Oxford Authors Series (London, 1984), or *'The Prelude': 1799, 1805, 1850*, ed. Jonathan Wordsworth, M. H. Abrams, and Stephen Gill (New York, 1979).

3. For De Quincey's account of the projected four-part work, based on the ministration of Our Ladies of Sorrow, and concluding in *The Kingdom of Darkness,* see *Confessions* 178–179n.

4. Drawing on *Lycidas,* line 192, Wordsworth had written, "The old man rose and hoisted up his load" (*Ruined Cottage,* line 534). Both Milton and Wordsworth thus signaled a departure to "fresh fields and pastures new."

5. *Boswell's London Journal,* ed. Frederick A. Pottle (New York, 1950), 4 June and 17 May, 1763.

6. Wordsworth uses his famous phrase, "spots of time," to refer to intense and intensely remembered experiences from early life, often disorienting, baffling, or frightening in themselves, which nevertheless "retain / A renovating virtue" for the mind of an adult who is depressed or oppressed by trivial concerns. This "efficacious spirit," he says, is chiefly found in those experiences where "we have had deepest feeling that the mind / Is lord and master, and that outward sense / Is but the obedient servant of her will" (*Prelude* 11.257–278).

7. The only texts of the fragmentary *Vale of Esthwaite* in print at the moment are partial ones in *The Poetical Works of William Wordsworth,* ed. Ernest de Selincourt and Helen Darbishire, 5 vols. (Oxford, 1941–1949), 1:270–283; and in *William Wordsworth: The Poems,* ed. John O. Hayden, 2 vols. (New Haven, Conn., 1981), 1:50–66. I should like at this point to acknowledge the work of my assistant editors on the forthcoming *Cambridge Wordsworth,* Nicola Trott and Duncan Wu.

8. I have discussed the uncanny importance of these *Hamlet* references in *William Wordsworth: The Borders of Vision* (Oxford, 1982), 63–65.

9. Grevel Lindop, "Pursuing the Throne of God: De Quincey and the Evangelical Revival," *Charles Lamb Bulletin,* new ser. 52 (Oct. 1985): 104.

10. Geoffrey H. Hartman, *Wordsworth's Poetry, 1787–1814* (New Haven, Conn., 1964), 5.

11. *The Ruined Cottage* and *The Pedlar,* ed. James Butler (Ithaca, N.Y., 1979), 275, lines 7–12.

12. Cf. J. Wordsworth, *Borders of Vision,* 60–62.

13. Thomas De Quincey, *Recollections of the Lakes and Lake Poets,* ed. David Wright (Harmondsworth, 1970), 161.

14. See *The Prose Works of William Wordsworth,* ed. W. J. B. Owen and Jane Worthington Smyser, 3 vols. (Oxford, 1974), 2:84: "If words be not . . . an incarna-

tion of the thought, but only a clothing for it, then surely they will prove an ill gift." De Quincey in his essay entitled *Style* in *Collected Writings of Thomas De Quincey*, ed. David Masson, 14 vols. (Edinburgh, 1890), 10:229–230, specifically recalls a conversation with Wordworth on the subject of language and incarnation: "His remark was by far the weightiest thing we ever heard on the subject of style."

Chapter 12. Wordsworth's Hedgerows: The Infrastructure of
the Longer Romantic Lyric

1. Rudolf Bultmann, *History of the Synoptic Tradition*, trans. John Marsh (Oxford, 1963), 166–167.

2. Martin Heidegger, *Was Heisst Denken?* (Tübingen, 1954), 41–42.

3. Martin Heidegger, *Einführung in die Metaphysik* (Tübingen, 1953), 130, 137, 138.

4. George Puttenham, *The Arte of English Poesie*, in *Elizabethan Critical Essays*, ed. Gregory Smith (1904; reprint London, 1937), 2:173–174.

5. Joseph Addison, *The Spectator*, ed. Donald F. Bond (Oxford, 1965), 3:535–536.

6. *Kritische Friedrich-Schlegel-Ausgabe*, ed. Ernst Behler (Munich, Paderborn, Vienna, 1958–   ), 2:182; *The Poetry and Prose of Blake*, ed. David Erdman (Garden City, N.Y., 1968), 2; *The Prose Works of William Wordsworth*, ed. W.J.B. Owen and Jane Worthington Smyser (Oxford, 1974), 1:126; *The Complete Works of Percy Bysshe Shelley*, ed. Roger Ingpen and Walter E. Peck (New York, 1965), 4:79; ibid., 6:88; *The Journals of Søren Kierkegaard*, ed. and trans. Alexander Dru (London, 1951), 25.

7. Friedrich Hölderlin, *Sämmtliche Werke*, ed. Friedrich Beissner (Stuttgart, 1946–   ), 2:236; *Friedrich Wilhelm Joseph von Schellings sämmtliche Werke*, ed. K.F.A. Schelling (Stuttgart and Augsburg, 1856–1861), 2:56.

8. Mary Moorman, *William Wordsworth, A Biography: The Early Years 1770–1803* (Oxford, 1957), 1.

9. John Crowe Ransom, *The World's Body* (New York, 1938), 333; John Crowe Ransom, *The New Criticism* (Norwalk, Conn., 1941), 333, 305–306.

10. Cleanth Brooks, *The Well-Wrought Urn: Studies in the Structure of Poetry* (1947; reprint London, 1971), 102; Yvor Winters, *Forms of Discovery: Critical & Historical Essays on the Forms of the Short Poem in Engilsh* (Denver, 1967), 171–172; F. R. Leavis, *Revaluation: Tradition & Development in English Poetry* (London, 1969), 184–185.

11. Cleanth Brooks and Robert Penn Warren, *Understanding Poetry*, 3rd ed. (1938; reprint New York, 1960), 377–380.

12. Ransom, *The World's Body*, 342; Brooks, *The Well-Wrought Urn*, 173.

13. Brooks, *The Well-Wrought Urn*, 15–16.

14. Ibid., 171.

15. Thomas McFarland, *Romanticism and the Forms of Ruin: Wordsworth, Coleridge, and Modalities of Fragmentation* (Princeton, 1981), 255–288; Robert Langbaum, *The Poetry of Experience: The Dramatic Monologue in Modern Literary Tradition* (New York, 1963), 53; S.T. Coleridge, *Biographia Literaria*, ed. J. Shawcross (London, 1907), 2:258; *The Letters of William and Dorothy Wordsworth: The Early Years, 1787–1805*, ed. Ernest de Selincourt, rev. Chester L. Shaver (Oxford, 1967), 641.

16. *Prose Works of Wordsworth*, 3:77; Wordsworth, *Letters: Early Years*, 641.

17. Winters, *Forms of Discovery*, 172.

18. Donald Davie, *Articulate Energy: An Inquiry into the Syntax of English Poetry* (London, 1955), 107.

19. *Oeuvres complètes de Jean-Jacques Rousseau*, ed. Bernard Gagnebin and Marcel Raymond, Pléiade ed. (Paris, 1959–1969), 1:1048.

Chapter 13. Wordsworth and the Victorians

1. Matthew Arnold, *The Complete Prose Works*, ed. R. H. Super, 10 vols. (Ann Arbor, Mich., 1960–1977), 9:181.

2. Hallam, Lord Tennyson, *Alfred Lord Tennyson: A Memoir*, 2 vols. (London, 1897), 1:338.

3. Arnold, *Complete Prose Works*, 9:40–41.

4. Quoted in Amy Cruse, *The Victorians and Their Books* (London, 1935), 176.

5. E* in *Westminster and Quarterly Review*, 54 (Oct. 1850): 272.

6. *The Poetical Works of Matthew Arnold*, ed. C. B. Tinker and H. F. Lowry (London, 1950), 229.

7. Eizabeth Browning, *Athenaeum*, 29 Oct. 1842, 932.

8. T. Hall Caine, *Recollections of Dante Gabriel Rossetti* (London, 1882), 148.

9. John Stuart Mill, *Autobiography* (London, 1924), chap. 5, p. 125.

10. *Autobiography of Charles Darwin*, ed. Sir Francis Darwin (London, 1929), 8; Cruse, *The Victorians and Their Books*, 176.

11. Arnold, *Poetical Works*, 271.

12. Arnold, *Complete Prose Works*, 9:54, 48. Arnold was President of the Wordsworth Society in 1883.

13. *Froude's Life of Carlyle*, ed. John Clubbe (Columbus, Ohio, 1979), 336.

14. Robert Langbaum, *The Poetry of Experience* (New York, 1957); "Soliloquy of the Spanish Cloister," *The Poems of Robert Browning* (London, 1928), 7.

15. "The King," *Rudyard Kipling's Verse, 1885–1918* (Garden City, N.Y., 1927), 430.

16. *Poems of Robert Browning* 636; from *Dramatis Personae* (1864).

17. Quoted in Gordon S. Haight, *George Eliot: A Biography* (Oxford, 1968), 29.

18. *The Writings of George Eliot*, 25 vols. (Boston, 1908), 19:271.

19. Haight, *George Eliot*, 341.

20. Stopford A. Brooke, *Theology in the English Poets*, 8th ed. (London, 1896), 93.

21. *Poems by William Wordsworth*, "Illustrated with One Hundred Designs . . . Engraved by the Brothers Dalziel," ed. Robert Aris Willmott (London, 1866).

22. *The Letters of William and Dorothy Wordsworth: The Later Years*, ed. Alan G. Hill (Oxford, 1979), 2:200.

23. Leslie A. Marchand, *The Athenaeum: A Mirror of Victorian Life* (Chapel Hill, N.C., 1941), 245–250, 275–283.

24. Merle Mowbray Bevington, *The Saturday Review, 1855–1868* (New York, 1941), 204–208.

25. Arnold, "In Harmony with Nature," *Poetical Works*, 5.

26. In "Fiction, Fair and Foul" (1880), John Ruskin wrote: "I have lately seen, and with extreme pleasure, Mr. Matthew Arnold's poems; and read with sincere interest his high estimate of them. But a great poet's work never needs arrangement by other hands. . . ," *The Works*, ed. E. T. Cook and Alexander D. O. Wedderburn, 39 vols. (London, 1903–1912), 34:318.

27. Algernon Charles Swinburne, "Byron," *Essays and Studies*, 5th ed. (London, 1901), 244, 245n.

28. Algernon Charles Swinburne, *Collected Poetical Works*, 2 vols. (London, 1924), 1:520, 748; 2:508, 567. Thais E. Morgan examined *By the North Sea* as an answer to Wordsworth in a paper at the annual meeting of the Modern Language Association on 28 December 1984.

29. H. Tennyson, *Alfred Lord Tennyson*, 2:70–71.

30. Mill, *Autobiography*, 126.

31. R. H. Hutton, "On Wordsworth's Two Styles," *Transactions of the Wordsworth Society* 6 (1884): 136–148.

32. James Kenneth Stephen, "A Sonnet," in *A Century of Parody and Imitation*, ed. Walter Jerrold and R. M. Leonard (London, n.d.), 376.

33. Jerrold and Leonard, *Century of Parody and Imitation*, 218.

34. Samuel Butler, "Quis Desiderio. . . ?" in *The Humour of Homer and Other Essays*, ed. R. A. Streatfield (London, 1913), 99–109.

35. *Transactions of the Wordsworth Society* 6 (1884): 169, 162.

36. H. Tennyson, *Alfred Lord Tennyson*, 2:69. Tennyson was paraphrasing Wordsworth, *A Poet's Epitaph*, lines 43–44.

37. N. S. Bauer, *William Wordsworth: A Reference Guide to British Criticism, 1793–1899* (Boston, 1978).

38. Bauer, *William Wordsworth*, 236, 294.

39. Henry James, *Literary Criticism* (New York, 1984), 770–775.

40. Among dissertations on the subject of this essay, see Eleanor C. Docherty, "The Influence of Wordsworth on the Verse of the Oxford Movement" (Radcliffe, 1934); Katherine M. Peek, "Studies in the History of Wordsworth's Fame" (Bryn Mawr, 1938); Robert E. Lovelace, "Wordsworth and the Early Victorians" (Wisconsin, 1952). Among articles, I am indebted to Barbara Garlitz, "The Immortality Ode: Its Cultural Progeny," *Studies in English Literature* 6 (Autumn 1966): 639–649.

Chapter 14. Wordsworth in America

1. James Fenimore Cooper [Anon.], *Notions of the Americans; Picked up by a Travelling Bachelor* (1828; reprint, 2 vols., Philadelphia, 1832), 313, 315.

2. See Leon Howard, "Wordsworth in America," *Modern Language Notes* 48 (1933): 359–365. Mark L. Reed, "Contacts with America," in *William Wordsworth, 1770–1970: Essays of General Interest on Wordsworth and his Time*, ed. Nesta Clutterbuck (London, 1970), 32–36, notes that *Goody Blake* was reprinted in the *Farmer's Museum* (Walpole, N.H.) in September 1799, though this was presumably taken over relatively indiscriminately from a British journal, as was the habit of the times. The fullest documentation of Wordsworth's American reputation is Annabel Newton, *Wordsworth in Early American Criticism* (Chicago, 1928). See also Linden Peach, *British Influence on the Birth of American Literature* (New York, 1982), 29–57; and William Charvat, *The Origins of American Critical Thought, 1810–35* (1936; reprint, New York, 1968), 71–76. For valuable assistance in the preparation of this essay, I thank Mark Walhout and Mark Reed.

3. *The Anti-Jacobin Review* 1 (1799): 1; 5 (1800): 334.

4. *The Complete Poetical Works of William Wordsworth*, ed. Henry Reed (Philadelphia, 1839), iii. I quote from the preface to the first (1837) edition, here reprinted.

5. *Wordsworth and Reed: The Poet's Correspondence with His American Editor, 1836–50*, ed. Leslie Nathan Broughton (Ithaca, N.Y., & London, 1933), 21.

6. John Stuart Mill, *Autobiography*, ed. Jack Stillinger (Boston, 1969), 86.

7. Orville Dewey, *The Old World and the New; or, A Journal of Reflections and Observations made on a Tour in Europe*, 2 vols. (New York, 1836), 1:89.

8. Richard Henry Data, Sr., *Poems and Prose Writings*, 2 vols. (New York, 1850), 2:263. A slightly (but only slightly) less rhapsodic version of this essay had first appeared in the *North-American Review* 8 (1819).

9. Henry N. Hudson, *Studies in Wordsworth* (Boston, 1884), 3.

10. *Journal of Richard Henry Dana, Jr.*, ed. Robert F. Lucid, 3 vols. (Cambridge, Mass., 1968), 1:36.

11. James McHenry, "American Lake Poetry," *American Quarterly Review* 11 (Mar.–June 1832): 154–174.

12. *The Letters of William Cullen Bryant,* ed. William Cullen Bryant II & Thomas G. Voss, 3 vols. (New York, 1975), 1:114, 235.

13. *Emerson's Literary Criticism,* ed. Eric W. Carlson (Lincoln, Neb., 1979), 199, 202, 113, 128, 139–140. See also Sheldon W. Liebman, "Emerson's Discovery of the English Romantics, 1818–1836," *American Transcendental Quarterly* 21 (1974): 36–44.

14. James Russell Lowell, *Among My Books,* 2d ser. (Boston, 1876), 223.

15. Henry T. Tuckerman, *Thoughts on the Poets,* 3d ed. (New York, 1848), 216.

16. Matthew Arnold, *Essays in Criticism,* 2d ser. (1888; reprint, London, 1935), 94, 97.

17. Geoffrey H. Hartman, *Wordsworth's Poetry, 1787–1814* (New Haven, Conn., 1964).

18. *Literary Essays of Ezra Pound,* ed. T. S. Eliot (1954; reprint, London, 1968), 7, 276–277, 373; *The Letters of Ezra Pound, 1907–41,* ed. D. D. Paige (New York, 1950), 90.

Chapter 15. 1800 and the Future of the Novel

1. M. H. Abrams, *The Mirror and the Lamp: Romantic Theory and Critical Tradition* (New York, 1953), 103.

2. William Wordsworth and Samuel Taylor Coleridge, *Lyrical Ballads,* ed. R. L. Brett and A. R. Jones, rev. ed. (London, 1965), 241, 250. Subsequent parenthetic citations of Wordsworth's prefaces and *Michael* are of this edition. Study of the dramatic properties of Wordsworth's *Lyrical Ballads* was largely initiated by Stephen M. Parrish, whose essays of the 1950s are incorporated into *The Art of Lyrical Ballads* (Cambridge, Mass., 1973). On the theoretical and political implications of Wordsworth's prefaces, see my own "Wordsworth on Language: Toward a Radical Poetics for English Romanticism," *Wordsworth Circle* 3 (1972): 204–211; Don H. Bialostosky, *Making Tales: The Poetics of Wordsworth's Narrative Experiments* (Chicago, 1984); and James K. Chandler, *Wordsworth's Second Nature: A Study of the Poetry and Politics* (Chicago, 1984), esp. 156–183.

3. Maria Edgeworth, *Castle Rackrent,* ed. George Watson, 2d ed. (Oxford, 1980), 1. Subsequent parenthetic citations are of this edition.

4. Coleridge, *Biographia Literaria,* in Brett and Jones, *Lyrical Ballads,* 289.

5. On the claim for ironically limited narration, I might grudgingly yield priority to Daniel Defoe's *Robinson Crusoe* (1719) and *Moll Flanders* (1722). The irony of these works is, however, a matter of continuing critical dispute.

6. Wordsworth's remarks are cited from a useful compendium, *The Critical Opinions of William Wordsworth*, ed. Markham L. Peacock, Jr. (Baltimore, 1950), 179, 243.

7. On the bonds of patriarchal descent in *Michael*, see Chandler, *Wordsworth's Second Nature*, 158–168, and Peter J. Manning, "'Michael,' Luke, and Wordsworth," *Criticism* 19 (1977): 195–211.

8. The outstanding history of Ireland in the late eighteenth century is R. B. McDowell, *Ireland in the Age of Imperialism and Revolution, 1760–1801* (Oxford, 1979). For a readable if somewhat less balanced account of Ireland in the 1790s, see Sean Cronin, *Irish Nationalism* (New York, 1981), 40–64.

9. *The Letters of William and Dorothy Wordsworth: The Early Years, 1787–1805*, ed. Ernest de Selincourt, 2d ed. rev. Chester L. Shaver (Oxford, 1967), 312–315. Two recent and very important articles use Wordsworth's letter to Fox as the fulcrum for their readings of *Michael*: Karl Kroeber, "Constable: Millais / Wordsworth: Tennyson," in *Articulate Images*, ed. Richard Wendorf (Minneapolis, Minn., 1983), 216–242; and Marjorie Levinson, "Spiritual Economics: A Reading of Wordsworth's 'Michael,'" *ELH*, 52 (1985): 707–731. Our arguments share a common vocabulary of interest in political economy, genre, biblical parallels, and representational strategies, but with markedly different emphases and conclusions.

10. Johnson's strictures from *The Life of Milton* are reprinted in *Milton's Lycidas: The Tradition and the Poem*, ed. C. A. Patrides, rev. ed. (Columbia, Mo., 1983), 60–61.

11. Michael Friedman, *The Making of a Tory Humanist* (New York, 1979), 187.

12. Thomas Flanagan, *The Irish Novelists: 1800–1850* (New York, 1959), 70.

13. Some critics find Thady's loyalty to the Rackrents suspect; see James Newcomer, *Maria Edgeworth the Novelist* (Fort Worth, Tex., 1967), 144–167; and Sandra M. Gilbert and Susan Gubar, *The Madwoman in the Attic* (New Haven, Conn., 1979), 146–154. Their readings, which I find unpersuasive, are at least tributes to the rich ambiguities of Edgeworth's tale. In *Heritage Now* (New York, 1982), 17–29, Anthony Cronin offers an ebullient response to Thady's voice that is able to balance his loyalty against his self-service.

14. The story of Edgeworth's role in running the estate is found in Marilyn Butler, *Maria Edgeworth: A Literary Biography* (Oxford, 1972), esp. 87–91, 179–180, 420–423, 426.

15. One critic has noted affinities between Jason's career in *Castle Rackrent* and Faulkner's saga of the upstart Snopeses; see W. B. Coley, "An Early 'Irish' Novelist," in *Minor British Novelists*, ed. Charles Alva Hoyt (Carbondale, Ill., 1967), 13–31. Similarities between the two novelists deserve further study.

16. Aldous Huxley, "Wordsworth in the Tropics," in *Do What You Will* (London, 1949), 114.

Chapter 16. "The Very Culture of the Feelings"

As my basic text for Wordsworth's poetry and prose, I have mainly relied on *William Wordsworth: Selected Poems and Prefaces*, ed. Jack Stillinger (Boston, 1965), except where earlier or unpublished texts were required. Stillinger's texts are usually the latest printed versions of Wordsworth's poetry. For earlier versions, generally from the year 1798, I have quoted from the following volumes: *Lines Left upon a Seat in a Yew-tree* and *The Thorn* are from *Lyrical Ballads 1798*, ed. W. J. B. Owen, 2d ed. (Oxford, 1969). The 1798 version of *The Discharged Soldier* is from *William Wordsworth*, ed. Stephen Gill (Oxford, 1984). This volume in the Oxford Authors Series generally reprints Wordsworth's earliest or first published versions. (Like Stillinger's and Owen's editions, it contains brief but useful notes.) For the two-part *Prelude* of 1798–1799, I have relied on the text edited by Jonathan Wordsworth and Stephen Gill and printed most accessibly in *The Norton Anthology of English Literature*, ed. M. H. Abrams, 3d ed. (New York, 1974). It is also available in a Norton Critical Edition of *The Prelude* put out by the same three editors. For the 1805 and 1850 versions of *The Prelude*, I have used the standard edition of Ernest de Selincourt, as revised by Helen Darbishire (Oxford, 1959). Johnathan Wordsworth's text of *The Pedlar* can be found in an appendix to his book *William Wordsworth: The Borders of Vision* (Oxford, 1982). What remains of the original text of *The Leech-Gatherer* can be found in Jared R. Curtis, *Wordsworth's Experiments with Tradition: The Lyric Poems of 1802* (Ithaca, N.Y., 1971). A small but convenient selection of Wordsworth's letters is included in the World's Classics series, ed. Philip Wayne (Oxford, 1954).

Coleridge is quoted from *The Portable Coleridge*, ed. I.A. Richards (New York, 1950). John Stuart Mill's comments on Wordsworth and the "culture of the feelings" can be found in his *Autobiography*, ed. Jack Stillinger (Boston, 1969). Matthew Arnold's most important views of Wordsworth were recorded in his *Memorial Verses: April, 1850* and in his great introduction to an 1879 selection of Wordsworth's poems, reprinted in *Essays in Criticism: Second Series* (1888). See the edition of S. R. Littlewood (London, 1938). Lionel Trilling's centenary essay, retitled "Wordsworth and the Rabbis," is readily available in *The Opposing Self* (New York, 1955).

1. Walter Benjamin, "The Storyteller," in *Illuminations*, ed. and trans. Harry Zohn (New York, 1968), 89; Wordsworth, Preface to *Lyrical Ballads*, in Stillinger, *Selected Poems and Prefaces*, 449.

2. Sending along his 1800 volume, Wordsworth drew the attention of Whig statesman Charles James Fox to *Michael* and *The Brothers* not as personal histories but for their social message (see his letter of 14 Jan. 1801).

3. "In all he said / There was a strange half-absence, and a tone / Of weakness and indifference, as of one / Remembering the importance of his theme / But feeling it no longer" (1805 *Prelude* 4.474–478).

4. Frederick A. Pottle, "The Eye and the Object in the Poetry of Wordsworth," in *Wordsworth: Centenary Studies*, ed. G. T. Dunklin (Princeton, N.J., 1951), 23–42. Also reprinted in Harold Bloom, ed., *Romanticism and Conciousness* (New York, 1970); see especially 274–281.

5. This line comes from a passage in *The Pedlar* later transferred to *The Prelude*. The text of *The Pedlar*, along with the best version of *The Ruined Cottage*, was published from manuscript by Jonathan Wordsworth, who notes that "despite its third-person narrative it is Wordsworth's earliest sustained piece of autobiographical and philosophical writing" (*William Wordsworth*, 382).

6. The term "boundary being" is one of Hartman's most suggestive phrases. See, for example, his *Wordsworth's Poetry, 1797–1814* (New Haven, Conn., 1964), 158, 198. Jonathan Wordsworth develops a similar idea in *William Wordsworth: The Borders of Vision*.

7. Yet, as Carl Woodring remarks, the dignity of these figures depends in some measure on their isolation. They are walled off from the routines of everyday life. "Not all his beggars are kings in disguise, but all of them are enhanced when isolated from the day's commotion" (*Wordsworth* [Boston, 1965], 53).

Select Bibliography

Editions of the Work of William and Dorothy Wordsworth

Darlington, Beth. *The Love Letters of William and Mary Wordsworth*. Ithaca, N.Y.: Cornell University Press, 1981. Attractively presented edition of thirty-one letters (all from 1810–1812) discovered in 1977.

Gill, Stephen, ed. *William Wordsworth*. Oxford Authors Series. London: Oxford University Press, 1984. Selection of poems and prose. Reprints, in order of composition, the earliest published versions (in some cases, earliest complete manuscript versions) of the poems. Useful notes.

Hayden, John O., ed. *William Wordsworth: The Poems*. 2 vols. New Haven, Conn.: Yale University Press, 1981. Complete edition (exclusive of *The Prelude*), arranged chronologically, follows the authorized 1850 texts. Originally published in Great Britain by Penguin, 1977.

Moorman, Mary, ed. *The Journals of Dorothy Wordsworth*. 2d ed. London: Oxford University Press, 1971.

Owen, W.J.B., and Jane Worthington Smyser, eds. *The Prose Works of William Wordsworth*. 3 vols. Oxford: Clarendon, 1974. Scrupulously edited and fully annotated.

Parrish, Stephen M., gen. ed. *The Cornell Wordsworth*. 12 vols. to date. Ithaca, N.Y.: Cornell University Press, 1975–. Makes available—in photographic facsimiles, printed transcriptions, and "reading texts"—the extant manuscript materials through which Wordsworth's composition of his major poems may be traced.

Selincourt, Ernest de, ed. *The Letters of William and Dorothy Wordsworth*. 6 vols. 1935–1939. Rev. ed. Oxford: Clarendon, 1967–.

Selincourt, Ernest de and Helen Darbishire, eds. *The Poetical Works of William Wordsworth*. 5 vols. 1941–1949. Rev. ed. Oxford: Clarendon, 1952–1959. Long the standard scholar's edition of Wordsworth's poetry, this edition must now be supplemented by available volumes of the *Cornell Wordsworth* (see Parrish) for detailed variants. Gives the final (1850) texts of the poems and follows Wordsworth's own (nonchronological) classification of his works.

Sheats, Paul, ed. *The Poetical Works of Wordsworth*. Boston: Houghton Mifflin, 1982. A revision of the 1904 *Cambridge Wordsworth*. Arrangement is largely chronological; texts of 1850. Useful notes.

Stillinger, Jack, ed. *William Wordsworth: Selected Poems and Prefaces*. Boston:

Houghton Mifflin, 1965. Superb annotation makes this an excellent classroom text. Arranged chronologically; texts of 1850.

Wordsworth, Jonathan, M. H. Abrams, and Stephen Gill, eds. *The Prelude.* New York: Norton, 1979. Contains the 1798–1799 version of the poem, with the 1805 and 1850 texts on facing pages. Includes a selection of critical commentary and the best general discussion of the genesis of the poem.

Books Primarily about Wordsworth

Abrams, M. H., ed. *Wordsworth: A Collection of Critical Essays.* Englewood Cliffs, N.J.: Prentice-Hall, 1972.

Averill, James H. *Wordsworth and the Poetry of Human Suffering.* Ithaca, N.Y.: Cornell University Press, 1980.

Beer, John. *Wordsworth and the Human Heart.* New York: Columbia University Press, 1978.

———. *Wordsworth in Time.* London: Faber, 1979.

Bialostosky, Don H. *Making Tales: The Poetics of Wordsworth's Narrative Experiments.* Chicago: University of Chicago Press, 1984.

Bloom, Harold, ed. *William Wordsworth.* New York: Chelsea House, 1985.

Chandler, James K. *Wordsworth's Second Nature: A Study of the Poetry and Politics.* Chicago: University of Chicago Press, 1984.

Ferguson, Frances. *Wordsworth: Language as Counter-Spirit.* New Haven, Conn.: Yale University Press, 1977.

Grob, Alan. *The Philosophic Mind: A Study of Wordsworth's Poetry and Thought.* Columbus: Ohio University Press, 1973.

Hall, Spencer, ed. *Approaches to Teaching Wordsworth's Poetry.* New York: Modern Language Association, 1986.

Hartman, Geoffrey H. *Wordsworth's Poetry, 1787–1814.* New Haven, Conn.: Yale University Press, 1964.

Havens, Raymond Dexter. *The Mind of a Poet.* Baltimore: Johns Hopkins University Press, 1941.

Heath, William. *Wordsworth and Coleridge: A Study of Their Literary Relations in 1801–1802.* New York: Oxford University Press, 1970.

Heffernan, James. *Wordsworth's Theory of Poetry: The Transforming Imagination.* Ithaca, N.Y.: Cornell University Press, 1969.

Hodgson, John A. *Wordworth's Philosophical Poetry, 1797–1814.* Lincoln: University of Nebraska Press, 1980.

Jacobus, Mary. *Tradition and Experiment in Wordsworth's Lyrical Ballads (1798).* Oxford: Clarendon, 1976.

Johnston, Kenneth R. *Wordsworth and "The Recluse."* New Haven, Conn.: Yale University Press, 1984.

Jones, John. *The Egotistical Sublime: A History of Wordsworth's Imagination.* London: Chatto and Windus, 1954.

King, Alexander. *Wordsworth and the Artist's Vision.* London: Athlone, 1966.

Lindenberger, Herbert. *On Wordsworth's Prelude.* Princeton, N.J.: Princeton University Press, 1963.

Moorman, Mary. *William Wordsworth, a Biography: The Early Years, 1770–1803.* London: Oxford University Press, 1957.

———. *William Wordsworth, a Biography: The Later Years, 1803–1850.* London: Oxford University Press, 1965.

Onorato, Richard. *The Character of the Poet: Wordsworth in* The Prelude. Princeton, N.J.: Princeton University Press, 1971.

Parrish, Stephen M. *The Art of the Lyrical Ballads.* Cambridge: Harvard University Press, 1973.

Perkins, David. *Wordsworth and the Poetry of Sincerity.* Cambridge: Harvard University Press, Belknap Press, 1964.

Reed, Mark L. *Wordsworth: The Chronology of the Early Years, 1770–1799.* Cambridge: Harvard University Press, 1967.

———. *Wordsworth: The Chronology of the Middle Years, 1800–1815.* Cambridge: Harvard University Press, 1975.

Sheats, Paul D. *The Making of Wordsworth's Poetry, 1785–1798.* Cambridge: Harvard University Press, 1973.

Simpson, David. *Wordsworth and the Figurings of the Real.* London: Macmillan, 1982.

Woodring, Carl. *Wordsworth.* Boston: Houghton Mifflin, 1965.

Wordsworth, Jonathan. *The Music of Humanity.* London: Oxford University Press, 1969.

———. *William Wordsworth: The Borders of Vision.* Oxford: Oxford University Press, 1982.

Books about the Age of Wordsworth

Abrams, M. H. *The Mirror and the Lamp: Romantic Theory and Critical Tradition.* New York: Oxford University Press, 1953.

———. *Natural Supernaturalism: Tradition and Revolution in Romantic Literature.* New York: Norton, 1971.

———, ed. *English Romantic Poets: Modern Essays in Criticism.* 2d ed. London: Oxford University Press, 1975.

Bate, Walter Jackson. *The Burden of the Past and the English Poet*. Cambridge: Harvard University Press, 1970.

Bloom, Harold. *The Visionary Company: A Reading of English Romantic Poetry*. Ithaca, N.Y.: Cornell University Press, 1961.

———, ed. *Romanticism and Consciousness: Essays in Criticism*. New York: Norton, 1970.

Butler, Marilyn. *Romantics, Rebels, and Reactionaries*. London: Oxford University Press, 1981.

Cameron, Kenneth Neil, ed. *Romantic Rebels: Essays on Shelley and His Circle*. Cambridge: Harvard University Press, 1973.

Clubbe, John, and Ernest J. Lovell, Jr. *English Romanticism: The Grounds of Belief*. Dekalb: Northern Illinois University Press, 1983.

Frye, Northrop. *A Study of English Romanticism*. New York: Random House, 1968.

Heffernan, James. *The Re-Creation of Landscape: A Study of Wordsworth, Coleridge, Constable, and Turner*. Hanover, N.H.: University Press of New England, 1985.

Hobsbawm, Eric. *The Age of Revolution: 1789–1848*. New York: New American Library, 1962.

Honour, Hugh. *Romanticism*. New York: Harper and Row, 1979.

Jordan, Frank, ed. *The English Romantic Poets: A Review of Research and Criticism*. 4th ed. New York: Modern Language Association, 1985.

Kroeber, Karl, ed. *Backgrounds to English Romantic Literature*. San Francisco: Chandler, 1968.

———. *Romantic Landscape Vision: Constable and Wordsworth*. Madison: University of Wisconsin Press, 1975.

Lefebvre, Georges. *The French Revolution*, 2 vols. New York: Columbia University Press, 1962, 1964. (Original French publication, Paris, 1957.)

McFarland, Thomas. *Originality and Imagination*. Baltimore: Johns Hopkins University Press, 1985.

———. *Romanticism and the Forms of Ruin: Wordsworth, Coleridge, and the Modalities of Fragmentation*. Princeton, N.J.: Princeton University Press, 1981.

Peckham, Morse. *The Triumph of Romanticism*. Columbia: University of South Carolina Press, 1970.

Perkins, David. *The Quest for Permanence: The Symbolism of Wordsworth, Shelley, and Keats*. Cambridge: Harvard University Press, 1959.

Woodring, Carl. *Politics in English Romantic Poetry*. Cambridge: Harvard University Press, 1970.

Contributors

JAMES K. CHANDLER, Associate Professor of English at the University of Chicago, has centered his scholarly work on the confluence between politics and literature in the Romantic period. He is the author of *Wordsworth's Second Nature: A Study of the Poetry and Politics* (1984). His current project is a study of English literature and politics in 1819.

MICHAEL G. COOKE is Professor of English at Yale University. He is author of *The Blind Man Traces a Circle* (1969), *The Romantic Will* (1980), and *Acts of Inclusion: A Theory of Romanticism* (1983). He also writes frequently on American, Afro-American, and Caribbean literature.

STUART CURRAN, Professor of English at the University of Pennsylvania, is best known for his work on Percy Bysshe Shelley. His books include *Shelley's* Cenci: *Scorpions Ringed with Fire* (1970), *Shelley's Annus Mirabilis: The Maturing of an Epic Vision* (1975), and *Poetic Form and British Romanticism* (1986). He is co-editor of *Blake's Sublime Allegory: Essays on the Four Zoas, Milton, and Jerusalem* (1973).

BETH DARLINGTON is Professor of English at Vassar College. She has edited Wordsworth's *Home at Grasmere* for the Cornell University Press series of Wordsworth texts, as well as *The Love Letters of William and Mary Wordsworth* (1981), from a discovery of old manuscripts made in 1977. She is currently at work on a biography of Dorothy Wordsworth.

MORRIS DICKSTEIN is Professor of English at Queens College and the Graduate School of the City University of New York. He is author of *Keats and his Poetry* (1971) and *Gates of Eden: American Culture in the Sixties* (1977). Besides English Romantic literature, he frequently writes on contemporary American culture for *Partisan Review*, the *New York Times Book Review*, the *Sewanee Review, American Film,* and other journals. He is a vice-president of the National Book Critics Circle, a fellow of the New York Institute for the Humanities, and a contributing editor of *Partisan Review*. He is currently working on a cultural history of America in the 1930s.

DAVID V. ERDMAN is Professor of English Emeritus at the State University of New York at Stony Brook and editor of the *Bulletin of Research in the Humanities*.

His first book was *Blake: Prophet against Empire* (1954; third edition, 1977); his most recent, *Commerce des Lumieres: John Oswald and the British in Paris, 1790– 1793* (1986). In between, he has produced a wealth of scholarship and criticism concerning especially the interrelations of art and society in the Romantic era, including: *The Poetry and Prose of William Blake* (1965; 1982), *A Concordance to the Poetry and Prose of William Blake* (1967), *Shelley and his Circle,* vols. 3–4 [Byron MSS] (1970), *The Notebook of William Blake* (1973), *The Illuminated Blake* (1974), three volumes in the *Collected Works of Samuel Taylor Coleridge* (1975), and many other essays, notes, and facsimile editions. He was honored by a special issue of *Studies in Romanticism.*

KENNETH R. JOHNSTON is Professor of English at Indiana University, where he has been a dean of Arts and Sciences and acting chairman of the English Department. He is author of *Wordsworth and "The Recluse"* (1984) and of several essays on Wordsworth, Blake, and other Romantic writers. He is currently working on a critical biography of the young Wordsworth and on a play dramatizing Wordsworth's role in English and French politics in the 1790s. He is a member of the executive committee for the exhibition "William Wordsworth and the Age of English Romanticism." He also writes frequently on topics in literary pedagogy and professionalism and on the history and structure of the institutions of "English" in America.

KARL KROEBER, Professor of English and Comparative Literature at Columbia University, has written widely on Romantic literature and culture from multi-disciplinary perspectives. His books include *Romantic Narrative Art* (1961), *The Artifice of Reality* (1964), *Styles in Fictional Structure* (1971), *Romantic Landscape Vision: Constable and Wordsworth* (1974), and *British Romantic Art* (1986). He has also edited *Images of Romanticism: Verbal and Visual Affinities* (1978) and *Traditional Literature of the American Indian* (1981).

THOMAS McFARLAND is Murray Professor of English Literature at Princeton University. Among his works on English Romantic literature are *Coleridge and the Pantheist Tradition* (1969), *Romanticism and the Forms of Ruin: Wordsworth, Coleridge and Modalities of Fragmentation* (1981), *Originality and Imagination* (1985), and "Romantic Imagination, Nature, and the Pastoral Ideal," in *Coleridge's Imagination,* ed. Richard Gravil, Lucy Newlyn, and Nicholas Roe (1985). He is at present engaged in editing Coleridge's *Opus Maximum* for the *Collected Works of Samuel Taylor Coleridge.*

STEPHEN M. PARRISH is Professor of English at Cornell University and general editor of the Cornell University Press editions of Wordsworth's poetry, which has produced twelve volumes to date, with another nine scheduled to appear. He is editor of *The Prelude, 1798–1799* in that series. He is author of *The Art of Lyrical Ballads* (1973) and is completing a study of Wordsworth's irony, from which his essay in this volume is adapted. He is a member of the executive committee for the exhibition "William Wordsworth and the Age of English Romanticism." He is a member of the Yeats Editorial Board, which has recently launched an edition of manuscripts, also to be published by the Cornell University Press.

GENE W. RUOFF is Associate Professor of English and Director of the Institute for the Humanities at the University of Illinois at Chicago. His contribution to this volume brings together two of his continuing interests, the poetry of Wordsworth and the fiction of the Romantic period. He has guest-edited two issues of *The Wordsworth Circle* devoted to British Romantic fiction. He has directed, for teachers, two summer institutes on Romanticism funded by the National Endowment for the Humanities, and he is a member of the executive committee for the exhibition "William Wordsworth and the Age of English Romanticism."

DAVID SIMPSON is Professor of English and Comparative Literature at the University of Colorado, Boulder. He is the author of *Irony and Authority in Romantic Poetry* (1979), *Wordsworth and the Figurings of the Real* (1982), *Fetishism and Imagination: Dickens, Melville, Conrad* (1982), *The Politics of American English, 1776–1850* (1986), and *Wordsworth's Historical Imagination: The Poetry of Displacement* (1987). He has edited *German Aesthetic and Literary Criticism: Kant to Hegel* (1984).

JACK STILLINGER is Professor of English at the University of Illinois at Urbana/ Champaign and a permanent member of the University of Illinois Center for Advanced Study. His scholarly work has been largely devoted to John Keats and his circle. He is the author of *The Hoodwinking of Madeline and Other Essays on Keats's Poems* (1971) and *The Texts of Keats's Poems* (1974). Among his many edited works are *The Poems of John Keats* (1978), the standard scholarly edition of the poet; *William Wordsworth: Selected Poems and Prefaces* (1965); and *The Letters of Charles Armitage Brown* (1966).

JOSEPH A. WITTREICH, JR., is Professor of English at the University of Maryland. His scholarly work has spanned the English Renaissance and Romantic periods, centering in John Milton and William Blake. His books include *Angel of Apocalypse:*

Blake's Idea of Milton (1974) and *Visionary Poetics: Milton's Tradition and His Legacy* (1979). Among his edited volumes are *The Romantics on Milton* (1970) and *Milton and the Line of Vision* (1975).

CARL WOODRING is George Edward Woodberry Professor of Literature at Columbia University and author of *The Politics of Coleridge's Poetry* (1962), *Wordsworth* (1965; corrected edition, 1968), *Virginia Woolf* (1966), and *Politics in English Romantic Poetry* (1970), as well as numerous articles on Romantic and Victorian literature and on the relations of literature and the visual arts. He is editor of Coleridge's *Table Talk* for the *Collected Works*. He was honored by his alma mater, Rice University, in 1986, and by a special issue of *Studies in Romanticism* (1987).

JONATHAN WORDSWORTH is Fellow and University Lecturer, St. Catherine's College, Oxford, and Chairman of the Wordsworth Heritage Trust, Grasmere. He is author of *The Music of Humanity* (1969) and *William Wordsworth: The Borders of Vision* (1982). He is editor of the forthcoming Cambridge edition of Wordsworth's poetry and is currently working on *"The Infinite I AM": Studies in Romantic Imagination*. He is a member of the executive committee for the exhibition "William Wordsworth and the Age of English Romanticism."

Index

Note: All works in this index are by William Wordsworth unless otherwise indicated.